Comparative Just War Theory

Explorations in Contemporary Social–Political Philosophy

Series Editors: Naomi Zack (University of Oregon) and Laurie Shrage (Florida International University)

As our world continues to be buffeted by extreme changes in society and politics, philosophers can help navigate these disruptions. Rowman & Littlefield's ECSPP series books are intended for supplementary classroom use in intermediate to advanced college-level courses to introduce philosophy students and scholars in related fields to the latest research in social–political philosophy. This philosophical series has multidisciplinary applications and the potential to reach a broad audience of students, scholars, and general readers.

Titles in the Series

Beyond Blood Oil: Philosophy, Policy, and the Future, by Leif Wenar, Anna Stilz, Michael Blake, Christopher Kutz, Aaron James, and Nazrin Mehdiyeva

Reviving the Social Compact: Inclusive Citizenship in an Age of Extreme Politics, by Naomi Zack

Comparative Just War Theory: An Introduction to International Perspectives, edited by Luís Cordeiro-Rodrigues and Danny Singh

Making and Unmaking Disability: The Three-Body Approach, by Julie E. Maybee

Comparative Just War Theory

An Introduction to International Perspectives

Edited by Luís Cordeiro-Rodrigues
and Danny Singh

ROWMAN & LITTLEFIELD
Lanham • Boulder • New York • London

Published by Rowman & Littlefield
An imprint of The Rowman & Littlefield Publishing Group, Inc.
4501 Forbes Boulevard, Suite 200, Lanham, Maryland 20706
www.rowman.com

6 Tinworth Street, London SE11 5AL

Copyright © 2020 by The Rowman & Littlefield Publishing Group, Inc.

All rights reserved. No part of this book may be reproduced in any form or by any electronic or mechanical means, including information storage and retrieval systems, without written permission from the publisher, except by a reviewer who may quote passages in a review.

British Library Cataloguing in Publication Information Available

Library of Congress Cataloging-in-Publication Data
Library of Congress Control Number: 2019952191

ISBN: 978-1-5381-2513-7 (cloth)
ISBN: 978-1-5381-2514-4 (pbk.)
ISBN: 978-1-5381-2515-1 (electronic)

Contents

Series Editors' Foreword: Contemporary Social–Political
    Philosophy and Comparative Just War Theory   vii
    Laurie Shrage and Naomi Zack

Foreword: Ethics and War in a Globalized World   xi
    Alex J. Bellamy

Introduction: International and Comparative Perspectives to Just
    War Theory   1
    Danny Singh and Luís Cordeiro-Rodrigues

1 Anarchism and Just War Theory   11
    Nathan Jun

2 "The Only Justifiable War": The Marxist Strategies of Lenin,
    Trotsky, and Blanco   31
    Andrew Ryder

3 A Pacifist Critique of Just War Theory   45
    Richard Jackson

4 Undertaking Critical Legal Theory to Examine Just War
    Intervention: A Smokescreen for Political Ambitions   61
    Danny Singh

5 An Examination of Nigerian, Sri Lankan, and Guatemalan Civil
    Wars in Light of the Law of Armed Conflict   81
    Jonathan O. Chimakonam and Victor C. A. Nweke

6 African Feminists' Critique of Just Wars and the Reality of
    African Women in Wars   95
    Olajumoke M. Akiode

7	Feminist Care Political Theory and Contemporary Just War Theory *Heleana Theixos*	115
8	An African Theory of Just Causes for War *Thaddeus Metz*	131
9	The Classical Confucian Ideas of *Jus ad Bellum* *Cao Qin*	157
10	Just War and the Indian Tradition: Arguments from the Battlefield *Shyam Ranganathan*	173
11	The Islamic War Ethic in Theory and Practice *Davis Brown*	191
12	Just War Thinking in Chinese Buddhism *Tong Sau Lin and King-Fai Tam*	209

Notes	227
Index	261
About the Editors and Contributors	263

Series Editors' Foreword

Contemporary Social–Political Philosophy and Comparative Just War Theory

Laurie Shrage and Naomi Zack

Now that my ladder's gone,
I must lie down where all the ladders start
In the foul rag and bone shop of the heart.
—"The Circus Animals' Desertion," William Butler Yeats

ABOUT THIS SERIES

From Plato to John Rawls, to Jürgen Habermas and Slavoj Žižek, philosophers have developed political philosophy as a stand-alone subfield in their discipline by focusing on political legitimacy, justice, and fundamental political institutions. The work of philosophers who focus on how societal practices and culture are related to politics or government is often subsumed under social philosophy, which has not been a strong, recognizable subfield. Nevertheless, scholars and students who critically examine social practices, traditions, and values, with the goal of improving the conditions of human life, are engaged with political philosophy—especially issues of inequality, oppression, and political power. For instance, philosophers who analyze racial and gender injustice have demonstrated how social norms and political principles can be productively investigated together. Such progressive, or liberatory, efforts have given rise to a number of questions, such as How are social values and culture related to political power structures? How do social identities of race, class, gender, ability, religion, and ethnicity affect both individual status and power as well as quality of life? Can justice be defined without close attention to actual oppression? The result of critical engagement with the questions of both social philosophy and political philosophy has been a new and growing body of method and content that is somewhat informally called social–political philosophy. This hyphenated name signals an intent to address political issues in combination with social and cultural criticism and/or to conduct social or cultural criticism with the goal of changing political structures.

The aim of this series is to present the best and most interesting work in social–political philosophy at this time for students, scholars, and general readers in accessible and clear prose and by authors who are transparent and self-critical about their methodologies.

Social–political philosophy should not be equated with the *application* of theoretical philosophy to social issues. This is because new subjects often call forth and support new ways of theorizing and pursuing knowledge, as we hope will be evident throughout this series. That is, contemporary social–political philosophy, as philosophy that evaluates the social and political conditions of human life, requires reassessing theoretical constructs and methods as well as addressing practical issues. If the traditional, canonical works and ideas of philosophers could directly be applied to the realities of contemporary human life, then this series would not be needed. As a series of books, Explorations in Contemporary Social–Political Philosophy will share important scholarly work and ideas with a multidisciplinary audience so that those ideas can be taken up to address some of today's most pressing problems.

ABOUT THIS BOOK

War is a recurring and ultimate arbiter involving organized armed conflicts ranging from large world wars to smaller regional and civil wars. Many observers believe that war and its tragic consequences are inevitable. Because Western just war theory derives and draws primarily from only one religious and philosophical tradition (Roman Catholicism), it fails to serve as a universal account of the acceptability of war or, much less, sustain a global dialogue about all the moral issues pertaining to war. *Comparative Just War Theory: An Introduction to International Perspectives*, edited by Luís Cordeiro-Rodrigues and Danny Singh, provides a much-needed intervention into debates about the moral dimensions of war. This collection includes neglected critical perspectives on the purpose and conduct of war that draw from Marxism, Confucianism, anarchism, African philosophy, and feminism. Alex J. Bellamy's foreword grounds the idea of war in evolutionary biology, which is another neglected perspective. This diverse and well-researched collection inaugurates a new subfield in social–political philosophy—debates about morality of war that acknowledge multiple religious, national, and cultural frameworks.

Foreword

Ethics and War in a Globalized World

Alex J. Bellamy

For as long as there has been, there have been efforts to control and limit war.[1] Wherever societies and whole civilizations have confronted war, they have become aware of its costs and developed moral principles, rules, and customs to limit and control war's violence and determine its victors. These normative conventions are constitutive of war itself because war is not just the practice of organized violence but a particular form of organized violence ordered by morals, rules, and customs. Indeed, it is war's character as a custom-governed activity that sets it apart from other types of organized violence, such as raiding, organized crime, and terrorism. It is not that these other forms of organized violence are not guided by their own customs, just that they are distinctive to the customs of war. Thus, while in every moral and cultural tradition we find those ready to argue that there is no place for morality in war—whether "realists," who insist that war is amoral, or "pacifists," who say it is inherently immoral—the fact is that the concept and practice of war itself has always been deeply imbued with moral principles, judgments, and arguments. Indeed, realist and pacifist positions are themselves moral positions on war.

Whenever societies are confronted by war, they are confronted by questions about whether it is legitimate to fight and how war ought to be conducted. We ask questions not only about whether we can fight but whether we ought to fight. It is not surprising, therefore, that each society or civilization has its own moral framework for thinking about war, most, if not all, comprising different traditions of thought. Until recently, scholarship on the ethics of war has focused almost entirely on the Western just war tradition, whose origins lie in Catholic theology. But, while it may help Westerners make sense of their own moral judgments and interaction between states and others within the Western world, just war cannot by itself support a global dialogue on the ethics of war. For that, we need conversations across different ethical traditions. That is why the essays contained in this volume are so important. They offer an important glimpse into some of the world's moral traditions and create the possibility for a new avenue of research—the comparative study of ethical thought about war—and, more importantly, for moral dialogue.

The essays here also highlight the importance of not treating moral traditions as homogeneous patterns of thought. They reveal that not only is there wide divergence of thought within the just war tradition itself; just war is but one of the moral traditions that inform Western approaches to war. Others include pacifism, Marxism, and anarchism but also legalism (and critical legal theory), liberalism, and, of course, realism. The same is true of other traditions. Confucian thinkers, such as Mencius and Xunxi, offered theories and principles, which differed from those of the Daoists, Mohists, and strategists of the Sun Tzu tradition. No matter where we look, we can find a rich variety of moral traditions about war that we have only just begun to understand and engage with. And most of these traditions arise out of patriarchal orders, which is why a feminist perspective is so crucial.

The problem of difference is central to the problem of war, which is why a global moral conversation—one inspired by better understanding of moral traditions and a comparativist to ethical enquiry and dialogue—is so important. Humans are divided into subgroups that lay claim to our loyalty. Group membership is—and always has been—fundamental to human survival and flourishing. From the time we first developed political communities, around 10,000 BCE, we have divided ourselves into groupings. Over time, the differences between groups—their values and interests—became deeply ingrained through language, culture, history, morality, religion, law, economics, and social hierarchies. Today, some groups hold radically different, and maybe directly contending, interests and values. These political communities coexist within an anarchical setting, one without government or enforceable law akin to that which exists within states. It is, I think, one of the great paradoxes of peace that the very social bonds that build harmony in our everyday lives within societies are so often sources of conflict between societies. It is a paradox rooted in the way we think, not in some timeless essence, yet we often like to think of the differences between groups and the potential for war these create as immutable and unchanging facts. Christopher Coker writes, "we tend to believe that . . . war has a nature which is eternal," while Azar Gat agrees that "[w]hile the forms of war may change with time, its spirit, or essence, remains unchanged."[2]

Human society was not "invented" out of a state of nature by self-interested and reasoning men, as Thomas Hobbes imagined. It emerged out of evolutionary biology.[3] Over time, the evolution of more internally coherent human groupings sharpened the differences between them, creating this tragic paradox: that some of the very qualities that helped promote peace *within* societies hardened the differences *between* them. As human minds grew, learning replaced natural selection as the principal driver of evolution.[4] Human groups learned to specialize and adapt to their environments in ways well beyond the capabilities of other species. They developed ways of living, cultures, moralities, and languages that enabled them to survive and thrive in their own particular contexts.[5] They developed explicit teachings about the value of community and the community's values. Myths and religious beliefs helped them understand life and the world around them.[6] Social qualities, such as a shared religion, something that many early political leaders tried to promote—often with themselves as the deity or in unique relation to it—helped bind early societies together.[7] The sacred and the secular emerged together, each dependent on the other. In this decidedly social context, the fittest were not necessarily the physically strongest or the most cunning but those that learned to cooperate most effectively for mutual support—something the Russian anarchist Peter Kropotkin recognized at the start of the twentieth century.[8]

With specialization came difference. We are hardwired to recognize our closest kin and to prioritize their needs and interests above those of others. The most effective groups extended those loyalties of kinship (albeit less intensely) to the group as a whole. The group is thus held together by an internal logic that pushes its members to be more concerned about the fate of other members than they are about the fate of nonmembers. Underpinning all this is an evolutionary logic that holds that the stronger a group's internal coherence, the better its members can cooperate and the greater the rewards that individuals reap from group membership. But internal coherence required external differentiation, sharpening rivalries, and reducing the common ground between the members of different groups. "Humanity" ceased being a salient frame of reference—it would have to be "invented" or perhaps discovered all over again.[9] The division of humanity pitted groups internally united by bonds of belief, language, and practice against alien outsiders, who were considered to be of less importance and value than insiders. Group selection favored those with the greatest internal coherence because they were best placed to harness the benefits of cooperation. Indeed, in-group solidarity was enhanced by hostility to out-groups.[10] The more defined and specialized groups became, the deeper the divisions between them turned out to be. The more effectively groups provided for the well-being of their members and the nourishment of their shared values, the stronger became the ties that bound them. The stronger the internal ties became, the weaker became the ties between those inside the group and those outside it. Language is a case in point. Language made communication and hence deep cooperation and shared morality possible. It underpinned huge leaps in social development, technology, and human well-being. But it also gave forceful practical meaning to human division because only those who comprehended a group's language could participate in the cooperation it engendered and moral bonds it forged. Communication became more intense within groups and sparser between them.

Groups developed a remarkable range of ways of living, moralities, and languages adapted by cultural evolution to the conditions in which they found themselves and shaped by their own internal and regional politics. Those groups that bonded together most tightly, held together by shared beliefs and common identities, profited more from their cooperation than those that did not while the bonds that held groups together imposed differences between them. From our earliest civilizations, humans developed different ideas not just about what is just and unjust but about the standard of justice itself. That is why we have no universal human account of justice and, because of that, no single vision of the morality of war.

War endures in part, therefore, because groups want or believe in different things and suppose that war will help them achieve it. Groups tend to start wars to satisfy their basic needs, enrich themselves and grow, fulfill what they understand to be their rights, or to correct what they understand to be grave injustices. Civil wars, meanwhile, occur when different groups—or subgroups—compete over the boundaries, shape, and control of a political order or proffer different accounts of what values should govern that order. The underlying problem here is that justice is not an objective standard. Groups can, and do, form different accounts of what justice is and how it applies in different situations. As a result, they can always find reasons to fight. It is a problem amplified by our limited understanding of different moral traditions, our tendency to privilege our own morality over that of others, and the lack of a common moral language with which to speak across difference. This volume opens up spaces for understanding and beginning just such a conversation.

How we understand morality is subjective and not objective, a product of language, culture, situation, and experience. It is not given from God or nature, knowable only through the application of proper method and contemplation. We often disagree about how justice is to be realized in any given situation. Sometimes, justice claims are not just incompatible; they are directly opposed. Sometimes, groups might point to equally valid principles of justice to make contradictory claims.

In their relations with each other, states and societies have found common ground on some shared principles to guide peaceful coexistence (e.g., international law and international organizations), express shared understanding about how people ought to be treated (e.g., human rights law), and establish procedures to manage disputes. These are what political theorist Michael

Walzer calls "conventions," sets of "articulated norms, customs, professional codes, legal precepts, religious and philosophical principles, and reciprocal arrangements" that shape judgments about morality and justice.[11] Some like-minded states and societies, especially regional groupings, have developed into deeply rooted "security communities" in which war between members becomes not just unlikely but unthinkable. The European Union provides a good example of a deep and substantive security community; ASEAN in Southeast Asia is an example of a more restrictive kind. Both, however, have been associated with significant declines of war and outbreaks of peace in their regions. But there are questions about whether these communities can be extended to embrace all of humanity. In 1903, for example, William Sumner argued that zones of peace could never be extended to all humanity because, whenever a group grows larger, animosities between insiders and outsiders grow and war inevitably follows.[12]

Thus far, global conventions have tended to be more procedural, designed to help manage points of difference and the disputes that inevitably arise. These conventions have contributed to the management of war but cannot by themselves resolve the problem of difference because radical disagreements over the fundamentals of justice may arise and, in those situations, groups may prefer to wage war than to accept the arbitration or judgments of others. Therefore, outside security communities, war remains the *ultima ratio* of disputes between groups. As Hannah Arendt explained, "the chief reason warfare is still with us is neither a secret death wish of the human species, nor an irrepressible instinct of aggression, nor, finally and more plausibly, the serious economic and social dangers inherent in disarmament, but the simple fact that no substitute for this final arbiter in international affairs has yet appeared on the political scene."[13] "For all its evil," George Orwell explained in *The Lion and the Unicorn*, war is "an unanswerable test of strength."[14] We have no government, no self-enforcing laws, that sits above states to regulate relations between them.

Yet war is an imperfect arbiter for at least two very different reasons that were identified by two very different Prussians. Immanuel Kant pointed out that war is an unjust and unreasoning arbiter. War turns contests over justice into contests of strength. A state's ability to wage war tells us as much about the justice of its cause as a schoolyard bully's ability to punch tells us about his. War is therefore inimical to the way that most of us would think is a fair way to settle a dispute—the application of law and reason. Carl von Clausewitz, meanwhile, observed that war is an unreliable arbiter. It is a dialectical process of attack and defense that produces "friction"—contingencies, uncertainties, and the unexpected things that occur in all war—which means that, once begun, war tends to be unpredictable. It generates unforeseen consequences. These qualities are the very opposite of those we normally look for in an effective arbiter of disputes.

The essays contained in this volume provide us with ways of thinking more deeply about moral traditions themselves and more widely about how these traditions speak to one another. In a globalizing world, where the capacity of one society to hurt another through violence is less and less restricted by physical distance, these are conversations that we desperately need to have.

Introduction

International and Comparative Perspectives to Just War Theory

Danny Singh and Luís Cordeiro-Rodrigues

The morality of war is of crucial importance to everyday social reality. For war is constantly present in political dynamics and, in an international globalized society like today's, the rules of war are a global concern. Precisely because of this global outreach, a comparative view of the values of war seems urgent. For if values of war do not look at different moral and cultural views, they may risk simply being an ethnocentric understanding of war. In the case of war, this comparative need is even more vivid; for the morality of war deals with extreme moral issues, such as the morality of killing and the possibility of violating a state's sovereignty. These issues are especially important because they deal with limits and as such they ought to be given special attention and comparative views on the morality of war seem significantly important. In other words, war involves addressing the morality of killing and using violence and these two are normally impermissible. Therefore, to justify something that is usually considered morally impermissible it is important to avoid biased perspectives and find a reasonable agreement.

On top of this, there is an increasing involvement of different countries in each other's security legislation. For instance, China has been cooperating substantially to develop existing peace and security structures in various African countries. Thus, common grounds on how to understand war are necessary to explore.

Despite this work being crucial, just war theory has been mostly addressed from a Western-centric perspective. In this edited volume, we wish precisely to carry out this task of looking at war from a comparative point of view. Most volumes on war so far have been focused on how different Western views address and conceptualize problems of morality in war. However, the diversity of these volumes has been reduced to the existing diversity in the Global North and, generally, from a liberal-informed point of view. This volume, instead, looks at radical traditions neglected in the Global North, such as Marxism and Anarchism, but also at the views from the Global South.

For this purpose, we argue that just war theory has mostly been studied from a Western viewpoint. After that, we will explain the value of the discussions in the book chapters and outline the chapters of the book. Based on the chapters of the book, the editors will then suggest how these views offer alternative approaches to contemporary just war theory and military ethics. Subsequently, suggestions of how such alternative approaches can be integrated in the phases of waging war (*jus ad bellum*) and methods used in war (*jus in bello*) will be provided. It will also be argued that although a critique of Western just war perspectives is relevant, non-Western just war theories can also be criticized. Critiques within those states and cultures of how just war theory have been applied in those cultures will be brought to attention.[1]

BRIEF OVERVIEW OF JUST WAR THEORY AND RELEVANCE OF NON-WESTERN APPROACHES

Just war theory has historical traditions and has been developed from major theological texts, humanists, and military ethics. Non-Western perspectives on just war theory include ancient Chinese philosophy and Hindu religious texts. In relation to Chinese philosophy, Confucius was skeptical about war but Mencius declared that war could be for righteous reasons such as the overthrow of a despot. In relation to Hindu texts, the *Mahābhārata* supports conventional morality but parasites are to be deprived of these values under just war such as fighting of Prince Rama against King Ravana (who captured his wife, Sita) or retaining independence from foreign occupational forces.

Just war theory has since been developed in the West to generate criteria, based on the archaic notions from Augustine and Aquinas, on the rules to wage war (*jus ad bellum*), and the conduct in war (*jus in bello*). To specify, Saint Augustine of Hippo (354–430) suggested that just war theory must rest on a punitive solution, measure moral ambitions of those engaged in (or deciding to wage) war and provide reference to Christian scriptures to legitimize a country's engagement in war.[2] However, Augustine argued that governments and their citizens must not wage war straightaway because God has given man the "sword" to govern a nation with a valid reason. The solid reason is associated with protecting peace and punishing wickedness instead of standing as pacifists.[3] According to Augustine, peace can function as an order to justify the use of force to preserve a government's order and avert chaos and to promote a more just order and rulership.[4]

Today's debates on the ethics of war are mostly divided into two groups; these are the traditionalists and the revisionists. The traditionalists, like Michael Walzer, have a strong influence from the Christian tradition of just war, which in turn largely informs current law.[5] Contrastingly, traditionalists, such as Jeff McMahan, challenge substantially the morality of traditionalism and tend to use the Rawlsian reflective equilibrium as a methodology to understand what is or not moral in war.[6] These philosophical and intertwined theological impositions of just war intervention and conduct concern contemporary legal principles of war. Various rules and international treaties are affiliated with rules of armed conflict which will not be discussed here. For readers who want or need some background to debates about the ethics of war, see the Stanford Encyclopedia of Philosophy entry on war or the Internet Encyclopedia of Philosophy entry on just war theory.[7] These texts and many other Western-based referenced works point to our argument that the philosophical literature on non-Christian or non-Western perspectives on the morality of war is extremely limited.

International law and Western interpretations of just war theory provide an increasing moral concern in contemporary politics and moral theory aims to address moral issues from a non-ethnocentric point of view. In terms of moral theory, this pattern is noticeable with the increasing relevance of comparative philosophy. For example, philosophers such as Chenyang Li, Thaddeus Metz, and Daniel Bell have compared African and Confucian ethical values and built up a moral theory based on the combination of both schools of philosophy.[8] Tongdong Bai, Joseph Chan, and Mario Wenning, among others, have equally compared Chinese philosophy with Western philosophy with the goal of finding a moral system that comprises East and West.[9] Thus, the concern of finding ethical values that are cross-cultural is an increasing concern in politics and moral philosophy.

One specific area where this concern is urgent is the morality of war. The morality of war/just war theory deals with the justification of how and why wars are fought. In this edited book, we will precisely address issues regarding the morality of war from a comparative perspective. In particular, the chapters in this book will look at two important debates regarding war ethics: (a) When is it morally justified to enter in war? (b) If one is in war, what are the morally acceptable violent methods? These topics have of course been debated substantially in the Western liberal context. What this volume does new is to address these topics taking into consideration concepts from non-mainstream Western and non-Western philosophical theories. Particularly, this means addressing those two issues taking into consideration concepts like Confucian Yi/Rightness, Ahimsa, Class Struggle, Ubuntu, Anarchism, Pacifism, Islam, Jihad, Buddhism, among other concepts. Moreover, critiques of these non-Western just war theories (with the use of concrete examples) will be provided because there are also problems within the countries and cultures they have been applied in. This book steps out from common edited volumes that only engage with liberal analytic philosophy as a response to these conflicts and tries to offer a wider conceptual framework to deal with the morality of war. Consequently, this book offers a comparative philosophical approach to just war theory.

Therefore, this collection of essays provides non-Western and alternative philosophical approaches of just war theory. Drawing on expert contributions that cut across different ideologies and philosophical traditions, this volume provides fresh insights into how the normative problems that arise from just war can be addressed. Filling this gap is needed so that ongoing debates concerning the morality of war can advance or alter debates, or at least introduce novel concepts or questions related to the permissibility of war *jus ad bellum* or actions in war *jus in bello*. The African view on war, for example, has as a guiding principle the idea that community harmony is the highest goal. Based on this perspective, the morality of killing, initiating war, and so forth, is guided not by individual values, but by community ones. In particular, the chapters will illustrate that alternative debates concerning the morality of war can avoid cultural bias, gender discrimination, and forms of structural violence targeted against vulnerable groups, ethnocentrism, and parochialism or other forms of ethnic, religious, and/or political bias.

OUTLINE OF THE CHAPTERS

The first chapter by Nathan Jun analyzes warfare from an anarchist perspective. This concerns an anti-militarist ideology that regards conventional warfare as an instrument of oppression and exploitation and rejects it accordingly. Yet, anarchists do not deem all wars to be unjust. People who are oppressed may wage a class or social war as their moral imperative. The chapter provides a novel critique of conventional just war thinking from an anarchist critique and argues in favor of anarchist conditions for entering war against the oppressive state and the normative (what it ought to be) meaning of engaging in warfare in practice. Concrete examples are provided to the Spanish Civil War and the Paris Commune. Therefore, this opening chapter provides an alternative critique to conventional just war theory and anarchist normative meanings in practice. This links to the subsequent chapter which focuses on revolutionary element of the oppressed rising up against their rulers.

The chapter by Andrew Ryder is centered on Marxist schemes of Lenin, Trotsky, and Blanco. Karl Marx stressed that throughout history, war can only be justifiable in revolutionary conflicts of exploited people against their rulers. This chapter provides a new reading of Marxist approaches to war and it has the merit of contrasting it with early classical Marxist treatment as well as critically engaging with the Russian civil war. Particularly, the Marxist approach is critical of just war involving conflicts between states, but an egalitarian revolutionary war can achieve socialist transformation. The concerns are based on the fear of the army substituting working-class self-organization and a military strategy while attaining the autonomy of workers. A comparison between the revolutionary leaders Lenin (Russian Revolution), Trotsky (Ukrainian head of the Red Army), and Blanco (Peruvian Trotskyist revolutionary) is made. The popular militia based on the Trotskyist tradition (later put into practice by Blanco) is a main apparatus of working people's emancipation, which operates on the people's behalf with no command structure. The organized militia provides mass political development, is democratically accountable, and fights to liberate working people from both class domination and national oppression. Marxian perspectives on just war theory provide criteria for military warfare that subordinates instant ends to emancipatory ends, and provides the potential direction to the end of war. The initial two chapters are fundamental to develop an understanding on anarchist and revolutionary interpretations of just war theory.

The third chapter provides a pacifist critique on just war theory based on the manipulation of politics and objectives. In this chapter, Richard Jackson contributes to understand the theoretical framework underlying just war theory. Particularly, Jackson contends that pacifists argue that just war theory is decontextualized, and the aims of just war theory do not thoroughly provide ethical guidance and conflict resolution to threats of war and engaging in war. Instead, pacifist theorists stress that just war theory is mainly utilized to provide investigations on the acceptance and legality on the use of force and principles of exercising it. Moreover, the nature of violence, the start and end of wars, the contention between legitimate and illegitimate violence, and not taking any action as the alternative to not using force are all uncertain normative and strategic goals of just war theory. Therefore, pacifists argue that just war theory is limited in international politics and needs to be replaced with more viable ethical and practical alternatives to challenge the use of force and decisions of nonintervention.

Danny Singh, in chapter 4, provides criticism on contemporary just war theory with a variety of examples concerning the legitimate versus illegitimate use of force. The interventions examined include NATO's bombing of the former Yugoslavia in 1999 and post-9/11 Afghanistan and Iraq counterinsurgency operations. The decisions of nonintervention include Rwanda in the lead up to the 1994 genocide and the Rohingya citizenship crisis in Myanmar due to the 1982 Burmese Citizenship Law. These concrete examples are threaded through the initially discussed international relations theories of realism and institutional liberalism. It will largely be argued that the world organization and regional security organizations often support contemporary interests of superpowers' security initiatives, counter-terrorist strategy, and interests in oil-rich countries. These are the reasons for the use of force (even if killing some civilians within the rule of "proportionality"), humanitarian intervention, and the promotion of the Responsibility to Protect (R2P).[10] If such interests and reasons for the use of force/intervention are not met, then the decision to do nothing is the likely outcome, even in the event of crimes against humanity and genocide. The alternative to contemporary just war theory serving as an instrument of geopolitical interests is to exercise institutional liberalism with R2P. This can place the UN and NATO in better positions to provide pressure on their powerful member states to intervene for traditional just war reasons, which can alleviate the cynicism of intervention as a political smokescreen for relative gains.

Jonathan Chimakonam and Victor Nweke, in chapter 5, similarly provide concrete examples on civil wars in three non-Western contexts: Nigeria, Sri Lanka, and Guatemala. This chapter is the first to point out similarities between these different wars fought in three different continents at different historical times. Particularly, they point out similarities regarding the crimes committed, external influences, and lack of will by the international community to prosecute those crimes. In fact, this chapter shows how in these wars humanitarian law, namely the Law of Armed Conflict (LOAC), was violated during the armed conflicts (*jus in bello*). Consequently, Igbo, Tamils, and Maya ethnic groups were ill treated in Nigeria, Sri Lanka, and Guatemala respectively. Economic blockades were exercised to starve civilians and crimes against humanity and potential genocides occurred due to predetermined mass executions. The humanitarian legal critique further stresses that the international community has done little to investigate the breaches of LOAC in these three non-Western countries and redress (including retrospective justice) has not been enforced (as in the former Yugoslavia and Rwanda).

Chapters 6 and 7 provide alternative critiques of just war theory from feminist philosophy. Olajumoke Akiode, in chapter 6, draws on feminist critiques of just war theory. The chapter more succinctly covers African feminist views with the provision of thematic cases, namely Nigeria and the Democratic Republic of Congo, to argue that the African reality of inclusion, interconnectedness, and empathy can better improve just war theory and potential peace settlements.

Heleana Theixos, in chapter 7, focuses on feminist care political theory. The chapter provides reference to the First Gulf War and the ticking time bomb hypothetical analogy of interrogation torture of a detained person who knows the location of a bomb. It argues that theoretical approaches to care and justice are compatible and feminist care political theory enhances morality beyond traditional just war theory. This chapter is perhaps the first to systematically apply the ethics of care to understanding the actions of the Iraqi Army invaders of Kuwait.

Thaddeus Metz, in chapter 8, analyzes the just war criteria of engaging in warfare (*jus ad bellum*) within the context of contemporary African philosophy. African philosophy has been growing but very little has been done on the field of just war theory, which is developed in this chapter. The chapter starts with an outline of African moral theory. This focuses on honoring people based on their capacity to relate and contribute to their community to govern violence and the use of force. This principle is applied within the context of the resistance to colonialism in Africa in the twentieth century. This is subsequently compared with contemporary Anglo-American philosophy. The African communal responses to military ethics differ from Anglo-American perspectives on sovereignty, prevention, bias, and innocence.

Chapters 9 and 10 provide non-Western philosophical interpretations to just war theory. These include Chinese philosophy and Hindu theology. In chapter 9, Cao Qin specifically covers Confucian criticism of war and Mencius's conceptions of war being thought for the right reasons thereby clarifying Confucian values on war. Shyam Ranganathan, in chapter 10, analyzes the *Mahābhārata* which supports traditional morality with the exclusion of "parasites" who must be deprived of certain rights and values during wartime. This can be applied to times when fighting for independence against oppressive regimes.

Davis Brown, in chapter 11, analyzes war ethics (both *jus ad bellum* and *jus in bello*) in traditional and contemporary Islamic thinking. The chapter offers an innovative way to look at war ethics in Islamic thought. Instead of simply looking through case studies, it articulates these with the study of Islamic scripture, Islamic classical literature, and the Islamic historical narrative. Deciding to engage in war (*jus ad bellum*) is slightly liberal but a radical approach on the holy war is beyond Islamic mainstream theory today, but Islamic thought spreads broad justifications for using force when compared to other contemporary secular or Christian just war theory. Islamic rules of conduct during war (*jus in bello*) are also slightly more permissive. Traditional Islamic theory, especially *taqiyya*, legitimizes some warfare tactics that are strictly prohibited in secular LOAC.

The final chapter by Tong Sau Lin and King-Fai Tam is the first in the field to systematically make a link between Chinese Buddhism, warfare, and contemporary discussions of just war theory. Specifically, the chapter provides a theological alternative approach to just war theory. This chapter focuses on Chinese Buddhism. Buddhism is largely hailed within all religions for its *ahisma* (non-harming) doctrine on nonviolence. Similar to the third chapter, Buddhism is largely based on pacificism and the promotion of peace. However, Gautama Buddha stressed that aggression must be avoided, even if protecting one's faith, but a cessation of violence is paramount. Based on this contradictory premise, entering war may be required to safeguard fellow civilians from aggression and thus must not be blamed when engaging in warfare. The Mahayana conception of mercy killing can be associated with an act of compassion and moral intentions to protect fellow people from brutality and further violence. The chapter goes on to argue that Chinese Buddhism provides an alternative approach mainstream just war theory.

CONCLUSION

This book offers the first comparative approach to just war theory, by including different authors who contrast arguments from different philosophical traditions and ideologies. Moreover, even though there is considerable literature on just war theory, there is no comparable work that deals with just war theory by using different concepts and ideologies. The chapters in *Comparative Just War Theory: An Introduction to International Perspectives* are innovative insofar as they provide new insights and approaches which are not usually employed in dealing with such a widely debated topic. As a result, this aims to make a significant contribution to the literature on war and comparative philosophy because it will provide the possibility to compare how different philosophical perspectives deal with the normative challenges that result from war. This, in turn, provides the necessary groundwork for the production of new scholarship that rests on the intersection of different philosophical traditions. Hence, a potential outcome of this volume will enhance new schools of thought that intercept different kinds of philosophy. For instance, a form of Confucian Marxism is a new school that would flourish from the comparative approach to war. In addition, as a result of the conceptual interchange of this volume, new insights for policy for war can appear. Thus, potentially, there is also a practical application of the literature of this volume to real-life cases as exemplified within the contexts of the former Yugoslavia and post-9/11, and cases of Iraq and Afghanistan. All principles regarding the international legality of intervention/waging war (*jus ad bellum*) and conduct and accountability during war (*jus in bello*) are particularly examined in these contexts. Other additional non-Western wars from Africa, Asia, and Central America are brought to attention. These include the Nigerian civil war, Sri Lankan civil war, and the Guatemalan civil war, which are analyzed with LOAC as international law to regulate behavior during armed conflict (*jus in bello*).[11]

BIBLIOGRAPHY

Bai, Tongdong. "What to Do in an Unjust State? On Confucius's and Socrates's Views on Political Duty." *Dao* 9, no. 4 (2010): 375–90.

Bell, Daniel A., and Thaddeus Metz. "Confucianism and Ubuntu: Reflections on a Dialogue between Chinese and African Traditions." *Journal of Chinese Philosophy* 38 (2011): 78–95.

Chan, Joseph. *Confucian Perfectionism: A Political Philosophy for Modern Times*. Reprint edition. Princeton, NJ, and Oxford: Princeton University Press, 2015.

Charter of the United Nations, adopted June 26, 1945, entered into force October 24, 1945, 1 United Nations Treaty Series (UNTS) XVI.

Holmes, Robert L. "A Time for War? Augustine's Just War Theory Continues to Guide the West." *Christianity Today*, September 1, 2001.

Internet Encyclopedia of Philosophy. "Just War Theory." n.d.

Langan, John. "The Elements of St. Augustine's Just War Theory." *The Journal of Religious Ethics* 12, no. 1 (1984): 19–38.

Li, Chenyang. "Confucian Harmony in Dialogue with African Harmony: A Response." *African and Asian Studies* 15, no. 1 (2016): 23–32.

Littlewood, Alex. "Marine Guilty of Afghan Murder." *BBC News*, November 8, 2013 [online].

McMahan, Jeff. "Innocence, Self-Defense and Killing in War." *Journal of Political Philosophy* 2/3 (1994): 193–221.

Stanford Encyclopedia of Philosophy. "War." May 3, 2016.

United Nations Summit Outcome Document. "2005 World Summit Outcome." UN General Assembly Doc. A/RES/60/1, 60th session, October 24, 2005.

Walzer, Michael. *Just and Unjust Wars: A Moral Argument with Historical Illustrations*. Third edition. New York: Basic Books, 2000.

Wenning, Mario. "Kant and Daoism on Nothingness." *Journal of Chinese Philosophy* 38, no. 4 (2011): 556–68.

Chapter One

Anarchism and Just War Theory

Nathan Jun

INTRODUCTION

Given that anarchism is a political ideology that categorically repudiates and actively seeks to abolish political authority in all its forms,[1] it comes as no surprise that anarchists have had comparatively little to say about traditional just war theory.[2] The latter, after all, is founded on two basic assumptions that anarchism rejects: first, that sovereign political authorities are (or at least can be) morally legitimate and, second, that the right to declare and wage war *justly* is the exclusive purview of morally legitimate political authorities.[3] Because anarchism maintains that all political authorities "by their nature, by all their conditions, and by the supreme aim and end of their existence . . . are completely the opposite of liberty, morality, and human justice,"[4] the question of whether and under what conditions their conduct qualifies as "just" is moot. If there is no such thing as "good, just, or virtuous" (i.e., morally legitimate) political authorities,[5] then *anything* and *everything* that issues from such authorities is unjust by definition.

As Andrew Robinson points out, it is more than a little ironic that anarchists have been routinely stereotyped as "bomb-throwers," whereas states and other political authorities are "generally viewed as a source of social peace" whose absence is "associated indissolubly with war."[6] The latter, after all, have been the foremost perpetrators of large-scale bloodshed in the history of the world, whereas the former have been among the most consistent and indefatigable critics of said bloodshed.[7] None of this is to say, however, that anarchism is inherently pacifistic, let alone that anarchists *qua* anarchists reject the presumed distinction between "just" and "unjust" forms of warfare. As Robinson notes, on the contrary:

> In general, anarchists identify the state [and other political authorities] as *inherently* violent and as a source of violence, and seek to end (or, failing this, to moderate) its violence through exercises of counter-power. Such counter-power is necessarily exercised by social movements or ethically-oriented individuals, not by states or other hierarchies, and can take the form of either nonviolent counter-power or of "popular defense."[8]

In other words, while "some anarchists are entirely nonviolent," anarchism itself has been consistently willing to "justify the use of force as means to defend against the oppressive violence of the state."[9]

All of this by way of saying that anarchist attitudes toward war—no less than their engagement with traditional theories of, and justifications for, warfare—are extremely multifarious and complex. Because providing an exhaustive overview and analysis of these attitudes would greatly exceed the scope of this chapter, I will instead attempt to highlight a few of the more significant themes that have featured in anarchist discussions of war since the nineteenth century as well as the various ways these themes have been expressed in anarchist political practice. Following a brief synopsis of traditional just war theory in the first section, the second section will discuss a range of general anarchist commitments that are especially salient to understanding its relationship to the former. This relationship is elucidated most clearly in the third section, which examines anarchist perspectives on war and violence in light of these commitments as well as representative examples of how they have been put into action.

TRADITIONAL JUST WAR THEORY

Although the term "war" is frequently used in reference to "any serious strife, struggle, or campaign," traditional legal, political, and sociological analyses have tended to define it more narrowly as a specific *kind* of armed conflict or violent altercation involving ostensibly sovereign political authorities.[10] In Oppenheim's classic formulation, for example, war is described as "a contention between two or more States through their armed forces for the purpose of overpowering each other and imposing such conditions of peace as the victor pleases."[11] This is more or less the prevailing understanding within so-called "just war theories," the common objectives of which have been (a) to determine when and under what conditions sovereign political authorities are morally justified in declaring and waging war (*jus ad bellum*) and (b) to identify the sorts of conduct that are morally permissible in the context of just warfare (*jus in bello*).[12]

Political authority in general involves the exercise of de facto power (i.e., the actionable capacity to compel or prevent behavior) on the basis of a presumed *right* to issue and enforce "binding" directives.[13] A directive is said to be "binding" when those subject to it have a "content-independent" duty or obligation to comply, where this, in turn, is a matter of their having reasons to do so independently of who or what issued the directive in the first place.[14] In this respect, a distinction is typically drawn between de facto political authority—which "consists merely in claiming, exercising, or being generally *believed* (by those subject to the authority)" to possess the right to issue and enforce "binding" directives—or to de jure authority, which consists in *actually* possessing it.[15]

Political authorities (i.e., governments) are entities that exercise de facto power over particular populations within specific bounded geographic areas and claim an exclusive right to do so. This right—which is generally referred to as "sovereignty"—entitles them to monopolize the exercise of de facto power within the scope of their own jurisdictions while simultaneously shielding them from interference by external entities.[16] Although all governments possess some degree of de facto authority in virtue of claiming and exercising sovereignty, this does not necessarily mean that they actually *are* sovereign. In other words, not all de facto political authorities possess de jure authority. Those that do are typically referred to as "legitimate."[17]

Since classical antiquity, Western political thinkers have proposed various theories of *normative* legitimacy, the common aim of which has been to determine the conditions for having an actual right to rule over others, which implies a correlative obligation on their part to obey. Although legitimate authorities tend to meet certain conditions for having de facto authority—for example, "popular support and representation of a people," "monopoly of violence and effective control of a people," "adherence to international legal standards," and "predisposition to strive for a lasting peace"[18]—this does not necessarily mean that they have de jure (i.e., legitimate) authority. Most of the aforesaid theories contend that legitimacy involves altogether distinct conditions related to the normative justification of political authority as such, though the nature and scope of this justification is itself a matter of considerable dispute. For some, legitimacy is a matter of fulfilling certain ends, bringing about certain consequences, or meeting certain responsibilities, as when Aquinas claims that political authorities exist for the sake of protecting the "common weal" of the "city, kingdom, or province subject to them."[19] For others—most notably social contract theories—legitimacy is a function of the voluntary consent of the governed.[20]

However legitimacy is defined and justified, legitimate political authorities are taken to have an exclusive right to exercise power within their own jurisdictions and defend themselves against real or imagined aggression. As we have already seen, the principal aim of just war theory is precisely to determine when and under what conditions warfare is a morally justifiable means of doing so. This presupposes that legitimate authority is a necessary (though not sufficient) condition for war to be declared and waged *justly*. As

Heinze and Steele note, the long-standing and deeply entrenched notion that nation-states alone have "legitimate" authority—and, by extension, a monopoly on the "legitimate" use of force—has proven difficult to sustain "in an era in which non-state actors are playing an increasingly prominent role in armed conflict."[21] From extremist groups like al-Qaeda and ISIS to private military contractors like Blackwater, the aftermath of the September 11, 2001, attacks has witnessed the emergence of a wide variety of actors that not only "operate largely independent of the sovereign jurisdiction of a state" but also "demonstrate[e] a striking array of state-like military capabilities and judicative capacities."[22] Notwithstanding their contemporary geopolitical significance—particularly in the context of the global "War on Terror"—such actors are difficult to accommodate within "prevailing normative frameworks" whose "moral vocabulary regarding war is primarily equipped to apply to the conduct of states."[23]

While nonstate actors have obviously employed violent means in pursuit of political, social, and religious objectives throughout human history, it was not until the nineteenth century that violence of this sort gained widespread attention from authorities and the general public alike in the form of politically motivated uprisings, riots, assassinations, and bombings. Then, as now, such acts were regularly described as "terrorism"[24]—a term that has tended to function less as a clear analytical category with a "precise, concrete, and truly explanatory definition" than a generic descriptor for any form of political violence perceived as morally illegitimate.[25] In response to the perceived inadequacies of this definition, Bruce Hoffman has proposed that terrorism is better understood as actual or threatened violence that is

> ineluctably political in aims and motives . . . designed to have far-reaching psychological repercussions beyond the immediate victim or target . . . conducted by an organization with an identifiable chain of command or conspiratorial cell structure (whose members wear no uniform or identifying insignia) . . . [and] perpetrated by a subnational group or non-state entity.[26]

Despite its pretenses toward greater precision, Hoffman's definition remains clearly indebted to the traditional notion that morally legitimate violence is the exclusive purview of the state. Hoffman would scarcely deny that state-sponsored violence is "political in aims and motives" and not infrequently "designed to have far-reaching psychological repercussions beyond the immediate victim or target," but this is ultimately immaterial as concerns its moral legitimacy. Whether legitimate or not, all such violence is "warfare" when it is perpetrated by states. When this same violence is perpetrated by a "subnational group or non-state entity," in contrast, it is considered "terrorism," the moral illegitimacy of which is invariably assumed regardless of its character or underlying motivations. This invites the problematic implication that there are no morally significant differences between different *kinds* of terrorism—in which case, "terroristic" acts marshaled in the service of Islamist "jihad" (e.g., the September 11 attacks) are morally indistinguishable from those employed in revolutionary struggles against an unjust oppressor (e.g., the American War for Independence).[27]

To circumvent this problem, some just war theorists have argued that traditional just war principles can and should be applied to "armed conflicts that involve non-state actors."[28] Of particular relevance here is the principle of discrimination (or distinction), which differentiates the moral evaluation of acts within war from their underlying causes. This principle is reflected, for example, in Article 4 of the Third Geneva Convention (1949), which allows for the protection of non-state actors, such as

> [m]embers of . . . militias and members of other volunteer corps, including those of organized resistance movements . . . provided that they fulfill the following conditions: (a) that of being commanded by a person responsible for his subordinates; (b) that of having a fixed distinctive sign recognizable at a distance; (c) that of carrying arms openly; (d) that of conducting their operations in accordance with the laws and customs of war.[29]

In these and similar cases, the fact that *all* combatants are considered equally beholden to the moral criteria of *jus in bello* is taken to imply that just war theory is applicable in principle to the conduct of state and nonstate actors alike.

The problem with this argument, as I see it, is that it assumes (if not explicitly asserts) that parties to armed conflicts must be sufficiently akin to state actors in their overall demeanor and conduct to qualify as "lawful" combatants. To this extent, it merely reinforces the presumption that state actors (and political authorities more generally) exercise a de facto monopoly over the "legitimate" use of force as well as over the right to morally evaluate the conduct of other actors.[30] The notion that such authorities (or the international legal bodies to which they belong) can and should apply just war principles to the conduct of nonstate actors is obviously compatible with the perpetuation of their already existing monopoly over the *right* to moral evaluation in general. Unless and until this right is extended to nonstate actors in a genuinely actionable way, merely broadening the scope of moral evaluation available to state actors fails to pose any real challenge to the state-centric framework.

Furthermore, the notion that just war principles can be neutrally applied to state and nonstate actors alike obscures the significant normative and conceptual differences between them. Inasmuch as these differences are presupposed in the very normative criteria that traditional just war theory seeks to articulate (i.e., criteria for morally evaluating the conduct of *state actors*), it is not clear how just war principles can be applied to the conduct of *nonstate actors* without presupposing that the latter act, or ought to act, like states via the principle of *discrimination*. This, of course, is precisely what traditional just war theory denies.

In fairness, the seemingly intractable association between sovereign political authorities and warfare comes as no surprise given the track record mentioned at the outset of this chapter. The same is true of our long-standing insistence—despite all evidence to the contrary—that this association is contingent rather than necessary (i.e., that war is something that particular authorities in particular circumstances *happen* to do from time to time as opposed to a constitutive element of political authority as such). After all, the notion that political authority is *founded* on pervasive, seemingly unending violence invites the uncomfortable prospect that this violence—no less than the entities that perpetrate it—is altogether irredeemable from the standpoint of morality.

Anarchism, for its part, has never had such misgivings. As we will see in the next section, this is a direct consequence of its traditional analysis of the nature and operation of political authority as such, the very essence of which it identifies as "war within and war without."[31] For anarchists, all political authority is compelled by necessity to seek "the augmentation of its power";[32] for this reason, Mikhail Bakunin writes, "it must be armed and ceaselessly on guard against both domestic and foreign enemies . . . [and] . . . is bound to regard all, both within and outside its borders, as enemies."[33] The fundamental problem for anarchists is that the acquisition and deployment of such power—including by means of war—is based on a presumed right to do so that does not and cannot exist.[34] Inasmuch as the moral legitimacy of political authority depends on such a right and the ability to acquire and deploy power *justly* depends on such legitimacy, it follows that *all* warfare prosecuted by political authorities is unjust by definition.

ANARCHISM AND POLITICAL AUTHORITY

Notwithstanding its considerable internal diversity, anarchism has consistently affirmed freedom and equality as its most fundamental and unassailable values. As I have argued at length elsewhere,[35] the prevailing understanding of these values within the broad anarchist tradition rests on four basic claims: first, that freedom is "a *state* or *condition* marked by the achievement of maximal human development or flourishing";[36] second, that the individual achievement of maximal human development or flourishing requires an actionable capacity for self-determined action (i.e., autonomy);[37] third, that the capacity for autonomous action is "inexorably social" insofar as it depends on political, social, and economic conditions that facilitate it;[38] and fourth, that the political, social, and economic conditions that facilitate autonomy are necessarily conditions of *equality*.[39]

According to the first of these claims, "true liberty" consists in "the liberty of actual and active opportunity"[40]—in other words, the "liberty to be, to do,"[41] to "grow to [one's] full stature . . . [to] learn to think and move, to give the very best of [oneself],"[42] to actualize the full range of one's latent "material, intellectual, and moral powers,"[43] to achieve "the all-around development and full enjoyment of [one's] physical, intellectual, and moral faculties."[44] While liberty of this sort obviously requires a capacity for autonomous action, such a capacity is actionable only in the absence of *domination* (i.e., a form of power that "inhibits or prevents people from participating in determining their actions or the conditions of their actions").[45] Inasmuch as domination is exercised by one group (or set of groups) over another group (or set of groups) in a way that "limits [the latter's] freedoms, choices, and abilities"[46] to the advantage of the former, it "invariably operates by means of the creation and maintenance of hierarchies—that is, structured relationships in which political, social, economic, etc. power is distributed unequally among those who are party to said relationships"[47] in a way that benefits some and harms others. In practice, the dominant groups within such hierarchies acquire, maintain, and augment their power over the subordinate groups through various kinds of coercion, violence, and repression as well as the denial of "significant political, social, or economic advantages."[48] Understood in this way, domination is necessarily incompatible with the conditions of possibility for the "full development of [individual] powers, capacities, and talents"[49] and, for this reason, is morally illegitimate by definition.

That anarchism regards political authority as a paradigmatic form of domination, as is made especially clear by the following well-known passage from Pierre-Joseph Proudhon's *The General Idea of Revolution in the Nineteenth Century*:

> To be governed is to be watched over, inspected, spied on, directed, legislated at, regulated, docketed, indoctrinated, preached at, controlled, assessed, weighed, censored, ordered about, by men who have neither the right, nor the knowledge, nor the virtue. . . . To be governed is to be at every operation, at every transaction, noted, registered, enrolled, taxed, stamped, measured, numbered, assessed, licensed, authorized, admonished, forbidden, reformed, corrected, punished. It is, under the pretext of public utility, and in the name of the general interest, to be placed under contribution, trained, ransomed, exploited, monopolized, extorted, squeezed, mystified, robbed; then, at the slightest resistance, the first word of complaint, to be repressed, fined, despised, harassed, tracked, abused, clubbed, disarmed, choked, imprisoned, judged, condemned, shot, deported, sacrificed, sold, betrayed; and, to crown all, mocked, ridiculed, outraged, dishonored. That is government; that is its justice; that is its morality.[50]

Given the prevalence of such ideas in anarchist literature, it comes as no surprise that anarchism has frequently been identified with antistatism. Anarchism's opposition to the state, however, is simply an extension of its rejection of domination more generally, and it is this, more so than anything else, that most clearly distinguishes it from other ideologies. For anarchists, political authority—no less than capitalism, sexism, racism, and homophobia—is simply one of the "multiple and mutually irreducible forms" that domination takes.[51] The state, accordingly, is simply "a particular (if particularly important) and unjustifiable instance of a more widespread social phenomenon."[52]

Inasmuch as domination in general involves a fundamental logic—the nature of which we will discuss in greater detail in the next section—it comes as no surprise that otherwise distinct instances of domination frequently operate in conjunction (or, better, *collusion*) with each other.[53] For anarchists, however, different forms of domination have different "qualities, interests, and dynamics"; unlike Marxists, they deny that all such forms are merely "consequences of 'relations of production' or, what comes to the same, that all [domination] is ultimately reducible to economic exploitation."[54] Political authorities, accordingly, are not just "committee[s] for managing the common affairs of the whole bourgeoisie"[55] or "organ[s] of class rule."[56] Their principal interest is not the perpetuation of class domination so much as the "the preservation of [their] exclusive governmental advantages and . . . personnel"[57]—chief among them, their monopoly over the exercise of de facto power. As noted previously, the principal function of de jure authority is precisely to justify and rationalize this monopoly.

Because the de jure authority that governments claim for themselves "does not *depend* on the voluntary compliance of those over whom it is exercised,"[58] the presumed right to issue binding, content-independent directives is, in practice, a right to command others as well as to compel their obedience through force if necessary. Anarchists reject such authority insofar as it implies an obligation or duty on the part of autonomous persons to surrender their private judgment and obey governmental directives regardless of what they themselves happen to think or desire. A truly autonomous person—a person who has both the ability and the right to decide what she will do or refrain from doing on the basis of her own private judgment—cannot possibly be obligated or duty bound in this way; thus, the very notion of de jure authority is fundamentally incompatible with autonomy and, by extension, with the fundamental values of freedom and equality.[59]

ANARCHISM AND CONVENTIONAL WARFARE

Anarchists are quick to point out that governments can and do exercise de facto power over their subjects regardless of whether the latter recognize their de jure authority to do so. This is because all governments—whether independently or in collusion with other dominating entities—are inexorably driven to acquire, maintain, and augment their power by seeking "ever greater control of territories and people."[60] Regardless of their particular "form, character, or color"—whether "absolute or constitutional, monarchy or republic, fascist, Nazi, or Bolshevik"[61]—they are "essentially based on domination . . . that is upon despotism"[62] and their "essential function in all times and in all places" has unfailingly been "that of oppressing and exploiting the masses" for the sake of "defending the oppressors and exploiters."[63] This suggests that the concept of legitimacy itself is little more than a "garment" with which governments "cove[r] themselves" to rationalize their behavior while simultaneously concealing the true nature and purpose of that behavior.[64] At the end of the day, anarchists contend, governments acquire and exercise their power to dominate people *in spite of* their claims to legitimacy—not *because* of it.

Like all forms of domination, the state is a "permanent conspiracy on the part of the minority against the majority," which "by its nature places itself outside and over the people and inevitably subordinates them to an organization and to aims which are foreign to and opposed to [their] real needs and aspirations."[65] As a result, "warlike relations often pertain between states and social forces inside societies. Indeed, in a state-controlled society, there is something like a situation of permanent social war."[66] Anarchists, accordingly, "refuse the division between external and internal, or the framing of war as a phenomenon occurring between already formed states."[67]

The same "inherent logic" that engenders "intrastate repression and violence" is the foremost cause of interstate warfare.[68] "By its very essence and by the goals which it fixes," Bakunin writes, "the modern state is necessarily a military state, and a military state is bound no less obligatorily to becoming a conquering state."[69] This is because every state, no matter its character, "must strive, under penalty of utter ruin, to become the most powerful of states . . . to devour others in order to not be devoured in turn."[70] In this respect, political domination is no different from economic domination or, indeed, any other form thereof:

> Just as capitalist production and banking speculation—which in the long run swallows up that production—must, under the threat of bankruptcy, ceaselessly expand at the expense of the small financial and productive enterprises that they absorb, and become universal monopolistic enterprises extending all over the world—so this modern and necessarily military state is driven by an irrepressible urge to become a universal state.[71]

A similar point is made by Errico Malatesta:

> There is, then, the dominating class only that counts; and this class, owing to its desire to conserve and to enlarge its power, even its prejudices and its own ideas, may find it convenient to excite racial ambitions and hatred, and send its nation, its flock, against "foreign" countries, with a view to releasing them from their present oppressors, and submitting them to its own political economical domination.[72]

Whatever sort of power they seek to acquire, maintain, and augment, all dominating entities "must be . . . ceaselessly on guard against both domestic and foreign adversaries . . . and . . . in a state of conspiracy against all of them."[73]

This reinforces a point made earlier, namely, that all conventional warfare—whether it is directed at foreign conquest or domestic repression—is ultimately an expression of the logic of domination. Anarchism obviously opposes warfare of this sort for the same reasons it opposes domination more generally.[74] More than this, it supports resistance on the part of those against whom such warfare is waged as well as proactive efforts to eradicate its source. That said, anarchists have often been divided over whether and to what extent violent means should be taken in pursuit of these ends. As Uri Gordon notes:

> When anarchists in the nineteenth and early twentieth century talked about political violence, they were typically referring to one of two scenarios: mass armed insurrection, or assassinations of heads of state and capitalist bosses. Today, in contrast, the primary context for discussion is the use of non-lethal violence during protests: scenes of property destruction and confrontations with police on the streets, in particular during demonstrations against summits of government leaders and international economic organizations.[75]

Insofar as anarchism *qua* anarchism does not have a single settled conviction on the morality of violence as such, let alone a uniform understanding of what violence *is*, it comes as no surprise that anarchists have disagreed over the use of such means. While some anarchists have categorically rejected them, the broad anarchist tradition itself has generally been accommodating of and receptive to violence—at least in certain circumstances.

ANARCHISM AND VIOLENCE

As a revolutionary ideology, anarchism seeks to abolish existing political, social, economic, ethical, and cultural institutions and replace them with something different.[76] Given that the institutions in question were created by the powerful for the sake of maintaining and augmenting their power—

usually over the course of centuries—it is naïve to expect that the defenders and beneficiaries of these institutions "will recognize the injustice of, the harm caused by" them, let alone "voluntarily renounce" the power they serve.[77] Although anarchists recognize that domination cannot be eradicated without struggle (violent or otherwise) and that this is not a realistic aspiration in the absence of mass counter-power, they have expressed a variety of ideas on how to build and mobilize this counter-power in practice, all of which seek to maintain fidelity to certain general and interrelated commitments.

The first of these commitments is to *prefiguration*. "[I]n its most general form," Benjamin Franks writes, prefiguration "denotes an identity between (anti-)political methods and (anti-)political goals or ends."[78] Anarchists "explicitly distance themselves from the position that the end justifies the means," demanding instead that the latter must be morally and politically consistent with the former. In other words, the means taken in the present must "prefigure" the very ends they hope to bring about in the future.

The second commitment, which follows from the first, is to *direct action*. Insofar as anarchism seeks to eradicate domination and to maximize individual autonomy, it is vitally important that those who share these aims strive to achieve them by and for themselves—that is, *autonomously*—rather than appeal to others to do so on their behalf. This lack of mediation "distinguishes direct action from . . . political strategies such as voting, lobbying, or rallying—which are activities that pursue certain results through one or more intermediaries."[79]

The third commitment is the *rejection of vanguards*, that is, "particular group[s] with claims to either superior knowledge or more fortunate location in the political terrain . . . which can take strategic priority and win battles for others (and often speak *on behalf of* the client group)."[80] As Peter Kropotkin writes:

> No handful of people, however energetic and talented, can evoke a popular insurrection, if the people themselves, through their own best representatives, do not achieve the realization that they have no other way out of a position with which they are dissatisfied except insurrection. Consequently, the business of any revolutionary party is not to call for insurrection but only to pave the way for the success of the imminent insurrection.[81]

Anarchists "do not want to liberate the people [from domination]" as much as they "want the people to liberate themselves."[82] They do not presume to know the people's interests or claim any right to act on behalf of those interests. Their principal task, accordingly, is that of "'pushing' [them] to demand and to seize all the freedom they can and to make themselves responsible for their own needs without waiting for orders from any kind of authority."[83] In practice, this is a matter of "demonstrating the uselessness and harmfulness of [domination], of encouraging and provoking by propaganda and action all kinds of individual and collective initiatives."[84]

The fourth and final commitment is to *revolution*, which Kropotkin defines as "a rapid modification of outgrown economic and political institutions, an overthrow of the injustices accumulated by centuries past, [and] a displacement of wealth and political power."[85] Revolutionary action, accordingly, is "radical rather than moderate, rapid rather than gradual, and emerges from without as-against dominant social arrangements rather than from within and in cooperation with them."[86] As proponents of such action, anarchists reject reformist strategies that seek to bring about "incremental change . . . through the provisions of existing power structures."[87] This includes everything from "constitutional [or] regulatory change driven by one or more branches of government" to "petitions for legislation or court action, the promotion of electoral candidates, and engagement between organized labor and employers."[88]

Taken together, these shared commitments constitute the foundation of anarchist practice and serve as the general framework within which ideas about anarchist practice are formulated and evaluated. It is in relation to this framework, accordingly, that anarchist attitudes toward violence must be understood. If we stipulate that violence in general refers to "any action or structural arrangement that results in physical or nonphysical harm to one or more persons"—including threats of harm that generate an "embodied sense of attack or deliberate endangerment in its recipient"[89]—it is trivially true that anarchists reject violence thus defined whenever it is employed as a means to domination and other morally illegitimate ends. Some have gone a step further, however, by rejecting the use of violent means in pursuit of the political aims of anarchism itself.

Here, a distinction must be drawn between those who reject (some or all) violent means on the grounds that violence as such is inherently wrong (i.e., pacifists) and those who do so because they consider such means to be inconsistent or otherwise at odds with the commitments enumerated above. It is true that certain notable anarchists have been pacifists and that anarchism itself has always contained pacifist currents.[90] For the most part, however, those anarchists who have opposed the use of violence have principally done so on the grounds that (some or all) violent means are incompatible with prefiguration. According to this view:

> [Anarchists] cannot say that violence, on whatever level, would be justified just because it helps achieve a free society. Rather, they believe that means and ends should always be of the same substance. The argument thus tends to take the following, straightforward form: "Anarchists want a non-violent society. Anarchists also believe that the revolutionary movement should prefigure the desired society in its means and ways. Therefore, anarchists cannot use violence to achieve a non-violent society."[91]

In response, some have argued that anarchism *qua* anarchism is not committed to eradicating violence per se (either because doing so is impossible or merely undesirable) as much as a particular form of violence (i.e., domination). It considers the latter to be morally illegitimate, moreover, not because it is *violent*, but because it is contrary to various fundamental moral and political values, such as freedom and equality. The same does not appear to be true of violence—at least not in all cases—which is why most anarchists have denied that the use of violent means is *necessarily* incompatible with anarchism in general or its commitment to prefiguration in particular.

However violence is defined, the prevailing view within the broad anarchist tradition is that "violence is justifiable when it is necessary to defend oneself and others from violence."[92] Inasmuch as domination in all its forms involves a kind of protracted warfare between those who dominate and those who are dominated, however, it follows that the latter are "always in a state of legitimate defense" and, consequently, that any violence they perpetrate against the former "is always justifiable and must be controlled only by such considerations as that the best and most economical use is being made of human efforts and human sufferings."[93] Being attacked themselves, "the oppressed . . . always have the right to attack the oppressors,"[94] to "react violently against [their] violence and to put lead against lead to crush [it]."[95] Indeed, such violence is not only justifiable but *necessary*: as Malatesta argues, it is "the only way to put an end to the far greater, the permanent, violence that keeps the majority of mankind in servitude."[96] Anarchism, after all, aspires to do more than *defend* people against the violence of domination; it seeks to eradicate domination altogether.

As Johann Most wrote in 1890, "It cannot and it shall be denied that most anarchists are convinced that the development of the present social order cannot be brought upon its right track by peaceable means. But that is a question of tactics which has nothing to do with principles."[97] Historically speaking, anarchists have tended to regard violence as a forgone conclusion in the revolutionary struggle against the state and other institutions that are themselves inherently violent. The main question, accordingly, has not been whether violence *as such* is a justifiable means of pursuing the goals of anarchism but whether particular kinds of violence that are otherwise consistent with fundamental anarchist commitments constitute an effective means of doing so.

Anarchists have proposed various answers to this question that reflect differing ideas about the nature of (the) revolution itself. Although they have generally agreed that the latter "seeks to alter the whole character of society"[98] by decisively abolishing domination in all forms (as opposed to merely changing the rulers or altering the form of government), they have vacillated over what this means in practice. In the late nineteenth century, most anarchists tended to understand revolution as a kind of event that would transpire rapidly and on a massive scale. Bakunin, for example, believed that it would take the form of a spontaneous uprising involving most or all members of the international working class and culminating in the total destruction of "all modern institutions," including "the state, church, courts, university, army, and police."[99] In practice, this would entail large-scale and extremely violent attacks on life and property that would continue indefinitely until the institutions in question were no longer able to defend themselves and thus were effectively overthrown.

Like other anarchists at this time, Bakunin rejected the "belief of the authoritarian communists . . . that a social revolution must be decreed and organized either by a dictatorship or by a constituent assembly emerging from a political revolution" and insisted that "revolution could neither be made nor brought to its full development except by the spontaneous and continued action of the masses, the groups and associations of the people."[100] As Uri Gordon notes, "By 'spontaneous' Bakunin does not mean impulsive, improvised, and undirected activity, but instead activity that is self-directed, voluntary, and therefore antagonistic to the imposition of artificial, pre-ordained structures."[101] Truly revolutionary activity is carried out "from the bottom up, by the free association or federation of workers"[102] and culminates in nothing less than "the immediate and direct actuation of full and complete social liquidation."[103]

The uprisings that precipitated the short-lived Paris Commune in the spring of 1871 are an oft-cited early example of the sort of revolutionary vision that Bakunin and other anarchists of his generation favored.[104] In the first place, the uprisings in question were large scale and all encompassing, resulting in the immediate (or nearly immediate) collapse of the existing order and corresponding transformation of virtually all aspects of life.[105] In the second place, they were almost entirely spontaneous and self-directed, erupting in a more or less spontaneous fashion following months of increasingly militant agitation by the Parisian working classes.[106] Although anarchists like Elisée Reclus and Louise Michel played important roles,[107] neither the uprisings themselves nor the particular forms they took were the work of any sort of ideologically motivated minority.[108]

All of this being said, because Bakunin and other anarchists had conflicting ideas about the failure of the Commune no less than the underlying causes that brought it about in the first place, they were naturally divided over its political implications. Given their belief that anarchism as such would never be consciously accepted by a majority of people, it seemed that revolution would necessarily be "the work of a conscious minority."[109] Because revolution cannot be *imposed*, however, such work would essentially be limited to "creat[ing] the conditions that make a rapid evolution toward anarchy possible."[110] As noted previously, this is principally achieved by "encourag[ing] the masses to act directly, to take possession of the means of production, to occupy housing, to perform public services without waiting for resolutions or commands from higher-ranking authorities."[111] The role of anarchists, accordingly, is to rouse people to action and fight *alongside* them—not *for* them.

It is by no means clear, however, how a minority of political actors who are essentially limited to propagandizing could possibly instigate a spontaneous, large-scale uprising like the Paris Commune. For this reason, many anarchists gradually abandoned the notion that the revolution should (or could) be made rapidly and all at once. Instead of an event, they came to see it as a *process* to be carried out over time. In practice, this would entail both sustained, long-term initiatives and episodic attacks on a smaller and more narrowly defined scale, all of which would serve to radicalize the wider population and impel them little by little to revolt. The salient questions became: what sorts of (long- and short-term) efforts should be pursued in this regard, and what is the best way of pursuing them?

With the notable exceptions of the Makhnovist Uprisings in the Ukraine (1917–1921) and the Spanish Civil War (1936–1939), anarchists have seldom participated directly in large-scale conventional warfare, presumably because modern military tactics, command structures, and the like are difficult to accommodate within anarchist political frameworks. In the aftermath of the Paris Commune, the anarchist movement gradually divided itself into two broad factions, the first of which favored sustained organizing and agitation within the wider labor movement and the second of which favored assassinations, bombings, and other forms of violent direct action, collectively known as "propaganda by the deed."[112] Many if not most of the representatives of the former faction—the so-called "anarcho-syndicalists"—had come to regard capitalism as the principal mechanism of domination in modern society. For this reason, they began to assert that the struggle to eradicate domination in general should be directed first and foremost against the major sources of capitalist power—hence, their emphasis on the use of various "method[s] of immediate warfare by the workers against their economic and political oppressors," including "the strike . . . the boycott; sabotage in its countless forms; anti-militarist propaganda; and in particularly critical cases . . . armed resistance of the people for the protection of life and liberty."[113] Many came to see the so-called general strike—an organized, all-encompassing refusal to work culminating in the expropriation of the means of production—as the chief means by which the revolution and its goals would be realized.

In a self-conscious effort "to create an atmosphere of struggle in which class enmities would sharpen and the workers would learn from experience the need for a revolutionary solution to the social problem,"[114] anarcho-syndicalists and other anarchists operating within the labor movement actively contributed to the explosion of militant labor activity that rocked Europe and the United States during the last two decades of the nineteenth century.[115] By the first decade of the twentieth century, anarcho-syndicalism had emerged as the dominant tendency within the labor unions of several countries, including Argentina, Brazil, France, Portugal, and Spain. Anarcho-syndicalists were at the forefront of organized opposition to the First World War and played leading roles in several notable actions, such as the Italian factory occupations of 1919–1920 as well as general strikes in Mexico (1916), Spain (1917), Portugal (1918), and Argentina (1918–1919).

Representatives of the other faction—who are most often referred to as "insurrectionists"—insisted that revolutionary action must be directed at all modern institutions simultaneously in the form of "immediate, destructive attack[s] on the structures, individuals and organizations"[116] that comprise them. Attacks of this sort—which typically included bombings, assassinations, and other "spectacular displays" of violence—were intended to illustrate the weakness and vulnerability of such institutions and, in so doing, inspire mass resistance to them.[117] To this extent, acts of "propaganda by the deed" functioned chiefly as a kind of "demonstrative communication" rather than as "substantive methods of socio-political change."[118]

At their peak in the 1880s, 1890s, and early 1900s, insurrectionists were involved in a wide array of politically motivated criminal activities (e.g., bank robbery and burglary[119]) and were directly and indirectly responsible for several high-profile acts of violence. These include, among others, the assassinations of Tsar Alexander II of Russia (1881), French President Sadi Carnot (1894), Spanish Prime Minister Antonio Cánovas (1897), King Umberto I of Italy (1900), President William McKinley of the United States (1901), and King Carlos I of Portugal (1908) and the bombings of the Liceu Theater in Barcelona (1893), the French National Assembly (1893), and the Café Terminus in Paris (1894).[120] These actions provoked severe government repression in Europe and the United States that dramatically weakened the anarchist movement. In the United States alone, "the newspapers drove a massive anti-anarchist propaganda campaign that fomented outright hysteria within an already xenophobic population. Meanwhile Congress passed numerous anti-radical bills, such as the Sedition Act of 1918, which led to the arrest, imprisonment, and deportation of thousands of suspected anarchists and other radicals."[121]

The two factions differed not only over particular tactics but also the overall role that organization plays or ought to play in revolutionary action. Virtually all representatives of the former emphasized participation "in mass workers' organizations and social movements," and many advocated the creation of explicitly anarchist groups, "based on theoretical unity, tactical unity, collective responsibility, and federalism," whose chief function "prior to [the] revolutionary transitional period" would be to "create the fullest possible extent of communistic alternatives (cooperatives, schools, cultural activities, etc.) and to fight to keep self-management at the centre of every political struggle."[122] Representatives of the latter, in contrast, endorsed a "strategy of informal and temporary organizations in affinity groups [as] base nuclei for . . . attacks on police stations, banks, and similar targets," abandoning organized "counter-hegemonic movement-building" in favor of episodic "riots and clandestine actions."[123] For the most part, these basic factional divisions have endured to the present and continue to express themselves in various ways within the contemporary anarchist movement.

CONCLUSION

Despite these and other internal disagreements, anarchism has always understood itself as a response to a perceived state of "ubiquitous 'social war.'" As I have taken pains to emphasize, anarchists of all stripes see themselves and the people they fight alongside as combatants in an ongoing struggle; for this reason, the means that they employ—whether violent or not—are ultimately *military* tactics that need to be evaluated in relation to this struggle and its aims. In a certain sense, this approximates just war theory, which involves a similar imperative because it concerns the behavior of state actors when waging war and their conduct during war. The crucial difference, as presented clearly in this chapter, is that, while the latter seeks to evaluate that behavior against the presumed moral justifiability of political authority itself, anarchism rejects that presumption on moral and political grounds of its own. It is these grounds, moreover, that serve as the ultimate standard by which anarchism evaluates its struggle against political authority and domination more generally.

BIBLIOGRAPHY

Allhoff, Fritz, Nicholas G. Evans, and Adam Henschke, eds. *The Routledge Companion of Ethics and War*. New York: Routledge, 2013.
Aquinas, Thomas. *Summa Theologica*. Edited and translated by the Fathers of the English Dominican Province. New York: Benziger Brothers, 1946.
Bach Jensen, Richard. *The Battle Against Anarchist Terrorism: An International History, 1878–1934*. Cambridge: Cambridge University Press, 2014.
Bakunin, Mikhail. *Bakunin on Anarchy*, edited by Sam Dolgoff. New York: Alfred A. Knopf, 1972.
———. *The Basic Bakunin*, edited by Robert Cutler. Buffalo: Prometheus Books, 1992.
———. *God and the State*. Mineola, NY: Dover, 1970.
———. *Michael Bakunin: Selected Writings*, edited by Arthur Lehning. London: Cape, 1973.
———. *The Political Philosophy of Bakunin*, edited by G. P. Maximoff. New York: Free Press, 1953.
Bantman, Constance. "The Era of Propaganda by the Deed." In *The Palgrave Handbook of Anarchism*, edited by Carl Levy and Matthew S. Adams, 371–87. Basingstoke, UK: Palgrave Macmillan, 2018.
Berkman, Alexander. *The Bolshevik Myth*. London: Pluto Press, 1989.

———. *Now and After: The ABC of Anarchist Communism*. New York: Vanguard Press, 1929.
———. *What Is Anarchism?* Oakland, CA: AK Press, 2003.
Bledsoe Robert, and Bolesław Boczek, eds. *The International Law Dictionary*. Oxford: ABC-CLIO, 1987.
Cudd, Ann. *Analyzing Oppression*. Oxford: Oxford University Press, 2006.
Dinstein, Yoram. *War, Aggression and Self-Defence*. 4th ed. Cambridge: Cambridge University Press, 2005.
Fiala, Andrew. *Against Religion, Wars, and States: The Case for Enlightenment Atheism, Just War Pacifism, and Liberal-Democratic Anarchism*. Lanham, MD: Rowman & Littlefield, 2013.
———. "Anarchism and Pacifism." In *Brill's Companion to Anarchism and Philosophy*, edited by Nathan Jun, 152–70. Leiden: Brill, 2017.
Fox, James, ed. *Dictionary of International and Comparative Law*. 3rd ed. New York: Oceana Publications Inc., 2003.
Franks, Benjamin. "Prefiguration." In *Anarchism: A Conceptual Approach*, edited by Benjamin Franks, Nathan Jun, and Leonard Williams, 28–43. London: Routledge, 2018.
———. "Vanguards and Paternalism." In *New Perspectives on Anarchism*, edited by Nathan Jun and Shane Wahl, 99–120. Lanham, MD: Lexington Books, 2009.
Franks, Benjamin, Nathan Jun, and Leonard Williams, eds. *Anarchism: A Conceptual Approach*. London: Routledge, 2018.
Goldman, Emma. *Anarchism and Other Essays*. New York: Mother Earth Publishing Company, 1910.
———. *Red Emma Speaks*, edited by Alix Kates Shulman. Amherst, NY: Humanity Books, 1998.
Gordon, Uri. *Anarchy Alive! Anti-Authoritarian Politics from Practice to Theory*. London: Pluto Books, 2008.
———. "Power and Anarchy." In *New Perspectives on Anarchism*, edited by Nathan Jun and Shane Wahl, 39–69. Lanham, MD: Lexington Books, 2009.
———. "Revolution." In *Anarchism: A Conceptual Approach*, edited by Benjamin Franks, Nathan Jun, and Leonard Williams, 86–98. London: Routledge, 2018.
Guérin, Daniel, ed. *No Gods, No Masters*. Translated by Paul Sharkey. Oakland, CA: AK Press, 2005.
Heinze, Eric, and Brent Steele, eds. *Ethics, Authority and War: Non-State Actors in the Just War Tradition*. New York: Palgrave Macmillan, 2009.
Hoffman, Bruce. *Inside Terrorism*. New York: Columbia University Press, 2006.
Jun, Nathan. *Anarchism and Political Modernity*. London: Bloomsbury, 2012.
———. "Freedom." In *Anarchism: A Conceptual Approach*, edited by Benjamin Franks, Nathan Jun, and Leonard Williams, 44–59. London: Routledge, 2018.
———. "On Philosophical Anarchism." *Radical Philosophy Review* 19, no. 3 (2016): 552–67.
———. "The State." In *The Palgrave Handbook of Anarchism*, edited by Carl Levy and Matthew S. Adams, 27–46. Basingstoke, UK: Palgrave Macmillan, 2018.
Kropotkin, Peter. *Anarchism: A Collection of Revolutionary Writings*, edited by Roger Baldwin. Mineola, NY: Dover, 1970.
———. *Direct Struggle Against Capital: A Peter Kropotkin Anthology*, edited by Iain McKay. Oakland, CA: AK Press, 2014.
———. *Fugitive Writings*, edited by George Woodcock. Montreal: Black Rose Books, 1993.
———. "Words of a Rebel." In *No Gods, No Masters*, edited by Daniel Guérin. Translated by Paul Sharkey. Oakland, CA: AK Press, 2005.
Lenin, Vladimir. *The Essential Works of Lenin*, edited by Henry Christman. New York: Dover, 1987.
Loadenthal, Michael. *The Politics of Attack: Communiqués and Insurrectionary Violence*. Manchester, UK: Manchester University Press, 2018.
Malatesta, Errico. *Anarchy*, edited by Vernon Richards. London: Freedom Press, 1974.
———. *Fra Contadini: A Dialogue on Anarchy*. Translated by Jean Weir. London: Bratach Dubh Editions, 1981.
———. *Life and Ideas*, edited by Vernon Richards. Oakland, CA: PM Press, 2015.

———. *The Method of Freedom: An Errico Malatesta Reader*, edited by Davide Turcato. Oakland, CA: AK Press, 2014.

Marx, Karl, and Friedrich Engels. *The Marx-Engels Reader*, edited by Robert Tucker. New York: Norton, 1978.

McLaughlin, Paul. *Anarchism and Authority: A Philosophical Introduction to Classical Anarchism*. London: Routledge, 2016.

Most, Johann. *The Social Monster*. New York: Bernhard and Schenck, 1890.

Oppenheim, Lassa. *International Law*. Vol. 2: *International Law, A Treatise*, edited by Hersch Lauterpacht. London: Longmans, Green & Co., 1952.

Ordóñez, Vicente. "Direct Action." In *Anarchism: A Conceptual Approach*, edited by Benjamin Franks, Nathan Jun, and Leonard Williams, 74–85. London: Routledge, 2018.

Peterson, Florence. Strikes in the United States, 1880–1936: Bulletin of the United States Bureau of Labor Statistics, No. 651. Washington, DC: United States Government Publishing Office, 1937.

Proudhon, Pierre-Joseph. *The General Idea of the Revolution in the Nineteenth Century*. Translated by John Beverly Robinson. London: Freedom Press, 1923.

———. *What Is Property?* London: William Reeves, 1969.

Robinson, Andrew. "The State as a Cause of War: Anarchist and Autonomist Critiques of War." In *The Ashgate Research Companion to War: Origins and Prevention*, edited by Oleg Kobtzeff and Hall Gardner, 131–51. Aldershot, UK: Ashgate, 2013.

Rocker, Rudolf. *Anarcho-Syndicalism: Theory and Practice*. Oakland, CA: AK Press, 2004.

———. *Nationalism and Culture*. Montreal: Black Rose Books, 1998.

Schwenkenbecher, Anne. "Rethinking Legitimate Authority." In *The Routledge Handbook of Ethics and War: Just War Theory in the Twenty-First Century*, edited by Fritz Allhoff, Nicholas G. Evans, and Adam Henschke, 161–70. London: Routledge, 2013.

Simmons, A. J. *Boundaries of Authority*. Oxford: Oxford University Press, 2016.

Van Crevald, Martin. *The Rise and Decline of the State*. Cambridge: Cambridge University Press.

Van der Walt, Lucien. "Anarchism and Marxism." In *Brill's Companion to Anarchism and Philosophy*, edited by Nathan Jun, 505–58. Leiden: Brill, 2017.

Woodcock, George. *Anarchism: A History of Libertarian Ideas and Movements*. Toronto: University of Toronto Press, 2009.

Young, Iris Marion. *Justice and the Politics of Difference*. Princeton, NJ: Princeton University, 1990.

Chapter Two

"The Only Justifiable War"

The Marxist Strategies of Lenin, Trotsky, and Blanco

Andrew Ryder

INTRODUCTION:
THE MARXIST CRITIQUE OF LIBERAL JUST WAR THEORY

Just war theory has taken on increasing prominence in the post–Cold War era. The classic work of contemporary liberal thought on the matter, Michael Walzer's *Just and Unjust Wars: A Moral Argument with Historical Illustrations*, was first published in 1977. Walzer aimed to provide a rational case for the unjust nature of the invasion of Vietnam by the United States but also to defend Israel's invasion of the West Bank and Gaza in the Six-Day War.[1] Walzer argues that there will likely be no end to war and that it is of paramount importance to determine rules for the correct instances in which wars can be waged (*jus ad bellum*) and for the ethical means of pursuing such a war (*jus in bello*).

In its basic orientation, his outlook is anti-Marxist in at least two respects. First, Walzer insists that we should not think from the perspective of ending war forever. In his view, the eschatological understanding that aims at the abolition of war has been employed by both the right and the left to justify crimes and atrocities on the grounds that they are necessary to hasten the elimination of war.[2] In contrast, Marxism fundamentally insists on the eventual building of an international socialist mode of production in which war will be obsolete. Second, Walzer relies on the classic international relations model in which nation-states function as rational, self-interested actors. In contrast, Marxism famously argues that the working class has no country.[3] From this viewpoint, class interests fundamentally cleave the integrity of nation-states. Walzer and other liberals would not generally see a civil war as just, but Marx and his followers consciously strive to create the conditions for a war between the working class and the capitalist state. Walzer argues that existing states should generally be kept in place, unless they are guilty of genocidal crimes: "Except when they are directed against Nazi-like states, just wars are conservative in character."[4] In this regard, Walzer and Marx have entirely incompatible views.

Walzer does attempt to address, briefly, Marx's understanding of war. He is aware that Marx rejects the political order of states but argues that Marx falls into conventionality in two ways, despite this. To demonstrate Marx's limitations, Walzer focuses on his analysis of the Franco-Prussian War. Walzer argues first that Marx personally took the side of Otto von Bismarck for his own modernist reasons: Prussian victory would unify state power, which would hasten a further centralizing of the working class. This is a justification on the basis of historical progress, of which Walzer is skeptical; he argues that this simply replicates Bismarck's own self-serving explanation.[5] However, in Marx's public pronouncements on the matter, which reject Bismarck's claims, Walzer discerns a reliance on a the "theory of aggression."[6] Walzer thinks that this is an unavoidable component of the just war theory, a moral rejection of unprovoked attacks on others. He notes that this is not necessarily embedded in Marxism as a doctrine but believes that Marx's practical viewpoint finds it indispensable.

Walzer, then, fundamentally rejects the revolutionary orientation of Marxism and argues that, in the world as we know it, we can search for correct moral justifications only for the practice of war rooted in a principle of self-defense or humanitarian necessity. This insistence has been enormously influential on the liberal opinion in the era following the Cold War. Marxists have generally rejected this tendency. For example, Michael Hardt and Antonio Negri argue that this ethical reframing of war tends to make it into a regular occurrence and one that is made *good*, an ethical instrument. Moreover, its ethical perspective names the enemy as the one who provoked war through aggression, making it fundamentally evil: "Today the enemy, just like the war itself, comes to be at once banalized (reduced to an object of routine police repression) and absolutized (as the Enemy, an absolute threat to the ethical order)."[7] In this view, the liberal just war theory may actually be conducive to a long line of bloody wars against demonized foes.

In his provocatively titled book *The Liberal Defence of Murder*, Richard Seymour has argued that this liberal just war theory has led to a continual abdication of the responsibility to oppose imperialist wars by many left-liberal intellectuals. He provides a long history of advocacy for wars by liberals and socialists against insurrections at the periphery of the world economy, going back to the Mexican-American War and the suppression of uprisings in South Africa, Algeria, and India.[8] In particular, like Hardt and Negri, Seymour opposes the contemporary mobilization of just war theory by

Walzer and others, such as Christopher Hitchens, Bernard Henri-Lévy, Michael Ignatieff, and American neoconservatives.[9] Seymour argues that these figures provide a moral justification for one or more of the following acts of violence: the bombing of Serbia and Libya by the North American Treaty Organization, the invasion of Iraq by the United States, and the shelling of Gaza by Israel, among other conflicts.[10]

In this century, the just war theory has been employed by capitalist powers. At present, revolutionary Marxism is a weak force, politically; there are very few self-designated Marxists capable of waging a military struggle.[11] As a result, it has generally served to criticize the blind spots and rationalizations found in liberal just war theory, rather than posing its own military codes. However, it may be necessary to confront the task of proposing an alternative theory of just wars, one that is rooted in the revolutionary claims of Marxist thought. To do this, we need to return to a time when socialist revolutionaries wielded military power. A discussion of the classical Marxist tradition that culminated in the victory of the Russian Revolution follows.

MARXISM AND REVOLUTIONARY WAR

To answer questions of the morality of war from a Marxist perspective, we first have to discover a Marxist position on what is "moral." This is not immediately apparent in texts of the Marxist tradition, and in fact many Marxist authors present criticisms of the assumptions of consensus moral codes. However, there is a clear ethical principle underlying Marxist practice—the rejection of illegitimate economic and political hierarchies and their limitations on the potential growth and activity of human beings. Marx asserts in his early, speculative work, "the *categorical imperative to overthrow all those conditions* in which man [sic] is an abased, enslaved, abandoned, contemptible being."[12] In his famous collaboration with Friedrich Engels, *The Communist Manifesto*, Marx demands "an association in which the free development of each is the condition for the free development of all."[13] Unlike the fundamentally conservative roots of liberal just war theory, then, Marxism generally acts to alter and transform political frameworks that confine human development.

This is most strongly evident in Marx's famous delineation of class struggle as a motor of history.[14] He argues that modern society, which appears to emancipate individuals, actually functions according to domination by a class (the bourgeoisie), which owns the means of production. This class impels the masses of working people to labor for wages and prevents them from sharing in the wealth that they produce.[15] Moreover, Marx argues that this exploitation will tend to grow worse and lead the vast majority of the population into desperate misery.[16] For these reasons, working people are correct to fight against the bourgeois class and, ultimately, against the state, which serves capitalist interests.

Nonetheless, the role of war in classical Marxism is not entirely clear. In his work on the Paris Commune of 1871, *The Civil War in France*, Karl Marx defines "the only justifiable war in history" as "the war of the enslaved against their enslavers."[17] This general principle animates his approach to war; a war can be said to be good if it is a clear contest between a group that is oppressed or exploited and the authors of that oppression. In particular, Marx aims to encourage the development of a coming civil war between the working class and the owners of capital, which will culminate in a dictatorship of the proletariat, capable of building a new socialist mode of production. For Marx, this will resolve the fundamental contradictions of history. However, this final war between classes is not the only type of war Marx indicates that he is willing to support. He also famously wrote letters to Abraham Lincoln, urging him to continue the war against the rebellious Southern states.[18] This was not a war against the bourgeoisie; in fact, it was waged on behalf of a bourgeois state. Nonetheless, Marx viewed the US federal government, in this instance, as a progressive force, crushing the slave society of the agrarian South.

The Marxist understanding of war had taken on a new form as analyses of imperialism became increasingly significant. Marx and Engels themselves approached imperial expansion and the resistance to it in a nonsystematic way. Other figures, such as Rosa Luxemburg and Nikolai Bukharin, supplemented and organized these analyses.[19] However, the most significant and lasting approach to this question was produced by Vladimir Lenin not primarily because of his characterization of imperialism, which is strongly indebted to Bukharin, but rather because of his emphasis on national liberation as a crucial necessity.[20] Lenin formulates his definition of just war very clearly:

> We fully regard civil wars, i.e., wars waged by the oppressed class against the oppressing class, slaves against slave-owners, serfs against land-owners, and wage-workers against the bourgeoisie, as legitimate, progressive and necessary.[21]

While Lenin championed these just civil wars, he reserved scathing criticism for wars of inter-imperialist rivalry. As a result, the First World War was decisive in the development of Marxist struggle. Famously, Lenin denounced Karl Kautsky, the leader of the Second International, for his decision to vote for German war credits, thereby endorsing participation in the war.[22] For Lenin, the Great War was a war between imperial powers by which the distinct bourgeois empires could compel proletarian armies to slaughter one another. In response to this challenge, Lenin counseled a strategy of "revolutionary defeatism"; the socialist organizations of each nation ought to oppose the war effort of their own state. In 1914, he wrote that the "only correct proletarian slogan is to transform the present imperialist war into a civil war."[23] Indeed, this was the eventual result of his practice in Russia; the world war led directly to the Russian Revolution and a subsequent civil war.

However, Lenin not only demanded civil wars within capitalist nation-states; he also argued that it was incumbent on socialists to support wars of decolonization, even if they were not clearly waged between the workers and bourgeoisie of these nations. In his view, distinct nations, defined by their language, culture, and territory, have the right to self-determination and ought not to be dominated by greater empires. This conviction led to Lenin's decisive significance for future processes of decolonization, like those that took place in China, India, Korea, Cuba, Algeria, Vietnam, and Nicaragua. Walzer, in principle, agrees with Lenin that national self-determination is a valid principle, although he frames this in terms of its earlier definition by John Stuart Mill.[24] However, Walzer primarily views this question by the conditions of intervention by other powers. In contrast, Lenin emphasizes the just war character of a war fought by a nation against a larger empire that would limit its sovereignty.

Joseph Stalin's leadership of the Union of Soviet Socialist Republics (USSR) led to a new policy among the various communist parties. From the 1930s onward, this leadership counseled a theory of "progressive" collaboration with national bourgeoisies; the theory of a popular front indicated that any nation-state that was opposed to the expansion of German Nazism ought to be supported.[25] In this period, a German Marxist, Erich Wollenberg, wrote a systematic approach to Marxist just war theory.[26] He argues that the just wars of the nineteenth century were generally wars of national unification against imperial division or control. In the twentieth century, just wars would primarily include civil wars of the proletariat, which would include a democratization of the army; wars of liberation by colonial and semicolonial populations as well as oppressed nations; and a war between a dictatorship of the proletariat and imperialist aggressors. Wollenberg argued that Stalinists had distorted this perspective toward an unprincipled *realpolitik*, following only the immediate interests of Stalin's USSR. This led to subsequent errors, such as the French Communist Party's support for the French efforts to retain control of Algeria.

Prior to Stalinization, the Soviet Union was born from a bloody and desperate civil war between the socialist government that came to power in the revolution and the various counterrevolutionary forces. Marxist theory clearly calls for this civil war and endorses it; it is, for Marx and Lenin, the inevitable final stage of class struggle. In their view, this war is the proper instance of *jus ad bellum* because it will overthrow the economic and political domination of the masses. Moreover, its success would eliminate the instance of future wars. However, the classical Marxists before Lenin expected this civil war to take place in an industrialized Western nation. In contrast, the civil war actually took place in a peripheral area, the complex and vast territory of the Russian Empire. It is necessary, then, to observe and study the process of the civil war in a finer grain of detail, beyond the more abstract prophecy provided by Marx himself. Leon Trotsky, the leader of the Red Army from 1918 to 1925, provides the most relevant, detailed, and consequential analyses and strategies for the Bolshevik approach to the war. These writings also give us a better understanding of a Marxist approach to *jus in bello*, the ethical considerations of what is permissible in a military situation, independent of the question of the just character of the war itself.

TROTSKY AND THE RED ARMY

Trotsky's leadership was controversial, and he encountered opposition to many of his policies from other Bolsheviks.[27] His decisions, questioned at the time and discussed critically today, include forced conscription, compulsory obedience, officers elected by the leadership rather than by troops, retaining officers from the old Tsarist army, and punitive mechanisms within the army (including the death penalty). He abolished the earlier, more organic form of self-defense—the Red Guards—and replaced it with a more conventional military command structure. In the emergency circumstances of a war for the survival of the socialist state, Trotsky believed that a conventional war machine was necessary, built from disciplined masses of soldiers.[28]

In this strategy, Trotsky ran the risk of cementing social relations that existed before the revolution, rather than revolutionizing the army itself and building a more popular and democratic force. Further, the ongoing conditions of war and decimation of the population of advanced workers increased the significance of the army such that it became the primary instrument of the socialist state—rather than the workers' councils that initially formed the basis of Soviet power. This course of events then provided many of the determinants that subtended Stalin's rise to power and the sidelining of Trotsky's more internationalist and classical views. The civil war, then, was a primary crucible of what Trotsky had previously criticized as "substitutionism"—the tendency of the centralized party and its coercive abilities to eventually act on behalf of the working class, ruling over it rather than enforcing its will.[29] This emphasis on the military as the defender of socialism, not the workers' organizations, threatened to redefine the socialist project itself. It appeared that victories of the Red Army could lead to the conquest of new territories in which "socialism" could be implemented by military decree from above. This suggestion, that soldiers could carry socialism rather than conscious workers, seemed to call into question the basics of socialist politics.[30] Most problematically, Trotsky even suggested a "militarization of labor" according to which the emergency situation would be overcome by implementing a chain of command into production as well as defense.[31]

Trotsky believed that victory was the primary concern that needed to be achieved at any cost. For a Marxist, a revolutionary war for socialism fits the greatest criteria of *jus ad bello*. Success could create the conditions for an international transformation in which exploitation and war could be overcome. In contrast, failure would lead to the reimposition of tyranny and abjection. For this reason, Trotsky emphasized victory over more immediate ethical concerns. For example, in 1923, he advised the necessity of research into chemical warfare.[32] No form of defense could be ruled out, and any potential weapon needed to be considered and developed.

In this respect, I disagree with Trotsky. While the exigency of the situation must be kept in mind, I argue that it is not justifiable, on Marxist grounds, to make victory the sole criteria of judging a military action. I would refer this to the basic Marxist ethical criteria of overcoming abjection. For this reason, I think that chemical warfare, torture, and the enlisting of child soldiers are incompatible with Marxist principles because they do not safeguard fundamental principles of human development. The Geneva Protocol of 1925 (against chemical weapons) and the Geneva Conventions, ratified in 1949, provide a fair guide to basic practices of war in a revolutionary situation.[33]

In these aspects of his activity, Trotsky began to deviate from the practical mechanisms of socialism. He maintained the ideal of socialism and continued to preserve it as the horizon of political goals, but it became something to be realized in the future. The exigencies of the present would require essentially nonsocialist measures. However, Trotsky's theory of warfare was not exhausted in this practice, limited in creativity by the civil war. He also suggested an alternative model of organization, which he believed would eventually develop as the socialist order stabilized itself. In some respects, he believed that the more conventional form of war and the relatively traditional army that he led would give way to another unit of military practice: the popular militia. This is a relatively underinvestigated aspect of his work.

I argue, then, that there are actually two approaches to war contained in Trotsky's work: first, the empirical facts of his leadership during the civil war, which were considered emergency measures, in contrast to a second theory, Trotsky's theoretical approach, which was only partially implemented in practice. I suggest that this second aspect is a much more valuable guide to a truly Marxist approach to war. As early as 1919, Trotsky argued for the eventual supersession of the standing army by a new "militia system," which would have a democratic character. This was not simply lip service; Trotsky began to put this new system into place in 1921, with the reforms continuing until their reversal by Stalin in the mid-1930s.[34] We should examine this other record of theory and practice to develop a military perspective that is less inclined toward substitutionism or administrative control.

Marx and Engels wrote little on the structure of the army. To supplement their approach, Trotsky took guidance from the French socialist Jean Jaurès and his book *L'Armée Nouvelle* (1910).[35] According to Isaac Deutscher (a Polish Marxist and Trotsky's biographer), Trotsky's "Theses" of March 1919 set forth the militias as the eventual replacement for the Red Army: "He looked forward to the time when men would receive their military training not in barracks but in conditions closely approximating to the workaday life of workers and peasants."[36] A chain of command would continue to exist, but officers would be elected by enlisted men and accountable to their judgment. Trotsky argued that this more democratic quality would have great benefits for morale and collective élan. He declared that militias "based on the natural, occupational-productive groupings of the new society, the village communes, the municipal collectives, industrial associations" and "inwardly unified by school, sports association, and circumstances of labour" would be "much richer in the 'corporate' spirit, in a spirit of much higher quality, than are barracks-bred regiments."[37] In 1921, he was able to produce three divisions, based on these principles, in Petrograd, Moscow, and the Urals.

Stalin's ascendency led to the abandonment of Trotsky's innovations regarding a democratic militia system. By World War II, the USSR's military pursued a strategy of total war, animated largely by nationalistic fervor and reliant on a conventional military hierarchy. Trotsky's alternative, here, vanished. However, in exile, Trotsky continued to advocate the militia form as the best means of working-class self-defense. This recommendation reappeared in 1934. Speaking specifically for the French context, he called for organized combat unit detachments to defend workers' organizations and to counterattack fascist groups.[38] Stalinist and social democratic parties disregarded this recommendation for the most part. However, we might find traces of its possibility in certain partisan deployments by national liberation movements during the war as well as in subsequent anti-fascist struggle.

A fascinating return to Trotsky's proposal took place in unexpected conditions, on the new terrain of Latin American peasant struggle. The complex and bloody decade of the 1960s saw a new wave of warfare in South America on behalf of socialist goals and inspired by the victory of the Cuban Revolution. While Trotsky's followers were uncertain of the correct approach to these developments, I will be particularly attentive to the practical and theoretical development of Trotsky's approach to militias, presented by Hugo Blanco in Peru.

TROTSKYISM AND GUERRILLA WARFARE IN LATIN AMERICA

Independently of Marxist practice, there is a long tradition of guerrilla warfare in Latin America. This began with the strategies of Pancho Villa and Emiliano Zapata during the Mexican Revolution. Augusto Sandino inherited this mode of warfare; his "crazy little army" fought the US Marines to a standstill in Nicaragua.[39] Drawing on these techniques, the July 26 Movement came to power in Cuba, overthrowing the US-supported dictator Fulgencio Batista. The theories of Che Guevara aimed to establish a Marxist grounding for this strategy of guerrilla warfare and to formalize it for use by others.[40] Régis Debray, a comrade of Guevara's during his campaign in Bolivia, wrote the most schematic development and defense of this approach in his work *Revolution in the Revolution?*[41] Guevara's and Debray's strategy was known as *foquismo*. It suggested that revolutionaries ought to take up arms, forming mobile units of soldiers in the countryside who could eventually encircle the cities and overcome their military defenses.[42]

Outside Cuba, this strategy was never successful. As a result, Latin American guerrillas, over time, began to supplement and redefine their military strategy along lines taken from the Chinese, Algerian, or Vietnamese wars of national liberation.[43] These strategies of protracted war had greater longevity but remained unsuccessful (with the singular exception of the Nicaraguan case).[44] Trotsky had been erased from history by the leadership of the world Communist movement, so his theories and practice had very little effect on these developments. However, some militants inspired by Trotsky proposed an alternative form of military engagement, drawing from his later advocacy of militias. I argue that this militia form constitutes a more authentically socialist approach to the demands and tests of warfare.

In *Just and Unjust Wars*, Walzer provides consideration of guerrilla war scenarios.[45] This is a point at which he confronts the Marxist tradition because many of history's guerrilla wars were wars of national liberation, as commended by Lenin and Trotsky. As noted, Walzer affirms the right to national self-determination.[46] He has some positive assessment of the codes of military behavior, practiced in the Chinese and Cuban struggles, and I think that the Marxist tradition would concur in this assessment.[47] However, the guerrilla strategies formulated by Mao Zedong and Che Guevara privileged mobile armies over the self-activity of working people themselves. As a result, their command structure was not in line with the priorities of the Marxist tradition. In this respect, from a Marxist perspective, they did not practice *jus in bello*. I argue that the Trotskyist tradition, which emphasizes popular militias rooted in self-governing communities, is superior and more authentically Marxist than the guerrilla method practiced in China and Cuba.

The Trotskyist movement was divided on the correct approach to Latin American guerrilla struggle, although the majority leadership decided to support the Guevarist strategy. However, Joseph Hansen, who had been Trotsky's secretary, raised a number of objections to this point of view. Hansen believed that it would lead further away from conscious political development.[48] He drew from Lenin's explicit guidance; in 1906, he had written that *"the party of the proletariat can never regard guerrilla warfare as the only, or even as the chief, method of struggle"*; "this method must be subordinated to other methods" and "ennobled by the enlightening and organising influence of socialism."[49] In contrast, Hansen believed that most of the guerrillas inspired by Guevara had simply extended the earlier tradition of warfare practiced by Villa and Sandino, which was populist in its aims but lacked a crucial dimension of political development and education. However, Hansen noted the existence of a distinct method of guerrilla warfare in Latin America, the struggle led by Hugo Blanco in Peru. This was not simply because Blanco voiced an adherence to Trotsky's theories but also because his practice was consciously distinct from *foquismo*. Other commentators and theorists, such as an Italian Trotskyist, Livio Maitan, endorsed and propagated Blanco's views.[50] In contrast to the emphasis on scattered mobile units of soldiers, evident in Guevara and Debray, Blanco argued for the self-defense and political development of rural communities.

Blanco practiced this brand of military organization from 1958 to 1963 in the mountains of Peru.[51] He systematically developed these insights in his book *Land or Death: The Peasant Struggle in Peru*, published in 1972. Blanco draws explicitly from Trotsky's insight into the democratic militia structure. However, he combines it with an attention to the communal structure of the traditional *ayllu*, according to which the peasants collectively own the land in which they work. For Blanco, this rural commune constitutes a "cell of primitive communism that has survived the Inca Empire, the Colonial period, and the Republic."[52] This *ayllu* can form the basis of a new socialist society, and arming it for self-defense will be a great contribution to revolutionary struggle; he believes that, in the future, "the *ayllu* will become one of the basic forms of the future workers' and peasants' government."[53] In protecting its autonomy, Blanco adhered to a political strategy of *indianismo*, a revalorization of indigenous culture and experience. This included the practice of the Quechua language as well as a championing of the indigenous worldview.[54] However, Blanco also rejected the strategy that would later become known as "localism." He did not believe that the peasant commune could secede and achieve self-sufficiency but rather that it would be necessary for it to provide a base for a national (and eventually international) revolution.[55] He believed that this focus on rural institutions stemmed from the awareness of a dual-power situation; the official state and economic framework could be contested by an independent and autonomous arrangement of popular self-government.

In the territory that Blanco led, his group was able to institute collective union ownership of the previous landlord's property, social distribution of uncultivated land, a new election for judges from within the community, and the construction of a new school. All of this required military defense from the state and the landlord class, which was supplied by "an embryonic armed force, the developing peasant militia."[56] Blanco rejected a sense of voluntarism and unearned vanguardism, which he found characteristic of those inspired by theories from the Cuban or Chinese experiences. He believed that the majority of guerrillas believed that it was necessary for only the armed leadership to risk death and violence, whereas, in fact, their political survival and success would depend entirely on the understanding and development of the popular masses.[57] Rather than guerrillas coming from without to install themselves, Blanco argued that the armed struggle could exist legitimately only as an outgrowth of the political education of communities and their need for self-defense. This strategy would remain rooted in the popular needs of the community rather than divorcing itself from it: "the militiaman stays at home, dedicating himself to his work, and when he has to fight, he fights."[58] He argued that this would certainly engender much greater popular support for socialist armed struggle, reporting that out of "one hundred peasants prepared to struggle, 99 would prefer to be militiamen, and only one a [*foquista*] guerrilla."[59]

In this instance, Blanco viewed the taking up of arms as the practice of a just war; the theories of Marx, Lenin, and Trotsky validate this view. The violence employed by the Peruvian peasants that Blanco led took place as a result of two linked struggles: the national oppression of the indigenous peasants by primarily *mestizo* landowners and their greater subordination by the North American state and the export of its capital, which rendered Peru a "semicolony of imperialism."[60] However, Blanco was unable to succeed in permanent self-defense of his community or in generalizing his activity toward an overthrow of the Peruvian state. In his own self-criticism, he partly attributed this to his inability to develop durable structures of a revolutionary party, which could generalize their struggle throughout the nation.[61] This was partly a result of political division with the official "Marxist" party, the Peruvian Communist Party, which followed a Stalinist line of class collaboration. The state exploited this division, which limited Blanco's political range. This led to his eventual capture in 1963 along with most of his comrades. Deported to imprisonment in Chile, Blanco was able to receive amnesty at the Swedish embassy in 1976; after an international solidarity campaign, he took refuge there.[62] He returned to Peru in 1978, where he was elected to parliament. In his most recent writings and interviews, he has endorsed the practice of the Zapatistas in Mexico.[63] Blanco, then, identified continuity between his own method—Marxist and Trotskyist—and that which would later be practiced by indigenous people in the Mexican federal state of Chiapas.[64]

REMARKS ON A GENERAL MARXIST CONCEPTION OF JUST WARS

Attention to Marx, Lenin, Trotsky, and Blanco reveals a consistent line of thought on how to wage war justifiably. The Marxist tradition first insists that the essential criterion is the rejection of oppression and exploitation. While wars between bourgeois states are illegitimate and should be resisted, violent struggle by workers can be necessary against class domination and by oppressed national groups against imperialist power. A war of national liberation can be waged until a national group obtains autonomy; a revolutionary civil war can conclude only with the formation of a workers' state, building a socialist society. The means by which these wars can be conducted varies and depends on historical and material circumstances. In the classic case of the Russian civil war, military strategy was largely conventional, with its ideals and ultimate goals as its relevant socialist component. The general principles of conduct in war, accepted by most societies since the mid-twentieth century, ought to be upheld. These are accomplishments of the democratic revolutions of that period.

The most truly Marxist approach is rooted in popular, democratic militias. These militias grow out of a principle of self-defense but must eventually confront the nation-state, aiming to smash it and replace it with a new socialist mode of production. The militias ought to be rooted in the collective activity of workers and may exist in rural, agrarian traditional societies or in urbanized settings. Unlike most theories of war, Marxism does not view the nation as the essential unit of defense. Instead, the nation is itself disrupted by the class struggle within it. However, the practical activity of the militias should include a revaluation of previously oppressed cultural forms of life, such as those belonging to indigenous people and racialized groups. This cultural self-defense will contribute to the self-confidence and activity of the armed militia. In this sense, Marxist theory is not indifferent to national belonging, but this approach to nation must always take place according to a criterion of resistance to oppression. The struggle of an oppressed nation is just, whereas an oppressor nation is necessarily in the wrong.

A revolutionary civil war is, in a sense, a necessary evil; it takes place with the goal of its own abolition. The socialist tradition believes that war will always be present in capitalist society but that victories over capitalism will lessen and eventually eliminate the potential for war. In this regard, socialist thought is optimistic in that war is not posited as an ahistorical tendency for nations or groups of people. However, this possibility is entirely contingent on the overcoming of capitalism, which is not preordained. For this reason, sobriety and courage are necessary for socialist leadership; victories will need to be consciously won to create a new, postmilitary society.

BIBLIOGRAPHY

Blanco, Hugo. "Indigenous People Are the Vanguard of the Fight to Save the Earth." *Links: International Journal of Socialist Renewal*. Published October 13, 2009. http://links.org.au/node/1304.

———. *Land or Death: The Peasant Struggle in Peru*. New York: Pathfinder, 1972.

———. "Militia or Guerrilla Movement?" In *Marxism in Latin America from 1909 to the Present*, edited by Michael Löwy, 255–58. New York: Prometheus, 1992.

———. *We the Indians: The Indigenous Peoples of Peru and the Struggle for Land*. London: Merlin Press, 2018.

Brewer, Anthony. *Marxist Theories of Imperialism: A Critical Survey*. New York: Routledge, 1990.

Bukharin, Nikolai. *Imperialism and World Economy*. New York: International Publishers, 1929. Accessed June 2, 2019. https://www.marxists.org/archive/bukharin/works/1917/imperial/index.htm.

Cliff, Tony. "Trotsky on Substitutionism." Accessed June 2, 2019. https://www.marxists.org/archive/cliff/works/1960/xx/trotsub.htm.

Debray, Régis. *Revolution in the Revolution? Armed Struggle and Political Struggle in Latin America*. New York: Grove Press, 1967.

Deutscher, Isaac. *The Prophet Armed: Trotsky 1879–1921*. London: Verso, 2003.

Dimitrov, Georgi. "Unity of the Working Class against Fascism." Accessed June 2, 2019. https://www.marxists.org/reference/archive/dimitrov/works/1935/unity.htm.

Greene, Doug Enaa. "The Communist Order of Samurai: Leon Trotsky and the Red Army." *Links: International Journal of Socialist Renewal*. Published May 17, 2016. http://links.org.au/node/4691.

Guevara, Che. *Che Guevara Reader: Writings on Guerrilla Strategy, Politics and Revolution*, edited by David Deutschmann. Melbourne: Ocean Press, 1997.

Hansen, Joseph. "In Defense of the Leninist Strategy of Party Building." *International Information Bulletin* 3, April 1971. Accessed June 2, 2019. https://www.marxists.org/archive/hansen/1971/indef.htm.

Hardt, Michael, and Antonio Negri. *Empire*. Cambridge, MA: Harvard University Press, 2000.

La Botz, Dan. *What Went Wrong? The Nicaraguan Revolution: A Marxist Analysis*. Boston: Brill, 2016.

Le Blanc, Paul. *Lenin and the Revolutionary Party*. New York: Humanity, 1993.

Lenin, Vladimir. *Collected Works*. Vol. 21: *Socialism and War: The Attitude of the Russian Social Democratic Labour Party Towards the War*. Peking: Foreign Languages Press, 1970. Accessed June 2, 2019. https://www.marxists.org/archive/lenin/works/1915/s+w/index.htm.

———. *Collected Works*. Vol. 26: *On the Slogan to Transform the Imperialist War Into a Civil War*. Moscow: Progress Publishers, 1977. Accessed June 2, 2019. https://www.marxists.org/archive/lenin/works/1914/sep/00.htm.

———. *Collected Works*. Vol. 28: *The Proletarian Revolution and the Renegade Kautsky*. Moscow: Progress Publishers, 1977. Accessed June 2, 2019. https://www.marxists.org/archive/lenin/works/1918/prrk/.

———. *Imperialism, the Highest State of Capitalism*. Moscow: Progress Publishers, 1963. Accessed June 2, 2019. https://www.marxists.org/archive/lenin/works/1916/imp-hsc/.

Luxemburg, Rosa. *The Accumulation of Capital*. London: Routledge, 1951. Accessed June 2, 2019. https://www.marxists.org/archive/luxemburg/1913/accumulation-capital/.

Maitan, Livio. "Major Problems of the Latin American Revolution: A Reply to Regis Debray." *International Socialist Review* 28, no. 5 (1967): 1–22. Accessed June 2, 2019. https://www.marxists.org/history/etol/writers/maitan/1967/05/debray.htm.

Marx, Karl. "Address of the International Working Men's Association to Abraham Lincoln, President of the United States of America." *The Bee-Hive Newspaper* 169, 1865. Accessed June 2, 2019. https://www.marxists.org/archive/marx/iwma/documents/1864/lincoln-letter.htm.

———. *The Civil War in France*. English edition of 1871. Accessed June 2, 2019. https://www.marxists.org/archive/marx/works/1871/civil-war-france/index.htm.

———. *The Portable Karl Marx*, edited by Eugene Kamenka. New York: Penguin, 1983.

Marx, Karl, and Friedrich Engels. *The Marx-Engels Reader*. 2nd ed. Edited by Robert C. Tucker. New York: W. W. Norton, 1978.

Ryder, Andrew. "Multiculturalism and Oppression: The Marxist Perspectives of Fraser, Lenin, and Fanon." In *Philosophies of Multiculturalism: Beyond Liberalism*, ed. Luís Cordeiro-Rodrigues and Marko Simendic, 80–96. New York: Routledge, 2017.

Seymour, Richard. *The Liberal Defence of Murder*. London: Verso, 2012.

Shawki, Ahmed. "China: Deng's Legacy." *International Socialist Review* 2, Fall 1997. Accessed June 2, 2019. http://www.isreview.org/issues/02/China_Part2.shtml.

Trotsky, Leon. *Fascism: What It Is and How to Fight It*. New York: Pioneer Publishers, 1964. Accessed June 2, 2019. https://www.marxists.org/archive/trotsky/works/1944/1944-fas.htm.

———. *Problems of Everyday Life*. New York: Pathfinder, 1973.

———. *Terrorism and Communism*. London: Verso, 2007.

UN Documents. Geneva Conventions of 12 August 1949 and Protocols Additional to the Conventions. Accessed June 2, 2019. http://www.un-documents.net/gc.htm.

United Nations Office for Disarmament Affairs. Protocol for the Prohibition of the Use in War of Asphyxiating, Poisonous or Other Gases, and of Bacteriological Methods of Warfare. 1925. Accessed June 2, 2019. https://www.un.org/disarmament/wmd/bio/1925-geneva-protocol/.

Walzer, Michael. *Just and Unjust Wars: A Moral Argument with Historical Illustrations*. 5th ed. New York: Basic, 2015.

Wollenberg, Erich. "Just Wars in the Light of Marxism." *New International* 3, no. 1, (1936): 2–5. Accessed June 2, 2019. https://www.marxists.org/history/etol/newspape/ni/vol03/no01/wollenberg.htm.

Chapter Three

A Pacifist Critique of Just War Theory

Richard Jackson

INTRODUCTION

There are a variety of ethical frameworks through which we might critically examine war, its conduct, and its consequences, including pacifism.[1] However, in practice, just war theory (JWT)—or some variant of it—is today the primary, if not the only, framework that is used to evaluate and guide the practice of war and the use of military force by states. JWT has become the unquestioned commonsense view of both the scholars and practitioners of international politics,[2] whereas pacifism, despite its continuing relevance to the contemporary evaluation of war and its analytical rigor,[3] remains marginalized and subjugated.[4] In addition to the virtual invisibility of pacifism in academic and public debate, perhaps the most significant indicator that JWT is the dominant paradigm "is the fact that the burden of justification concerning value judgements of conflict rests on pacifists, not warists."[5]

However, the dominance of JWT is not without critical engagement. Both historically and in recent times, substantial criticisms have been made of JWT and in favor of pacifism.[6] The aim of this chapter is to build on this literature and summarize some of the main procedural and substantive objections to JWT as a means of both destabilizing its normalization and opening up new questions and avenues of investigation into the contemporary practices of war. As I will attempt to demonstrate, the ethical and analytical horizons of JWT are extremely narrow and, as a consequence, distorting of the real-world practices they purport to study and advise on. Moreover, the ethical and political questions they pose, far from being objective and reasonable, function primarily to distort and deflect an honest and properly ethical evaluation of war as a central feature of international politics and contemporary society.

THE LIMITS OF JUST WAR THEORIZING

Before I consider some of the more substantive problems with the actual content of JWT, it is important to note the limitations inherent to the dominant mode of theorizing that JWT relies upon. The way in which just war theorists approach and formulate the questions they ask, as well as the mode of reasoning they use to answer those questions, is directly linked to the distortions and inadequacies of the theoretical formulations produced.

The first problem here is that just war theorizing tends to proceed in a top-down manner[7] and often on the basis of "wildly imaginative hypothetical situations"[8] or highly abstracted principles[9] and normally starts with the question of means rather than ends. That is, it starts with the question, under what conceivable circumstances is it legitimate for states to use violent force as a political means? One of the problems with this mode of theorizing, apart from loading the question, is that, "while such philosophical niceties about intention [for example] seem plausible when reflecting on war from a distance, they are disloyal to the lived experience of war."[10] By way of example, an alternative approach would begin on the foundation of a more realistic anthropology of war, violence, and conflict,[11] recognizing that the same actions performed at different times and in different contexts may have different consequences and, hence, require a different ethical assessment.[12] More specifically, in contrast to JWT, a pacifist approach starts by asking, what is the most effective and ethical thing to do in response to a threat in a specific cultural–historical context? The point of reformulating the question in this way is to focus on the concrete real-world problem and determine the primary reason for acting in the first place,[13] rather than privileging the use of violence and then searching for reasons and occasions for its use, as JWT tends to do.

A particular problem here is that, in its ethical reasoning, JWT tends to reduce moral agency to the singular reactive moment when it is too late to do anything else,[14] rather than recognizing that moral agency encompasses continuous everyday actions in the present that can be oriented toward preventing the conditions that give rise to just war scenarios in the future. That is, JWT waits until an invasion is about to take place or a population is under immanent threat of genocide before asking, what is the ethical thing for states to do, and can they use military force to do it? A more realistic and holistic ethical reasoning would ask, how can states act now to prevent the possibility that a conflict won't escalate into war or a genocide won't take place?

Another critical part of this decontextualized mode of theorizing involves the promiscuous use of analogy, especially the tendency to analogize nation-states to individual persons.[15] In fact, in many contemporary versions of JWT, the entire basis for the justification of employing force is based on the analogy that, if an individual is attacked, he or she has the right of self-defense and, therefore, so do states. The problems and failures of this analogy are well known and need not be repeated here.[16] The key point is that there are serious limitations to relying on analogical and hypothetical theorizing, rather than the historical record and academic research into real-world cases of war. Of course, the problem for JWT is that, in the real world, wars are messy, complicated affairs that confound attempts at clarity and certainty. Cheyney Ryan, in an examination of JWT, notes that, out of around 3,200 recorded wars, JWT seems to agree on WWII as being the one clear example of a just war.[17] And yet, even in this case, the atomic attacks on Japan, the terror bombing of German civilians, the failure to stop the genocide of European Jews, and the preventable Bengali famine that killed 2 to 4 million people because food supplies were sent elsewhere for military reasons are facts that tend to be excluded from the theoretical calculations about justice, relative evils, or saving lives within JWT.

A second related simplification often made in JWT is the arbitrary limitation of war to the period of lethal fighting between protagonists. Apart from the often arbitrary nature of determining the beginning and end of wars (even when limiting it to the period of military combat), reducing war to this narrow time frame is incredibly distorting of reality given that it fails to consider the nature of the effects and costs of war preparations and the long-term consequences once the fighting is over.[18] Any realistic and honest evaluation of the costs of going to war must also consider the excess annual deaths caused by the diversion of public funds from health care and social welfare to military preparations; the well-documented suicides of former veterans for decades after deployment during war; the deaths attributable to the structural violence caused by the disruption to social systems of food production, medical care, and economic development; and so on.[19] More broadly, it can be reasonably argued that going to war makes subsequent wars more likely through the spread of weaponry, the creation of new grievances, and the reinforcement of the belief among political actors that violence is a way to achieve political goals.[20]

The problem here is that JWT has an ontology of war that is divorced from the real world and mistakes the phenomenon of war for one small part of it. However, it is rare to see any discussion of the broader war system or the long-term real-world consequences and effects of war and the use of military violence in JWT. Instead, discussions tend to be based on an a priori acceptance that militaries preexist and that the ethical consequences of war do not extend into the future beyond the end of hostilities. For example, in the single case that JWT agrees is an example of a just war, there is no acknowledgment or accounting in that justification for the way in which that war led directly to the Cold War, the division of Europe, nuclear proliferation, Cold War proxy wars in Africa and Asia, and many other conflicts.

Another related problem with just war theorizing is what Michael Neu describes as its tendency toward "analytical atomism." That is, JWT fails to do justice to the complexities of the moral world in which human beings actually live.[21] Instead, JWT tends to view the world as being composed of neatly separable analytical categories, such as aggressors and innocent defenders or combatants and noncombatants, rather than as interconnected actors, social structures, and processes bound together in complex and shifting ways.[22]

Perhaps more importantly, in its ahistorical, decontextualized mode of reasoning, JWT also assumes that the agents making the moral decisions about the use of force have played no part in the production of the moral dilemma they are faced with but rather are neutral agents who must now decide what the most ethical response is. This is evident with the recent international condemnation of Syria to stop mass-scale atrocities conducted by the al-Assad regime. Instead, it has been argued that the ethical problem entails too little military intervention to protect populations at risk, rather than too much external military intervention, which then creates violence and human rights abuses.

From another perspective, it can be argued that JWT limits itself to considering only some of the consequences of ethical judgments in war and not others.[23] For example, JWT will commonly discuss the ethical consequences of failing to act in situations where vulnerable populations are at risk of direct harm from an immediate threat but will not discuss the longer-term consequences for vulnerable populations of preparing for war or the consequences of war long after the fighting has ended. In the view of JWT, the possibility of children being killed by a dictator carries a heavier ethical burden than the possibility of children dying from the effects of depleted uranium after the humanitarian intervention is over. At root, JWT involves a consequentialist (and, hence, utilitarian) set of calculations about the costs of certain actions or inaction. And yet, as several scholars have pointed out,[24] JWT severely limits which costs to include in its calculations.

Finally, some critics have noted that JWT is often characterized by a certain degree of moral and epistemological certainty and an implicit claim to universality. For example, rather than starting from a position of objective uncertainty about whether wars can or cannot be just, JWT presupposes that some wars are just and some wars are unjust and then asks how to differentiate the two. Additionally, ignoring that there are other moral theories that could be employed to evaluate the justness of war, it simply assumes that "JWT is the correct theory from which to evaluate war."[25] In fact, given that killing involves consequential irreversibility (unlike nonviolent action, there is no going back from killing people), JWT displays breathtaking moral certainty in its prescriptions about when people can be killed deliberately or with foresight (in terms of expected collateral deaths).

Lastly, JWT, in its dominant expression, appears to be simultaneously Western centric and universalistic. That is, the principles on which JWT is based are assumed to be universal ethical and moral principles, but, in virtually all instances, they are applied solely to the consideration of Western wars and never to the victims of Western aggression. For example, it would be surprising to see JWT being used to evaluate the justness of North Vietnam's military campaign or the insurgent campaign following the 2003 invasion of Iraq. The use of JWT to evaluate Lebanese resistance to Israeli military intervention[26] is a rare exception within the literature.

QUESTIONING THE ASSUMPTIONS OF JWT

In addition to the problematic epistemological and ethical assumptions in theorizing about just war noted above, there are a number of other, more serious problems with some of the fundamental concepts and categories employed in JWT. Perhaps the most problematic assumptions relate to JWT's naïve and simplistically normative assumptions about the nature and effects of direct physical violence and whether it can be employed as a tool or an instrument of politics. That is, in a great deal of the JWT literature, it is assumed that military force—organized violence—can be employed as a rational instrument of policy and as a political tool that leaves no lasting effects on the society that employs it. These are highly problematic assumptions for a number of reasons.

In the first instance, these assumptions about the nature of violence misunderstand and confuse the relationship between violence, force, and power and, therefore, how violence can or cannot be used in politics. More specifically, they misunderstand the relationship between brute force and coercion[27] and how the effectiveness of violence depends entirely on how people respond to violence, not the violence itself. That is, the capacity of a state or group of states to harm and destroy bears no direct relation to the ability to coerce[28] because the application of violence can provoke either deterrence or retaliation, intimidation or rage, submission or resistance, and the desired response can never be assured. This explains in part why proponents of violence, including just war theorists, often mistake the reliability of violence as a political tool for things such as self-defense of the nation or humanitarian intervention to protect vulnerable populations. It also explains why so many real-world humanitarian interventions launched on the justification of JWT, such as the interventions in Somalia, DRC, Haiti, Syria, and elsewhere, faced resistance and created unpredicted results, such as the violent instability following the Libyan intervention in 2011.

Directly related to this, and following Hannah Arendt,[29] Stellan Vinthagen explains how power and violence are analytically distinct given that violence is unilateral action, whereas power is by definition relational and operates through the approval of the subordinate.[30] This is important because part of the justification for just war is that states have the power to ensure swift success in their military campaign so as not to prolong the inevitable suffering caused by war. For the most part, JWT assumes that the main source of state power lies in military strength. This misunderstanding of the relationship among violence, power, and coercion is powerfully illustrated by the empirical studies that show that states with greater material capabilities are no more likely to win wars than those with weaker capabilities[31] and are, in fact, winning wars less often.[32] This more realistic, historically grounded understanding of the nature and limits of violence as a political tool raises serious questions for the credibility of JWT.

In addition, close analysis of JWT writings reveals a lack of understanding about the performative, message-sending dimension of violence, that is, how violence requires a broader discourse to make it both possible in the first place[33] and meaningful to its perpetrators and its audience. This is because physical violence, even when undertaken in pursuit of ostensibly just reasons, is a brutal, incomprehensible, traumatic, world-shattering experience that is devoid of meaning in its material experience.[34] It requires tremendous discursive effort to legitimize, obscure, or aestheticize its sheer brutality and highlight instead its positive, redemptive, or least legitimate dimensions. From this perspective, it can be argued that JWT, particularly in terms of its abstracted and decontextualized mode of theorizing, functions to obscure and legitimize the intentional, organized destruction of human bodies. At the same time, JWT contributes to the broader discourse that makes collective violence possible in the first place through its provision of a justificatory framework for killing.

In part, this relates to the more important criticism of JWT's naïve assumptions about violence, namely, that violence can be used as a tool or instrument by states that then remain unaffected by participating in violence. In fact, basic social theory tells us that violence is never purely instrumental but, rather, is *constitutive* of identities, ethics, and social and political practices. As Frazer and Hutchings put it, the idea that violence can be employed instrumentally as a tool "misses the link between violence as doing and violence as being," especially "when we take into account that our bodies themselves are prime instruments of violence." They conclude that "violence is not actually very much like a tool at all."[35] At the very least, the employment of political violence constitutes society through the social embedding of war preparation, such as militaries, war memorials, arms factories, and the like, in society and the normalization of the resort to violence as an essential part of politics.[36]

The questions this raises for JWT are troubling. Apart from including the costs of the war system and the way it functions to constitute actors, identities, and ethics, it suggests that, in employing violence to protect a group of innocent people in the present, for example, the long-term effects will be to reinforce the discourses and psychological mechanisms that encourage future resorts to violence and the entrenchment of an ongoing cycle of violence. This means that the practice of just war will likely perpetuate rather than relieve the suffering of the innocent in the long term and that the costs in innocent lives of future wars need to be accounted for in the calculations of the justness of present wars. As Laurie Calhoun puts it,

> Even in a particular case where it appears that waging war will maximise the utility of the people immediately concerned, it might still, in reality, be better not to resort to the use of deadly force, since the very example set by doing so reinforces the tendency in others to do so, and these effects extend far into the future.[37]

In a sense, this criticism of JWT's limited understanding of violence follows Arendt's observation that "[t]he practice of violence, like all action, changes the world, but the most probable change is to a more violent world."[38]

A final but not unrelated problem here is that JWT focuses exclusively on physical, usually military violence, and ignores the possibility or nature of structural violence or the ways in which societies can be violent.[39] There are normative and material dimensions to this, and they are in a way related to the real costs of violence, which are rarely, if ever, acknowledged by JWT. For example, the logic of JWT can bleed over into other areas of human interaction so that sweatshops or torture become accepted and legitimized on the basis of similar ethical reasoning to that of JWT. More broadly, there is evidence that seemingly different types of violence—domestic, criminal, and military—are constituted in a broader culture of violence such that high levels of external military violence appear to result in increased levels of domestic violence. In any event, the simplistic assumption that violence is constituted solely by direct physical combat and that military violence can be treated separately from the broader context in which it exists functions to distort a more complex reality.

A related problem with the major assumptions inherent to JWT include its failure to problematize or properly account for the inseparability of means and ends in its ethical deliberations. Instead of acknowledging that the outcomes of all political actions, including just war and humanitarian intervention, are prefigured in the means, JWT instead assumes that an inherently evil means—the organized killing of humans in war—can nevertheless be used to achieve a good end—the defense of the nation or the protection of vulnerable people, for example. The common separation of means and ends seen in JWT is an ontological and epistemological failure because it mistakes a necessary heuristic practice with the nature of reality. What this means is that the outcomes of all political actions are already *prefigured* in or an extension of the means employed to achieve them; "[h]owever hard we try to separate means and ends, the results we achieve are extensions of the policies we live," and, most importantly, ontologically speaking, "Means and ends are aspects of one and the same event."[40] Understanding social action in this way helps to explain the ways in which wars create the conditions for further wars: World War I creates the conditions for World War II, which in turn creates the conditions for the Cold War and its proxy conflicts in the developing world; World War I and the Cold War create the conditions for today's wars in the Middle East, Eastern Europe, and elsewhere; and so on.

Partly as a consequence of these and other assumptions, as well as the separation of *jus in bello* and *jus ad bellum* in ethical terms, contemporary versions of JWT have produced a whole series of "inconsistent moral prescriptions," "incompatible practical guidance,"[41] and internal contradictions in the theory. There is not the space to explore all of them here; others have done this in some detail elsewhere.[42] Instead, a few examples will suffice to illustrate. For example, the separation of *jus in bello* and *jus ad bellum* creates the paradoxical (or absurd) situation that, even if an invasion of a state is unjust, as long as the invading soldiers act justly, the population has no right to defend itself against the invading soldiers without violating JWT. More broadly, this means that "if unjust combatants fight without violating the rules governing the conduct of war, all their individual acts of war are permissible; yet these individual acts together constitute a war that is unjust and therefore impermissible."[43] Within JWT, therefore, there is no problem with asserting "that an unjust war can be fought justly."[44] Related to this because, according to Waltzer, soldiers participating in an unjust war are not responsible for that injustice and are obligated to participate, they are equally justified in killing soldiers fighting a just war of defense.[45]

Similarly, under the JWT principle that wars have to be authorized by a legitimate authority, a rapid invasion that dissolves a sitting government means that, without direction from a functioning government, the civilians of that country have no right to forcefully resist their invaders, even if the invasion itself is completely unjust. In another contradiction, just war theorists conclude that villagers who are being bombed have no right to defend themselves by shooting down a plane that will knowingly kill them as "collateral damage" if the pilot of that plane is acting under orders and in accordance with JWT. Or, once civilians do attempt to defend themselves, they then pose a threat and satisfy JWT's criterion of liability to attack; that is, "by engaging in self-defense, they cease to be innocent and become legitimate targets."[46] Finally, contemporary forms of JWT recognize a "supreme emergency" in which unjust means can be used in pursuit of (the just cause of) preventing the destruction of the political community. In other words, in this situation, JWT both prohibits and permits the deliberate targeting of noncombatants.⁴⁷ These are just a few of the absurdities and oddities produced by the ethical reasoning based on JWT's simplistic assumptions, narrow focus, and consequentialist calculations.

THE EFFECTS AND CONSEQUENCES OF JWT IN THE REAL WORLD

Critics of JWT argue that, in the real world, the widespread acceptance of the theory and its frequent use as the justificatory basis for wars and interventions functions to reify the use of violence as a tool of politics and maintains the current system of militarized states. As Neu puts it, JWT contributes to "maintaining a moral climate in which violence is not just taken for granted but considered *just*."⁴⁸ Within this moral climate and broader discursive system of war, JWT also contributes to the maintenance of moral hierarchies of the victims of war.⁴⁹ That is, in making some forms of violence just, at the same time, some of the victims of violence become "ungrievable" lives, in the words of Judith Butler;⁵⁰ those defined as combatants can be killed, as can intended collateral damage. Moreover, the foreseen victims of peacetime military forces, such as the victims of sexual assault around military bases, are not even acknowledged as worthy of inclusion in the moral calculations of JWT. This is the constitutive function of JWT in which a broader political culture and way of life is constructed around militarism, war, and worthy/worthless lives. In this and other ways, the theory helps to reinforce the maintenance of what has been called the war system, or the culture of violence. In turn, given the significant carbon emissions produced by the world's military forces and the huge national resources diverted from social programs to the military, there is a further indirect but not insignificant impact on climate change and inequality. The point is that these effects are rarely, if ever, given due consideration within ethical reasoning about the use of force by states.

More prosaically, it has been argued that JWT has not infrequently provided discursive cover for self-interested states and great power geopolitics. JWT is a handy justification for states that want to employ military force in pursuit of their own interests, justifying their invasions on the basis of saving endangered people or self-defense works to deflect criticism by claiming just motives for what would normally be considered unjust motives. In particular, self-defense has been used on multiple occasions to justify invasions, including Japan's invasion of Manchuria, Italy's invasion of Ethiopia, the United States' invasion of Grenada, and many more. In the 2003 Iraq invasion, after the Coalition failed to find the weapons of mass destruction, which were the basis for its initial JWT claim of self-defense, it switched to the argument that Saddam's human rights abuses provided the justification for the invasion. The point is that JWT is not equipped nor does it intend to interrogate real-world historical events and, therefore, cannot provide useful ethical or practical guidance when states go to war in the name of justice.

From this perspective, it can be argued that JWT contributes to making war and the use of military force more, rather than less, likely in the international system, thereby increasing the pool of direct and indirect global suffering. Certainly, it can be reasonably argued that, since the formulation of JWT several centuries ago, it has failed to significantly reduce the number of wars or to noticeably improve conduct within wars. It has also failed to halt or reduce global militarism and the spread of military weapons. Even attempts to ban weapons, which cannot be justified in JWT because of their indiscriminate nature, such as nuclear weapons, chemical weapons, and land mines, have met with limited success.

A final criticism to make here is that JWT is predicated on the assumption that war will be fought by duly constituted authorities. In other words, it is a theory for evaluating wars between states or when a state confronts a powerful nonstate actor. In the real world, increasing numbers of wars are fought between nonstate actors, such as when a state government collapses and factions struggle to assert their claims to be the legitimate authority. Somalia has been in this condition since the early 1990s and Libya, since the 2011 intervention that toppled Gaddafi. It is difficult to see how JWT can contribute to the resolution of these kinds of conflicts beyond the banality of appealing to combatant groups to fight according to *jus in bello*. Similarly, as war evolves from territorially defined battle zones between state militaries to hybrid forms of multi-actor warfare, again, it is difficult to see exactly what JWT can contribute.

JWT AND ALTERNATIVES TO VIOLENCE

For pacifists, a major criticism of JWT is that it appears to dismiss the efficacy of nonviolent responses to real-world threats and crises and, instead, axiomatically assumes that using force is the only alternative to "doing nothing." This is directly related to JWT's simplistic assumptions about what violence can and cannot do and the unproven (and empirically incorrect) assumption that violence can be deterred or defeated only by counterviolence or that coercing an opponent into desisting from unwarranted behavior necessitates military capabilities. In fact, we know from a great many real-world cases that collective action by unarmed protestors or the imposition of other kinds of sanctions (economic or moral, for example) can coerce, deter, or persuade actors to change their behavior.

The issue here is that JWT often starts from a position of either ignoring or actively rejecting pacifism on the grounds of a series of common objections.[51] For example, it is not uncommon that just war theorists and other defenders of military force will argue that pacifism cannot be considered as a relevant moral theory for international politics because it entails passivity in the face of evil, or "doing nothing" when faced with a violent threat. However, "pacifists do not claim that it is wrong to resist violence. On the contrary, they claim that *violence should be resisted*. They just believe that there are strong moral grounds for preferring to do so nonviolently."[52] In fact, pacifism entails both a negative and a positive action orientation: a negative refusal to participate in organized political violence or offer it legitimacy and a positive determination to actively build more peaceful forms of political life and methods for resolving contemporary threats and challenges. From this perspective, it can be argued that reflexively relying on violence to resolve problems is ultimately more passive than nonviolence given that it entails doing nothing until situations have deteriorated to the point of requiring urgent action.[53] Pacifism and nonviolence, by contrast, mean active engagement in the present to construct more just and peaceful societies so that violence does not emerge in the first instance.

Another common narrative from just war theorists and advocates of military force is that pacifism and nonviolence do not work or would not work in many of the situations of international politics. A response from pacifists is simply to point to all the cases throughout history when nonviolent actions have worked, as documented in the large case study literature[54] as well as in the data sets on which the quantitative literature is based.[55] In other words, following Cady, "[w]hen faced with the objection 'it won't work,' the pacifist response must be, simply, that nonviolent action does work and has a history to document the claim."[56] Another approach is to admit that

> we simply do not *know* whether there is a viable practical alternative to violence, and will not and cannot know unless we are willing to make an effort, comparable to the multibillion-dollar-a-year effort currently made to produce means of destruction and train young people in their use, to explore the potential of nonviolent action.[57]

Related to this, just war theorists, such as Michael Walzer, argue that nonviolence would not work against a brutal, unprincipled opponent and that previous historical cases, such as Gandhi in India and King in America, worked only because their opponents were democracies. However, this argument is belied by both the evidence of the kind of brutality Gandhi's and King's movements faced[58] but also robust empirical research demonstrating the success of nonviolent movements against a great many brutal dictatorships,[59] findings that hold even under situations of severe forms of repression.

Perhaps the most common argument employed to dismiss pacifism is the Nazi analogy, although the example of the Islamic State has recently been used in a similar manner. While it is a challenging argument given its seeming self-evidence, it can be responded to in a number of ways. First, as Holmes reminds us, "we should remember that there need be no inconsistency in holding that the war against Nazi Germany was justified but that war today is unjustified."[60] Wars today are fought under different circumstances, with different weapons, by different actors, and under the constant threat of nuclear weapons, and there are nonviolent mechanisms and options for dealing with international threats that were not available in 1939. Second, it is important to recognize the temporal assumptions of the argument and the way in which the analogy is most often framed. That is,

> While nonviolence obviously could not have pushed back German armour on the battlefield once the institutions of militarism had been allowed to mature and the self-propelling mechanism of a military state put into motion, it might have been effective at an earlier stage in preventing the rise to power of those responsible. If the historical fact is that military means stopped Hitler once he began to march, it is also an historical fact that reliance upon such means on the part of the world's nations did not prevent his rise to power in the first place . . . [and] had military action not been taken, say, until 1943 (or if Germany . . . [had] perfected the atom bomb first), it is unlikely that Hitler could have been stopped this way either.[61]

Lastly, it can be argued without contradiction that there will always be cases when nonviolence cannot succeed, just as there will always be cases when violence cannot succeed either. Certainly, there are always going to be circumstances when nonviolence (or violence) will not succeed immediately but might succeed if sustained over many years. In the case of Hitler and the Nazis, it is also important to question what the aims of employing violence against the Axis powers were. If it was simply to defend against or repel foreign invasion by destroying the enemy's will to continue fighting, then the military campaign obviously succeeded (after many years of struggle). On the other hand, if the violence of the Western Allies had normative goals, such as protecting civilians, saving European Jews, ending future military aggression, defeating the forces of fascism, or creating a more peaceful world, then it clearly failed. From this perspective, pacifists argue that the moral burden is not on those who oppose violence to show that it is wrong; it is upon those who advocate for its use, such as just war theorists, to show that it is right.[62]

In the end, JWT willfully fails to acknowledge the ethical validity and historically proven efficacy of pacifism and nonviolence. Today, there are important and growing literatures on nonviolent political change,[63] establishing nonwarring communities in the midst of violent civil conflict,[64] nonviolent approaches to peacekeeping and civilian protection,[65] nonviolent national self-defense,[66] nonviolent political theory,[67] responding to terrorism nonviolently,[68] and more. All these literatures provide important evidence and arguments regarding nonviolent ways of responding to contemporary violence and threats in international politics. As a consequence of the willful ignorance of these literatures, JWT grossly overestimates the number of situations where the employment of violence is the only realistic option for achieving some kind of just end. In the real world, it also greatly limits the ethical and policy imagination of policymakers,[69] who instead reflexively turn to military options, despite the long-term constitutive and destabilizing effects of employing military force. It can be argued that taking seriously the ethical and practical advantages of pacifism and nonviolence would force JWT to seriously reconsider many of its primary claims, particularly the arguments that are frequently made about war being a last or final resort.

CONCLUSION

If only even a portion of the myriad problems with JWT that I have identified in this chapter are correct—and I believe they are all correct—then the scholars and practitioners of international politics need to urgently rethink their unquestioned and unreflexive adherence to the theory. JWT is an extremely limited and conceptually poor basis for thinking ethically about war and violence in international politics or, indeed, for analyzing the practices of actual wars. In fact, it is worse than that; JWT and the widespread belief that collective violence is both just and a moral duty in some cases is most likely one of the reasons war as a practice, and the war system that supports it, persists today. As such, it can be argued that JWT and its proponents are implicated in the immense harm and suffering caused by continued warfare and militarism.

There is, therefore, an urgent need for normative international relations scholars and ethicists, just war theorists, and war studies scholars to engage seriously with the literature on pacifism and nonviolence and to take seriously fundamental issues, such as the constitutive nature of political violence and the inseparability of means and ends. Such an engagement would not only open up new questions and analytical avenues; it would also open up the policy imagination to new possibilities for action. Taking up nonviolence would in turn have positive benefits for the world's climate as well as for social justice and greater equality. This would likely result, in turn, in a reduction in violent conflicts and war, exactly the outcome that JWT claims to support.

BIBLIOGRAPHY

Aboultaif, Eduardo. "Just War and the Lebanese Resistance to Israel." *Critical Studies on Terrorism* 9, no. 2 (2016): 334–55.
Alexandra, Andrew. "Political Pacifism." *Social Theory and Practice* 29, no. 4 (October 2003): 589–606.
Arendt, Hannah. *On Violence*. New York: Harcourt, Brace and World, 1970.
Arreguin-Toft, Ivan. *How the Weak Win Wars: A Theory of Asymmetric Conflict*. New York: Cambridge University Press, 2005.
Bartkowski, Maciej, ed. *Recovering Nonviolent History: Civil Resistance in Liberation Struggles*. Boulder, CO: Lynne Rienner Publishers, 2013.
Biddle, Stephen. *Military Power: Explaining Victory and Defeat in Modern Battle*. Princeton, NJ: Princeton University Press, 2004.
Bird, Colin. *An Introduction to Political Philosophy*. Cambridge, UK: Cambridge University Press, 2007.
Burrowes, Robert. *The Strategy of Nonviolent Defense: A Gandhian Approach*. New York: State University of New York Press, 1996.
Butler, Judith. *Precarious Life: The Powers of Mourning and Violence*. London: Verso, 2006.
Cady, Duane. *From Warism to Pacifism: A Moral Continuum*. 2nd ed. Philadelphia, PA: Temple University Press, 2010.
Calhoun, Laurie. "How Violence Breeds Violence: Some Utilitarian Considerations." *Politics* 22, no. 2 (2002): 95–108.
Chenoweth, Erica, and Maria Stephan. *Why Civil Resistance Works: The Strategic Logic of Nonviolent Conflict*. New York: Columbia University Press, 2011.
Frazer, Elizabeth, and Kimberley Hutchings. "On Politics and Violence: Arendt Contra Fanon." *Contemporary Political Theory* 7 (2008): 90–108.
Goerzig, Carol. *Talking to Terrorists: Concessions and the Renunciation of Violence*. Abingdon: Routledge, 2010.
Holmes, Robert L. *The Ethics of Nonviolence: Essays by Robert L. Holmes*, edited by P. Cicovacki. New York: Bloomsbury, 2013.
———. "The Metaethics of Pacifism and Just War Theory." *The Philosophical Forum* 46, no. 1 (2015): 3–15. https://doi.org/10.1111/phil.12052.
———. *Pacifism: A Philosophy of Nonviolence*. London: Bloomsbury, 2017.
Howes, Dustin. "The Failure of Pacifism and the Success of Nonviolence." *Perspectives on Politics* 11, no. 2 (2013): 427–66.
———. "The Just War Masquerade." *Peace Review: A Journal of Social Science* 27, no. 3 (2015): 379–87.
———. *Toward a Credible Pacifism: Violence and the Possibilities of Politics*. Albany, NY: SUNY Press, 2009.
Hutchings, Kimberly. "Pacifism Is Dirty: Towards an Ethico-Political Defence." *Critical Studies on Security* 6, no. 2 (2018): 176–92.
Ihara, Craig. "Pacifism as a Moral Idea." *The Journal of Value Inquiry* 22 (1988): 267–77.
Jackson, Richard. "Commentary & Debate: CTS, Counterterrorism and Nonviolence." *Critical Studies on Terrorism* 10, no. 2 (2017): 357–69.
———. "Pacifism: The Anatomy of a Subjugated Knowledge." *Critical Studies on Security* 6, no. 2 (2018): 160–75.
———. "Pacifism and the Ethical Imagination." *International Politics* 56, no. 2 (2019): 212–27.
Jackson, Richard, and Helen Dexter. "The Social Construction of Organised Political Violence: An Analytical Framework." *Civil Wars* 16, no. 1 (2014): 1–23.
Julian, Rachel, and Christine Schweitzer. "The Origins and Development of Unarmed Civilian Peacekeeping." *Peace Review: A Journal of Social Justice* 27, no. 1 (2015): 1–8.
Kaplan, Oliver. *Resisting War: How Communities Protect Themselves*. Cambridge, UK: Cambridge University Press, 2017.
Kemp, Graham, and Douglas Fry. *Keeping the Peace: Conflict Resolution and Peaceful Societies Around the World*. London: Routledge, 2003.

Mantena, Karuna. "Another Realism: The Politics of Gandhian Nonviolence." *American Political Science Review* 106, no. 2 (2012): 455–70.

May, Todd. *Nonviolent Resistance: A Philosophical Introduction.* Cambridge, UK: Polity, 2015.

McMahan, Jeff. "Rethinking the 'Just War,' Part 1." *New York Times Opinionator*, November 11, 2012. https://opinionator.blogs.nytimes.com/2012/11/11/rethinking-the-just-war-part-1/.

———. "Rethinking the 'Just War,' Part 2." *New York Times Opinionator*, November 12, 2012. https://opinionator.blogs.nytimes.com/2012/11/12/rethinking-the-just-war-part-2/.

Miniotaite, Grazina. "Lithuania: From Non-Violent Liberation towards Non-Violent Defence?" *Peace Research: The Canadian Journal of Peace Studies* 48, no. 4 (1996): 19–36.

Nepstad, Sharon. *Nonviolent Revolutions: Civil Resistance in the Late 20th Century.* New York: Oxford University Press, 2011.

Neu, Michael. *Just Liberal Violence: Sweatshops, Torture, War.* London: Rowman & Littlefield, 2018.

———. "Why There Is No Such Thing as Just War Pacifism and Why Just War Theorists and Pacifists Can Talk Nonetheless." *Social Theory and Practice* 37, no. 3 (July 2011): 413–33.

Parsons, Graham. "The Incoherence of Walter's Just War Theory." *Social Theory and Practice* 38, no. 4 (October 2012): 663–88.

Phillips, Robert, and Duane Cady. *Humanitarian Intervention: Just War vs. Pacifism.* Lanham, MD: Rowman & Littlefield, 1996.

Roberts, Adam, and Timothy Garton Ash, eds., *Civil Resistance and Power Politics: The Experience of Non-Violent Action from Gandhi to the Present.* Oxford: Oxford University Press, 2009.

Ryan, Cheyney. "Pacifism, Just War, and Self-Defense." *Philosophia* 41 (2013): 977–1005.

———. "Pacifism(s)." *Philosophical Forum* 46, no. 1 (2015): 17–39.

Scarry, Elaine. "Injury and the Structure of War." *Representations* 10 (Spring 1985): 1–51.

Schock, Kurt. *Unarmed Insurrections: People Power Movements in Nondemocracies.* Minneapolis: University of Minnesota Press, 2005.

Vinthagen, Stellan. *A Theory of Nonviolent Action: How Civil Resistance Works.* London: Zed Books, 2015.

Wallace, Molly. *Security without Weapons: Rethinking Violence, Violent Action, and Civilian Protection.* Abingdon, UK: Routledge, 2016.

Chapter Four

Undertaking Critical Legal Theory to Examine Just War Intervention

A Smokescreen for Political Ambitions

Danny Singh

INTRODUCTION

The chapter initially covers just war theory. This involves military, theological, and political ethics when engaging in war and the conduct in war and account of civilian casualties for military advantage (proportionality). The next section covers critical legal theory, which addresses the need for criticism of laws that discriminate against certain groups. The example of the 1982 Citizenship Law in Myanmar, which denies Rohingyas in the Rakhine state of basic citizenship rights, has caused international pressure but remains unrevoked. Next, two international relations theories, realism and institutional liberalism (the latter includes the Responsibility to Protect [R2P] doctrine), are discussed. This allows an examination of the weak interventions in Bosnia and Rwanda and nonintervention in Darfur. I go on to argue that there was a good argument made by the UN Secretary-General and the Commander of the United Nations Assistance Mission in Rwanda (UNAMIR) to intervene under just war theory once hate messages from Hutu radio had been reported. However, major troop-contributing countries (TCCs) did not commit human and financial capital to avert the genocide because there were no resources or material gain to attain from such intervention. The international relations theory of realism supports this explanation of selfish state interests and an international anarchic system of self-help. I then provide a critique on the rule of "proportionality" when the North Atlantic Treaty Organization (NATO) decided to attack a Belgrade media center in 1999, killing civilians but justifying the bombing because the broadcasting also served Serbian military intel.

The penultimate section analyzes the cases of both post-9/11 interventions in Afghanistan and Iraq. I go on to critically argue that the interveners utilized their *just* reasons as a political umbrella for realist ambitions, more specifically, relative gain and power, for oil and counterterrorist strategy. US foreign policy also manipulated the UN to back the United States and its coalition of willing states in both contexts.

The examples and cases presented in this chapter are based on humanitarian intervention, the War on Terror, and internationalism. Such intervention (and nonintervention, if lack of geopolitical interests) is part of the liberal analytical approach of just war, which has caused a threat to the traditional principles of just war theory. To counter contemporary criticism of the liberal analytical doctrine of just war interventions (and noninterventions), I conclude that institutional liberalism can place the UN and NATO in a stronger position to pressure their member states to intervene in the name of just war ethics via the normative dimensions of the R2P doctrine. This can reduce international skepticism of intervention as a political umbrella/smokescreen to extract resources and destroy military communication and other political gain. Adopting such an approach can morally justify (1) the legality to wage war (*jus ad bellum*), (2) the methods of conduct during war (*jus in bello*), and (3) the democratization and/or reconstruction process in the aftermath of intervention (*jus post bellum*).

JUST WAR THEORY

Traditional military ethics are undertaken by leaders of armed forces, theologians, and policymakers. These ethics are part of the just war theory doctrine, which aims to morally justify a war to be deemed as *just* when certain criteria are met. Just war theory has archaic origins. It originally derived from Hinduism and, later, Christian theology. Saint Thomas Aquinas (1225–1274) outlined the conditions of when a war could be justified. Aquinas combined philosophical reasoning with faith and ranked three pillars of a just war under the medieval thought of Scholasticism. First, a just war must be ordered by an institutional authority, such as a state, to represent a common good for the sake of God. Second, war must be waged for a just end by "just means," instead of self-interests or state gain, to honor the view that killing innocent civilians cannot be justified.[1] For instance, waging war in pursuit of national interests is not justified, and exercising power to merely restore denials, such as loss of territory or goods or punishing a government, army, or civilians who have committed evil acts, is not justified. Third, during a violent conflict, peace must be the principal objective as part of the right intention. The right intention consists of an authority and its soldiers vying for just reasons to support its initial justification of war.[2] Aquinas also argued that a just war can be outlined with philosophy and theology and both are not contradictory. Later, in the sixteenth and seventeenth centuries, additional fourth, fifth, and sixth conditions of just war theory were proposed by de Vitoria and Suárez. They argued that the loss of human lives should be proportionate to the injustice that is prevented or resolved by war, peaceful means to prevent war must be exhausted, and a just war should have a high chance of success.[3]

In contemporary philosophical thought and basic international law, just war theory has two main categories. Initially, there has to be a moral justification, or a right, of waging and/or entering a war (*jus ad bellum*). *Jus ad bellum* is also judged on the legality of a war, which means norms are determined and violation of the legal process rests on the irresponsibility of states.[4] Article 2 (4) of the 1945 Charter of the United Nations (hereinafter, the UN Charter) stresses that all UN member states must refrain from their international relations threatening or using force against another territory. Once engaged in war, the morality of conduct during the war is judged (*jus in bello*) to provide "justice in war."[5] As part of *jus in bello*, just conduct in war has two main principles. First, discrimination covers who legitimate targets are in war. Second, proportionality concerns a threshold of force that is deemed as morally applicable.[6] This principle forbids attacks countering military aims that have a high chance of causing either or a combination of fatalities, injury, or property damage to civilians. The predicted military advantage that is desired needs to outweigh these repercussions against civilians. The concept of military necessity may contradict *jus in bello*. Military necessity is when a military has no other option but to overrule *jus in bello* and justify using powerful weapons, such as nuclear weapons and poisonous gas, as "morally permissible" for utilitarian purposes.[7] Such purposes are based on clear military advantage.

In recent times, there has been pressure to include a third thread of contemporary just war theory to deal with the morality of settlement and reconstruction in the aftermath of war (*jus post bellum*).[8] These military ethics assume that war is abysmal but is not the worst action to undertake. An authority, such as a state and its supporting military, has moral responsibilities, unwelcome consequences, or avoidable atrocities to consider that may justify waging war.

The world organization also adheres to discrimination and proportionality principles within just war theory. The UN Charter aims to settle disputes pacifically between states under Chapter VI of its Charter to avert wars. However, when Chapter VI of the UN Charter has applied diplomatic efforts but such measures are exhausted to no avail, then Chapter VII undertakes sanctions and the legitimate use of force *erga omnes*. In international law, *erga omnes* describes an obligation of states toward the international community to protect undeniable and universal interests when critical rights are violated.[9] States may signal a complaint against such breaches, and examples of these norms include piracy, genocide, an act of aggression, and property rights.[10] Under Chapter VII of the UN Charter, the UN authorizes states to undertake legitimate self-defense against states to maintain international peace and security. The UN Charter also upholds that collective self-defense with consent of the UN Security Council (UNSC), which usually includes *erga omnes* norms, must respect the limitations of proportionality and military necessity.

Hence, according to contemporary international law, *jus ad bellum* consists of a state defending itself by going to war. However, this requires clear evidence of an aggressor state, or else questions based on the morality of waging war and legality will commence. The international legality on the use of armed force is strictly assessed with justifiable motivations. Such legal justification can be provided only by the authorization of a competent body, usually the UNSC. Article 53 (1) of the UN Charter, under Chapter VIII, Regional Arrangements, states that the Security Council can utilize regional arrangements for enforcement action but no enforcement action can be undertaken from any regional arrangement or agency without consent of the Council. The UNSC is assigned the role of identifying particular conditions as threats to international peace and security. Subsequently, the Council can authorize interference into the sphere of independence, which is frequently reserved to a state.

CRITICAL LEGAL THEORY

The UN Charter is in support of just war theory and the reasons for waging war (*jus ad bellum*). This includes enforcement action to be undertaken, with consent of the UNSC, with good reason for a state's self-defense and weight of proportionality (potential civilian fatalities and injury and property damages taken into consideration). Despite these intentions of the UN Charter and affiliated international legal instruments, critical legal theory[11] offers an evaluative legal tool. It analyzes laws as a means to preserve the status quo of a given society's or international society's structures of power and law and is codified to postulate societal and political biases against marginalized groups.[12]

I argue that critical legal theory can be applied to international legal preference on state sovereignty. I agree that states must remain sovereign and powerful states or security organizations, and even economic trading organizations if the state is deregulated, must be respected. However, if a state is denying its citizens basic rights or massacring them, then intervention should be permitted. Intervention can be permitted under Chapter VII of the UN

Charter *erga omnes*, but state sovereignty has dominance since the Treaties of Westphalia (1648) up until Article 2 (7) of the UN Charter.[13] This is why 193 states have signed up to the UN so they can have security and other protections from member states and have legal standing from other states to *not* interfere in their internal affairs under the rule of state sovereignty. State sovereignty, with international legal support, is to preserve the status quo of the international community and that of individual states, but domestic laws may have biases against marginalized groups.

To provide one example, Myanmar has ratified the UN as a member under the former name Burma and has a 1982 Citizenship Law, which was enacted under a military dictatorship. This law deprives the Muslim minority group, an estimated 800,000 Rohingyas, from the Rakhine state and refugees in Bangladesh of basic civil and political rights.[14] Despite such international norms and legal instruments being raised as a consequence of the 1982 Citizenship Law, the Myanmar government has claimed that revising its citizenship law would breach its state sovereignty. Therefore, a critical legal approach would support the argument that state sovereignty is to preserve the status quo, with the 1982 Citizenship Law, which discriminates against the marginalized Rohingya ethnic group. The following section will cover the notion of state gain and decisions made to intervene in states under realist theory in international relations.

REALISM IN INTERNATIONAL RELATIONS

Realism is an archaic doctrine in international relations. Classical realism argues that moral perceptions are not applicable when a state is considering waging war or pursuing foreign policy,[15] whereas neorealists try to view international politics through an empirically based approach. Structural realism/neorealism argues that power dictates international relations.[16] Morgenthau and Waltz both perceive that international relations is driven by competitiveness and hostility where power conquers the global stage.[17] This is why power is central to the theory of structural realism. Morgenthau argues that the national armed forces hold influential power but the nation's characteristics on morale and the efficiency of governance hold more significance.[18] Morgenthau further goes on by arguing that power is largely cemented on military stature.[19] Alongside military strength, Waltz provides additional modes of power and abilities, which also include the size of a population, economic ability, political stability, resources, and competency.[20] Waltz's conception of power is mainly narrow but is not based solely on material components.

The main concept of structural realism that is relevant to this chapter is based on the international anarchic system. This means that states are vying for survival and prerequisites to reach additional goals. The aim of their own survival drives their offensive military competences and their foreign policy, usually foreign interventions, to intensify their relative power. Relative gain concerns a state's actions in response to power balances to *not* only increase their wealth, power, or utility (absolute gain) but also to increase the gap of such absolute holdings and those of other states.[21] States do not trust one another because they are run in an anarchic world.[22] As neorealists argue, states are cautious with relative power losses, which could lead to other states' threatening their survival, because, even if two states expect "large absolute gains," each state will fear how the other will use that power.[23] This is referred to as the security dilemma caused by rivalry, fear, inaccurate threats, and the need for self-help for a state's own security within an international system of anarchy.[24]

Relative gains can be made by other states, which creates fear, insecurity, and the thought of potential dependency with emerging and potential predominant powers. As a consequence, states are less likely to cooperate with one another. Relative gain results in a balance of power because every state aims to maximize its relative power, which dictates international politics. This increases the security dilemma because other states might be maximizing their utility, wealth, or military power to cause a threat to the concerned state's security. In contrast to this approach, liberalism is based on the conception of states to benefit their security and economy. Liberalism will now be covered.

LIBERALISM IN INTERNATIONAL RELATIONS THEORY

Neoliberals undertake an absolute gain approach when studying international relations, unlike neorealists, who focus on relative gains.[25] Absolute gain is the opposite of relative gain. It concerns the decision-making of a state or organization to increase its own wealth, power, or utility that disregards gains that have been made by other states or organizations.[26] Neoliberals support absolute gain because they believe that it measures the full picture, consisting of economic, security, and cultural impacts of an action for a state, rather than perceive other states' power as a possible threat or competitor to them. Neoliberals believe that there are international structures to govern the behavior of states, rather than what realists argue of an absence of an international order (anarchy), and, thus, in a worst-case scenario, a state can lose gains if it fails to cooperate.[27] Liberal international relations theory stresses that the absolute gains describe what influences the interests of international actors and considers the complete impact of a decision on either a state or an organization, and the actors behave in view of that.

INSTITUTIONAL LIBERALISM

Institutional liberalism is a new strand of international relations theory. It is largely based on idealism from the onset of the League of Nations, founded in 1920 in the aftermath of the Great War, and is criticized for being overoptimistic from realists.[28] The theory, based on Immanuel Kant, stresses that international organizations and institutions can create an organization of states to enhance state cooperation and the preservation of peace.[29] Such global organizations include the UN, NATO, and the European Union (EU). Institutional liberalism is based on utilitarian ideology (i.e., for the greater good of society) and is rationalistic (i.e., relies on reason and experience to establish truth as the source of knowledge without relying on perceptions). All states within international institutions are equal, and hierarchy is nullified, which represents diplomacy on a level playing field. Liberals believe that such a global political system, with the use of institutions, can reduce conflict and enhance economic prosperity. Therefore, states can exercise freedom with liberalism.

The thought behind institutional liberalism is an appealing one to reduce conflict and increase diplomacy in the event of human suffering, persecution, and economic despair. Even though the theory may appear too idealistic, the goals promoted by international organizations and institutions can support states to better their economic and security measures. I will now focus on the UN providing support with diplomacy and collective security measures when a state fails to protect its own citizens from mass-scale human rights violations.

THE UNITED NATIONS AND THE RESPONSIBILITY TO PROTECT

The UN had significant shortcomings by failing to protect civilians during two genocides in the mid-1990s. In Rwanda, the UNAMIR comprised only a 2,500-troop lightly armed peacekeeping contingent, which took five months to put together.[30] UNAMIR's commander, Lieutenant General Roméo Dallaire, signaled the signs of genocide based on Hutu hate messages broadcast on Rwandan radio stations to kill the cockroaches (i.e., the Tutsis). Dallaire then liaised with the UN secretary-general (UNSG), Boutros Boutros-Ghali, to call for more support from TCCs in finances, resources, and personnel.[31] Dallaire argued for a rapid deployment of a well-equipped contingent of 5,000 troops, with a robust mandate to use force to prevent the massacres in South and West Rwanda.[32] On April 29, 1994, the United States and the United Kingdom notified the UNSG to undertake African states' efforts to avert the violence in Rwanda, which led to the UNSG's writing to over thirty African states for more troops, and Dallaire cynically stated this was due to a lack of political will from Western governments.[33] The secretary-general of Médecins Sans Frontières, Alain Destexhe, argued that the UNSC left the lives of Tutsis in the hands of the United States. However, the United States was reluctant to strongly intervene because over thirty of their armed forces had been killed during the UN peacekeeping operation in Somalia a few years earlier.[34] Ultimately, UNAMIR did not receive adequate support, and the peacekeeping troops were forced to surrender Tutsis like cattle to be slaughtered by Hutus. As a consequence, 800,000 people (mostly Tutsi and some Hutu pacifiers of Tutsi) were killed over a 100-day period from April–July 1994 due to the Hutu government's support of the Interahamwe (i.e., Hutu paramilitary organization).[35]

Moreover, in the summer of 1995, Bosnian Serb President Radovan Karadžić's ethnic cleansing policy targeted Muslims in Bosnia. A UN protection force was deployed during the civil war in Bosnia. A Dutch contingent stayed in accommodation in Potočari, a village in the Srebrenica municipality, to protect the safe haven in Srebrenica. However, the Bosnian Serb army commander, Ratko Mladić, continued the ordering of the systematic killing of 8,000 Bosniak (i.e., Muslim) men and boys.[36] Therefore, the UN had weak forces and mandates in Rwanda and Bosnia and thus failed to protect Tutsis and Bosnian Muslims.

In 2005, the UN then failed to intervene in Darfur, West Sudan. This was due to the failure of the UNSC to label it as genocide, calling it crimes against humanity of an ethnic essence, despite tens of thousands being massacred and 1.8 million being displaced.[37] This was because genocide would have led to the international community's intervening *erga omnes*. Such an intervention would have been vetoed in the UNSC due to alleged Chinese military lorries and A5 Fantan fighter jets in Darfur supporting President Bashir and the Arab Janjaweed militia, despite a UN arms embargo, in exchange for oil deals.[38]

Therefore, weak intervention (e.g., in Rwanda and Bosnia) or nonintervention (e.g., Darfur) are due to the lack of political will. Under structural realism, the lack of political will, in these cases, may have been because of powerful states having no relative power (i.e., expansion of own economy over other countries or enhancing security within an area) to intervene or because robust intervention would have hindered their own resources and gains. One could also argue that a neoliberalist cooperative intervention via a security organization for absolute gains was also not perceived possible by a collection of states, which is why intervention was weak. Because of these shortcomings, the theory of institutional liberalism was further emphasized from the 2005 World Summit to avert additional international humanitarian law (IHL) abuses: genocides, ethnic cleansing, crimes against humanity, and war crimes. All UN member states endorsed R2P at the summit.

The principle of R2P accepts that sovereignty is to be respected as a traditional foundation of international law. However, R2P proposes that with sovereignty comes the state's responsibility to protect all its populations from widespread atrocity crimes. Based on this condition, human rights are directly intertwined with state sovereignty, rather than being traditionally in opposition.[39] R2P also provides rhetoric on other mass atrocity crimes, including crimes against humanity and breaches of IHL in noninternational armed conflicts (NIAC), which must be protected by sovereign states.[40] Therefore, international legal norms are respected regarding sovereignty, peace, and security to maintain basic standards in armed conflict and human rights.

R2P consists of three interconnected pillars, which are mentioned in the World Summit Outcome Document.[41] In relation to the document, the UN member states unanimously approved upholding state R2P. Pillar I is concerned with the state's responsibility to protect the state. This concerns every state protecting its populations from the four crimes mentioned in IHL: war crimes, crimes against humanity, ethnic cleansing, and genocide.[42] It is a fallacy that R2P attempts to undermine a state's sovereignty; rather, it attempts to reinforce the responsibilities that come with state sovereignty.[43] Most states have the institutional strength and capacity to prevent such mass atrocity crimes. If states do not have the capacity to assist populations before the outbreak of a crisis, then the international community can assist under Pillar II of R2P. This pillar concentrates on international support and capacity building to help states that are willing to uphold their own R2P. Pillar III is based on an appropriate and decisive response, which concerns measures adopted in Chapter VI (i.e., diplomacy) followed by Chapter VII (i.e., collective security) of the UN Charter. This liberalist movement aims to institutionally promote R2P and its three pillars within states under the auspices of the UN to prevent mass atrocities and human rights abuses when states fail to protect their populations.

INTERVENTIONS

This section will critically examine the decisions to go to war (*jus ad bellum*), modes of warfare, and particularly the rule of proportionality (*jus in bello*) in the contexts of Kosovo, Afghanistan, and Iraq.

Kosovo

In the case of Kosovo, a three-month NATO bombing campaign from March 24 to June 10, 1999, was begun on the grounds of humanitarian intervention to retaliate against Slobodan Milošević's ethnic cleansing policy regarding Kosovar Albanians.[44] NATO failed to gain the authorization of the UNSC (which is the most relevant authority in the case of humanitarian intervention) yet proceeded to intervene anyway. That clearly breached Article 53 (1) of Chapter VIII in the UN Charter. Despite international legal criticism, NATO justified the intervention as a just humanitarian war. However, on the grounds of proportionality, moral intention, and legitimate authority, it is debatable whether the intervention of Operation Allied Force qualified as a just war. Waltzer claimed that ethnic cleansing was already under way, with visible Serbian armed forces on Kosovo's borders and refugees moving, and thus military intervention was justified and compulsory.[45] The term "humanitarian" was not used, but the intervention in the literature concerns the nature of a "humanitarian intervention." Holzgrefe defines humanitarian intervention as the actual use or threat of force that goes beyond a state's borders by either another state or a collective group of states to prevent serious human rights abuses without the consent of the state in which the force has intervened.[46] A collective group of states was evident in NATO's bombing against the former Socialist Federal Republic of Yugoslavia (SFRY) because a collection of states, including the United Kingdom and United States, permitted the campaign, despite failure to obtain authorization from the UNSC; thus, debatably, they acted outside of international law.[47] NATO considered the action to be a military intervention to protect a small group of people, based on moral grounds, to prevent a genocide and, thus, was humanitarian.[48] The legitimate objectives were military targets and communications of Serbian military forces, which debatably avoided breaching the discrimination and military necessity principles in *jus in bello*.

The NATO-led airstrikes targeted media systems that served military purposes. However, this strategy led to civilian casualties. On April 23, 1999, Belgrade's leading government-supported Serbian radio and television broadcasting station, Radio Television Serbia, was bombed by aircraft.[49] NATO justified the bombing even though sixteen civilians, who were employees of Radio Television Serbia, were killed at its headquarters during these coordinated attacks.[50] NATO argued that the station had a dual military and civilian purpose. Based on this argument, it was a warranted target because of its military use, which encompassed more than 100 radio relay sites across Serbia.[51] NATO argued that this case was lawful because of the fact that the destruction of the military communications command structure outweighed civilian harm, which was not excessive. Yet the International Criminal Tribunal for Yugoslavia (ICTY) contended that the bombing, which gained a meager three hours of media coverage, in contrast to the fatalities of sixteen civilian workers, was disproportionate. Despite such criticism, the Office of the Prosecutor for the ICTY did not recommend NATO to be investigated for negligence.[52] The rule of proportionality, *jus in bello*, is thus a confusing and subjective topic.

Therefore, under a critical legal theory, it can be argued that the former SFRY intervention was to preserve the security objectives of NATO, which failed to consult the UN, making it illegal under international law (Article 53 (1) of Chapter VIII of the UN Charter). Because of the absence of UNSC authorization, NATO's intervention was deemed illegal by the Kosovo Report Commission.[53] Malone and Wermester also argued that the intervention was debatably illegal under international law, but as the then UN secretary-general, Kofi Annan, argued, NATO provided a more rapid response with "more teeth."[54] For Wheeler, in conditions of humanitarian emergency (i.e., *jus ad humanitarianism*), waiting for authorization from a legal system is not as important as rapid action.[55] A just cause for humanitarian intervention can be based on genocide alone as a peremptory norm in international law (i.e., *jus cogens*) to act against heinous atrocity crimes *erga omnes*. Moreover, the intervention cannot be under a pillar of just war theory only if proportionality of targeting media and military targets in Serbia was to avert further ethnic cleansing and discrimination against Kosovo Albanians. The lives of innocent Serbs and property damage being justified under just war theory's rule of proportionality and military necessity *jus in bello* provides a contentious debate. The rule of proportionality was applied by NATO states when deciding to aerially strike Belgrade's radio station, a military communication media for Milošević's forces, despite killing civilian workers. However, the notion of targeting military targets should not result in excessive civilian casualties and property damage. This rule of proportionality came into effect in the 1977 Additional Protocol I (International Armed Conflicts) to the Four Geneva Conventions of 1949.[56]

Afghanistan

After the September 11, 2001 (hereinafter, 9/11), terrorist attacks on the World Trade Center and the Pentagon bombings, which took the lives of 2,997 civilians and those of the 19 hijackers of the passenger planes, US foreign policy took a robust approach.[57] Osama Bin Laden was the prime suspect; his group, al-Qaeda, was suspected to be hiding in Afghani mountains with the backing of Taliban pacifiers who rejected the then US President George W. Bush's ultimatum to surrender Bin Laden.[58] This resulted in the United States seeking UNSC authorization for UN member states to support the US War on Terror. UNSC Resolutions 1368 and 1373 were passed after 9/11 within the same month as a measure for the United States and Coalition forces to pursue collective security for self-defense against al-Qaeda. Articles 39, 42, and 51 in Chapter VII of the UN Charter were referred to, which pertain to a UN member state's right to exercise collective self-defense due to a threat against it that violates international peace and security. However, al-Qaeda is a nonstate actor; therefore, military intervention utilizing Chapter VII of the UN Charter can be challenged by international lawyers. First Lady Laura Bush also justified the war in Afghanistan as an opportunity to liberate women against the patriarchal informal dispute systems, which appealed to feminists.[59]

Bush's rhetoric on the War on Terror to fight against the axis of evil, Afghanistan, Iraq, Iran, and North Korea, was initiated as a counterinsurgency strategy.[60] This war was promoted as being just to deter and combat evil as a last resort, which can be traced to Saint Augustine's theological Christian ethics.[61] However, Kamrany and Greenhalgh argue that the war in Afghanistan does not comply with St. Augustine's ethics of just war because the intervention *jus ad bellum* was not clear, had unclear just aims, and was illegitimate.[62] In addition, the war was based on capturing Bin Laden, despite his absence in Afghanistan. Bin Laden and his combatants had fled to Pakistan via the Tora Bora Mountains in December 2001.[63] Moreover, Pashtun tribes were underrepresented after the intervention and the Bonn peace process because they were wrongly perceived as being anti-American, and Tajiks (many part of the Northern Alliance) were overrepresented due to security and patronage ties.[64] Furthermore, the war served as a first resort, rather than a last resort whereby diplomatic measures had been exhausted, and, thus, Chapter VII of the UN Charter was triggered under aggressive US foreign policy.[65] Finally, there was no estimation on the success of the intervention. It was not thoroughly considered whether the intervention would serve the good of the people for whom the intervention was undertaken, as Aquinas outlined in just war ethics, and thus there has been limited success.

On October 7, 2001, airstrikes began with Operation Enduring Freedom, mainly US and British military forces collaborating with anti-Taliban Northern Alliance warlords on the ground, and full UN backing to target al-Qaeda and overthrow the Taliban regime.[66] This was the longest direct involvement of the United States in a war, and the United States withdrew its forces only recently, rather than in 2014, which was the proposed date. There have been thousands of civilian casualties as well as the deaths of international soldiers. An estimated 225,000 Afghan civilians died, and 365,000 were wounded; a minimum of 3,315,000 Afghans were also displaced because of the war affecting Afghanistan and neighboring Pakistan and Iran.[67] Furthermore, the methods of conducting war during the intervention *jus in bello* have been criticized. Chomsky has convincingly argued that the United States, aided by anti-Taliban Tajik Northern Alliance militia's pointing out the whereabouts of al-Qaeda, used illegal biochemical weapons to "smoke out" the Taliban in the remote mountains.[68] The use of illicit arms can be challenged under rules pertaining to conduct in war, more narrowly, the Hague Conventions of 1899 and 1907 and the 1925 Geneva Protocol for the Prohibition of the Use in War of Asphyxiating, Poisonous or Other Gases, and of Bacteriological Methods of Warfare.

Therefore, in the context of Afghanistan, skepticism exists around the motives of the United States and the legality of the intervention *jus ad bel-*

lum. Moreover, the conduct of war *jus in bello* has been criticized due to the use of drone attacks and illegal biochemical weapons, which caused mass civilian casualties and extensive destruction of agricultural land. Under the rule of proportionality, the Taliban was successfully ousted from power but only by the end of 2001; therefore, protracted involvement caused excessive deaths and property and land damage. In addition, prohibited weapons were utilized as part of military necessity *jus in bello*. The United States and its Coalition forces could argue that the war was just and that extended intervention was required *jus in bello* to continue fighting the radicalized Taliban, which had been resurging in Pakistan from late 2005 to 2006, and to assist with reform of the Afghan military and police *jus post bellum* so they could stand alone once intervention had ceased.

The United States and international supporters could have exercised R2P as an instrument for intervention because most Afghans were dissatisfied with strict Taliban rule, which had been in effect since September 1996. To specify, the Taliban were committing serious human rights abuses by prohibiting female professionals from working, closing education facilities for girls, and arresting men in the streets for having beards deemed too short.[69]

Based on this premise, the Taliban was not upholding its claim as a sovereign state because Mullah Omar's rule was not legally recognized by the international community. Hence, if R2P had arrived before the World Summit in 2005, then R2P could have been exercised in ousting the Taliban, regardless of the political smokescreen from the United States and its pacifiers. Under international relations theory, structural realism is the doctrine associated with the Afghan war because the United States pursued relative power in securing the area by ousting the Taliban out of power and forcing an interim democracy. More could have been done on promoting the just war ethics on the last, rather than first, resort; the legality of the intervention; and the conduct of armed conflict during the war.

Iraq

The second Iraq intervention began in March 2003, and international military forces formally disbanded in December 2011.[70] Justification was required to topple the totalitarian Saddam Hussein regime, eliminate the threat of an Iraqi nuclear enrichment program, defeat pacifiers of al-Qaeda, and debatably extract oil reserves to maximize relative power and military gain.[71] *Jus post bellum* focused on forming a new democracy to enhance trading ties with the West. The United States pressed its concerns to the UN. In response, the UNSC authorized Resolution 1441 in November 2002, recalled Resolutions 660 and 678 from 1990, and recognized that Iraq held a security threat due to its noncompliance with previous resolutions. Resolution 1441 further stated that Iraq's "proliferation of weapons of mass destruction (WMD) and long-range missiles poses" a threat "to international peace and security." Subsequently, UN weapons inspectors did not find any WMD. However, the United States formed a coalition of willing states, which included Britain, to invade Iraq without direct UNSC authorization (as permitted under Chapter VII of its Charter). The intervention later destroyed large parts of Iraq, including the devastation of Baghdad due to strong civilian support for further aggressive action.[72] Saddam Hussein was later captured, tried, and hanged at the Iraqi Special Tribunal for crimes against humanity on December 30, 2006.[73]

Therefore, the justification for intervention *jus ad bellum* in Iraq can be challenged under international law. Clearly, Article 2 (4) of the UN Charter has been breached because the United States and its Coalition forces did not refrain from its international relations for foreign policy, security, and resource reasons when deciding to intervene in Iraq. Moreover, the actions during the Iraqi intervention *jus in bello* resulted in widespread civilian casualties and property damage, which can be challenged under the proportionality principle. Realist theory in international relations is useful for explaining the political imperatives of the United States and its Coalition forces to overthrow a despot and form a democracy to benefit oil ties in the Middle East with the West. The just war argument of a last resort was not credible because no WMDs were found by UN weapons inspectors.

Similar to the post-9/11 intervention in Afghanistan, the axis of evil rhetoric and the War on Terror was utilized in aggressive US unilateral and foreign policy. In addition, Article 2 (7) related to Chapter VII of the UN Charter, as later reiterated with R2P, could argue that the Iraqi dictatorship had not respected its own sovereignty by participating in atrocity crimes, particularly against the Kurdistan region. However, the intervention failed to appeal on the atrocity crimes, warranting intervention, which was later scrutinized by both US and UK citizens, civil society groups, and nongovernmental organizations. This critical approach from within states can be referred to as constructivism in international relations theory, which is useful to point out the criticism of international military intervention from their own citizens. A political smokescreen was not achieved by George Bush and Tony Blair. Blair had to report to the Iraq Inquiry.[74] In the aftermath of 9/11, counterinsurgency strategy was dominating the UN and foreign policy of Western states. It was fairly clear that *erga omnes* was exercised in the Afghan context under the umbrella of Chapter VII of the UN Charter and a coalition of willing states without direct UNSC consent for Iraq. This contemporary liberal analytical approach to just war theory counters the legality and morality of engaging in war *jus ad bellum*. Consequently, the traditional principles of *jus ad bellum* were under threat.

CONCLUSION

Institutional liberalism can utilize powerful security organizations, such as NATO and the UN, to undermine a state's sovereignty when it is posing a threat to its citizens rather than merely acting out of foreign policy. However, this debate was contested with counterinsurgency post-9/11 in Afghanistan and Iraq. For R2P to have prominence as a norm, because it is not legally binding, the UN can strive for major TCCs to exercise stronger political will as a means of just war intervention to avert a huge loss of lives. This could have been done with the mid-1990s genocides in Bosnia and Rwanda.

The intervention (for structural realist relative power or neoliberalist absolute gain) and methods of military benefit (proportionality) that states and organizations institute must be consistent with just war theory and R2P to support military, political, and legal decisions to enter war. The legality of engaging in war *jus ad bellum* is pivotal to enhance the credibility of intervention and decisions to destroy military communications for military advantage; these military decisions should conform to proportionality and military necessity *jus in bello*. Both principles were hotly contested with NATO's intervention and destruction of Belgrade's radio and television broadcasting station in the SFRY. War must not be waged by a state or a coalition of states for national or collective interests or self-gain, as outlined in Aquinas's second pillar of just war theory. Aquinas argued that some groups or persons must be protected and that war must be waged solely as retaliation against a governmental foe. Ethnic groups must not be protected over others due to stronger political will, based on the absolute gains (including economic, resource, and security advantages), under offensive realism or structural realist relative power on security policy. Kosovo-Albanians and, debatably, the people of Afghanistan and Iraq were protected under the justified just war theory (even if for relative power and/or absolute gains), but Rohingyas, Tutsis, and Bosnian Muslims did not receive adequate military intervention to protect them. The application of just war theory must be consistent in scenarios when states decide to wage war and not driven merely by realist geopolitical interests (i.e., intervention) and/or the lack of political will (i.e., weak intervention or nonintervention).

Institutional liberalism and R2P represent a step in the right direction for powerful states to apply just war theory and, cautiously, the rule of proportionality to avoid another Rwandan genocide and Srebrenican massacre. In the aftermath of the mid-1990 genocides, Bill Clinton and powerful political actors claimed that this would never occur again; thus, international ad hoc criminal tribunals were established for both the former Yugoslavia and Rwanda. However, under critical legal theory, it can be argued that these tribunals are used to retain the status quo of the supported parties. For instance, the Kagame regime in Rwanda was accused of utilizing the now dissolved International Criminal Tribunal for Rwanda to merely hunt Hutu commanders and avoid prosecuting those who killed Hutu refugees in Zaire during the genocide.[75] Based on this argument, law and international criminal law can bring a victor's justice, as in the Nuremberg military tribunals, *jus post bellum*, but liberalist political pressure can better lead to intervention to save human lives when it is justified under the ethics of just war theory.

On the other hand, advocates of realism could argue that R2P can be used as a political umbrella for foreign interests and national security strategy *erga omnes*. The interventions in Afghanistan and Iraq could have attempted to apply R2P if it had been introduced earlier than 2005. It could have been argued that both states were undermining their sovereignty due to mass human rights violations and atrocity crimes. This might have encouraged a better political smokescreen of internationalist realist security and economic ambitions.

However, this proposed solution to utilize R2P to mask geopolitical interests would undeniably contradict advocates of Aquinas's classical just war criteria and contemporary international law. Aquinas would argue that waging war must be done for just ends, rather than self-interest. Article 2 (4) of the UN Charter also states that members must refrain from threatening or using force in another territory based on their international relations.[76] Despite this obvious criticism, realists could support this potential solution because realism has dictated international relations since the days of the Melian dialogue, the Cold War bipolar security axis between the United States and Soviet Union, and post-9/11 foreign policy.

BIBLIOGRAPHY

Andersson, Hilary. "China 'Is Fuelling War in Darfur.'" *BBC News*, July 13, 2008. http://news.bbc.co.uk/1/hi/world/africa/7503428.stm

Aydin, Mustafa, and Kostas Ifantis. "Introduction." In *Turkish-Greek Relations: The Security Dilemma in the Aegean*, edited by Mustafa Aydin and Kostas Ifantis, 1–18. London: Routledge, 2004.

Badescu, Christina Gabriela. *Humanitarian Intervention and the Responsibility to Protect: Security and Human Rights*. London: Routledge, 2011.

Bartrop, Paul Robert. *A Bibliographical Encyclopedia of Contemporary Genocide: Portraits of Evil and Good*. Santa Barbara, CA: ABC-CLIO, 2012.

Boutros-Ghali, Boutros. "Supplement to an Agenda for Peace: Position Paper of the Secretary-General on the Occasion of the Fiftieth Anniversary of the United Nations." UN Doc. A/50/60-S/1995/1, January 3, 1995.

Burri, Nina. *Bravery or Bravado? The Protection of News Providers in Armed Conflict*. Leiden: Brill Nijhoff, 2015.

Charter of the United Nations, adopted June 26, 1945, entered into force October 24, 1945, 1 United Nations Treaty Series (UNTS) XVI.

Chesterman, Simon. *Just War or Just Peace? Humanitarian Intervention and International Law*. Oxford: Oxford University Press, 2001.

Chilcot, John, Lawrence Freedman, Roderic Lyne, and Usha Prashar. *The Report of the Iraq Inquiry: Executive Summary*. Report of a Committee of Privy Counsellors, HC 264, July 6, 2016. London: House of Commons.

Chomsky, Noam. *9/11*. New York: Pluto Press, 2001.

Cohen, Jared A. *One Hundred Days of Silence: America and the Rwanda Genocide*. Lanham, MD: Rowman & Littlefield, 2007.

Cottle, Simon. *Global Crisis Reporting: Journalism in the Global Age*. Maidenhead, Berkshire: Open University Press, 2009.

Cutler, David. "Timeline: Invasion, Surge, Withdraw; U.S. Forces in Iraq." *Reuters*, December 18, 2011. https://www.reuters.com/article/us-iraq-usa-pullout/timeline-invasion-surge-withdrawal-u-s-forces-in-iraq-idUSTRE7BH08E20111218.

Danju, Ipek, Yasar Maasoglu, and Nahide Maasoglu. "The Reasons behind U.S. Invasion of Iraq." *Procedia – Social and Behavioral Sciences* 81 (2013): 682–90. https://doi.org/10.1016/j.sbspro.2013.06.496

Destexhe, Alain. *Rwanda and Genocide in the Twentieth Century*. East Haven, CT: Pluto Press, 1995.

De Wet, Erika. *The Chapter VII Power of the United Nations Security Council*. Portland, OR: Hart Publishing, 2004.

Diesen, Glenn. *EU and NATO Relations with Russia: After the Collapse of the Soviet Union*. London: Routledge, 2015.

Donnelly, Jack. *Realism and International Relations*. Cambridge: Cambridge University Press, 2000.

Drury, Shadia B. *Aquinas and Modernity: The Lost Promise of Natural Law*. Lanham, MD: Rowman & Littlefield, 2008.

Eko, Lyombe S. *New Media, Old Regimes: Case Studies in Comparative Communication Law and Policy*. Lanham, MD: Rowman & Littlefield, 2012.

Fotion, N. *Military Ethics*. Stanford, CA: Hoover Institution Press, 1990.

Garcia, Denise. *Disarmament Diplomacy and Human Security: Regimes, Norms and Moral Progress in International Relations*. New York: Routledge, 2011.

Gardam, Judith. *Necessity, Proportionality and the Use of Force by States*. Cambridge: Cambridge University Press, 2004.

Gareau, Frederick H. *State Terrorism and the United States: From Counterinsurgency to the War on Terror*. London: Zed Books, 2004.

Grant, Reg G. *1001 Battles That Changed the Course of History*. New York: Chartwell Books, 2017.

Herold, Marc W. "Urban Dimensions of the Punishment of Afghanistan by US Bombs." In *Cities, War, and Terrorism: Towards an Urban Geopolitics*, edited by Stephen Graham, 312–29. Malden, MA: Blackwell Publishing, 2004.

Herro, Annie. *UN Emergency Peace Service and the Responsibility to Protect*. London: Routledge, 2015.

Holzgrefe, Jeff L. "The Humanitarian Intervention Debate." In *Humanitarian Intervention: Ethical, Legal and Political Dilemmas*, edited by Jeff L. Holzgrefe and Robert O. Keohane, 15–52. Cambridge: Cambridge University Press, 2003.

Human Rights Watch. *Human Rights Watch World Report 2000: Events of 1999 (November 1998–October 1999)*. New York: Human Rights Watch, 2000.

International Convention on the Elimination of All Forms of Racial Discrimination, adopted December 21, 1965, General Assembly Resolution 2106 (XX), 660 UNTS 195.

International Criminal Tribunal for the Former Yugoslavia. "Final Report to the Prosecutor by the Committee Established to Review the NATO Bombing Campaign Against the Federal Republic of Yugoslavia," ICTY, 2000. http://www.icty.org/en/press/final-report-prosecutor-committee-established-review-nato-bombing-campaign-against-federal.

Independent International Commission on Kosovo. *The Kosovo Report*. Oxford: Oxford University Press, 2008.

Jackson, Robert, and Georg Sørensen. *Introduction to International Relations: Theories and Approaches*. 6th ed. Oxford: Oxford University Press, 2016.

Kamrany, Nake M., and Jessica Greenhalgh. "Afghanistan War Is Not a Just War?" *Huffington Post*, July 6, 2013, https://www.huffingtonpost.com/nake-m-kamrany/afghanistan-war-just-war_b_3220799.html.

Kramer, Matthew H. *Critical Legal Theory and the Challenge of Feminism: A Philosophical Reconception*. Lanham, MD: Rowman & Littlefield, 1995.

Larson, Eric Victor, and Bogdan Savych. *Misfortunes of War: Press and Public Reactions to Civilian Deaths in Wartime*. Santa Monica, CA: RAND Corporation, 2007.

Leaning, Jennifer. "Was the Afghan Conflict a Just War?" *British Medical Journal* 324, no. 7333 (2002): 353–55.

MacAskill, Ewen. "Sudan's Darfur Crimes Not Genocide, Says UN Report." *The Guardian*, February 1, 2005. https://www.theguardian.com/world/2005/feb/01/sudan.unitednations.

Malone, David M., and Karin Wermester. "Boom and Bust? The Changing Nature of UN Peacekeeping." *International Peacekeeping* 7, no. 4 (2000): 37–54. https://doi.org/10.1080/13533310008413862.

Mastanduno, Michael. "Do Relative Gains Matter? America's Response to Japanese Industrial Policy." *International Security* 16, no. 1 (1991): 73–113.

Mattox, John Mark. "The Just War Tradition in Late Antiquity and the Middle Ages." In *The Cambridge Handbook of the Just War*, edited by Larry May, 13–32. Cambridge: Cambridge University Press, 2018.

Morgenthau, Hans Joachim. *Politics among Nations*. New York: Alfred A. Knopf, 1956.

Murphy, Colleen, and Linda Radzik. "*Jus Post Bellum* and Political Reconciliation." In *Jus Post Bellum and Transitional Justice*, edited by Larry May and Elizabeth Edenberg, 305–26. Cambridge: Cambridge University Press, 2013.

Nsia-Pepra, Kofi. *UN Robust Peacekeeping: Civilian Protection in Violent Civil Wars*. New York: Palgrave Macmillan, 2014.

Orend, Brian. *The Morality of War*. Peterborough, ON: Broadview Press, 2006.

Paterson, Thomas G., J. Garry Clifford, Shane J. Maddock, Deborah Kisatsky, and Kenneth J. Hagan. *American Foreign Relations*. Vol. 2: *A History since 1895*. 7th ed. Boston, MA: Wadsworth Cengage Learning, 2010.

Petersen, Alexandros. *Integration in Energy and Transport: Azerbaijan, Georgia, and Turkey*. Lanham, MD: Lexington Books, 2016.

Piiparinen, Touko. *The Transformation of UN Conflict Management: Producing Images of Genocide from Rwanda to Darfur and Beyond*. Oxon: Routledge, 2010.

Protocol Additional to the Geneva Conventions of August 12, 1949, and Relating to the Protection of Victims of International Armed Conflicts (Protocol I), adopted June 8, 1977, 17512 UNTS 4.

Protocol Additional to the Geneva Conventions of August 12, 1949, and Relating to the Protection of Victims of Non-International Armed Conflicts (Protocol II), adopted June 8, 1977, 17513 UNTS 610.

Regan, Richard J. *Just War: Principles and Cases*. Washington, DC: The Catholic University of America Press, 1996.

Report of the Secretary-General. "Implementing the Responsibility to Protect." UN General Assembly Doc. A/63/677, 63rd session, January 12, 2009.

Richardson, James L. *Contending Liberalisms in World Politics: Ideology and Power*. Boulder, CO: Lynne Rienner Publishers, 2001.

Ronzitti, Natalino. "Reparation and Compensation." In *Research Handbook on International Conflict and Security Law*, edited by Nigel D. White and Christian Henderson, 638–60. Cheltenham, Glos: Edward Elgar, 2013.

Sandal, Nukhet A., and Jonathan Fox. *Religion in International Relations Theory: Interactions and Possibilities*. Oxon: Routledge, 2013.

Scheuer, Michael. *Osama Bin Laden*. Oxford: Oxford University Press, 2011.

Security Council Resolution 660 (August 6, 1990) UN Doc S/RES/660, adopted 2932nd meeting.

Security Council Resolution 678 (November 29, 1990) UN Doc S/RES/678, adopted 2959th meeting.

Security Council Resolution 1368 (September 12, 2001) UN Doc S/RES/1368, adopted 4730th meeting.
Security Council Resolution 1373 (September 28, 2001) UN Doc S/RES/1373, adopted 4936th meeting.
Security Council Resolution 1441 (November 8, 2002) UN Doc S/RES/1441, adopted 4644th meeting.
Sharan, Timor. "The Dynamics of Elite Networks and Patron-Client Relations in Afghanistan." In *Elites and Identities in Post-Soviet Space*, edited by David Lane, 185–204. Oxon: Routledge, 2012.
Simmons, William Paul. *Human Rights Law and the Marginalized Other*. Cambridge: Cambridge University Press, 2011.
Skaine, Rosemarie. *The Women of Afghanistan under the Taliban*. Jefferson, NC: McFarland and Company, 2002.
Spellman, William M. *A Concise History of the World since 1945: States and Peoples*. New York: Palgrave Macmillan, 2006.
Stover, Eric, Victor Peskin, and Alexa Koenig. *Hiding in Plain Sight: The Pursuit of War Criminals from Nuremberg to the War on Terror*. Oakland, CA: University of California Press, 2016.
United Nations Summit Outcome Document. "2005 World Summit Outcome." UN General Assembly Doc. A/RES/60/1, 60th session, October 24, 2005.
United States Commission on International Religious Freedom. *Annual Report of the United States Commission on International Religious Freedom*. Washington, DC: Diane Publishing Co., May 2010.
Waltz, Kenneth N. *Theory of International Politics*. New York: McGraw-Hill, 1979.
Waltzer, Michael. *Arguing about War*. New Haven, CT: Yale Nota Bene, 2005.
Wardak, Ali, and John Braithwaite. "Crime and War in Afghanistan. Part II: Jeffersonian Alternative?" *British Journal of Criminology* 53 (2013): 197–214. https://doi.org/10.1093/bjc/azs066.
Wheeler, Nicholas J. *Saving Strangers*. Oxford: Oxford University Press, 2000.
White, Richard D., Jr. "Military Ethics." In *Handbook of Administrative Ethics*, edited by Terry L. Cooper, 629–48. 2nd ed. New York: Marcel Dekker, 2001.
Widdows, Heather. *Global Ethics: An Introduction*. London: Routledge, 2014.
Worley, Will. "9/11 Anniversary: Rare Images Show the Aftermath of World Trade Centre Attack That Killed 2,997." *The Independent*, September 11, 2018. https://www.independent.co.uk/news/world/americas/9-11-anniversary-images-aftermath-world-trade-center-terror-attack-responders-emergency-al-qaeda-a8530611.html.

Chapter Five

An Examination of Nigerian, Sri Lankan, and Guatemalan Civil Wars in Light of the Law of Armed Conflict

Jonathan O. Chimakonam and Victor C. A. Nweke

INTRODUCTION

Human beings often enact and enforce laws to regulate their conduct in different spheres of life. Conduct that is consistent with the law is legally recognized as right or just conduct. Conversely, any conduct that is contrary to the law is legally wrong and unjust; every conduct that is legally wrong or unjust amounts to a form of injustice that needs to be redressed. The way a given law is defined, promulgated, or enforced can be a source for critical reflection and evaluation. Such reflections fall within the scope of the philosophy of law, or jurisprudence. A philosopher or theorist of law may reflect on the morality of a given law or how it is enforced in different contexts. Through such reflections, some forms of injustice may be unveiled. The focus of this chapter borders on the enforcement of *jus in bello*, right conduct in war, in the Global South using selected armed conflicts, namely, the Nigerian Civil War (1967–1970), the Sri Lankan Civil War (1983–2009), and the Guatemalan Civil War (1960–1996), as points of reference. Our aim is to evaluate these wars and, in the process, draw attention to some forms of injustice in the way these wars were conducted. This will help to unveil the bias of the international community in relation to ensuring justice for the citizens of countries in the Global South.

Generally, just war theory (*jus bellum justum*) is often divided into two concepts, *jus ad bellum*, the right to go to war, and *jus in bello*, right conduct in war.[1] They respectively deal with when a war is permissible and how a war should be conducted. If the rationale for the first is to prevent unnecessary wars, that of the second will be to prevent unnecessary harm during war. For any war to count as just within the confines of international law, it must meet the criteria for a permissible war and comply as well with the rules of right conduct in war. A war that fails to meet the criteria for permissibility is apparently unjust. A permissible war is just if its conduct complies with the rules of right conduct in war. The underlying presupposition is that there is a limit to how human beings should treat another human being, even during a period of war. We accordingly seek to buttress that the conduct of the three mentioned civil wars violated some of the rules of right conduct in war as enshrined in the Law of Armed Conflict (LOAC). The corollary is that none of these wars meets the minimum criteria for a just war. Hence, the inability or unwillingness of the requisite international institutions to investigate the conduct of these wars and punish violators of the LOAC amounts to a form of injustice.

To substantiate the above claim, we present a succinct account of the three mentioned civil wars. We also present an exposition of the LOAC as a system of rules for right conduct in war. Therefrom, we use the basic provisions of the LOAC to evaluate how the selected wars were conducted. We then proceed to conclude concerning how the conduct of the wars violated some of the basic provisions of the LOAC.

AN OVERVIEW OF THE THREE ARMED CONFLICTS IN THE GLOBAL SOUTH

The Global South is perhaps a better description for countries in Africa, Latin America, and Asia that are still classified as "underdeveloped" or "developing" countries. The common denominator is mainly socioeconomic similarity as opposed to geographic proximity. Nigeria, Sri Lanka, and Guatemala are among the countries that belong to the Global South. Hence, the Nigerian, Sri Lankan, and Guatemalan civil wars are typical examples of armed conflicts that occurred in the Global South between the last decades of the twentieth century and the first decade of the twenty-first century. We employ the term "armed conflict" to refer to a violent combat that involves at least two armed groups seeking to gain or maintain control of a specific territory. The said territory may be a nation, a country, a state, or a specific part of any of these. Seen in this perspective, armed conflict is synonymous with war.

A civil war is a form of armed conflict between citizens of the same country who belong to different political units or organized groups. It is an intrastate war that is often triggered by political purposes, such as the move for political independence or the control of political power by a specific region/organized group and the struggle against such demands or dominance by another region(s)/organized group(s). This is true of the Nigerian, Sri

Lankan, and Guatemalan civil wars. Our main interest concerns how these wars were conducted. To understand how these wars were conducted, we shall, where necessary, provide background information about the composition of the respective countries and what led to the wars. We begin with the Nigerian Civil War.

THE NIGERIAN CIVIL WAR (1967–1970)

Nigeria is a country of many nations, located in West Africa. The various nations that make up Nigeria were existing and interacting as independent nations with distinct languages, peculiar cultures, and unique histories prior to the era of European colonial conquest. The British Empire conquered and then amalgamated the diverse nations into one country it called Nigeria. The final stage of the amalgamation and christening happened in 1914 when the northern and southern protectorates were merged. This merging was done without the consent of the inhabitants or leaders of the diverse nations. With the emergence of Nigeria, the diverse nations became ethnic groups (often misconstrued as "tribes"). The country was later administratively divided into three major regions: (1) the northern region, dominated by the Hausa-Fulani ethnic group; (2) the western region, dominated by the Yoruba ethnic group; and (3) the eastern region, dominated by the Igbo ethnic group. What this amounts to is that Nigeria as a country was solely a creation of the British through colonial administrators. The British also divided and ruled Nigeria along ethnic lines. The effects of the divide and rule policies of the British colonial administration in Nigeria on the question of national consciousness and integration became vivid when the British agreed to grant political independence to Nigeria. Nigerian nationalists who were fighting for independence became regionalists (i.e., ethnic nationalists) who were willing to delay the political independence of the country until their region was prepared to struggle for public offices with other regions. As a result, the three regions were granted internal autonomy separately.

When Nigeria gained political independence on October 1, 1960, all its major political parties were ethnically based. The colonial structure of the country was neither renegotiated nor transformed. Ethnicity and regionalism were at the forefront of political decisions, including the issue of elections and appointments into significant public offices. Most politicians and public office holders became committed to the interest of their ethnic groups (i.e., their primordial nation) and region, even to the detriment of the country, Nigeria.[2] Rivalry between political parties easily transformed into rivalry among different ethnic groups and regions. Political moves were also interpreted using the lens of ethnicity and regions. It was the interpretations of the political moves of some Nigerian military officers by their military colleagues that led to the Nigerian Civil War.

On January 15, 1966, a group of mutinous Nigerian soldiers led by two Igbo officers, Major Chukwuma Kaduna Nzeogwu and Major Emmanuel Arinze Ifeajuna, toppled the government of President Nnamdi Azikiwe and Prime Minister Tafawa Balewa on the grounds of salvaging the country from corrupt and inefficient political leaders.[3] Top politicians, including the prime minister and premiers of the western and northern regions, and some military officers were killed in the process. However, no top Igbo politician or military officer was killed. Although the mutiny was not successful in Lagos, the then federal capital where the seat of political power was located, the surviving senior government officials (mainly Igbo) decided to hand over power to the military until political stability was restored. In addition, the person to wield political power was the most senior military officer at that time, who happened to be Major-General J. T. U. Aguiyi-Ironsi, an Igbo man. Neither the efforts of Aguiyi-Ironsi nor the role that other Igbo military officers played against the January 15 mutiny stopped politicians and military officers from the northern region from interpreting the uprising as an Igbo mutiny. Hence, on July 28, 1966, military officers from the northern region staged a countercoup that not only killed Igbo political leaders and military officers but metamorphosed into the massive killing of many Igbo civilians living in various parts of the northern and western regions. "It is generally admitted that the size and scope of the killings gave them 'genocidal proportions' and there exists ample evidence to show that they were planned, directed and organized."[4]

The inability of the northern commanded military administration of Yakubu Gowon to curb the senseless killings of Igbo people living in the northern region and the destruction of their properties led to the mass exodus of the Igbo, including military officers, civil servants, and traders, from other regions back to the eastern region. Some were attacked and killed as they attempted to escape from the northern region. Igbo political leaders and military officers interpreted the said inability to mean unwillingness of the northern-led federal military government to protect the lives and properties of the Igbo. Consequently, on May 30, 1967, the military governor of the eastern region of Nigeria, Lieutenant Colonel Chukwuemeka Odumegwu Ojukwu, declared the eastern region of Nigeria to be a sovereign state, the Republic of Biafra. On July 6, 1967, head of the Nigerian military government, General Yakubu Gowon (from northern Nigeria), declared war (i.e., "police action") to reclaim the secessionist eastern region, the Republic of Biafra. Works that contain accounts of the Nigerian Civil War include Frederick Forsyth (1969),[5] Alexander Madiebo (1980),[6] and H. B. Momoh (2000).[7] The question is whether it was conducted in line with the LOAC. We shall return to this question after our exposition of the basic provisions of the LOAC. Before this critical analysis, we offer an overview of the Sri Lankan and Guatemalan civil wars.

THE SRI LANKAN CIVIL WAR (1983–2009)

Sri Lanka is an island country located in South Asia. The country comprises various ethnic nationalities. It was also conquered and colonized by the British Empire. It gained its political independence on February 4, 1948, and became a republic on May 22, 1972. The colonial name of the country, which is Ceylon, was replaced with Sri Lanka when the country attained the status of a republic in 1972. The civil war was fought between the Sinhalese (the dominant ethnic group that has the largest population) and the Tamils (the main minority ethnic group that challenged the discriminatory policies of the Sinhalese-led government).

After political independence, the Sinhalese-led government started to introduce discriminatory policies against the minority ethnic groups. Even prior to independence, there were such laws as the Ceylon Citizenship Act of 1948, which made it impossible for the members of the Indian Tamil minority ethnic group to obtain citizenship in their country. The act rendered about 700,000 Indian Tamils stateless. Another policy was the Sinhala Only Act of 1956, which replaced English with Sinhala, the language of the Sinhalese ethnic group, as the only official language of the country. The language act affected the Tamil-speaking population in relation to employment, education, and civil/public services in Sri Lanka. The crises and confrontational politics that followed the promulgation of such acts led to the demand for a separate Tamil state, Tamil Eelam. July 23, 1983, is often considered to be the beginning of the Sri Lankan Civil War because it was on that day that one of the many Tamil militant groups that were committed to the goal of a separate state, the Liberation Tigers of Tamil Eelam (LTTE), launched a deadly ambush that killed thirteen Sri Lankan soldiers. In response to the ambush, an anti-Tamil pogrom started on the night of July 24, 1983. This led to the prolonged armed conflict that lasted until 2009. Works that contain accounts of the Sri Lankan Civil War include R. Hoole et al. (1990),[8] Adele Balasingham (2003),[9] and Gordon Weiss (2011).[10] The fundamental question is still the same, namely, was the prolonged armed conflict conducted according to the provisions of the LOAC? We shall come to this later.

THE GUATEMALAN CIVIL WAR (1960–1996)

Guatemala is the most populated country in Central America. The country was conquered and colonized by the Spanish in the sixteenth century. It later regained political independence from the Spanish on September 15, 1821.

Guatemala is also a multiethnic country. The ethnic composition of the country at the dawn of political independence consisted of the Mestizo (i.e., people of mixed native and European ancestry, who are the biggest group), the Maya (i.e., the dominant indigenous ethnic group), the non-Maya indigenous ethnic groups (e.g., the Mam, the Afro-Mestizo, the Garifuna, and the Afro-Guatemalans), and the people of European ancestry. The civil war was between the Guatemalan government and rebel groups supported mainly by the Maya ethnic group.

The civil war came after a period of enduring instability and civil strife, which the country experienced from the mid- to late nineteenth century into the twentieth century. Beginning in the early twentieth century, Guatemala was ruled by a series of dictators backed by the United Fruit Company (UFCO) and the US government. In 1931, General Jorge Ubico, with the support of the United States came into power. Ubico was a brutally repressive military dictator and a staunch anti-communist who consistently sided with the UFCO, Guatemalan landowners, and urban elites in disputes with peasants. His government marginalized the indigenous population. He gave away hundreds of thousands of hectares to the UFCO, exempted it from taxes in Tiquisate, and allowed the US military to establish bases in Guatemala.[11]

Attempts to remove him led to a series of political protests and military coups d'état that aggravated the political repression, widespread socioeconomic discrimination, and racism practiced against Guatemala's indigenous peoples, such as the Maya. Ubico and his protégés were finally overthrown in 1944 by a pro-democratic military coup. This initiated a decade-long revolution that led to sweeping social and economic reforms that benefited and politically strengthened the civil and labor rights of the urban working class and the peasants in many ways. Although the reforms of the revolutionary government were deemed progressive, they affected the interests of the UFCO, landowners (generally, descendants of Spanish and other European immigrants to Guatemala and some mestizo people), and the US government. Hence, in 1954, a military countercoup backed by the United States ended the revolution and installed another dictatorship.[12] On November 13, 1960, a group of left-wing junior military officers of the *Escuela Politécnica* national military academy led a revolt against the autocratic government of General Ydígoras Fuentes, who enjoyed the support of the United States. Besides the question of gross corruption of the Ydígoras regime, the immediate reason for the revolt was Ydígoras's decision to allow the United States to train an invasion force in Guatemala without consulting the Guatemalan military and without sharing with the military the payoff he received in exchange from the US government. The young officers were concerned about the infringement on the sovereignty of their country. The failure of the revolt compelled the surviving rebellious officers to flee to the hills of eastern Guatemala and neighboring Honduras. They later contacted the Cuban government of Fidel

Castro and established an insurgent movement known as the MR-13 (*Movimiento Revolucionario 13 Noviembre*), named after the date of their revolt. The Guatemalan government continued to fight against MR-13 and other rebel groups until 1996. Works that contain accounts of the Guatemalan Civil War include Victor Perera (1993),[13] Beatriz Manz (2004),[14] and Greg Grandin (2011).[15]

A common similarity concerning the remote causes that led to these wars is the composition and political structure of the three countries. The composition and political structure of the three countries were primarily designed to favor the interest of their European colonizers.[16] Chinua Achebe pointed out that the creation of tension-prone states is one of the most lethal legacies of European colonialism.[17] Another factor that is common to the three wars is the imperialistic interference of some leading countries of the Global North. Britain and the United States played significant roles in the Nigerian and Guatemalan civil wars, respectively, based on their vested interests, to the detriment of justice. Besides, military equipment that was used in all the wars was not locally produced in the Global South. All these indices underscore the fact that, though the three wars took place in the Global South, they were not fought without external interference. However, our hunch is that neither the Nigerian, Sri Lankan, nor Guatemalan civil war was conducted according to the provisions of the LOAC. To buttress this point, an exposition of the basic provisions of the LOAC is needed.

UNDERSTANDING THE LOAC

The LOAC refers to the international humanitarian law (IHL), which is applicable in armed conflicts. The LOAC has a long history dating back to ancient civilizations. Its principles stem from international laws and treaties that many independent states have come to accept as required rules that should govern the conduct of military operations and armed conflicts in a civilized world. A relevant international treaty in this regard is the Geneva Convention of 1949, comprising four treaties and three additional protocols, which established the standards of international law for humanitarian treatments in war after World War II. The Geneva Convention of 1949 is deemed to be a product of universal participation because it was ratified, in whole or with reservations, by 196 countries. However, one should note that the treatises were basically informed by ideas in the history of Western (i.e., Anglo-American and European) philosophy.[18] Irrespective of the acclaimed universal participation and acceptance of the Geneva Convention of 1949, the LOAC is predominantly founded on the Western conception of what a just war should look like. That said, we now proceed to look at the basic principles of the LOAC.

As part of international law, the LOAC has certain principles that regulate the conduct of armed conflicts to prevent senseless killings. We shall explicate three cardinal principles of the LOAC that apply to international armed conflicts and the conduct of military operations in relation to internal armed conflicts, such as counterinsurgency and civil war. These principles are distinction, military necessity, and proportionality.

The principle of distinction differentiates between lawful targets (i.e., valid military targets) and unlawful targets (i.e., civilians, civilian property, prisoners of war, hospitals, and wounded personnel who are out of combat). It requires that combatants always distinguish between valid military targets and civilian objects and ensure that they attack only military objectives (i.e., valid military targets). The principle of military necessity requires that armed forces adopt only such measures as are necessary to overpower the enemy and to bring about its surrender. It suggests that the aim of armed conflict should not be seen as the destruction of as much of the property and killing of as many members of the adverse armed forces as possible; rather, "the proper aim is to destroy and to kill as few as possible and to cause such damage only to the extent necessary to overpower the enemy."[19] This goes to show that even valid military targets are not to be attacked without limitations. The principle of proportionality prohibits an attack on a valid military target in situations where civilian casualties would clearly outweigh military gains. It specifically obliges combat forces to minimize collateral damage—the incidental, unintended destruction that occurs as a result of a lawful attack against a legitimate military target. All military measures taken by armed forces must be proportionate to the aim they seek to accomplish.[20]

Accordingly, the above three principles are not coextensive with the entire principles of the LOAC. They are, however, the most fundamental principles that capture the main goal of the LOAC. The primary focus of the principles of the LOAC is humanity. Hence, violations of the LOAC are seen as crimes against humanity. Robert Kolb and Richard Hyde outlined "the fundamental purposes of the LOAC, which are, to a large extent, reflected in these principles" as follows:

> (a) to prevent "unnecessary suffering" of combatants and noncombatants alike. Such suffering may be seen as unnecessary in relation to the war aims or in relation to general humanitarian considerations; (b) to avoid an escalation or a spread in the conflict and to prevent the horrors that accompany total warfare; and (c) to protect noncombatants, particularly the civilian population, civilian objects, and civilian property and those combatants rendered *hors de combat* by the conflict.[21]

Compliance to the LOAC is ensured through a variety of preventive and disciplinary measures. An utmost preventive measure involves disseminating knowledge of the LOAC within the armed forces, training and equipping forces in accordance with LOAC requirements, and establishing an effective system for taking LOAC considerations into account in military planning and decision-making. Disciplinary measures, which may include the prosecution of military officers, economic sanctions, arms embargoes, demand for compensation, and various types of military action, taken under the authority of international bodies, including the UN Security Council, against offending states or armed groups have been set in place for violators of the LOAC.

THE LOAC AND ARMED CONFLICTS IN THE GLOBAL SOUTH

Ordinarily, the LOAC is a product of the international community, and the international community is mainly controlled by powerful European and North American countries that make up the Global North. It is, therefore, logical to expect that the international community will always be willing to enforce compliance to the LOAC in the Global South as an unbiased umpire. This appears not to be the case. The international community seems to be indifferent to the reports about violations of the LOAC in the selected "civil" wars that took place in different parts of the Global South due mainly to their vested interests and complicities to the humanitarian crimes committed in those wars. It is well known that the powerful countries profited from the wars economically through huge arms deals. They also profited immensely in terms of cheap supply of mineral resources. So wars in the Global South, like the three cases under discussion in this work, are good for business for the powerful nations who have what it takes to enforce compliance to the principles of the LOAC.

The most explicit violation of the LOAC that is common to the Nigerian, Sri Lankan, and Guatemalan civil wars is the employment of strategies that promote indiscriminate attacks, including direct strikes on noncombatants, which apparently contradicts the principle of distinction. Negligence of the principle of distinction can pass as the most heinous violation of the LOAC because whoever makes noncombatants a direct target for military operations has already abused the principle of military necessity and most likely cares less about the principle of proportionality. Writing as a survivor of what is often referred to as the "Asaba Massacre"—one of the towns in which there was senseless murdering of many Igbo civilians, including women and children, and selectively all males in every household by Nigerian troops during the war[22]—Emma Okocha described the Nigerian Civil War as "the first Black on Black Genocide."[23] The works of revered journalists and writers who witnessed the war, such as Frederick Forsyth[24] and Chinua Achebe,[25] support this claim. Frederick Forsyth outlined some of the unaddressed charges against the Nigerian government as follows:

> The Biafran charges against the Nigerian Government and armed forces rest on their behavior in five fields: the pogroms of the North, the West and Lagos in 1966; the behavior of the Nigerian Army towards the civilian population they encountered during the course of the war; the behavior of the Nigerian Air Force in selection of its targets; the selective killings in various captured areas of chiefs, leaders, administrators, teachers, technicians; and the allegedly deliberate imposition of famine, which was predicted in advance by foreign experts and which during 1968 carried away an estimated 500,000 children between ages of one and ten years. . . . The widespread killing of Biafran civilians and Ibo [Igbo] inhabitants of the Midwest State is incontrovertible.[26]

It was not only children between the ages of one and ten years that died as a result of the "deliberate imposition of famine" on Biafrans by the Nigerian government through total economic blockage; the whole population of Biafra were victims. Over three million civilians were estimated to have died for lack of access to food. Similar charges of selective killings, kidnapping, assassination, economic blockage, and indiscriminate strikes on civilians have also been made about both the Sri Lankan[27] and the Guatemalan civil wars.[28]

In Sri Lanka, there were pogroms against the civilian population of Tamils; attacks on civilian targets, such as hospitals; attacks on international humanitarian programs; and massive human rights abuses, especially at the tail end of the war by government forces, which were clearly against the LOAC. The International Crisis Group reports that the government of Sri Lanka undermined the UN and assaulted the IHL in its conduct during the war.[29] The government forces repeatedly violated the terms of the "no fire zones (NFZs)," that is, the designated centers where Tamil civilians went to get food and medical treatments supplied by international humanitarian missions. These zones were reported to have been regularly shelled by the government forces, leading to the maiming and killing of many noncombatant civilians. Unfortunately, the weapons that the government of Sri Lanka used in committing these humanitarian atrocities were supplied by powerful nations. According to Shlomi Yass, "[M]any countries have provided Sri Lanka with weapons, including the Ukraine, Iran, Russia, Pakistan, China, England, and the United States."[30] Thus, even in the midst of pogroms and possible genocide against the Tamils, powerful nations continued to equip and assist the government of Sri Lanka, which partly explains why war crimes in that country have largely been ignored by the UN. This was debatably in breach of *jus in bello* principles.

The primary victims of these alleged attacks on humanitarian targets were Tamil civilians, who, according to a report by American University's Washington College of Law,[31] suffered what qualifies as genocide during the war. Crisis Group, another global war crimes watchdog, "collected evidence that provides reasonable grounds to believe the repeated shelling of civilians in the three NFZs, combined with the obstruction and undersupplying of food and medical care for civilians, was part of the government's overall military strategy in the Vanni."[32] Yet the human rights violations that led to the death of Tamil civilians were not perpetrated by the government forces alone. The International Crisis Group also reports that the LTTE forces resorted to violence and even shooting of civilian populations to deter many Tamil civilians who wanted to cross over to the government-controlled side.[33] These actions also were clearly in violation of humanitarian laws of the LOAC, but the worrisome part is that, as the Crisis Group reports, almost all crimes against humanity, which are in violation of the LOAC, committed during the conduct of the Sri Lankan Civil War have gone unpunished, thus, once again, demanding answers from the powerful nations in the Global North who control global resources for maintaining IHL.

The case in Guatemala was no different. Several sources report that indiscriminate killings of indigenous peoples and several war crimes characterized the civil war in that country, especially between 1980 and 1983, during the dictatorship of General Ríos Montt as well as the period when the US government under Ronald Ragan offered military assistance to the Guatemala government. Those who were found guilty of human rights violations include the guerrilla forces, successive government forces, and the CIA. The Guatemalan truth commission blamed the country's army for most of the human rights abuses. It also blamed the US government and the guerrilla groups for various human rights violations. The United States, specifically, was blamed for its part in escalating the war.[34]

The difference between the Guatemalan case, on the one hand, and the Biafra and Sri Lanka cases, on the other, is that, in the former, the UN-backed International Commission against Impunity in Guatemala (CICIG) was able to collaborate with the office of the attorney general of that country to prosecute several human rights violation cases. One thing they all have in common is the influence of powerful nations through military assistance and supply of weapons that killed several million innocent people. In Sri Lanka, there was a naval blockade against the Tamil area, resulting in the discrete use of hunger as a war strategy. Even though limited relief materials were allowed in by the government, it continued to shell the NFZs, thus hampering and jeopardizing humanitarian efforts. In Biafra, the case was odious because the government of Nigeria clearly and boldly used deliberate starvation as a tool in that war, which led to the starvation of about three million Biafrans mainly from the Igbo nation. These humanitarian crimes of genocidal proportions are yet to be prosecuted.

What happened in Sri Lanka and especially in Biafra was a human catastrophe. Biafra specifically was a human calamity comparable to the genocide conducted by King Leopold of Belgium in the Congo. In Biafra the statistics of the dead in three years of war was about three million, most of whom died through deliberate starvation inflicted by the government of Nigeria. Of the 233 independent countries and semiautonomous territories in the world, about 95 have less than three million population each. Countries such as Georgia in Europe and Uruguay in South America have a little over three million in their populations. What happened in Biafra was like wiping out the entire population of Georgia or Uruguay, not to mention the other 95 territories with less than three million in their populations each. Several powerful nations, such as Great Britain, the former Soviet Union, the United States, and even Israel, that sold weapons and assisted the Nigerian government were complicit in this genocide against the Igbo.[35] This partly explains why there was a lukewarm attitude from the Global North and UN toward prosecuting war crimes in the Biafra–Nigeria war.

On the whole, these alleged violations of the LOAC have yet to be properly investigated by relevant national or international institutions for the purpose of prosecuting and punishing culpable persons without bias. The unwillingness or inability of relevant international institutions to investigate reports about alleged violations of the LOAC and prosecute and punish defaulters portrays a selective approach to justice, namely *jus post bellum*.

CONCLUSION:
A CASE TO OBEY THE PRINCIPLE OF OSITADIMMA

Our analysis of the LOAC shows that it is basically aimed at ensuring the prevention of unnecessary suffering that combatants may inflict on themselves and other human beings and entities within their territories and beyond through the protection of fundamental human rights and dignity. While human beings may resort to armed battle to settle deep-seated differences, they ought to do so in a civilized way that befits their status as reasonable beings. Enforcing compliance to the LOAC amounts to the protection of our common humanity in an intricately interconnected world. To violate the LOAC is to commit a crime against humanity. Our discussion on the respective wars in different parts of the Global South reveals that they were not conducted according to the principles of the LOAC. Despite the existence of media reports and formal complaints about gross violations of the principles of the LOAC, the international community seems unwilling to investigate and prosecute alleged violators accordingly. We condemn the attitude of the international community and then implore respective institutions to heed to the principle of *ositadimma*.

The principle of *ositadimma* stems from Igbo–African intellectual heritage. It simply admonishes that it is never too late to start doing what is right. It is always early enough for an individual or a group that was unjust or indifferent to a just cause to start acting right. The tenets of African relational ethics[36] would rightly suggest that indifference in the face of injustice amounts to complicity. We therefore submit that the seeming indifference of the international community to alleged gross violations of the LOAC in many armed conflicts in the Global South will pass as complicity when viewed from the context of African relational ethics. Nonetheless, it is not too late for them to do the needful. Many countries in the Global South, and indeed many critical individuals in the world, have lost faith in the integrity of international institutions, such as the International Court of Justice to try states guilty of violating the LOAC and international criminal tribunals to try individuals responsible for war crimes, crimes against humanity, and genocides. Nothing less than honest responses to unaddressed demands for justice by many victims of manifold injustices in the Global South will help to restore hope in the integrity of the international system.

BIBLIOGRAPHY

Achebe, Chinua. *There Was a Country: A Personal History of Biafra.* New York: Penguin Group, 2012.

Ademoyega, Adewale. *Why We Struck: The Story of the First Nigerian Coup.* Ibadan: Evans Brothers, 1981.

American University, Washington College of Law. *Justice for Genocide: Sri Lanka's Genocide against Tamils.* Washington, DC: UNROW Human Rights Impact Litigation Clinic, 2014.

Amnesty International. *Guatemala: All the Truth, Justice for All.* Published May 13, 1998. Accessed December 22, 2018. https://www.refworld.org/docid/3ae6a9ba4.html.

Anthony, Douglas. "Ours Is a War of Survival: Biafra, Nigeria and Arguments about Genocide, 1966–70." *Journal of Genocide Research* 16, no. 2–3 (2014): 205–25. doi:10.1080/14623528.2014.936701.

Balasingham, Adele. *The Will to Freedom—An Inside View of Tamil Resistance.* 2nd ed. Mitcham, UK: Fairmax Publishing, 2003.

Ball, Patrick, Herbert F. Spirer, and Louise Spirer. *Making the Case: Investigating Large Scale Human Rights Violations Using Information Systems and Data Analysis.* Washington, DC: American Association for the Advancement of Science, 2000.

Bird, S. Elizabeth, and Fraser M. Ottanelli. *The Asaba Massacre: Trauma, Memory, and the Nigerian Civil War.* Cambridge: Cambridge University Press, 2017.

Boyle, Francis. *The Tamil Genocide by Sri Lanka: The Global Failure to Protect Tamil Rights.* Atlanta: Clarity Press, 2010.

Brockett, Charles D. *Political Movements and Violence in Central America.* Cambridge: Cambridge University Press, 2005.

Cordeiro-Rodrigues, Luís. "Towards a Tutuist Ethics of War: Ubuntu, Forgiveness and Reconciliation." *Politikon* 45, no. 3 (2018): 426–35.

Desgrandchamps, Marie-Luce. "Dealing with 'Genocide': The ICRC and the UN during the Nigeria–Biafra War, 1967–70." *Journal of Genocide Research* 16, no. 2–3 (2014): 281–97. doi:10.1080/14623528.2014.936705.

Doron, Roy. "Marketing Genocide: Biafran Propaganda Strategies during the Nigerian Civil War, 1967–70." *Journal of Genocide Research* 16, no. 2–3 (2014): 227–46. doi:10.1080/14623528.2014.936702.

Ekeh, Peter P. *Colonialism and Social Structure: An Inaugural Lecture.* Ibadan: Ibadan University Press, 1983.

———. "Colonialism and the Two Publics in Africa: A Theoretical Statement." *Comparative Studies in Society and History* 17, no. 1 (1975): 91–112.

Forsyth, Frederick. *The Making of an African Legend: The Biafran Story.* New York: Penguin Books, 1969.
Grandin, Greg. *The Last Colonial Massacre: Latin America in the Cold War.* Chicago: University of Chicago Press, 2011.
Hoole, Rajan, Daya Somasundaram, K. A. Sritharan, and Rajani Thiranagama. *The Broken Palmyra—The Tamil Crisis in Sri Lanka: An Inside Account.* Claremont: The Sri Lanka Studies Institute, 1990.
International Crisis Group. "War Crimes in Sri Lanka." *Asia Report*, No. 191, May 17. Brussels: ICG, 2010.
Kolb, Robert, and Richard Hyde. *An Introduction to the International Law of Armed Conflicts.* Oxford: Hart Publishing, 2008.
Landman, Todd. *Studying Human Rights.* London: Routledge, 2006.
Madiebo, Alexander. *The Nigerian Revolution and the Biafran War.* Enugu: Fourth Dimension Publishers, 1980.
Manz, Beatriz. *Paradise in Ashes: A Guatemalan Journey of Courage, Terror, and Hope.* Oakland: University of California Press, 2004.
McClintock, Michael. *The American Connection: State Terror and Popular Resistance in Guatemala.* London: Zed Books, 1985.
McNeil, Brian. "And Starvation Is the Grim Reaper: The American Committee to Keep Biafra Alive and the Genocide Question during the Nigerian Civil War, 1968–70." *Journal of Genocide Research* 16, no. 2–3 (2014): 317–36. doi:10.1080/14623528.2014.936723.
Metz, Thaddeus. "Toward an African Moral Theory." *Journal of Political Philosophy* 15, no. 3 (2007): 321–41. doi:10.111/j.1467-9760.2007.00280.x.
Momoh, H. B., ed. *The Nigerian Civil War: 1967–1970: History and Reminiscences.* Ibadan: Sam Bookman Publishers, 2000.
Okocha, Emma. *Blood on the Niger: The First Black on Black Genocide.* New York: Gomslam Books, 2012.
O'Sullivan, Kevin. "Humanitarian Encounters: Biafra, NGOs and Imaginings of the Third World in Britain and Ireland, 1967–70." *Journal of Genocide Research* 16, no. 2–3 (2014): 299–315. doi:10.1080/14623528.2014.936706.
Perera, Victor. *Unfinished Conquest: The Guatemalan Tragedy.* California: University of California Press, 1993.
Permanent Peoples' Tribunal. *Peoples' Tribunal on Sri Lanka: 07–10 December 2013.* Bremen: Permanent Peoples' Tribunal and the International Human Rights Association, 2014.
Sanford, Victoria. *Buried Secrets: Truth and Human Rights in Guatemala.* New York: Palgrave Macmillan, 2003.
Simpson, Brad. "The Biafran Secession and the Limits of Self-Determination." *Journal of Genocide Research* 16, no. 2–3 (2014): 337–54. doi:10.1080/14623528.2014.936708.
Streeter, Stephen M. *Managing the Counterrevolution: The United States and Guatemala, 1954–1961.* Athens, OH: Ohio University Press, 2000.
Weiss, Gordon. *The Cage: The Fight for Sri Lanka and the Last Days of the Tamil Tigers.* New York: Random House, 2011.
Weld, Kirsten. *Paper Cadavers: The Archives of Dictatorship in Guatemala.* Durham, NC: Duke University Press, 2014.
Winn, Peter. *Americas: The Changing Face of Latin America and the Caribbean.* Berkeley: University of California Press, 2006.
Yass, Shlomi. "Sri Lanka and the Tamil Tigers: Conflict and Legitimacy." *Military and Strategic Affairs* 6, no. 2 (2014): 65–82.

Chapter Six

African Feminists' Critique of Just Wars and the Reality of African Women in Wars

Olajumoke M. Akiode

INTRODUCTION

Just war theory (JWT) is a theory that tackles the ethics of the use of force or of going to war in three parts. These are when it is right to resort to armed force (*jus ad bellum*), what is acceptable in using such force (*jus in bello*), and the management of the justice of war termination and peace agreements and the prosecution of war criminals (*jus post bellum*). JWT originated in the fourth century from Greek and Roman philosophy, with substantial input from Christianity, then from the Enlightenment era and contemporary Western academia, giving it a long and rich history.

JWT does not describe the world as it is, but it provides an outline for the assessment of the justice of particular wars. Thus, theorists and leaders have shaped and augmented its principles to adapt to the requirements of their particular societies and times.[1] These augmented JWT principles may or may not include adaptation to their respective geopolitical interests. If it were, adaptation to particular societies, times, and geopolitical interests may create an environment for or may enhance the masking of JWT for ulterior motives. However, this same supposed value, that is, abstraction, is perceived to be a major flaw of JWT.

In the discourse of JWT, a series of criticisms have been leveled against it, some of which necessitate adjustment to it. This chapter will examine the feminists' critique of JWT. It will then look at the African feminists' critique of JWT, highlighting their contextual differences and similarities. It will also provide a historical analysis of war in African countries beginning with the era in African history before colonial intrusion followed by the pre- and postindependence periods. It will examine lived experiences of women during wars in African countries from the past to contemporary times. It aims to propose the way forward with JWT from an African feminist perspective. This chapter is more of a thematic examination of African reality as it pertains to JWT and African women's experience. It is divided into seven sections: feminists' critiques of JWT; African feminists' critique of JWT; historical appraisal of war in African countries; African women's experience; JWT and war in contemporary African countries; the reality of African women in war; analysis of the failures of JWT vis-à-vis the experiences of African women in war-ravaged African countries; and the conclusion.

FEMINISTS' CRITIQUES OF JWT

Feminists, such as Carol Gilligan, Laura Sjoberg, Sara Ruddick, Margaret Coady, Carol Cohn, Jean Bethke Elshtain, and Virginia Held, have over time criticized JWT. The fulcrum of their critiques rests on issues such as the role realism plays in JWT and its inability to assert that all conditions have been satisfied in accordance with rigorous standards, especially in relation to attempting nonviolent alternatives. That is, JWT rests on the assumption that aggression is embedded in the nature of man, hence, the use of force, which makes armed conflict inevitable. In the same vein, the assumption that it is nearly impossible to satisfy all conditions requisite to the commencement of just war is one of the main issues critiqued by feminists in JWT. They also critiqued JWT's propensity for abstraction and dichotomizing reality in accordance with gendered distinctions as well as the priority it accords to the state and to state authority vis-à-vis the individual.[2] Feminists reject the dichotomized speechmaking characteristic of current discussions of war that refuse to admit the interrelationship between domestic, national, and international violence.[3]

The immunity principle is simply the criterion of proportionality and discrimination stipulated in *jus in bello*, which requires mitigating the magnitude and violence of warfare to minimize destruction and casualties and the kind of force that is morally permissible (i.e., proportionality) as well as the determination of legitimate targets of war that require the avoidance of killing noncombatants (discrimination).[4] It defines as noncombatants citizens such as women, children, and elderly people. However, Sjoberg opines that the immunity principle is ineffective due to the embedded gender stereotypes and gendered just war narrative, which, on close analysis, fails to afford any civilians protection. She proposed a more effective, feminist reformulation based on empathy.[5]

Krcek also asserts that, though the stipulations of JWT may be good, its flaws derive from its patriarchal framework, "it's male-derived understanding of ethics, single mode of ethical interpretation," and the consequent insensitivity and denial of the "concrete, horrific reality of war. Moreover, it perpetuates the gendered assumptions about women's role in warfare."[6]

The just war tradition, in particular, has long neglected concerns and feelings that raise awareness of harsh reality behind the sanitized abstractions of war.[7] That is, the abstraction insulates policymakers or constituted authorities deciding about use of armed conflict from the impact on adults, children, and elderly people and on animals, the environment, and resources essential for dignified existence.

This abstraction and its insulating effect enhances the prevalence of low and sometimes no report of war crimes, especially war crimes against women and children. These crimes were not only ignored or underreported, but their perpetrators went unpunished. Rape was not even considered a war crime. In fact, "for centuries, sexual violence in conflict was tacitly accepted as unavoidable. A 1998 UN report on sexual violence and armed conflict notes that historically, armies considered rape one of the legitimate spoils of war."[8] It is only recently that rape became both a war crime and a crime against humanity.

> On 18 December 1992, the Council declared the "massive, organized and systematic detention and rape of women . . . an international crime that must be addressed." Subsequently, the Statute of the International Criminal Tribunal for the former Yugoslavia (ICTY, 1993)[9] included rape as a crime against humanity, alongside other crimes such as torture and extermination, when committed in armed conflict and directed against a civilian population. In 2001, the ICTY became the first international court to find an accused person guilty of rape as a crime against humanity. Furthermore, the Court expanded the definition of slavery as a crime against humanity to include sexual slavery. Previously, forced labour was the only type of slavery to be viewed as a crime against humanity.[10]

Unfortunately, before 1992, rape of women and children was to just war theorists, policymakers, and combatants mere collateral damages of war. This perception is also a consequence of abstraction and dichotomy in JWT. If the tables were turned and it were their family members and communities that were being raped and sexual violence were being perpetrated against them and not "the other," it definitely would be a crime and not just collateral damage of war.

In the same vein, the Geneva Convention IV (1949), ratified by 195 countries, extensively defined the basic rights of wartime prisoners (i.e., civilians and military personnel) and established protections for the wounded and sick and protections for noncombatants, that is, the civilians in and around a war zone. However, because the GC IV is about people in war, the articles do not address warfare proper, especially the use of weapons of war.

These views represent mainly those of Western feminists; African feminists' critique is absent from the mainstream literature.

AFRICAN FEMINISTS' CRITIQUE OF JWT

African feminism is a brand of feminism that is embedded in the lived reality of women feminists on the African continent. "A non-radical brand that strategically eliminated the masculine radix of suffixing the second sex with male/man, fe/male and wo/man," but is not antagonistic toward men.[11] African feminists seek to deconstruct gendered sociocultural constructs as well as assimilated imperialists' constructs and influence. They attempt a mainstream deconstruction of stereotypes that enhances passivity and precludes women's voices from decision-making and their efforts as complementary members of their societies from being recognized. These efforts range from their everyday contributions in the private sphere to their contributions in the public sphere, which may include peace building, conflict resolution, or strategizing for war.

African feminists speak "in a different voice" from those of men, as advocated by Carol Gilligan,[12] and in a more culturally contextualized voice compared to that of Western women. Women's discourses prioritize the notion of nonviolence and a strong sense of responsibility toward the world. Male-orientated discourse prioritizes abstract notions of universal rights and justice. African feminists speak from the perspective of an ontologized ethics of care and womanhood in such a way that balances violence and nonviolence within the paradigm of an interrelated sense of responsibility first to one another and then to the community.

African feminists challenge binary formulations and dichotomous thinking that oversimplify postcolonial African realities and the messiness of war. They underscore frequently neglected interconnections, contesting either/or conceptualizations, such as "traditional" versus "modern" African societies, soldiers/civilians, freedom fighters/terrorists, rebels/murderers, victims/perpetrators, "just wars"/"dirty wars," and "state" versus "individual" violence.[13]

African feminists' critique of JWT encompasses the entirety of the theory through its various adjustments. This critique stems from its patriarchal underpinning to its feeble attempt at gender consciousness as contained in the immunity principle. Through the critical lens of African feminism, JWT is adjudged *not* an effective means of preventing, executing, and terminating moral or just wars.

Malone recognizes that contemporary JWT lacks the depth and breadth to confront the type of intra- and interstate wars and civil wars raging in African countries. It is more appropriate to theorize within a domestic context, instead of international and transnational contexts. In the same vein, Omotosho argues that the relative multidimensional nature of wars in Africa, which is more intrastate than interstate, necessitates a collective redefinition of *jus pos bellum* for it to be relevant in an African war context.[14] For example, Michael Walzer's[15] justification of war relies on the protection of human rights, but wars within the African continent do not commence in a bid to protect any human right. They instead promote protection of splintered political interests and, in the process, perpetrate sexual violence and rape. This justification of war in a bid to protect human rights tramples more on women's fundamental human right to life and, therefore, defeats the justification for war. In addition, seeing that African wars fail to comply with the principles of JWT, Omotosho proposes a brand of morality that is nonpacifist, based on realist pragmatism coupled with womanist principles of care, love, compassion, and resilience. The African feminists' review of JWT reorders its sequence to prioritize *ante bellum*, planning for peace ahead of initiation of war because this prioritization suits the African context much more.[16] This reordering of JWT, which prioritizes *ante bellum*, is based on African feminists' claim that consideration of recourse to war should be contextual and on a situational merit basis. Furthermore, their reflection on the consequences of war on individuals and quality of communal existence and on their livelihood and environment as well as the primacy of preservation of life are paramount in deciding whether to resort to war or continue to seek peace. This consideration also informs feminists' persistence on seeking peace through strategic cultural, legal, and moral frameworks. Therefore, *ante bellum* (i.e., planning for peace) would entail the meaningful inclusion of women, visibly and audibly, in decision-making in all spheres, especially in governance, such that the deciding authority would include the voice of women, which would ensure all peacemaking efforts are persistently employed. Moreover, the inclusion of women in decision-making about war would ensure new peace plans are initiated through a systemic analysis of the enablers and inhibitors of conflict before approval of war.

HISTORICAL APPRAISAL OF WAR IN AFRICAN COUNTRIES: THE WOMEN'S EXPERIENCE

In precolonial times, African kingdoms warred against one another for reasons ranging from expansionist tendencies, to righting of wrongs, to subduing errant subservient kingdoms and territorial protection. These wars were inclusive in their planning, implementation, and ending. Their moral codes for war conduct were based on their cultural beliefs and values. Victims were captured, sacrificed to their gods, or enslaved. Both men and women effectively led wars and conquered territories. The Moremi of Ile-Ife; the Efunsetan Aniwura Iyalode of Ibadan, who was a revered war promoter who provided war horses and mercenaries; Omu Okwei of Aba; Queen Amina of Zaria; Tiye of Nubia and Egypt; and Yaa Asantewa of Ghana[17] are examples of women warlords in Nigerian history. Moremi of Ile-Ife was a beautiful woman married to Oranmiyan, the king of Ile-Ife, Osun State Nigeria. Ile-Ife town was consistently raided at night by Ugbo dressed in strange masquerade attire. Moremi was unhappy at the incessant loss and difficulty faced by her people. She offered herself to be captured by the raiders. She consulted with the god of Esimirin River about the success of such a mission and pledged to make a sacrifice if she was successful. Upon her capture, she understudied the raiders and discovered they were not masquerades but Ugbo people whose attire was made of grass. She escaped and informed the Ile-Ife warriors, who later attacked the Ugbo raiders with burning bundles of elephant grass. The raiders fled and never returned to Ile-Ife, and so the Ile-Ife people lived in peace afterward.[18] Queen Amina of Zaria was born in the fifteenth century, was trained the art of war by Chief Karama, and went with him on many warring raids. She reigned for thirty-four years, expanded her state, and opened the East–West trade routes. Her wealth was mostly from tributes from conquered kingdoms. She is remembered as Amina, daughter of Nikatau, a woman as capable as a man.[19]

Wole Soyinka gleaned the following information about warfare in the Yoruba kingdom from the Ifa corpuscle:

> The justification for war is justice. The Ifa corpuscle claims that justice is the mortar that kneads the dwelling-place of man. Can mere brick on brick withstand the bloodied cries of wrong from the aggrieved?—Sango restores.[20]

What this means is that warfare occurs as a result of pursuit of justice, which sets the condition for war, for engaging in war in the traditional Yoruba society or kingdom.

Moreover, Ogun, the acclaimed warlord, is set to conduct his warfare in comradeship, "comradeship in strife . . . the hardy route of self-sacrifice."[21] This Ifa verse could mean only comradeship, friendship with others either as partners or in opposition. This sets the tone for the perception and the conduct of war. It does not alienate the opposition as the "other," who is less than human, who should be dehumanized and annihilated, whose community should be totally destroyed and erased from history, and whose lineage should be contaminated with poisons that cannot be undone. Rather, it is a condition of friendship that admits that conflict is a temporary situation that does not alter the ontology of the opposition. These people will not conduct warfare in a way that removes them from the communal enclave of beings, interrelated, interconnected beings. Furthermore, because warfare is intrinsically camaraderie with partners, this understanding reflects in the actions of the winners in war. Surviving losers are mostly enslaved, sacrificed to their gods, sold, and imprisoned.

In the traditional Yoruba society, the condition for the engagement in warfare is the pursuit of justice, and the implementation requires friendliness. In the face of comradeship, there will not be inhuman aggression against victims of war, especially vulnerable women and children.

In addition, within those kingdoms, there were cultural rules guiding warfare that enabled them to peacefully exist, which did not necessarily target women but, rather, provided a modicum for peaceful coexistence. For instance, the Yoruba traditional kingdom had proverbs that provide glimpses into possible cultural warfare codes. Some examples are listed below:

1. *Moja Mosa ni kii je ki akinkanju o bogun lo-*

    - Literal interpretation: Knowing when to start warfare and the appropriate time to call it off or escape from it; preserves the life of the brave warrior.
    - Meaning: There is an order to warfare that gives room for calling off warfare by a weakened party or the opportunity to escape to safety.

2. *Ogun awitele ki I pa aro to ba gbon*

    - Literal interpretation: A wise invalid is never consumed by or destroyed in warfare.
    - Meaning: The conditions of war, the prerequisite announcement and preparation for warfare, afford the invalid enough time to prepare for safety or to crawl to a safe hiding place.

3. *Ogun ni sini mu, epe kii sini pa, ko seke kii fi eke ku.*

    - Literal interpretation: A person could be an unintended victim of warfare, but a curse affects only a deserving person; he who does not transgress does not die from the consequence of the transgression.
    - Meaning: The war environment is chaotic and so gives room for accidents, including accidental targets, or unintended victims.

These proverbs indicate the following:

- Warfare is almost always planned and prepared for. That is, the aggressors secure their communities before commencing war while the defending communities usually have watchmen who announce the advancement of invaders, which gives time for preparation by all members either to participate or to flee to safety. The preparation ensures protection for the noncombatant members of society or at least enables them to hide in safe places. Most African communities had such safe hiding places, which are potential tourist sites today.
- Warfare engagement allows for the acceptance of peace treaties irrespective of the stage of the warfare.
- There is an acknowledgment of the unpredictability of a war situation, the acceptance of a high probability of occurrence of accidents and accidental victims. This enables warring parties to prepare for unplanned eventualities as well as to fortify their communities to reduce the unintended casualties of war and protection of noncombatants.

From the foregoing, the experience of women in war times in traditional African societies was complementary as stakeholders in the affairs of state and in engagement in war. The atmosphere of war was of comradeship, of strategic contemplation and provision for the vulnerable members of society. There was no dehumanization agenda of the opposition and victims of war. In these times, women were not targets for sexual violence.

During the colonial occupation of Africa and postcolonial era, the wars were mostly against the colonial government and the perceived injustices by the natives. This type of warfare is at best civil, tribal, and intratribal wars and quests for freedom and emancipation from colonial rule. In this category and probably in this era, warfare was still largely inclusive. Both men and women participated; women supported their freedom-fighting husbands, brothers, and fathers. Moral codes were still in place to guide the conduct and termination of war. As an example, Angolan women participated prominently in their freedom struggles.

However, at a point during this era, the hold of the moral code for warfare was already waning. Both parties engaged in nonconventional violent conflict. For instance, the French government provided nothing more than a public apology to the Algerian government and people for its cruelty during the independence war. "France acknowledged for the first time it was responsible for systematic torture during the Algerian war of independence in the mid-1950s."[22]

The proliferation of nonconventional fighting forces across Africa, from the colonial through the postcolonial era to contemporary times, contributes to high levels of community violence. Violent societies are associated with increased violence against women.[23] From this period onward, the dehumanization of women became prominent. Women were arrested, tortured, and violated alongside their men. Violence against women was part of a systematic method of warfare employed to demoralize the opponents' women, "to terrorize the population, break up families, destroy communities, and, in some instances, change the ethnic make-up of the next generation. Sometimes it is also used to deliberately infect women with HIV or render women from the targeted community incapable of bearing children."[24]

JWT AND WAR IN CONTEMPORARY AFRICAN COUNTRIES

In contemporary times, there are about fifteen African countries that are involved in war, just out of war, or are experiencing postwar conflict and tension. In West Africa, these countries are Cote d'Ivoire, Guinea, Liberia, Nigeria, Sierra Leone, and Togo. In East Africa, these countries are Eritrea, Ethiopia, Somalia, Sudan, and Uganda. In Central Africa, these countries are Burundi, Democratic Republic of the Congo, and Rwanda. In North Africa, the country engaged in strife is Algeria, and, in South Africa, the countries are Angola and Zimbabwe.[25]

Developing African countries have peculiar challenges of weak democracies and institutions, which make the principles of JWT difficult to implement. The weak institutions enable warring communities to disrespect the rule of law and further break down law and order in these countries. This situation of lawlessness fosters the injustices suffered by citizens, especially noncombatant groups, which should be protected under GC IV. The noncombatant groups should not be targeted due to the legal principles of distinction and discrimination during conflict, terror attacks, civil war, and territorial disputes. In these countries, a flawed JWT worked within a framework that exacerbated its flaws, and the impact of those flaws on the lived experiences of women is enormous. They are the most affected victims of conflict and war as they battle to save their lives and ensure the safety of their children, husbands, and means of livelihood.

JWT is readily applicable to sovereign nations going to war against one another. In Nigeria, however, as in other African countries, the wars are within communities, states, and ethnic groups. Unlike with international war engagement, as stipulated in JWT, African countries engage in intrastate warfare, thereby making it not applicable to them in the real sense. Most of these wars and clashes are essentially reprisal attacks to avenge wrongdoings or perceived infractions and revolution or rebellion to constituted authorities in coups d'état, guerrillas, nationalist militias, and freedom fighters. This situation leaves no room for discussions or negotiations of the type that could begin to weigh the compliance or noncompliance to *jus ad bellum*. There is usually no constituted authority on either side to determine the criteria that is sufficient to make warring permissible as well as the accurate timing to commence war and the permissible duration of the warfare.

For instance, the northeastern part of Nigeria has been embroiled in intra-community warfare between herdsmen and local farmers for over two years with no end in sight. This is because every time cattle rustlers attack the herdsmen, they attack the nearest farming community at night by killing and destroying their farms, farmlands, and homes, killing hundreds of people, most of whom are women and children. This pattern has remained in the war for some years now. It contravenes JWT principles of *jus ad bellum* and *jus in bello* because the punishment for cattle rustling, such as the ransacking, killing, and maiming of farming communities, far outweighs the loss of cattle. African feminists' proposition of *jus ad bellum* would have introduced the consideration of arbitration to ensure peace and prevent repeated destruction of lives and properties.

These war situations in African countries also do not comply with the principles of just cause of war. "War is permissible only to confront a 'real and certain danger,' to protect innocent life, to preserve conditions necessary for decent human existence, and to secure basic human rights."[26] The civil war in Nigeria in 1967, also known as the Biafra war, came about to prevent the eastern region from breaking away. It was not because the Nigerian state or the citizens were in any "real and certain danger," nor was it to preserve innocent lives, especially noncombatant citizens, nor was it to preserve conditions necessary for decent human existence and to secure basic human rights. The international community ignored the Biafra agitation and supported the Nigerian government to suppress the agitation through supply of ammunition.[27]

While the civil war (i.e., Biafra war) was declared by competent authority, the incessant intraethnic and communal clashes between herdsmen and farmers and others were not declared by competent authority.

In most African wars, comparative justice is usually not a consideration because the rights and values being protected do not justify the killings that take place. How can the rights of the herdsmen to herding, without loss of their cattle, override the presumption against killing and ransacking entire farming villages? How does the right of the Nigerian state to maintain territorial unity by keeping all its regions within it intact justify the killings that take place against those who are exercising their right to self-determination?

Moreover, the intention of war in most cases cannot be said to be right, even for the aggressor and the victim. The pursuit of peace and reconciliation is often not in the agenda; neither are the warring parties consumed with the conscience or consciousness to avoid unnecessary or unreasonable destructive acts. They are keen on inflicting the worst pain and causing the most irreversible destruction as possible. Unfortunately, the weakness of the institutions in these countries, their lack of requisite political will to check and strongly sanction perpetrators, makes unjust wars possible without commensurate penalty. Consideration of peaceful alternatives that makes going to war a course of last resort is hindered by insufficient peace-building architecture in the governance of the existing polity.

Furthermore, consideration for the probability of success in warfare is usually overridden by the thirst for holding on to power, punishment, revenge, self-determination, perceived entrenchment of justice, and so on. There is a prevalence of irrational resort to force or hopeless resistance, and the outcome is usually futile, an endless cycle of attack and reprisal.

The concept of proportionality in JWT is problematic. The basis for a logical, comparative analysis of the damages inflicted in warfare and the cost of procuring and engaging in war against the good it is expected to achieve cannot be universally accepted because the value placed on human life, either universally or culturally, has a role to play in rendering life immeasurable. Hence, the illogical consideration of proportionality is not just an African country's issue; it is universal.

Wars in contemporary African countries also clearly flout the prescription of the principle of *jus in bello*, which stipulates "how the war should be conducted" and entails the following:

- Discrimination is a condition to avoid killing noncombatants.
- Proportionality, that is, each action must be judged according to the level of force required, with the least possible force used to achieve victory, which avoids needless civilian casualties and property damage.

Unfortunately, the savagery that accompanies these types of warfare seems to target the vulnerable noncombatant. The Democratic Republic of Congo (DRC) war is famed for being an antiwoman war because forty-eight women were said to be raped every hour during the war. The northeastern Nigerian herdsmen did not spare women and children; pregnant women were cut open and fetuses and babies were slaughtered.

In the face of this reality, what then is the fate of the citizens caught in the crossfire of these intrastate/state wars? What is the fate of the women?

THE REALITY OF AFRICAN WOMEN IN WAR

Women and children and other vulnerable groups, such as the sick, the disabled, and the elderly, are usually the most negatively affected in every situation of resort to armed force or war. The UN and international aid agencies say women are among the worst victims of war. Tens of thousands suffer from sexual violence, rape, and lack of access to life-saving health care.[28] In all fifteen African countries currently or recently involved in war, women in the thousands were the worst hit. In every instance of conflict or full-blown war, women do not worry about just their own safety but also that of their husbands, children, parents (i.e., hers and her in-laws), neighbors, and community members. Depending on their circumstances, ensuring their preservation is a burden they bear, and they put this above their own well-being. This commitment informs their position on warfare either in defense or in attack.

Historically, African women were traditionally part of the governance architecture; they were involved in decision-making, which included deciding about war. So they have not always been mere victims of warfare but were also war protagonists, such as Efunsetan Aniwura, Moremi, Queen Amina of Zaria, Tiye of Nubia and Egypt, and Yaa Asantewa of Ghana.[29]

Whatever role they played in warfare, the following experiences were characteristic of the lived experiences of African women in conflict and war situations.

Disruption of Family Life and Work

The chaos and insecurity prevalent in conflict and war situations bring with them panic and disruption of erstwhile peaceful family lives and work. Work is suspended or becomes minimal, depending on the type of work a woman does and the location. Keeping the family and home front together is one of the cultural roles of a woman, and a war situation hinders her from carrying this out.

Insecurity of Self and Family

The security of her family, dependents, and herself is threatened in war situations. Unfortunately, paramount to a woman's well-being is a sense of security in her life and home, and conflicts and war threaten this security or snatch it from her.

Loss of Husband, Children, and Relatives

Similar to the threat to a woman's security in warfare is the loss of husband, children, and family members. Such loss could be due to death or enlistment in the army, militia, and rebel groups willingly or by coercion.

Restrained Mobility Due to Danger or Cultural Limitations

Restrained mobility affects women's ability to freely go about their daily chores due to the danger induced by war or conflict; they are forced to run or hide from danger. Women's mobility could also be restrained due to cultural practices that restrict women's movement, especially outside their homes, such as having women chaperoned outside their homes or covering themselves up from prying eyes and staying indoors. In the midst of chaos, there may not be willing or available men to chaperone women to safety.

Displacement

In war situations, women, children, and vulnerable people become displaced. They suffer the loss of their homes and livelihoods and end up in displaced people's camps or makeshift settlements. Displacement is a harrowing experience for pregnant women; nursing mothers; women with young children who need to be carried or are terrified and distraught; and women with disabled, sick, or elderly dependents.

Hunger

Women suffer hunger and thirst during wars. Following the loss of husband, family life, and livelihood, there is bound to be lack of food and water. It is disheartening for women who are mothers watch their children suffer hunger and thirst and, worse still, become emaciated and die from hunger. Many women in countries with protracted warfare, such as Sudan and DRC, suffer hunger and watch their children become walking skeletons who eventually die.

Lack of Access to Health Care

During wars and ensuing chaos, normal living routines are disrupted, so doctors and nurses cannot provide care for those in need of it. Pregnant women do not have access to antenatal and postnatal care, which increases the mortality rate of women and children. According to Nadine Puechguirbal, the Red Cross advisor on women and war, pregnant women in war zones who face serious medical emergencies and need immediate care too often are unable to reach a health care facility.[30]

Sexual Violence and Rape

During war, the risk of occurrence of sexual violence, including rape, is very high for women and, sometimes, children. "Sexual violence can be used as a form of reprisal, to create fear, or as torture. It may also be used systematically as a method of warfare, to destroy the social fabric of a community by causing shame for the victim and community. In short, sexual violence is a tool of power and humiliation."[31] Rape and other forms of sexual violence during armed conflict are now acknowledged as "weapons of war, designed not only to inflict bodily harm on primarily—but not exclusively—female victims, but also to terrify and humiliate them and their families and communities."[32]

Women who experience sexual violence and rape, especially during warfare, are not just devastated; they also suffer from a lifetime of physical and mental health problems. "Health issues may include fistulas, chronic pain, HIV infection, anxiety, severe depression, a sense of helplessness and hopelessness, insomnia, or recurring nightmares. Such problems can even lead to suicide."[33]

The UN reported over 6,700 rape cases, 43 percent of which involved children, "between June 2007 and 2008" in Ituri province, South Sudan; about 20 percent of rape incidents are never reported.[34] As previously stated, the DRC war is famed for being an antiwoman war because forty-eight women were raped every hour during the war. DRC is the world's rape capital.[35] In Rwanda, between 100,000 and 250,000 women were raped during the three months of genocide in 1994; more than 60,000 during the civil war in Sierra Leone from 1991 to 2002; more than 40,000 in Liberia from 1989 to 2003; and at least 200,000 in the DRC since 1998.[36]

Silence, Stigmatization, Ostracizing, and Lack of Care for Survivors of Sexual Violence

Because of the cultural implications of being raped, most rape cases go unreported. Health care is usually readily available for wounded victims of war, but none is readily available to cater to the needs of victims of rape and sexual violence. Health care services, where available, are rendered discreetly to avoid public detection. With the incidences of rape that are public knowledge, the victims become stigmatized and ostracized. Married rape victims get divorced, and unmarried ones are deserted and labeled as tarnished. There is no family or communal sympathy for their pain and plight.

Death

During these wars, women die. The clashes between the herdsmen and farmers in northeast Nigeria leave women and children dead. The massacre does not spare pregnant women. Women as victims or perpetrators of warfare die. Unfortunately, these atrocities and death of women and children are not always recorded or are underreported, and perpetrators are usually never apprehended nor penalized.

On the other hand, women had experiences other than being victims. To say of women that they were mainly victims of war is to paint a distorted view of African women and their experience in war. Countries such as Liberia, DRC, and Angola witnessed their women standing up as revolutionists and advocating women's movement for peace and reconciliation in their respective countries. Women of Liberia Mass Action for Peace is a remarkable example. Its activities are described as follows:

> Women of Liberia Mass Action for Peace is a peace movement started in 2003, which worked to end the Second Liberian Civil War. Organized by Crystal Roh Gawding and social workers Leymah Gbowee and Comfort Freeman, the movement began despite Liberia having extremely limited civil rights. Thousands of Muslim and Christian women from various classes mobilized their efforts, staged silent nonviolence protests that included a sex strike and the threat of a curse.

Their statement of intent reads as follows: "In the past we were silent, but after being killed, raped, dehumanized, and infected with diseases, and watching our children and families destroyed, war has taught us that the future lies in saying NO to violence and YES to peace! We will not relent until peace prevails."[37]

Indeed, they successfully got the warring factions together and talking; the result was a peace agreement that ended the infamous war in Liberia, thanks to these great women and their experience of war and resolution to make a difference.

The Algerian revolutionists' efforts are also noteworthy accomplishments and examples of the experience of women in war. "Revolutionary war, as the Algerian people refer to it, was a total war in which the woman does not knit for or mourn the soldier. The Algerian woman is at the heart of the combat. Arrested, tortured, raped, shot down, she testifies to the violence of the occupier and to his inhumanity."[38]

However, women as actors in war do not yield as much intrinsic value to the cause of women as women as actors in peace building. According to Aaronette M. White,

> African women combatants, for all the progress some have made as individuals, represent a fraction of the total female population of their countries. Yet, when any woman fights in a military force, we [women] are forced to examine the complexities and interrelationships of gender and war. Merely becoming involved in a military force does not automatically liberate African women or any woman from exploitive relationships.[39]

The sad reality is that, especially as it played out for the Angolan women, their participation alongside their men in the revolution did not change the stifling gender stereotypes in their communities.

ANALYSIS OF THE FAILURES OF JWT VIS-À-VIS THE EXPERIENCES OF AFRICAN WOMEN IN WAR-RAVAGED AFRICAN COUNTRIES

Having highlighted the lived experiences of African women in war-torn African countries and their communities, it is expedient to examine these experiences alongside the flaws of JWT. This analysis will focus on just one of the outlined flaws, which is the abstract and hypothetical view of war.

The proponents of the just war tradition focus their ethical views on abstract notions of universal rights and justice and the abstract, hypothetical view of war. By concentrating primarily on universal rights and seeking universal justice, particular rights of individuals, especially the vulnerable members of society and the noncombatant members, were often ignored and trampled on. Their rights to life, peaceful existence, and bodily dignity are not accounted for in the preconditions for war in JWT. The abstract thinking of war is similar to a video simulation of war scenarios, as in a video game that numbs the mind to reality.[40] Abstract thinking makes possible the denial of suffering, especially of noncombatants. Following are the consequences of the highlighted flaws:

- They shroud the real impact of war on noncombatant citizens, especially women and children. They distance the reality of war from the consciousness, making war's reality and possible impact a surreal experience. Like in a video game, the abstraction in JWT makes the effect of war seem like fiction. "It makes the atrocities of war and its impact on individual bodies, the perception of the enemy as 'other' surreal and enhances concentration on principles of justice and rights rather than needs and interest of specific persons in particular conflicts."[41] It numbs the reality of the effect of warfare that will most certainly cause "burning, explosions, flesh-tearing, radiation poisoning, life-annihilating devastation"[42] on fellow human beings, especially women and children and other noncombatants. If these bodily and environmental injuries as well as the dehumanization through sexual violence and rape were ever calculated in the comparative cost analysis of war, nothing would have justified warfare.
- The ripple effect of war that reaches beyond the field of warfare is the unintended, unplanned, and sometimes planned effect of war on human beings, their farmlands and other means of livelihood, and the destruction of existing infrastructure provision, the economy, sociopolitical life, and the environment.
- The deplorable condition of African women and vulnerable groups of people during and after the termination of war is not considered in the details and calculations of JWT. The central focus of care ethics is on the moral salience of recognizing persons as human beings of whom we take

responsibility rather than abstract and independent agents.[43] No one takes responsibility for the women's deplorable condition during the war and even after the war has ended. Rather, if it becomes public that they were raped, they not only suffer emotional, physical, and psychological trauma; they also become stigmatized and ostracized.

- The seeming invisibility of these atrocities, their underestimation and underreporting, locally and internationally, is intentional. For a very long time, the atrocities committed during wars in African countries did not attract international attention, especially if the country in question did not have any potential or actual economic value to the super countries and their news agencies. Even local news glosses over the gory tales, and details of death casualties and violence to noncombatants were largely underestimated.

This analysis brings to the fore the fallout of JWT regarding the experience of African women during wars in their countries. It portrayed the implication of the abstraction of war, that is, the hypothetical war, on the engagement of war, the conduct of war, and even its cessation. The consequences negate the purpose of JWT because it alienates the fundamental human rights of the people involved, both combatants and noncombatants. The real cost of war if calculated without abstraction cannot be said to be adequate for the pursuit of a just war.

CONCLUSION

This chapter has identified the implication of the hypothetical view of war in JWT and how it contributes to the deplorable lived experiences of women during and after war. This chapter concludes by proposing an African feminists' perspective that draws from the African reality of inclusion, interconnectedness, and empathy. This perspective will bring together other feminists' views, including non-African feminists, in forging a forward-looking improvement of JWT or an outright alternative to it.

It is a consensus proposition to remove the abstract or hypothetical view of war from JWT and replace it with an actual relatable conception of warfare and its impact and consequences in real life and not in a surreal atmosphere. Doing this enables the introduction of an empathic understanding and perception of warfare, thereby making JWT humane. Sjoberg proposes the notion of "empathetic war-fighting," which stresses that the belligerent party is responsible for preventing any reasonably foreseeable impact of its warfare and not merely intend to do so. The current version of the immunity principle (i.e., proportionality and discrimination) allows for civilian damage as long as it is unintended.[44]

In addition, if an empathic understanding and perception of war is incorporated into JWT, as proposed by African feminists' perspective, it will ensure realistic appraisal of the impact and consequences of war. It will consider the short- and long-term consequences of warfare on real men and women, children, and elderly people in the society. Furthermore, it will bring a new level of determining the principles of proportionality and probability of success as well as the criterion for last resort. This empathic understanding and perception of war goes beyond consideration for immediate survival to also encompass the quality of the survivors' lives and relationships and the environment and its ability to sustain their food and water demands as well as other basic infrastructure provision. It calls for a critical evaluation of the short- and long-term actual and potential benefits as well as forecasts for peace and security.

This empathic understanding and perception enhances the possibility of seeking peace treaties and peaceful settlements of crisis and conflicts as a priority. This perception requires the use of strategic and innovative cultural and moral peace frameworks that involve systemic analysis of the inhibitors and enablers of conflict and wars, thereby resorting to humane just wars only as a true last resort. This approach will ensure considerable protection for women who are currently mass-scale victims in fifteen African countries' conflicts as well as children, the socioeconomic infrastructure, and the environment.

BIBLIOGRAPHY

Adetunji, Jo. "The Democratic Republic of Congo: Forty-Eight Women Raped Every Hour in Congo, Study Finds." *The Guardian*, May 12, 2011. https://www.theguardian.com/world/2011/may/12/48-women-raped-hour-congo.

African Sun News. "About Wars and Post-War Conflicts." Accessed May 14, 2019. http://africasunnews.com/wars.html.

Aljazeera News. "France Admits Torture during Algeria Independence War." Published September 13, 2018. https://www.aljazeera.com/news/2018/09/france-admits-torture-algeria-war-independence-180913140641963.html.

Brossault, Aurore. "South Sudan: Working with Communities to Help Victims of Sexual Violence." Published April 8, 2016. https://www.icrc.org/en/document/south-sudan-communities-help-victims-sexual-violence.

Cockburn, Cynthia. "The Gendered Dynamics of Armed Conflict and Political Violence." In *Victims, Perpetrators or Actors? Gender, Armed Conflict and Political Violence*, edited by Caroline Moser and Fiona C. Clark, 13–29. London: Zed Books, 2001.

Cohn, Carol. "Emasculating America's Linguistic Deterrent." In *Rocking the Ship of State: Toward a Feminist Peace Politics*, edited by Adrienne Harris and Ynestra King, 153–70. Boulder, CO: Westview Press, 1989.

Eboh, Marie Pauline. "From Fowl to Feminism: Snippets of Gynist Issues in Non-Gendered Narrative." In *Discourses in African Philosophy*, edited by Ike Odimegwu, Martin Asiegbu, and Maurice Izunwa, 13–15. Akwa: Fab Anieh Nigeria Ltd., 2015.

El Saadawi, Nawal. "War against Women and Women against War: Waging War on the Mind." *The Black Scholar: Journal of Black Studies and Research* 38, no. 2–3 (2008): 27–32.

Fanon, Frantz. *A Dying Colonialism*. Translated by Haakon Chevalier. New York: Grove, 1967.

Gilligan, Carol. *In a Different Voice*. Cambridge, MA: Harvard University Press, 1982.

Global Nonviolent Action Database. "Liberian Women Act to End Civil War." Published October 22, 2010. Accessed May 14, 2019. https://nvdatabase.swarthmore.edu/content/liberian-women-act-end-civil-war-2003.

Halim, Asma Abdel. "Attack with a Friendly Weapon." In *What Women Do in Wartime: Gender and Conflict in Africa*, edited by Meredeth Turshen and Clotilde Twagiramariya, 85–100. New York: Zed Books, 1998.

Held, Virginia. *The Ethics of Care: Personal, Political, and Global*. Oxford: Oxford University Press, 2005.

Hun, Sinem. "An Evaluation of Feminist Critiques of Just War Theory." *DEP* 24 (2014): 76–86. https://www.unive.it/media/allegato/dep/n24-2014/Ricerche/05_Hun.pdf.

International Criminal Tribunal for the Former Yugoslavia. UN Security Council Resolution 827, May 25, 1993. Accessed May 19, 2019. http://www.icty.org/en/documents/statute-tribunal.

Krcek, Jiri. "What's Wrong with Just War Theory? Examining the Gendered Bias of a Long-standing Tradition." *Inquiries Journal* 4, no. 5 (2012): 1–2. Accessed May 14, 2019. http://www.inquiriesjournal.com/articles/648/whats-wrong-with-just-war-theory-examining-the-gendered-bias-of-a-longstanding-tradition.

Legit. "10 Things You Should Know about Biafra and the Biafran War." Accessed February 14, 2019. https://www.legit.ng/629644-10-things-need-know-biafra-biafran-war.html.

Madden, Annette. *In Her Footsteps*. New York: Gramercy Books, 2001.

Malone, Naomi. "From Just War to Just Peace: Re-Visioning Just War Theory from a Feminist Perspective." Master's thesis. University of South Florida, 2004. https://scholarcommons.usf.edu/cgi/viewcontent.cgi?article=2145&context=etd.

Mama, Amina, and Margo Okazawa-Rey "Editorial: Militarism, Conflict and Women's Activism." *Feminist Africa* 10 (2008): 1–8. http://www.agi.ac.za/sites/default/files/image_tool/images/429/feminist_africa_journals/archive/10/feminist_africa_10.pdf.

Ochieng, Ruth Ojiambo. "The Scars on Women's Minds and Bodies: Women's Role in Post-Conflict Reconstruction in Uganda." *Canadian Woman Studies* 22, no. 2 (2003): 23–27. Accessed May 19, 2019. https://cws.journals.yorku.ca/index.php/cws/article/view/6482/5670.

Oluwole, Sophie Bosede. "Short Notes on the Characters." In *African Myths and Legends of Gender*, edited by Sophie Bosede Oluwole and J. O. Akin Sofoluwe, 67–72. Lagos: Ark Publishers, 2014.

Omotosho, Sharon A. "African Womanist View of Just War Theory in Tunde Kelani's Narrow Path." *African Notes: Bulletin of the Institute of African Studies* 42, no. 1–2 (2018): 56–74.

Peach, Lucinda. "An Alternative to Pacifism? Feminism and Just-War Theory." *Hypatia* 9, no. 2 (1994): 152–72.

Schott, Robin. "Gender and 'Postmodern War.'" *Hypatia* 11, no. 4 (2009): 19–29.

Sinem, Hun. "An Evaluation of Feminist Critiques of Just War Theory." *DEP* 24 (2014): 76–86. Accessed January 19, 2019. https://www.unive.it/media/allegato/dep/n24-2014/Ricerche/05_Hun.pdf.

Sjoberg, Laura. "Gendered Realities of the Immunity Principle: Why Gender Analysis Needs Feminism." *International Studies Quarterly* 50, no. 4 (2006): 889–910.

Sofoluwe, J. O. Akin. "Heroes and Heroines in African Classical Thought." In *African Myths and Legends of Gender*, edited by Sophie Bosede Oluwole and J. O. Akin Sofoluwe, 22–37. Lagos: Ark Publishers, 2014.

Soyinka, Wole. *The Seven Signposts of Existence: Knowledge, Honour, Justice and Other Virtues*. Ibadan: Bookcraft, 1999.

UN Outreach Programme on the Rwanda Genocide and United Nations. Department of Public Information. Published March 2014. Accessed June 11, 2019. https://www.un.org/en/preventgenocide/rwanda/preventing-genocide.shtml.

UN Women. "The Contribution of UN Women to Increasing Women's Leadership and Participation in Peace and Security and in Humanitarian Response." Published September 2013.

Accessed June 7, 2019. http://www.unwomen.org/en/about-us/evaluation/~/media/3A55D8A0FCB64F98997D99A95A616F6A.ashx.
VOA News. "UN Says, Women, Children Are Biggest Victims of War." Published November 2, 2009. Accessed January 30, 2019. https://www.voanews.com/a/a-13-2009-03-08-voa9-68678402/408727.html.
Walzer, Michael. *Just and Unjust Wars: A Moral Argument with Historical Illustrations*. 2nd ed. New York: Basic Books, 1977.
White, Aaronete M. "All the Men Are Fighting for Freedom, All the Women Are Mourning Their Men, But Some of Us Carried Guns: Fanon's Psychological Perspectives on War and African Women Combatants." *Journal of Women in Culture and Society* 32, no. 4 (2007): 857–84. Accessed January 19, 2019. https://genderandsecurity.org/sites/default/files/aaronette_white_working_paper_302.pdf.

Chapter Seven

Feminist Care Political Theory and Contemporary Just War Theory

Heleana Theixos

This chapter will look at contemporary just war theory (JWT) with resources in feminist care political theory. This focus highlights how feminist care theorists see much of contemporary JWT as a traditionally male, masculine, or male-biased moral approach to analyzing the justice of war. Feminist care political theory is interested in values of care, which is to say, it is an approach that deeply considers the voices of those most affected by war and how it is incumbent upon the architects of war to care about and for their experience. This chapter stipulates that a care ethical approach is a legitimate foundation for interrogating the traditional justice approach of liberal human rights theory. This feminist care approach will provide a critique of Operation Desert Storm during the First Gulf War and a critique of the ticking time bomb thought experiment. What this chapter is interested in is how both traditional and revisionist JWT, that is to say, *contemporary just war theory* (CJWT), can enrich itself by appealing to the principles in feminist political theory, broadly, and feminist care ethics, more specifically.

Wars have long been waged without mutually agreed-upon moral principles, and so the evolution and emergence of a formal just war framework writ large is an important step in ethics. While *historical* JWT is an accumulation of philosophies of Christian, Kantian, and the consequences and rights brought to bear on war, *contemporary* traditional and revisionist JWT is an application of those historical principles with rigorous analysis of human rights in contemporary wartime.[1] In traditional JWT, the moral mechanisms for war are separate and outside our commonplace morality; for revisionist JWT, our common morality and war morality overlap, although moral principles that occur in war rarely occur in common morality.[2]

Theorists in traditional JWT formulate a separate moral code that applies to war and isn't easily transferable to other human endeavors, for example, the moral principles in individual self-defense or in policing are considered to be separate moral codes from self-defense moral codes of war.[3] Revisionist JWT theorists are responding and evolving their principles toward a unified, objective moral theory.[4] For revisionists, morality extends within our social circles and within the parameters of war, albeit rarely do the demands and moral principles of war occur in our everyday lives. Most contemporary just war theorists, both revisionist and traditional, include the principles of minimizing collateral damage; conducting war within the confines of agreed-upon rules; and how to ethically respond to illegal, nonstate combatants, stateless agents, and/or terrorists.

Insofar as CJWT is a framework about just cause, action, intention, consequences, liabilities, necessity, duty, and a host of other concerns, feminist political theory notices that the framework is set against systems and structures that are themselves unjust so that what justice looks like can be male centric and rational to the exclusion of the emotional and experiential. Feminist political theory looks to expand what can be seen as a masculine framework of moral rightness and wrongness in CJWT by offering insights and asking questions about moral motivations, interpersonal relationships, and individual pressures and constraints.

Feminist care political theory notices that wars are most often organized and fought by men; so this theory sees CJWT principles as having a problematically male-centric, or patriarchal, ethic to its core.[5] Problematic to this male-centric core is that wars are often experienced most brutally by women, civilians, noncombatants, the elderly, and people with disabilities and can be waged with particularly anti-feminist tactics, such as rape of women and children. Feminist political theory also notices how social structures, such as housing, sanitation, banking, families, food supplies, and individual security, are effected by war but that those interests are perhaps only tangentially accounted for in CJWT before, during, and after war. Insofar as feminist interventions recharacterize dominant discourses, they also reformulate political analysis; in that way, a feminist political theory can address CJWT on its own terms with an aim toward broadening CJWT analysis.

Feminist care theorists do not commonly argue that theories of justice be replaced with theories of care. Feminist care political theory contributes to CJWT by emphasizing the aspects of relational, care, and social reasoning in addition to the justice reasoning of CJWT. It offers a perspective on how individuals are not neutral actors but rather contextualized people with histories and lived experiences, such as experiencing shame, regret, and remorse for their previously justified actions. Feminist care analysis maintains that individuals bring their moral agency and sentiments to every action and decision and that, however rational a decision might be and justified through the rubric of CJWT, the agents themselves may not live their lives committed and satisfied by those justifications.

SECTION ONE:
AN OVERVIEW OF FEMINIST POLITICAL THEORY

Feminist political theory emphasizes a personal and contextual view of humans and humanity; from that foundation emerge principles of compassion, care, recognition, standpoint, and equity/equality and criticism of modes of exclusion, inequality, abuse, and oppression. Feminist political theorists begin from a position that accepts that humans are contextual and subjective. Feminist political theorists are concerned with social factors, such as structural oppression and its effects on the most marginalized; social norms and expectations and how they influence, or manipulate, moral norms; and how political decisions can be formed with a variety of influences and factors such as inadequate access to education, wealth disparities, and recognizing autonomy, mobility, and disability. Race, sex, gender, sexual orientation, and bodily autonomy and how they are socially constructed and relate to mechanisms of social power are central to feminist political theory. Thus, feminist political theory is, broadly, a process of understanding, questioning, challenging, and changing dominant political frameworks of justice and freedom. Table 7.1 characterizes the different areas of interest for different feminist political theories.

Table 7.1. Feminist Approaches to Political Practices and Theories

Feminist interventions into political discourse, called feminist political theory, prioritizes what might be called a gendered perspective and methodology. These investigations recognize and prioritize insights of feminist, or female, concerns. A feminist political perspective and methodology is an observation and a critique of ways in which political theories frame themselves in traditional male-centric language. Following are the theoretical schools of feminist theory, which focus on power applied to political issues, such as international relations and war theory, but also on cultural, social, societal, and organizational issues:

Phenomenological Feminist Theory
Phenomenological feminist political approaches engage with Simone De Beauvoir's *The Second Sex* and draw on how women's physiology connects to social roles. Maurice Merleau-Ponty, Iris Young, and others engage with the ways in which the female body situates women in the world as self-conscious, embodied existence interacting with culture and social tensions. Phenomenological approaches ask how a male body–dominated culture interacts with female bodies in social, cultural, historical, economic, and environmental terms and environments and how those terms and environments define value.

Radical Feminist Theory

Theorists such as Catharine MacKinnon and Judith Butler criticize the cultural norms of sex/gender distinctions. They argue that both sex and gender are social constructions, shaped by power relationships, largely male–female relationships, which are analogous to master–slave relationships. The analysis of power is thus central to radical feminist analysis.

Intersectional Feminist Theory

Intersectional feminist political theories have the goal of developing theories for analyzing political cultures and power by examining how sexism/heterosexism, racism, class oppression, and other components of social and cultural oppression intersect. The aim is to collapse separate and distinct loci of control and power and instead examine how they overlap and intersect.

Poststructural Feminist Theory

Poststructural feminist political theories engage with the middle-period work of Michel Foucault. Poststructural feminists analyze political power and power writ large as social systems emerging and reemerging within society, embraced by some members of society while others are excluded, reimagined, or constant.

Postmodernist Feminist Theory

Postmodernist feminist political theories build on the central premise that how we engage with political power and aspects of our political lives is inextricably connected to the narratives we tell, the truths we choose to believe, and the psychological processes and cultural components that influence us.

Analytic Feminist Theory

Analytic feminist political approaches are a combination of empirical, social–scientific research and normative philosophical theorizing. Central to these modes of theorizing is engaging with how political power functions within the conditions of social dynamics and individual psychology.

Liberal Feminist Theory

Liberal feminist approaches see political power as a positive resource that ought to be distributed fairly. Liberal theorists argue that women can preserve their own equality from male-centric power structures so marginalized people can share political and legal rights.

Socialist Feminist Theory

Socialist feminist political approaches are interested in how economics plays a vital role in theories of gender exploitation. Social feminist theorists, such as Alison Jaggar, prioritize how economic oppression and subordination are intertwined. Usually through a Marxist lens, socialist feminist theorists look at political power as a component of class oppression; exploitation, in particular unpaid domestic labor; and capitalist appropriation.

Feminist Pacifist Theory

Pacifist political theories argue that there is no such thing as a just war. These theorists argue that war and morality do not overlap or intersect and that, if one is interested in moral principles, then one must be abolitionist regarding war and the primary aim is always deterrence. Feminist pacifist theorists see war as architected by men disproportionately affecting women and the most marginalized.

Feminist International Political Theory
International feminist political theorists, such as Laura Sjoberg, Alison Jaggar, Grace Clement, Nancy Hirschmann, and others, integrate feminist theory with political theory and international relations. Intersecting gender studies, standpoint epistemology, and race and economic theory with moral theory and justice theory, these theorists argue that systems of power, of which war is one example, can countermine feminist ethical values.

Feminist Care Theory
Feminist care theorists, such as Carol Gilligan, Nel Noddings, Annette Baier, Virginia Held, Eva Feder Kittay, Sara Ruddick, Fiona Robinson, and Joan Tronto, are some of the most influential among many contributors to care ethics, a branch of feminist philosophy and philosophy of education, which explores a female-oriented value system and moral philosophy.

Feminist Care Political Theory
Feminist care political theory intersects with feminist care ethics and feminist political theory and is interested in centering feminine and feminist care ethics in the domain of political theory, in particular in analyzing the justice of war. Virginia Held, Fiona Robinson, Grace Clement, and others work in feminist care ethics applied to a number of moral issues and ethical fields, including caring for animals and the environment; bioethics; and, more recently, public policy, political theory, and JWT.

SECTION TWO:
FEMINIST CARE POLITICAL THEORY AND JWT: SANCTIONS

Traditional and revisionist just war theories differ in their methodology, but, for the purposes of this chapter, these two philosophical traditions within CJWT are largely grouped together. Examining CJWT reasons for going to war, *jus ad bellum*, involves questions about legitimate authority, just cause(s), necessity, autonomy, and rights. Considerations about engaging in war, *jus in bello*, involve questions about proportionality, double effect, discrimination, and the rights and protections for noncombatants, which is in contrast to feminist political scholarship, which interrogates the prevailing justifications for war before, during, immediately after, and long after its completion. Feminist care political theory emphasizes principles of lived experience narratives, commitment to the values of others, policies that are open to dialogue, recognizing and elevating marginalized voices, empathy, cooperation, peaceful resolution, deterrence, and caring. This chapter reviews feminist political theory, in particular *feminist care* political theory, to interrogate and intervene in CJWT principles with the aim of adding moral texture to our decision-making processes about justice. It is important to recall that CJWT offers a moral lens for examining and determining just acts, primarily before and during war, but not a legal or legislative lens. Feminist care political theory is also a process for examining, analyzing, and making determinations about justice before, during, and after war but with a set of moral values different from those of CJWT. This section articulates how CJWT and feminist political scholarship recognize and/or prioritize different values from each other, and offer different judgments in the narrow case of multilateral sanctions against Iraq before and after America's Operation Desert Storm (ODS).

The George H. W. Bush administration was acutely aware of the failed engagement of the United States in Vietnam, so ODS was tasked with adhering to principles within CJWT.[6] In the wake of Iraq's refusal to withdraw from Kuwait, the Bush administration, in conjunction with the UN Security Council, broadly considered two options: harsher UN sanctions above and beyond the already harsh UN Security Council embargo on all Iraqi-controlled territories or military force to defend the Kuwaitis.[7] The decision was a military action. ODS was operationally successful; Iraq withdrew from Kuwait and the UN established Resolution 687, a conditional and comprehensive regimen of sanctions, in effect continuing and escalating the pre-ODS embargo on Iraq.

Taking into consideration both pre- and post-ODS UN sanctions, Iraq was under one of the longest and most restrictive, coercive diplomacy protocols in modern history.[8] Over 100,000 Iraqi civilians were dead or dying who were directly connected to the effects of the pre- and post-ODS sanctions, most of the deaths caused by the breakdown of social services, such as lack of access to clean water and disruption to sewage disposal.[9] Communicable diseases, highly predictable in areas of degraded sanitation, surged, and the death toll was compounded by the decimation of responsive social services, such as medical facilities.

The United States and the UN were responding to a violent, undemocratic, belligerent state led by a despot, Saddam Hussein, who had been in US favor just twenty years prior; the aims of a CJWT-constrained military approach were to remove Iraq from Kuwait. These constrained and measured goals were achieved. CJWT constraints and permissions were integrated throughout the UN and Bush administration's response. Therefore, ODS was, through the lens of CJWT, largely considered a *just war*. Feminist approaches in international relations and security studies use a different lens and resources and came to a different conclusion regarding the justice of ODS.

Feminist care political theory takes seriously how the powerless, impoverished Iraqi civilians respond to both the coercive diplomacy of the UN embargo and the propaganda, conditions, and motivations for invading Kuwait. Feminist care political philosophy is especially interested in the reports of desperation and destitution wrought by a despotic Iraqi government before the invasion and during Kuwait's occupation and how those reports are connected to a despotic leader's policies and embargoes. A feminist care lens asks about harsh sanctions on civilians, about how desperate situations foster blaming others, and how best to motivate Iraq to withdraw from Kuwait without threatening war or harsher sanctions. To those goals, feminist care political scholarship would pay very close attention to what the Iraqi people (i.e., *moral stakeholders*) were saying about their experiences with coercive diplomacy and their reasons for blaming Kuwait.

Neither the international community nor the Bush administration is known to have robustly recognized the motivations for why the decimated Iraqi community supported its despotic leader *as a result* of such harsh sanctions before and after ODS, but feminist political scholarship does.[10] Devastating sanctions, among myriad decimations to the functions of daily life, are *demoralizing*, and demoralized people are desperate to find blame.[11] When multilateral sanctions produce deep and broad desperation among civilians, those civilians can be susceptible to scapegoat propaganda, and a susceptible, demoralized, blame-finding community expresses its attitude in stories and narratives that feminist philosophy takes seriously. A feminist care political approach asks questions about attitudes and desires, pride and scapegoating, and impoverishment and aggression to understand Iraq's aggression and why sanctions had "failed." An ethics of care can articulate how the pre-ODS embargo was not only economically and socially devastating but also that devastated people can react aggressively.

CJWT is not clearly the theory to appeal to for uncovering these civilian narratives. CJWT-connected language explained the failed sanctions as being caused by the strong-armed control of the Hussein government, to the lack of information and education of the Iraqi people, and to tribal histories blaming Kuwait.[12] Resources in CJWT do not reveal how engagement with stakeholder stories reveals the reasons for blame and aggression. A feminist care analysis asks about the private pain of the most marginalized and affected. It prioritizes the stories about suffering families, interrogates male-centric stories about unjustified aggression, and counters a male-centric narrative focused on rationality with female-centric stories of suffering.

In sum, feminist care inquires about the everyday lives of everyday people profoundly transformed by sanctions and explains how these stories explain scapegoating, aggression, and a confused loyalty to a despotic regime. This inquiry can be transformative for powerful state actors who are deciding between, primarily, two options: more sanctions or war. Borrowing from postmodern feminism, a feminist care political approach is a process of discourse and of narratives, of telling stories about facts in the world and about what matters to moral stakeholders; this approach uncovers a multitude of considerations and augments narrow decision-making.

For example, the feminist care political approach would prescribe a *jus ante bellum* UN commission of moral stakeholders.[13] Historically, the UN has played the part of such a commission, but how to organize an external body, what terrain it represents, and what sort of review it engages in is enriched with an appeal to recognizing demoralized aggressor stories. Engaging with the moral stakeholders in dialogue, with the aim of preventing war and diffusing harm, is a robust *jus ante bellum* perspective, something CJWT does not clearly prescribe. This dialogue must differ from dialogue about penalizing and punishing the Iraqi government. This commission must involve international moral stakeholders across state boundaries to Iranian, Jordanian, and American communities. This commission must arrange and prioritize dialogue with moral stakeholders aimed at understanding aggression and deescalating sanctions and war. It is not the point of this chapter to dissect the UN's prewar methodology; its only point is to make clear that such a commission of moral stakeholders is prescribed through feminist care analysis, which is not true for CJWT frameworks.

SECTION THREE: SANCTIONS CONCLUSION

Prominent just war theorist Michael Walzer addresses traditional JWT's limitations regarding what is morally demanded *after* the just war is concluded. Walzer writes that "[o]nce we have acted in ways that have significant negative consequences for other people (even if there are positive consequences), we cannot just walk away," but, he further says, that in the real world the international community often does just walk away *post bellum* and that JWT can justify leaving the decimated community to its own repair. Walzer argues that discussions about *jus post bellum* are limited in part because the aggressor states bear the costs and responsibilities of rebuilding and that, while this appears morally problematic, it can be justified on principles of justice and self-determination.[14]

One can take Walzer's view and apply it to how limited CJWT is *ante bellum*, how prioritizing considerations of justice and self-determination is not always a sufficiently robust consideration. Feminist care political theory is able to draw out moral principles about valuing dialogue about oppression, desperation, and confusion in an *ante bellum* environment and, in so doing, can offer entities such as the UN and the US government more options. CJWT, with an infusion of feminist care political theory, does not become a new moral system but rather becomes a new moral orientation; as such, ODS looks less conclusively just.

SECTION FOUR:
CALIBRATING THE TICKING TIME BOMB HYPOTHETICAL WITH FEMINIST CARE POLITICAL THEORY

Earlier, this chapter characterized the ways in which feminist political theory, in particular feminist care theory, values moral stakeholder narratives. Feminist care political theory values the stories told by the moral stakeholders, who are also aggressors, as well as the stories told by the victims. Thus, the previous section provided a framework for how feminist care political theory raises different concerns from the concerns raised by CJWT including a concern about how coercive diplomacy affects civilians, even the aggressor state's civilians. An appeal to CJWT does not reveal the importance of narratives within its methodology, and so feminist care political theory augments and enriches CJWT methods.

This next section looks at how CJWT may not robustly consider the experiences of another kind of moral stakeholder in a just war: interrogators. The next section examines the ticking time bomb hypothetical situation, which is often characterized as an airtight just war thought experiment. This section examines how the thought experiment can be further enriched with an appeal to resources prescribed within feminist care political theory and, in particular, examines and demands a parity of moral concern for interrogators, detainees, and innocent bystanders.

Example of Interrogation Torture in the Ticking Time Bomb Case

The moral permissibility of interrogation torture is commonly made by an appeal to the ticking time bomb (TTB) thought experiment. The TTB clarifies our decision-making process about what matters morally and how to act justly.[15] The CJWT-augmented TTB thought experiment is most commonly characterized like this: The military forces of a just war have detained someone who they reasonably believe knows the location of a ticking time bomb.[16] If the bomb explodes, many innocent lives will be lost. It is stipulated that the detainee *likely* knows the bomb's location but refuses to divulge the information. It is stipulated that an interrogator could use interrogation methods to get the detainee to reveal the bomb's location. It is stipulated that the detainee is morally *liable* to interrogation by refusing to cooperate, that there is *urgency* to interrogating the detainee, and that the *necessity* of the situation demands that some form of limited interrogation torture can be justified.

CJWT takes into account principles of justice, such as rights, duties, permissions, restraint, and liabilities, and also includes considerations of the greatest good. Therefore, CJWT theory, applied to the TTB hypothetical, checks for legitimacy of the interrogator, for probability of success, for liability of the detainee, for urgency of force, and for proportionate use of force. In sum, the CJWT-enriched hypothetical asks us to weigh the benefits of harming the one unjust, liable, informed, knowledgeable, recalcitrant detainee by using force, which is proportionate, necessary, and likely to be effective.[17] A CJWT-enriched TTB thought experiment is used widely in legal, procedural, and social analysis.[18] On this circumspect application of the TTB hypothetical, most theorists and political analysts, policymakers, and architects of war conclude that interrogation torture can be morally justified.[19]

The TTB hypothetical is more than an intellectual exercise; it does the moral work of framing our moral intuitions into a digestible scenario wherein we develop significant moral decisions, those decisions become clear to us, and we apply those decisions in areas of significance, such as international policy.[20] Jeremy Waldron's meta-analysis of decision-making in war shows just how ubiquitous use of the TTB thought experiment is.[21]

Feminist care theory is interested in whether this hypothetical—and whether our subsequent moral beliefs about interrogation torture more broadly—is sufficiently robust in considering the moral experience of, at a minimum, the most central stakeholders. Under a narrow set of CJWT conditions, the TTB hypothetical seems to deliver a clear, if wildly rare, case where interrogation torture is permissible. Insofar as the thought experiment is a hypothetical for justifying interrogation torture, feminist care theory asks different moral questions and prioritizes different moral concerns, and so under feminist care analysis the TTB's moral calculus looks different.

One of the most compelling components of the TTB hypothetical is weighing the calculus of harms to innocent civilians against the harms to the detainee, after and including checks for CJWT components, such as liability and urgency. What is missing is parallel, moral concerns for harms to the interrogator. Thus a feminist care approach to the TTB hypothetical would ask questions similar to what CJWT theorists would ask: questions about the ways interrogation methods can be proportionate and constrained, about the rights the interrogator has to refuse an order, and/or about what sort of psychosocial effects interrogators have experienced in the past. Feminist care asks questions different from those the CJWT theory asks while recognizing CJWT principles: questions that take into account the interrogator's liability to posttraumatic distress, considerations for the interrogator's posttorture regret if the detainee is not in fact liable to torture, questions about the proportionality of significant bad effects to the interrogator as well as to the detainee.

Feminist care asks us to reconstruct the TTB hypothetical with a parity of CJWT moral concern for the interrogator. Enhancing the TTB hypothetical with robust and informed CJWT concern for interrogators seems incumbent upon those of us who use the hypothetical as both a policy-guiding and an intuition-guiding thought experiment. For example, in the usual CJWT-enhanced construction of the TTB, we stipulate that the detainee likely knows the bomb's location and this contributes to the detainee's liability to torture. On parity of reasoning, we must also stipulate that the interrogator is aware of the psychosocial effects of interrogation on interrogators and that their knowledge contributes to their liability to any posttraumatic harms. As it is commonly used, the CJWT-enriched TTB thought experiment does not prescribe a moral concern for the interrogator. This is not to say that a justice-based analysis can't have moral concern for the interrogator, only that it is not clear that CJWT requires that step. Furthermore, feminist concerns for the interrogator go beyond a calculus of moral concern that parallels that for the detainee. For example, CJWT asks whether the detainee is *liable* to being interrogated. Insofar as the detainee has satisfied some liability conditions, a determination of liability can be met. Such analysis can also be applied to the interrogator by determining whether the interrogator is liable to the harms of posttraumatic stress disorder (PTSD), moral injury, or other psychosocial harms involved when one human inflicts serious harm on another; this enriched CJWT analysis would be a moral improvement, having a parity of moral concern for both detainee and interrogator. Feminist care political analysis is interested in how justifications for liability to harm are calculated and how they're revisited, reanalyzed, and expressed throughout time. To illustrate this point, we can turn to the resources in military psychology, where the depth and degree of the effects of interrogation torture on interrogators is well documented and researched. Damien Corsetti, known in military circles as the monster of Bagram, says that he is suffering from PTSD for having been involved in interrogation torture: "It's done to drive them crazy.... The cries, the smells, the sounds are with me. They are things that stay with you forever.... I almost went crazy myself."[22] Adam Gray and Jonathan Millantz, army soldiers who interrogated Iraqi detainees, describe how their justifications for their actions were steadfast, until they were not.[23] Millantz describes his and Gray's reflections on the experience of interrogation as leaving them with self-hate, deep remorse, and an inability to reconcile themselves back into the moral community: "I think he [Gray] hated who he was when he was there ... he couldn't deal with what he had done. And I still have trouble with that. It haunts me every day, and it's something I'll never get away from."[24]

Millantz and Gray, both suffering from PTSD and moral injury, are characterized by their families and colleagues as having been committed to service, to the mission, and to the moral correctness of their actions—all analytic JWT conditions we might include in a more robust TTB thought experiment. Additionally, both Gray and Millantz changed those beliefs over time and developed new, debilitating psychological and emotional difficulties, and so *postinterrogation regret* would be an important component for consideration in a feminist care approach to the TTB hypothetical.[25]

As it stands, we commonly perform a TTB analysis without determining what interrogator-relevant considerations should or should not be included. Whether we include these considerations for the interrogator into our TTB calculation is a separate consideration from whether we are acting legitimately in deciding not to include those interrogator-relevant considerations. Much of moral theorizing about actions in political theory in general and within the TTB hypothetical specifically centers on checking our justifications for actions, the moral rightness or wrongness of acts and decisions. Feminist care political theory looks to expand traditionally rationalistic frameworks of moral rightness and wrongness by checking moral motivations; interpersonal relationships; and the individual's pressures, constraints, and contexts. For the TTB hypothetical to have normative validity, feminist care theory demands parity of concern metrics for the central agents effected within the moral scope of the TTB: interrogator, detainee, and civilians.

That feminist care political theory would argue for equitable moral concern for the torturer seems counterintuitive: the interrogator is in a position of power over the victim, the interrogator can make more choices than the victim, the interrogator (per the TTB stipulations) is engaging in a just war intending to save many innocent lives. Indeed, the interrogator is an agent of power and clearly not a victim. Ultimately, in theory and practice, the TTB hypothetical offers us moral justification for causing harm to a detainee without a calculus for harms to the interrogator, and, in that analytical sense, the TTB hypothetical is lopsided. Insofar as we consider ourselves allies to the interrogator, it is incumbent upon us to consider how we apply our moral concern unequally. This is not to say that the interrogator is a victim of power (although that is an argument feminist political theorists could make); it is to acknowledge how harms are distributed within a torture scenario and how our moral concern is unequally applied.

Furthermore, the commonly constructed "agent-neutral" formulation of the thought experiment is insufficient in light of both the serious moral concerns for the interrogator and how the interrogator acts on our behalf such that we are implicated in harms to the interrogator. Without feminist care political theory considerations, and specifically without feminist care components, the TTB hypothetical is analytically impoverished. Feminist care theory is valuable in its ability to emphasize the moral concerns for those most affected by just war decisions. Feminist moral theories are concerned about the moral justifications for harming the detainee, innocent civilians, *and* the interrogator. Insofar as both detainee and interrogator are eligible for serious harms in the process of interrogation, feminist care theory is as concerned for the interrogator as it is for the detainee.

There could be objections to feminist care demands for robust moral concern for the interrogator, objections that highlight the professionalism, training, and just cause of the interrogator, a *good soldier objection*. The objection might be that parity of moral concern for the interrogator is trivial, considering the interrogator's own informed, willing, and committed consent. A feminist care theory approach interrogates this traditionally male-centric narrative about consenting good soldier and questions whether the interrogator is best served by this kind of consent analysis. It considers how the phenomenology of violence affects perpetrators and asks whether this good soldier is *fully* informed as to those experiences such that consent is robust. Without feminist political theory considerations, and specifically without feminist care concern metrics equitably applied to all moral stakeholders, the TTB hypothetical is analytically and morally incomplete. Feminist care theory's concern for the interrogator complements the analytics of CJWT in that it demands concern for the psychosocial effects the interrogator is genuinely liable to, which effects are proportionate, and, thus, which actions are morally justified. The commonly constructed *agent-neutral* formulation of the thought experiment is morally insufficient.

There might be some concern that feminist care political analysis of the TTB is overly paternalistic, that it is a process of the good soldier's perspective. This paternalism, or *maternalism*, to use a more feminist care–appropriate term, may appear to diminish the good soldier's training, commitment to the cause, and self-determination. Within the perspective of feminist care theory, maternalism is addressed and validated. Feminist theory acknowledges the worry about maternalism/paternalism and counters that moral stakeholders are entitled to have their perspective taken seriously while accounting for the ways in which their perspectives may be better informed.

SECTION FIVE:
TTB CONCLUSION

Insofar as we criticize and analyze the justifications for wars, we have a duty to those who act on our behalf to take their morally relevant concerns into account. Feminist care political theory provides the resources for recognizing that the TTB thought experiment demands more from us. The TTB case is praised as a concrete and rational (despite its being wildly improbable) thought experiment, but, insofar as TTB helps clarify our justifications for interrogation torture, it must have parity of concern for the interrogator.

FEMINIST CARE POLITICAL THEORY
CHAPTER CONCLUSION

Both traditional and revisionist JWT appeals to the principles grounded in Kantian deontological ethics and in utilitarian/consequentialist ethics. CJWT is, for the most part, a theory that appeals to principles within these two philosophical/ethical traditions, and so it is in many ways a dichotomous ethical tradition. This chapter highlights how theories about just war are enriched when they appeal to moral concerns not clearly articulated within these traditions. This chapter recognizes what CJWT takes into account moral concern for the consequences to moral stakeholders in war, the rights of the moral stakeholders in war, and the duties and limitations placed on decision-making at the military and political levels. This chapter highlights how principles within feminist political theory, and feminist care political theory specifically, enrich the moral texture and responsibility of moral just war reasoning.

Feminist care political theory principles are scalable and transferrable, thus augmenting, not replacing, CJWT. Moral theory in general aims at extending common moral principles so that at some point in our human achievements we can say that we, as a humanity, have ethical principles that apply rationally, emotionally, analytically, and subjectively. The assumption in this chapter is that theories of justice and care are conceptually compatible and that theories of justice can be morally enriched by appealing to principles in feminist care political theory.[26]

BIBLIOGRAPHY

Buchanan, Allen, and Robert Keohane. "Pre-Commitment Regimes for Intervention: Supplementing the Security Council." *Ethics & International Affairs* 25, no. 1 (Spring 2011): 41–63.

Cortright, David, and George A. Lopez. *Sanctions and the Search for Security: Challenges to UN Action*. Boulder, CO: Lynne Rienner Publishers, 2002.

Gándara, Alejandro. "Memorias de los Monstruos." *El Mundo*. Published November 11, 2011. Accessed May 19, 2019. https://www.elmundo.es/blogs/elmundo/escorpion/2011/11/17/memorias-de-los-monstruos.html.

Haas, Richard N. *War of Necessity, War of Choice: A Memoir of Two Iraq Wars*. New York: Simon and Schuster, 2009.

Hassan, Hamdi A. *The Iraqi Invasion of Kuwait: Religion, Identity and Otherness in the Analysis of War and Conflict*. London: Pluto Press, 1999.

Luban, David. "Liberalism and the Unpleasant Question of Torture." *Virginia Law Review* 91, no. 6 (2005): 1425–61.

McAfee, Noëlle, and Katie B. Howard. "Feminist Political Philosophy." The Stanford Encyclopedia of Philosophy. Modified October 12, 2018. Accessed March 10, 2019. https://plato.stanford.edu/archives/win2018/entries/feminism-political.

———. "Torture in Principle and in Practice." *Public Affairs Quarterly* 22, no. 2 (2008): 111–28.

McMahan, Jeff. *Killing in War*. Oxford: Oxford University Press, 2009.

———. "Torture in Principle and in Practice." *Public Affairs Quarterly* 22, no. 2 (2008): 91–108.

Meagher, Robert Emmet. *Killing from the Inside Out*. Eugene, OR: Cascade Books, 2014.

Nunner-Winkler, Gertrud. "Two Moralities? A Critical Discussion of an Ethic of Care and Responsibility versus an Ethic of Rights and Justice." In *An Ethic of Care*, edited by Mary Jeanne Larrabee, 143–56. New York: Routledge, 1993.

Phillips, Joshua A. S. *None of Us Were Like This Before: American Soldiers and Torture*. New York: Verso Books, 2010.
Rejali, Darius. *Torture and Democracy*. Princeton, NJ: Princeton University Press, 2009.
Selden, Zachary A. *Economic Sanctions as Instruments of American Foreign Policy*. Westport, CT: Praeger Publishers, 1999.
Sjoberg, Laura. *Gender, Justice, and the Wars in Iraq*. Oxford: Lexington Books, 2006.
United Nations Human Rights. "Convention against Torture and Other Cruel, Inhuman or Degrading Treatment or Punishment." United Nations Treaty Series, 1465 (December 10, 1984). Accessed March 12, 2019. https://www.ohchr.org/EN/ProfessionalInterest/Pages/CAT.aspx.
United Nations Security Council Resolution 678. Adopted by the Security Council at its 2963rd meeting. November 29, 1990. Accessed March 12, 2019. https://documents-dds-ny.un.org/doc/RESOLUTION/GEN/NR0/575/28/IMG/NR057528.pdf?OpenElement.
Waldron, Jeremy. *Torture, Terror, and Trade-Offs: Philosophy for the White House*. Oxford: Oxford University Press, 2012.
Walzer, Michael. *Just and Unjust Wars*. New York: Basic Books, 1977.
———. "The Triumph of Just War Theory (and the Dangers of Success)." *Social Research* 69, no. 4 (2002): 925–44.

Chapter Eight

An African Theory of Just Causes for War

Thaddeus Metz

INTRODUCING AFRICAN VALUES

It is literally in the past few years that theoretical discussions of violence, with some clear reference to military conflict, in the light of characteristically African norms have begun to sprout.[1] Substantial texts in African philosophy originated only in the post-independence era of the 1960s, with the rise of literacy and the demise of colonialism, which means that some debates that have been long-standing in other global traditions have yet to receive much attention in this one. Just war theory is one such debate, having received virtually no analysis by professional philosophers working in the African tradition until quite recently.[2] As one scholar has remarked, "The literature on political theory and moral philosophy in Africa offers very little resources on the subject matter of the morality of war. This situation is paradoxical, given the almost incessant occurrence of war in the continent."[3] In this chapter, I aim to develop African just war theory by reflecting on some topics that have yet to be considered and by advancing perspectives different from what have been suggested so far.

About the only thing concerning African values that philosophers and related theorists beyond the continent are likely to know is that they are characteristically communitarian. As I indicate below, that is true, but the form the communitarianism takes, at least in a fairly distinct and attractive form, is relational. That is, communal or harmonious relationships are what tend to be prized, in contrast to both a corporate ascription of value to a group and an individualist ascription of it to autonomy or rationality as per much of the modern Western moral tradition.

My approach in this chapter is to spell out a foundational African ethic, according to which one must treat people's capacity to relate communally (or harmoniously) with respect, derive some principles from it to understand the just causes for war,[4] and compare and contrast their implications with other recent African views and some prominent accounts in contemporary Anglo-American philosophy. Just causes for war are considerations that in principle can justify initiating military (and similar kinds of) conflict, with common Western accounts of them including rebutting aggression, punishing the guilty, and protecting certain human rights. Drawing on African values, I argue that respectfully treating people's capacity for communion grounds the principles that a large degree of discord (i.e., the antisocial opposite of communion) is justified, insofar as it is directed toward those who have been initially discordant and the discord is the least amount essential and expected to rebut a no greater discord on their part; otherwise, substantial discord is usually[5] unjust.

Although this approach will be broadly familiar to readers in the Western tradition, its ethical foundation is distinct, and I work to highlight contours of it that differentiate it in some plausible ways from the views of thinkers such as Thomas Hurka, David Luban, Larry May, Jeff McMahan, and Michael Walzer. For example, I argue that the Afro-communal approach is naturally understood to entail that some forms of military conflict could be justified to protect a people's culture from being suppressed or, perhaps most radically different, even for the sake of the *aggressors*. In addition, I argue that it forbids going to war to punish aggressors for the purposes of either retribution or general deterrence, and also rules out doing so merely to protect territory from incursion.

As for the African credentials of my approach, this is not a work of intellectual or sociological history; it does not empirically recount the nature of sub-Saharan cultures in general or military practices in particular. I ground the ethic on the remarks of contemporary African philosophers and illustrate its implications for warfare by applying it to familiar armed conflicts in southern Africa and appealing to the ideas of some African military leaders, including King Moshoeshoe I, Kenneth Kaunda, and Amilcar Cabral. However, this work is constructive and normative and not so much representative; I draw on ideas salient in African philosophical thought to advance a novel and promising theory of just cause, setting aside descriptive issues such as what the indigenous worldviews informing contemporary African philosophy are like and whether Africans have tended to accept the theory's prescriptions in respect of military and related forms of conflict.

In the following text, I begin by sketching an ethic of communion (or harmony) informed by the African tradition and then derive from it principles about when, why, and how much to be antisocial (discordant) and illustrate them by applying them to two African conflicts that are particularly known to a global audience. One is the guerrilla war that was waged against the apartheid regime in South Africa, and the other is the forcible ejection of white farmers from Zimbabwe (which, while not having become full-blown warfare, did involve a recent deployment of systematic violence). Then, I apply the Afro-communal approach to a variety of issues regarding the just causes for war and similar sorts of deadly force, highlighting respects in which its implications merit consideration as rivals to views that others working in the African tradition have recently suggested and some salient Western views. I conclude by noting topics that pertain to *jus in bello* and *jus post bellum*, which African reflection on just war has yet to address thoroughly, and suggesting some argumentative strategies in respect of them.

AN AFRICAN ETHIC[6]

Of the various philosophical interpretations of sub-Saharan moral thought, I appeal to a fundamentally relational one,[7] spelling it out here but applying it to military conflict in the following section. Instead of conceiving of morally right action in terms of what honors or promotes a good intrinsic to a person, such as her welfare, autonomy, or life, my favored ethic places a certain way of relating between individuals at the ground of how to treat others. The following comments by scholars of African ethics, from places as diverse as Uganda, South Africa, Zimbabwe, and Kenya, suggest such a relational approach to morality:

> [I]n African societies, immorality is the word or deed which undermines fellowship.[8]

> Social harmony is for us [Africans] the *summum bonum*—the greatest good. Anything that subverts or undermines this sought-after good is to be avoided like the plague.[9]

> [O]ne should always live and behave in a way that maximises harmonious existence at present as well as in the future.[10]

> A life of cohesion, or positive integration with others, becomes a goal, one that people design modalities for achieving. Let us call this goal communalism, or, as other people have called it, communitarianism. In light of this goal, the virtues... become desirable.[11]

I do not take these comments about fellowship, harmony, and communalism at face value because doing so has counterintuitive implications regarding human rights. As they stand, they variously suggest that certain (harmonious or communal) relationships are good for their own sake, that it is always wrong to undermine them, and that one should promote them as much as possible. However, if existing relationships alone were finally valuable and ethically relevant, then a person not in the relevant relationship with an agent, such as a stranger in a foreign land, would seem to lack moral standing relative to her and to be legitimately attacked for selfish gain. If it were always wrong to act in ways that undermine the relevant relationship, then threats, violence, and other forms of force would be categorically impermissible, even when directed against aggressors to protect innocents. Moreover, if one were supposed to maximize the relevant relationships, then it would be permissible to use any means whatsoever, including intentionally harming innocents in severe ways whenever doing so would promote harmony in the long run.

To avoid these implications while retaining a relational approach, I advance a principle according to which individuals have a dignity in virtue of their communal nature, or capacity for harmony, that demands respect. By "communion" or "harmony," I mean the combination of two logically distinct relationships that are often implicit in African characterizations of how to live well.[12] Consider these quotations from another group of philosophers, theologians, and related theorists from Nigeria, Ghana, and South Africa:

> Every member is expected to consider him/herself an integral part of the whole and to play an appropriate role towards achieving the good of all.[13]

> [H]armony is achieved through close and sympathetic social relations within the group.[14]

> The fundamental meaning of community is the sharing of an overall way of life, inspired by the notion of the common good.[15]

> [T]he purpose of our life is community-service and community-belongingness.[16]

> If you asked *ubuntu* [the Nguni catchword for African morality] advocates and philosophers: What principles inform and organise your life? What do you live for? ... the answers would express commitment to the good of the community in which their identities were formed, and a need to experience their lives as bound up in that of their community.[17]

Notice that, in these characterizations of how to commune, or harmonize, two logically distinct relationships are repeatedly mentioned. First, there is considering oneself part of the whole, being close, sharing a way of life, belonging, and experiencing oneself as bound up with others, which I label "identifying with" or "sharing a way of life with" others. Second, there is achieving the good of all, being sympathetic, acting for the common good, serving the community, and being committed to the good of one's society, which is labeled "exhibiting solidarity with" or "caring for" others. Note how they are different ways of relating; one could cooperate with others on projects that are not good for them, and, conversely, one could act in ways that are good for others but do not include participating with them evenhandedly.

For the purposes of this chapter, it will be enough to work with the following representation of communion or harmony shown in Figure 8.1.

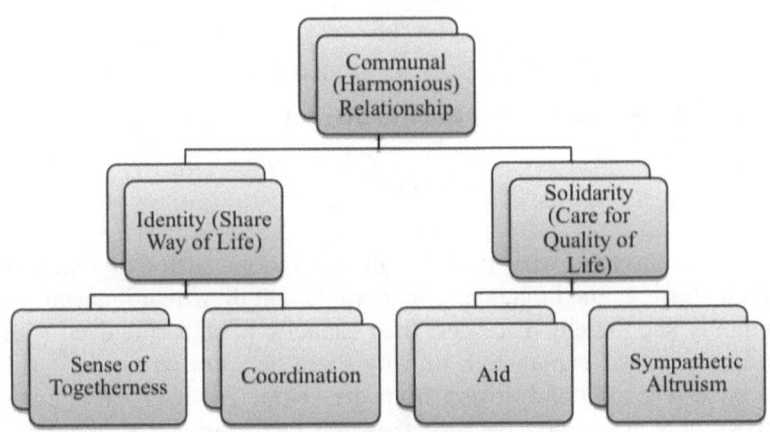

Figure 8.1. Schematic Representation of Harmony

By the ethic advanced here, it is not this communal *relationship* that has a basic moral value, but rather an individual's natural *capacity* for it. Typical human beings, for example, have a dignity insofar as they are in principle *able* to be communed with and to commune. The highest moral status accrues to us, beings that by nature can be both *objects* of a harmonious relationship (i.e., able to be identified with and cared for by others) and *subjects* of it (i.e., able to identify with and care for others).

Turning from moral status to normative theory, I propose that an act is right insofar as it respects others by virtue of their natural capacity to relate harmoniously; otherwise, an act is wrong. Equivalently, an act is wrong if and only if it degrades others who can in principle be party to relationships of identity and solidarity, especially insofar as (roughly) it treats innocent parties in extremely antisocial or discordant ways, with enmity. Discord consists of the opposites of identity and solidarity whereby, instead of togetherness and coordination, there is distance and subordination (together constituting division) and, instead of altruism and aid, there is cruelty and harm (ill will) (see Figure 8.2).

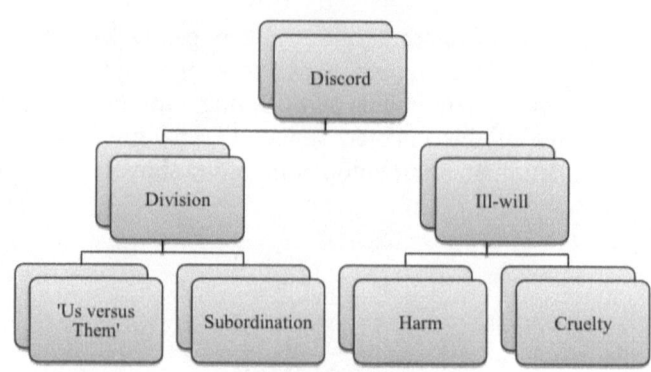

Figure 8.2. Schematic Representation of Discord

From this perspective, what typically makes actions such as lying, promise breaking, abusing, and kidnapping immoral is that they treat innocent parties discordantly and thereby disrespect their capacity to be harmonized with and to harmonize. That explanation of why these acts are wrong is, I submit, prima facie plausible and differs from the characteristically Western ideas that these acts are wrong because they are degradations of autonomy, or failures to maximize well-being in the long run, or forbidden by what parties would agree to in a social contract.

In other work, I have argued that this moral–theoretic interpretation of the sub-Saharan value of communion/harmony entails and well explains a variety of salient practices among indigenous sub-Saharan peoples, ones that have some intuitive moral pull even for those outside the African tradition. For example, the idea that people merit moral consideration in virtue of their capacity for relationships of identity and solidarity makes good sense of the frequent search among African peoples for reconciliation in the face of wrongdoing; if our relational nature is what is important about us, then the priority should be to repair broken relationships.[18] For another example, African peoples are well known for resolving political conflicts by seeking consensus, which is also well explained by a drive to foster a sense of togetherness, to interact on a cooperative basis, and to do what is expected to be good enough for everyone.[19]

In prescribing that we treat with respect persons who have the capacity to be party to communal/harmonious relationships, consequentialism is rejected, and in at least two respects. For one, a person should not aim to promote harmony wherever she can to the maximum degree that she can but, instead, should give priority to those with whom she has already enjoyed a harmonious relationship. Although the relational ethic includes an impartial dimension, according to which everyone with the ability to relate harmoniously has a dignity, it also has a partial dimension, according to which there is extra reason for an agent to harmonize with those already tied to her. The longer and stronger the harmonious relationship, the more reason there is to continue it, even if, from a more neutral perspective, greater harmony could be produced otherwise. This account of partiality is a philosophical reconstruction of the traditional African practice of according priority to blood relations.[20]

For another respect in which the ethic is deontological and not consequentialist, the way in which harmony is promoted matters morally in itself. An agent may not use any means whatsoever to maximize the net amount of harmony in the world. As I explain in the next section, it would normally be wrong to treat innocent parties discordantly, even if a greater long-term harmony would result from treating them that way. In addition, it would often be right to treat guilty parties discordantly, even if doing so would prevent a greater long-term harmony.

DERIVING PRINCIPLES TO GOVERN WARFARE

In the previous section, I advanced a foundational ethic with a sub-Saharan pedigree according to which one must respect others in virtue of their ability to be party to communal or harmonious relationships. Although what is special about us, by this moral theory, is our capacity for harmony, it does not follow that we may never act in opposite, discordant ways. In this section, I explain why respect for the capacity for harmony in fact sometimes justifies discordant behavior, spell out how the ethic's prescription of discord grounds normative principles to regulate military and related forms of conflict, and illustrate the principles by applying them to two cases of social upheaval in sub-Saharan Africa. It is only in the following sections that I show how their implications differ from recent statements by others working in the African tradition and by those who hold more characteristically Western perspectives.

Wrong acts by the present ethic are those failing to treat people as special in virtue of their capacity for harmonious relationships. Often, then, indifference and isolation are immoral while worse are discordant actions involving subordination consistent with an "us versus them" attitude and harm consistent with a selfish motivation. However, it does *not* follow that discordant actions are *always* wrong. They are instead wrong only when they fail to express respect for the dignity of people's communal nature, which they need not do.

It is one thing to act discordantly toward someone who has not herself acted that way. If someone has not initially acted in a discordant way and instead has related harmoniously with others (who themselves have not been discordant, let us suppose), then she counts as "innocent" and is liable for only harmonious treatment. Were one to treat an innocent person in a severely discordant way, most often one thereby would be violating her human rights, even if in the long run more harmony would be fostered in society. What killing, torture, slavery, rape, human trafficking, apartheid, and other gross infringements of civil liberties and equal opportunities arguably have in common is that they are instances of substantial discord directed to those who have not acted this way themselves, thereby denigrating their special capacity to be party to relationships of identity and solidarity.

Concretely, one who engages in such practices treats a person who has herself been harmonious with great discord (enmity) and does so along all four major dimensions of it. The actor treats the other as separate and inferior, instead of in ways that express a sense of togetherness. He undermines the other's ends, as opposed to engaging in mutually supportive projects with her. He harms the other for his own sake or for an ideology, as opposed to doing what is likely to make her better off in either welfarist or perfectionist terms. Finally, he acts in ways that evince negative attitudes toward the other's good, rather than acting out of a sympathetic reaction to it. By the African ethic advanced here, acting discordantly in respect of an innocent party is *pro tanto* degrading and wrongful, even if one would promote more long-term harmony by doing so. This account of what constitutes a human rights violation plausibly rivals utilitarian and Kantian rationales.

However, severe discord can be justified at least when it is essential to rebut another's initial and, hence, wrongful discord.[21] Consider an analogy with Kantianism. If the point of infringing a person's wrongful employment of autonomy is to sustain another's autonomy, then there need not be degradation of autonomy nor any treatment of it merely as a means or otherwise as less than a superlative final value. Similar remarks apply to harmony: if the only way to rebut disrespectful treatment of a person's harmonious nature in the form of discord is to use discord, then harmony is not necessarily degraded.

Suppose that someone has initially acted in a discordant manner (including threatening to subordinate and harm or having authorized others to do so) and therefore counts as "guilty" or an "aggressor" in respect of an innocent party. Suppose further that only the use of discord would rebut his discord, by which I mean that only subordination and harm of him would serve functions such as incapacitating him from subordinating or harming his victim, deterring him from doing so, getting him to compensate his victims, or reforming his character so that he would not act similarly again. In that event, treating him with comparable discord would not degrade his capacity for harmony, which he has wrongfully failed to employ.

Furthermore, directing discord against a discordant party to protect or compensate his victims is well understood as expressing respect for them. Indeed, if one could, at little cost to oneself, direct discord against an aggressor and thereby protect innocents from or compensate them for severe discord, respect would seem to obligate one to do so. By the respect-based African ethic, the innocent should be protected from or compensated for severe discord even if more harmony would be promoted in the long run by not doing so. For example, if one had to gravely wound three aggressors seeking to abuse an innocent woman, which would mean somewhat less long-term harmony in the world upon considering the former's families, one should nonetheless do so to save the latter; otherwise, one would be failing to treat her as having dignity, viewing her interests as relevant only insofar as they promote good outcomes.

Putting these ideas together, I propose the following principles to regulate force that is large (e.g., loss of life, limb, or mind at both the individual and collective levels). First, substantial discord directed toward a party is justified if it is the least amount necessary and likely to rebut a comparable initial discord on his part; equivalently, one may significantly subordinate or harm another if that is essential and expected to prevent or compensate for a similar or greater degree of subordination and harm that he initiated.[22] While that principle governs how to treat aggressors, this second one deals with innocents: if a person has not acted in a substantially discordant way or been responsible for such,[23] she is not liable to be treated in a substantially discordant way; equivalently, it is a *pro tanto* grave wrong to subordinate or harm another person significantly if she has not herself acted similarly, been responsible for others doing so, and the like.[24]

The reader will notice that the first principle posits merely sufficient conditions for the use of compulsion, violence, and threats of such. The reason I do not consider them to be necessary conditions is that I believe that severe punishment of the guilty can be justified but not merely on grounds of defensive force. Although I maintain that punishment should do some good, in the form of labor that serves to compensate victims and reform offenders, I deny that punishment has to be necessary to bring about these goods in order to be justified.[25] Instead, as long as punishment is sufficient to pay back victims and rehabilitate those who are guilty, it is justified not merely as one way to bring those conditions about but also for expressing that an offender acted in wrongful ways abjured by the political community as well as that a victim should have been treated otherwise.

Although punishment can be justified even when it is unnecessary to produce desirable outcomes, war is different. The degree of mayhem that accompanies military conflict, and especially the grave risks to nondiscordant parties (but also the risks of disproportionately great subordination of and harm to certain aggressors), means the substantial discord of that nature must be necessary, not merely sufficient, to bring about desirable outcomes.

Beyond following from a prima facie plausible moral theory with an African pedigree, these principles governing deadly (or otherwise large) force account for intuitive reactions to some globally well-known anti- and postcolonial struggles in the sub-Saharan region. As an example, they make sense of the way the rebellion against apartheid was on the whole justly conducted by Nelson Mandela and much of the African National Congress (ANC).[26] By these principles, military force, such as sabotage and violence, directed against those responsible for apartheid was justified as necessary and likely to overcome it, but it was unjustified when targeting those not responsible for it. This ethical analysis coheres well with Mandela's decisions to fight the apartheid regime with violence as well as his explicit statements about them.

First, the white South African government was of course the one that was initially discordant toward black people. Starting in earnest with the Natives Land Act of 1913, which declared the majority of land to belong to the white population, and intensifying with apartheid statutes and the prohibition of political gatherings, the government was the one to distance itself from people it considered not white, to subordinate them, knowingly harm them, and act out of indifference to their well-being. "If there was not the violence of apartheid, there never would have been violence from our side."[27]

Second, Mandela sought to use violence against government and more generally political targets (i.e., against those most responsible for the oppression of blacks). Now, in practice, the ANC sometimes did target civilians, which the Truth and Reconciliation Commission hearings made clear. And Mandela himself approved of the targeting of infrastructure, such as electric power stations[28] as well as telephone lines and transportation links.[29] However, as far as I can tell, Mandela never deemed it permissible to use violence against those who were not initially being unjust or were not particularly responsible for injustice. He instead tends to speak of violence being properly used against "the state"[30] or "government installations, particularly those connected with the policy of apartheid and race discrimination."[31] In *Long Walk to Freedom* Mandela recounts this about the decision to found Spear of the Nation (*uMkhonto weSizwe*, abbreviated "MK"), the military wing of the ANC: "Violence would begin whether we initiated it or not. Would it not be better to guide this violence ourselves, according to principles where we saved lives by attacking symbols of oppression, and not people?"[32]

Third, Mandela had used nonviolent forms of struggle against apartheid for about fifteen years, and the ANC and black resistance movements generally had used nonviolent responses for several decades. However, they had been ineffective, and Mandela often emphasized the point that he and the ANC deemed violence to be permissible only as a last resort. Most famously, consider his statement at the famous Rivonia Trial when he said, for just one short line, "It was only when all else had failed, when all channels of peaceful protest had been barred to us, that the decision was made to embark on violent forms of political struggle."[33] He reiterated this point, about the necessity of violence to rebut violence, in the speech in which he rejected the government's offer to release him from prison in exchange for a renunciation of violence on his part[34] and continued to make it repeatedly in later years.[35]

Fourth, and finally, Mandela sought to use the least force necessary to accomplish his aim of achieving freedom and equality for all those in South Africa. In *Long Walk to Freedom* he says:

> Our intention was to begin with what was least violent to individuals but most damaging to the state. . . . It made sense to begin with the form of violence that inflicted the least harm against individuals: sabotage. . . . Strict instructions were given to members of MK that we would countenance no loss of life. But if sabotage did not produce the results we wanted, we were prepared to move onto the next stage.[36]

All these elements of Mandela's advocacy of violence accord with the principles above.

The Afro-communal principles justify the use of violence against the apartheid regime as well as the guerrilla war conducted against the colonial Rhodesian government in the 1970s (although not insofar as it involved the targeting of civilians at department stores and on airplanes). In contrast, they appear to entail that it was unjustified for Robert Mugabe's government in post-Rhodesia Zimbabwe to confiscate land from white farmers in 2000, which involved violence, coercion, and physical removal. Despite the transition to a more democratic government and to black rule in Zimbabwe in 1980, land reform had not been well effected, leaving much arable farmland in the hands of white descendants of those who had not acquired it legitimately. In the year 2000, the Zimbabwean government supported guerrilla war veterans in their ejection of white people from these commercial farms and without compensation. Although it was not outright warfare, there was substantial discord, including the use of deadly force, employed to redistribute the farms.

It is fair to have viewed many of the white farmers not to have been innocent; they were retaining land that they should have shared with the black population. However, it does not follow that force was justified as a way to effect land reform for the glaring reason that the means taken were foreseeably counterproductive in respect of the legitimate end. That is, it was unlikely that the lives of many victims of colonialism would have been improved as a result of "fast-track" or "en masse" land reform; in fact, it made (and was likely to have made) many of their lives worse. It is well known that a number of the farms were allocated to political elites and those connected to them and not so much to the common black person. In addition, upon land being redistributed, often the new holders of it lacked the knowledge and capital needed to farm, which meant a drastic drop in production and consequent widespread hunger in Zimbabwe. Furthermore, there was predictable capital flight, to the point of creating grotesque hyperinflation, reported rates of 90 percent unemployment, and a much greater difficulty of purchasing essential goods.[37] According to one estimate, about a decade after the land confiscations, the private sector was "operating at 10 percent of its former capacity" and about fifteen years later "Zimbabwe's per capita GDP is $600, the third lowest in the world."[38]

Instead of reducing the harmful effects of colonial land dispossession, the Zimbabwean approach to land reform foreseeably caused more harm, particularly to the black population, which was innocent. Note that, even if things were to get better in Zimbabwe after twenty or twenty-five years, that would mean little to those who suffered most directly from colonialism; they would not have been compensated (beyond knowing their descendants might come out well), instead having lived worse lives for those decades (and then many soon to die given their age).[39] The Afro-communal approach entails that, in principle, discord could have justifiably been used to effect land reform in Zimbabwe but not of a sort that was likely not merely to fail to help but also to harm seriously innocent parties to such a great extent.

CONTRASTS WITH OTHER AFRICAN VIEWS

I now reveal more about what the Afro-communal principles entail in respect of why and when to engage in military conflict by showing how they constitute sensible alternatives to views suggested lately by others working in the African tradition. Some thinkers seem to maintain that African norms support the view that war may be justly fought to bring about certain goods, such as welfare or virtue, whereas my favored principles imply that only rebutting certain "bads" can justify war. Others appear to contend that a good justification for going to war is the need to protect one's country or people, regardless of how it or the other party being attacked has behaved, but I argue that partial considerations plausibly play a different role when thinking about whether to go to war.

Above, I sometimes spoke about severe discord being justified only if certain "desirable outcomes" were forthcoming, by which I meant, more carefully, ones such as the prevention of a comparable discord or compensation for it. Such an approach to just cause is on the face of it attractive for clearly entailing that it is wrong to go to war to purify the race, uphold the glory of the king, spread Christian piety, obtain booty, or hold onto political power. One way to put this point is that the bad of military conflict can be justified only by rebutting a comparable bad, not to promote a (perceived) good.

Some African thinkers have implicitly questioned this approach, however, and are naturally read as suggesting that armed struggle can be justified as a means to achieve the end of certain intrinsically desirable states, not merely the end of avoiding certain undesirable ones. For example, one thinker appeals to the southern African ethic of ubuntu to aver that violence can be justified as a means to "promote the just advancement of the welfare of societies"[40] or so that people "can experience personhood,"[41] where talk of "personhood" in the African tradition signifies virtue or human excellence (often contrasted with an animal existence). Another thinker who appeals to ubuntu in respect of war maintains that "acts of violence can be justified if the outcome is one that leads to social harmony."[42]

However, I submit that violence, at least in the form of military conflict, cannot be justified for the sake of bringing about goods such as well-being and harmony, and probably not any good at all. I agree it can be permissible to impose minor to moderate burdens on innocent parties to foster benefits and not merely to remove other burdens. For example, it is justified for the state to institute a scheme of threatening drivers for not keeping left so as to improve coordination or to tax the superrich to foster the arts for the public. What I deny is that the burdens placed on innocents may (usually) be large, even if the expected benefits from doing so would be large. That is, it is (normally) wrong to threaten the life, limb, or mind of those who have done no wrong to bestow pure goods (i.e., benefits beyond the removal of burdens) onto them or others.[43] It would intuitively be wrong for political leaders to go to war so that the research and development sectors would invent new technologies likely to have consumer gadget spin-offs, or for the sake of developing the virtues of courage and determination in their people, or to prompt citizens to enjoy a sense of togetherness and to cooperate in their efforts against a perceived common enemy.

Although I do not believe that the goods of welfare, personhood (virtue), or even harmony can be just causes for war, their disvaluable antipodes can. For instance, if a country is being discordant or causing another one woe, say, by blocking a vital river that they had shared for centuries, that could justifiably ground war as essential to regain access to water.[44]

A second salient respect in which my favored principles differ from the views of other Africanists concerns the status of one's country. As indicated above, African morality has characteristically included a partial dimension, prescribing favoritism to one's people. Some have suggested that this means taking a "My country, right or wrong" approach to military force. For example, speaking of indigenous sub-Saharan ethics, Godwin Sogolo notes that it could include a code that

> requires members of the group to abstain from violence in relation with fellow members without necessarily subjecting them to such requirements in their relation with non-members of the group. . . . [T]he ability of an individual to lie, to trick or even to kill a non-member of his group may carry high "moral" approval.[45]

If the lives of outsiders do not count, then war will often be justified in respect of them, even if they have not been discordant. Sogolo does not quite defend this extremely partial approach as appropriate, but he does work to show that it conceptually counts as a "moral" perspective and to explain its adoption among some African peoples.[46]

More clearly approving of an extreme partialism are Francis Kasoma's remarks: "The basis of morality in African society is the fulfilment of obligations to kins-people, both living and dead. . . . What strengthens the family, the clan and the tribe or ethnic group is generally morally good."[47] Taken at face value, this principle appears to warrant treating out-group members merely as a means to the strengthening of one's in-group.

Sogolo and Kasoma are largely appealing to anthropological, historical, and sociological data about what certain indigenous Africans believed and how they acted. I believe that counterevidence is available, e.g., many African peoples showed great hospitality when visitors would arrive at their village,[48] and many also ascribed a dignity to all persons as children of God or members of a common human family.[49] However, a thorough empirical reckoning is beside the point. I am seeking to provide a philosophically attractive normative ethic, and so I submit that a better interpretation of the African moral tradition is one that recognizes the superlative final value of characteristic human persons and makes guilt or innocence central to determining whether violence is justified in respect of them.

The Afro-communal principles normally forbid inflicting severe discord on innocent parties who may be strangers if they are not being discordant. So, in my view, partiality is not sufficient to warrant attacking innocents.[50] However, partiality can ground a kind of reason for a country to go to war, namely, to attack a guilty party that has attacked those in relation to that country. Respecting people in virtue of the ability to relate communally/harmoniously means that a particular agent has extra reason to fight in defense of an innocent party with whom the agent has so related. The fact that two countries have identified with each other and exhibited solidarity with each other to a substantial degree in the past provides some moral reason for them to help each other that is missing in the case of countries without such ties. Friends have extra moral reason to help friends in need.

So, when it comes to the question of *who* has a just cause for war, partial considerations answer it to some extent: *this country has additional reason to help the (innocent) one with which it has communed*, where such communion need not have taken the form of a formal pact, such as the North Atlantic Treaty Organization (NATO). Considerations of *which agents* have a just cause to fight is underexplored in just war theory; the focus has nearly exclusively been on the content of the just cause. The African philosophical tradition that prizes communal relating helps to open up this dimension of thinking about justice.[51] Some moral reasons for action, including going to war, are agent relative and, specifically, are a function of prior relationships between agents that need not include having made a promise.

Furthermore, with respect to the question of *why* one party ought to fight a war, part of the answer can sometimes be that this country ought to help defend that one (from an unjust attack) *because they have communed*. It can be permissible for Country A to be severely discordant in respect of Country B because B was initially severely discordant in respect of Country C, broadly in the manner of the doctrine of the responsibility to protect (R2P[52]). However, the fact that A has identified with and exhibited solidarity toward C and vice versa in the past provides the former additional *pro tanto* reason to do now what it is permitted to do to B. One consideration that should move a political leader to put the lives of her innocent soldiers in harm's way when not necessary for defense of her own country is the fact of a communal bond with another country.[53]

In sum, the way that relationality is interpreted here does not mean that it can be just, on grounds of communion, for one country to attack innocents to foster harmony locally or otherwise support one's people, as is suggested by the remarks of some Africanists. Instead, communion can, plausibly, ground some additional moral reason for one country to fend off an unjust attack against another with which it has communed.

CONTRASTS WITH WESTERN VIEWS

Whereas the previous section contrasted my Afro-communal approach to armed conflict with other readings of African norms and presented some reason to favor it, this section does something similar in respect of more Western perspectives. Here, I compare and contrast my approach with those who think of just cause in terms of rebutting aggression, effecting punishment, or protecting human rights, at least the first and third of which are central to recent Euro-American thought and international law more broadly.

Conceiving of the just cause for war in terms of preventing or compensating severe discord directed against innocent parties has some obvious similarities with the standard conception of it in the postwar era in terms of fending off aggression. Aggression has usually been taken to include mere encroachment into a state's territory,[54] whereas substantial discord, as roughly the combination of severe subordination and harm, probably has a different implication. Merely flying or sailing into a state's territory, or even taking over some portion of it, such as the Falkland Islands, need not constitute such discord and so would not be a good enough reason to start war, *contra* Thomas Hurka.[55] Maintaining the integrity of a state's territory is not covariant with rebutting severe discord. The point is not merely that the harms or, more broadly, disadvantages of engaging in warfare to reclaim the Falkland Islands in this particular case outweighed the good (or reduction of other bad) to be achieved by doing so, but rather that this good of merely reclaiming territory and sheep was not the sort of thing that could in principle justify the bad of war. It is not merely the risks to innocent parties that this good fails to justify but even the killing of guilty soldiers.[56]

Conversely, aggression is not usually understood to include recklessly or negligently cutting off another country's major water supply.[57] Aggression is normally construed as some kind of use of military force against a state, even if not a strike against it (as in using the navy to impose an economic blockade). However, the Afro-communal approach entails that, say, building a dam on a vital river without any military engagement could be a just cause for war. The amount of harm we can imagine that the dam would likely cause to a country's people would be great enough to justify in principle an armed response, for instance, bombing the dam or threatening deadly force against those responsible for its construction.

Punishment has been another salient just cause for war in Western thought. Some laypeople might think in terms of retribution, giving a country the suffering it deserves because it deserves it. However, my interpretation of African morality (and any influential reading of it) eschews imposing harm in the absence of any expectation of some kind of desirable outcome; protection of the innocent and reconciliation with the guilty are much more prominent themes in sub-Saharan philosophical reflection on criminal justice. Some other philosophers working in the African tradition have maintained that, after a war, reconciliation should be the aim, not the retributive infliction of suffering for its own sake.[58] For a classic example of this orientation, consider the tale of a nineteenth-century southern African military leader, King Moshoeshoe I, who, upon having successfully repelled an unjust attack, sent the losing party cattle as a present.[59]

Besides not having imposed retribution on the defeated soldiers for their wrongful attack, the king also did not seek to make an example of them. However, a salient view these days among Western philosophers is that general deterrence, roughly punishing some to scare off others, is one just cause for war. The Afro-communal approach to permissible warfare, and to deadly force and violence more generally, allows substantial discord to be directed against the initially discordant to rebut *their* substantial discord. Just causes for military conflict include preventing serious degrees of subordination and harm and compensating the victims of it when it has already been effected. This position contrasts with some influential Anglo-American just war theorists who contend that it can be justified to direct deadly force against aggressors to instill fear into *others* so that they will not engage in aggression, with Jeff McMahan being a clear proponent.[60]

For a more qualified instance of this view, Hurka has argued that, although general deterrence is not in itself sufficient to justify going to war in the first place, if a party has gone to war for some other, justifiable reason, such as rebutting aggression, then it may attack aggressors to advance the further aim of deterring others from aggressing against it.[61] Sometimes, this point is put in terms of unconditional versus conditional ends or justifying versus attendant aims. The end of general deterrence, for Hurka, is not sufficient on its own to justify using the means of war, but, upon the means of war having been rightly employed for the sake of some other (unconditional or justifying) end, it may be additionally used to advance the former (conditional or attendant) one of general deterrence.

Despite the qualification,[62] I maintain that respect for people's capacity to commune probably forbids such an approach. To see this, consider first some of this approach's counterintuitive implications. If a thief wrongfully enters my house and the only way to get him to leave and without taking my things is to use a certain degree of force, I may do so. However, it would intuitively be wrongful (not merely illegal in all jurisdictions I am familiar with in North America, Europe, and South Africa) to haul him out into the street and give him an additional beating intended to scare off other, potential thieves. The logic of defensive force allows me to get him out of my house and to prevent any unjust takings and probably to instill fear *in him* with an eye to preventing future housebreaking on his part ("special deterrence") but does not permit additional force beyond those aims, such as instilling fear in others.

For another counterexample, consider why many are inclined to think that deadly force can often be permissible but that the death penalty is not (or only rarely is). The best explanation of the difference is something to the effect that one may kill a person to prevent comparable wrongdoing of which he is a part but not to prevent wrongdoing of which he is not a part. Otherwise, the death penalty would be justified upon showing that it generally deters. Of course, some are inclined to bite the bullet on this score,[63] but many are not.

Furthermore, other acts that appear impermissible would be permissible, by analogy, with general deterrence. For example, if force against aggressors may be used to stop them *and* deter others from using force, then it would likely be justifiable to kill a would-be killer for the state to harvest his organs and thereby save the lives of innocents he has not threatened. Perhaps someone has shot a person in the liver, and the latter needs the former's liver to survive. While I accept that there is real moral reason to take a wrongful shooter's liver if truly necessary to save the life of his victim, it would not be justifiable, I think, to take the shooter's organs for the purpose of saving the lives of those shot (or otherwise needed) by others who were not part of his criminal plan.

In sum, to rule out counterintuitive practices, such as public thrashings of subdued thieves, the death penalty for convicted murderers, and the harvesting of organs of attempted killers, a principle governing violence probably has to forbid its use for purposes of general deterrence (and similar public goods), even if the violence were directed against only the guilty. Furthermore, consider the plausible rationale for *why* it would be wrong to direct violence against the guilty for the sake of general deterrence: one is not liable (and usually should not be held responsible) for the misdeeds of others. There is no disrespect in using substantial force or other discord if necessary to get a wrongdoer to stop his discordance or to compensate his victims for it (or probably to get him to reform or be fearful of committing such wrongs in the future). However, I, at least, intuit a kind of disrespectful treatment when substantial force is used against a wrongdoer for some purpose other than getting him to "clean up his own mess." The Afro-communal principle is consistent with, indeed, partially motivated by this broad interpretation of respect for persons.[64]

For a third and final common suggestion from the contemporary Western, and particularly Anglo-American, literature on just cause, consider the view that war is justified only as a way to protect certain human rights, a view advanced by, among others, David Luban[65] and Larry May.[66] This view has a number of advantages relative to the others discussed in this section. It enables one to maintain the following claims, which are attractive in the light of prior analysis in this chapter. A just cause for war need not involve a state or at least not its territory but instead can be a function of how people considered apart from being citizens have been (or would be) wrongfully harmed. A just cause for war could include obstructing a waterway vital to satisfy a human right to life. Retribution is never a just cause for war because by definition it does not essentially involve aiming to realize any state of affairs besides proportionate suffering. Being violent toward an aggressor for the sake of general deterrence might count as a violation of that person's rights.

There is substantial overlap between the Afro-communal principles advanced here and a human rights approach. Recall the suggestion above that human rights violations are often well construed as forms of severe discord directed toward innocent parties; they are characteristically instances of substantial subordination and harm inflicted on those who have not acted in these ways. What difference, then, does the Afro-communal approach make relative to this view?

Here, I discuss two respects in which a characteristically African perspective on violence differs from a standard human rights approach in the West.[67]

First off, consider that the usual human rights invoked when thinking about what would justify military conflict are what one might call "structural" or "basic" ones. By this I have in mind that they are rights that make lots of other rights possible. So, for example, the right to life, on which arguably all other rights depend, justifies war, if any right does. Similarly, the right to self-governance is essential for the realization of a host of other rights that would come in the wake of that ability to make decisions in a certain territory, and its violation is routinely invoked as a justification for warfare. I accept that the violations of these rights would constitute severe discord but submit that the latter is not exhausted by the former.

In particular, some of those in the African tradition have emphasized the idea that one justification for violence is a need to protect people's cultures.[68] Most prominent has been Amilcar Cabral, an intellectual and revolutionary who had fought against the Portuguese colonial presence in Guinea-Bissau. When it comes to using violence against colonial governments, Cabral's view is usefully summed up this way: "[T]he concept of national liberation was to be defined not so much as the right of a people to rule itself, but as the right of a people to regain its own history."[69] Although there are occasions in Cabral's writings where he deems the reinvigoration of an oppressed people's cultures to be a particularly useful tool to combat colonialism, there are also clear passages where he indicates that armed struggle against colonialism is justified, if necessary, as a way to protect indigenous cultures for their own sake.[70] Just consider section headings such as National Liberation, an Act of Culture[71] and Armed Struggle, an Instrument for Unification and Cultural Progress.[72] From this standpoint, the need to defend a culture can warrant a kind of violence that a desire to retain sheep on an island cannot.

I think Cabral's perspective would have broad resonance among African thinkers, particularly in the light of the way that they have often described colonialism's effects on indigenous cultures. For just a few examples, apartheid in South Africa and colonialism on the rest of the continent have been labeled forms of "spiritual genocide,"[73] "cultural violence,"[74] and "epistemicide."[75]

On the interpretation here, the idea is not that *enriching* a culture could justify violence; the claim is not that terror bombing is permissible when essential and likely to produce artworks, such as Picasso's *Guernica*. Instead, the suggestion is that violence can sometimes be justified as necessary to rebut discordant actions that would gravely *impair* culture. For a recent illustration, consider the attack in Mali on the Timbuktu Manuscripts. Did anyone bat an eyelash at the thought that military force would have been justified if it were the only way to protect them from destruction by Islamic extremists?

Now, some would deny that there is a human right to culture, although the idea is of course more commonly accepted these days. If it is a human right, however, it is not a basic one, not one responsible for the realization of many other human rights. In this respect, therefore, the Afro-communal principles support a rationale for war that differs from a prominent Western appeal to human rights. Specifically, they justify a violent response necessary and expected to rebut at least the intentional suppression of people's culture because that would consist of severe discord. One central way to identify with others or to share a way of life with them is to participate in a common culture. Where people have freely adopted common ways of speaking, interpreting the world, making art, and celebrating meaningful events to the point of thinking "This is who we are," trying to destroy those lifestyles counts as truly discordant; it is not merely the undermining of political self-rule that can impair a shared way of life.

Here is a second interesting respect in which the Afro-communal approach to just cause probably differs from a standard Western human rights approach. By the latter, the end for which the means of war is alone justified is a function of helping victims. It is in the name of those whose human rights are being (or would be) violated that war is in principle permissible. However, in the African tradition one also encounters the fascinating idea that war can be justified, at least in part, on the ground that it would help the aggressors.

Such an approach is hinted at when Desmond Tutu points out that apartheid degraded not merely black people but also the white people who of course in one respect benefited from it. "The humanity of the perpetrator of apartheid's atrocities was caught up and bound up in that of his victim whether he liked it or not. In the process of dehumanising another, in inflicting untold harm and suffering, the perpetrator was inexorably being dehumanised as well."[76] The logic of this position, in which one's humanness or virtue is a function of whether he has communed with others, suggests that one reason to fight back against apartheid was for the sake of the humanness of the oppressor.

Such a rationale for violence is more explicit in Kenneth Kaunda's reflections on anticolonial armed struggles in Africa. Kaunda fought against British colonialism in Zambia and wrote a book about why he considers use of violence justifiable in having done so and more generally for the purpose of overthrowing European domination in the sub-Saharan region. The book includes this perspective:

> Now, it is not hard to show that liberating the oppressed by the use of force is an act of love, but can our minds grasp the unthinkable idea that the oppressors also need to be re-humanized possibly by the use of force which destroys their claim to be superhuman? . . . If it is right to use force on behalf of the oppressed to give them back their humanity, why is it wrong to use force against the oppressor to restore him to true humanity also and make him capable of love?[77]

In addition to posing these rhetorical questions, elsewhere in the same text, Kaunda remarks, "[S]omeone has got to save these whites in Southern Africa from themselves."[78]

The suggestion is not that violence could be justified merely to produce more virtue in people, say, by making them more courageous. That position, focusing on promoting a pure benefit, I rejected above. Instead, the more plausible idea is that violence can be justified to reduce people's vice manifested by having been severely discordant in respect of innocents. Implicit in the concept of rebutting discord is the idea that one way to do so would be to reform the bad character of the discordant. The thought that military conflict might be justified not merely to protect victims but also to stop aggressors from living like animals has not been salient in Western just war theory but is a striking feature of the relational African normative thought that grounds the present account of just cause.

CONCLUSION: SOME NEXT STAGES OF REFLECTION

In this chapter I have argued that a certain interpretation of the moral significance of communal or harmonious relationship provides a novel and promising African foundation for thinking about the just causes of war, one that merits being weighed up against competitors in both the African and Western traditions. I close this chapter by briefly mentioning some topics pertaining to just war theory that remain underexplored in the light of characteristically sub-Saharan values and norms[79] and by suggesting some strategies to explore in respect of them.

Most glaring and in need of attention is the absence of any real literature on *jus in bello*, how to conduct a war. Central to Western discussions of this matter are how to understand the nature of discrimination, that is, which parties are legitimate targets, as well as what a proportionate use of force is, say, what counts as a "good" to be weighed up against the "bad" of specific military options. There is nothing in the African philosophical tradition that is systematic on these matters, and I can mention only the suggestion that war should be conducted in ways that do not undermine the prospect of reconciliation afterward.[80]

This principle is, furthermore, prima facie dubious, at least considered as the "main standard" when evaluating acts of war,[81] because it is likely that judgments about the prospects of reconciliation are tracking more basic judgments about, say, using the least force necessary and not targeting innocents. That is, the best explanation of why reconciliation would be hindered by certain uses of violence is that parties to the conflict have prior, independent views about how force ought to be employed, where it is these that have normative force. For example, deeming terror bombing to be wrong would be why those who have been terror bombed would be disinclined to reconcile with terror bombers.

I do, however, believe that Afro-communalism or relational considerations more broadly can plausibly figure into thinking about *jus in bello*. Here are two lines that merit exploration. Consider innocent threats, those who are faultless for posing a serious risk of death to oneself and must be killed to save one's life, and innocent shields, those who are faultless for protecting aggressors and must be inflicted with deadly force to protect one's life. Much contemporary Anglo-American theorizing about such cases is absolutist in the sense of contending that it is either always permissible or always impermissible to kill innocent threats or shields in self-defense. In contrast, it might be that considerations of communal relationship entail that large differences in the degrees to which innocents have communed or will commune can be a way to "break the tie" between them, sometimes, providing reason to kill to save oneself and, sometimes, not. Perhaps it would be wrong for the proverbial hermit to kill an innocent threat with substantial ties to family and friends if that person would live if he did not. Such an approach makes sense of why people tend to mention that they have families when pleading not to be killed and why in societies facing extreme scarcity, often those who would soon die anyway, ending their relationships, make the tough decision to exit.

Another way in which the relationality characteristic of African normativity might be revealing when it comes to *jus in bello* concerns whom to save in respect of other parties, excluding oneself. Suppose that in the middle of a war, an unjust aggressor, W, began to attack two different innocent countries, X and Y, and that a fourth country, Z, could help only one of these two. Communal factors might entail that Z would have some extra (but not necessarily conclusive) moral reason to help X fend off attack if, and because, Z and X had communed in the past while Z and Y had not.

Finally, it is well worth exploring further the ideas that *jus post bellum* should be focused on reconciliation rather than retribution and what that might involve. Tutu famously contrasts reconciliation with punishment of any sort, maintaining that it instead prescribes forgiveness.[82] Such an approach is admittedly suggested by the inspiring actions of King Moshoeshoe I, mentioned above. Here, however, is another angle, which appeals to the idea of "restorative sanctions"[83] or "reconciliatory sentencing."[84] By this approach, part of what it means to reconcile is for offenders to express remorse by taking on burdens likely to compensate their victims or a state making them take on such burdens if they will not do so willingly. Such penalties could involve, say, clearing unexploded ordnance, repairing infrastructure, or working with one's hands on a farm. Instead of forgoing hard treatment altogether or imposing it in the manner of "an eye for an eye," this approach would impose hard treatment on those responsible for serious wrongdoing during war as a way to disavow the wrongdoing productively, by improving victims' quality of life. Better this for war criminals than either getting off scot-free or doing nothing in prison, so one might suggest.

The relational considerations mentioned in this conclusion can be intuitively appreciated by those beyond the African philosophical tradition. However, it is the African one, at least relative to the Western, in which considerations of communion and harmony have been salient and particularly promise to make good theoretical sense of them.[85]

BIBLIOGRAPHY

Aja, Egbeke. "Crime and Punishment: An Indigenous African Experience." *Journal of Value Inquiry* 31, no. 3 (1997): 353–68.

Appiah, Anthony. "Ethical Systems, African." *Routledge Encyclopedia of Philosophy*. Accessed May 31, 2019. https://www.rep.routledge.com/articles/thematic/ethical-systems-african/v-1.

Baker, Deane-Peter. "Rebellion and African Ethics." *Journal of Military Ethics* 15, no. 4 (2016): 288–98.

Balogun, Oladele Abiodun. "A Philosophical Defence of Punishment in Traditional African Legal Culture." *Journal of Pan African Studies* 3, no. 3 (2009): 43–54.

Bujo, Bénézet. "Differentiations in African Ethics." In *The Blackwell Companion to Religious Ethics*, edited by William Schweiker, 423–37. Malden, MA: Blackwell, 2005.

Cabral, Amilcar. "National Liberation and Culture." In *Unity and Struggle: Speeches and Writings*, edited by PAIGC, translated by Michael Wolfers, 138–54. New York: Monthly Review Press, 1979.

Cordeiro-Rodrigues, Luís. "African Views of Just War in Mandela and Cabral." *Journal of Speculative Philosophy* 32, no. 4 (2018): 657–73.

———. "Towards a Tutuist Ethics of War: Ubuntu, Forgiveness and Reconciliation." *Politikon* 45, no. 3 (2018): 426–35.

Chasi, Colin. "Tutuist Ubuntu and Just War." *Politikon* 45, no. 2 (2017): 232–44.

———. "Provisional Notes on Ubuntu for Journalists Covering War." *International Communication Gazette* 78, no. 8 (2016): 802–17.

———. "Ubuntu and Freedom of Expression: Considering Children and Broadcast News Violence in a Violent Society." *Journal of Media Ethics* 30, no. 2 (2015): 91–108.

Farrell, Daniel. "Capital Punishment and Societal Self-Defense." In *Philosophy and Its Public Role*, edited by William Aiken and John Haldane, 241–56. Charlottesville, VA: Imprint Academic, 2004.

Gathogo, Julius. "African Philosophy as Expressed in the Concepts of Hospitality and Ubuntu." *Journal of Theology for Southern Africa* 130, no. 1 (2008): 39–53.

Gbadegesin, Segun. *African Philosophy*. New York: Peter Lang, 1991.

Government of the Republic of Colombia and the Revolutionary Armed Forces of Colombia—People's Army. "Final Agreement to End the Armed Conflict and Build a Stable and Lasting Peace." Published November 24, 2016. Accessed May 31, 2019. http://especiales.presidencia.gov.co/Documents/20170620-dejacion-armas/acuerdos/acuerdo-final-ingles.pdf.

Gyekye, Kwame. "African Ethics." Stanford Encyclopedia of Philosophy. Published September 9, 2010. Accessed May 31, 2019. http://plato.stanford.edu/entries/african-ethics/.

———. *Beyond Cultures*. Washington, DC: The Council for Research in Values and Philosophy, 2004.

Hill, Thomas, Jr. *Virtue, Rules, and Justice*. Oxford: Oxford University Press, 2012.

Hobbes, Michael. "How Did Zimbabwe Become So Poor—and Yet So Expensive?" *The New Republic*. Published January 5, 2014. Accessed May 31, 2019. https://newrepublic.com/article/115925/zimbabwe-prices-why-are-they-high-new-york-citys.

Holland, Heidi. *Dinner with Mugabe: The Untold Story of a Freedom Fighter Who Became a Tyrant.* Johannesburg: Penguin Books, 2008.

Hurka, Thomas. "Liability and Just Cause." *Ethics and International Affairs* 21, no. 2 (2007): 199–218.

———. "Proportionality and Necessity." In *War: Essays in Political Philosophy*, edited by Larry May, 127–44. New York: Cambridge University Press, 2008.

Iroegbu, Pantaleon. "Beginning, Purpose and End of Life." In *Kpim of Morality Ethics*, edited by Pantaleon Iroegbu and Anthony Echekwube, 440–45. Ibadan: Heinemann Educational Books, 2005.

Kasenene, Peter. *Religious Ethics in Africa*. Kampala: Fountain Publishers, 1998.

Kasoma, Francis. "The Foundations of African Ethics (Afriethics) and the Professional Practice of Journalism." *Africa Media Review* 10, no. 3 (1996): 93–116.

Kaunda, Kenneth. *Kaunda on Violence*. London: Collins, 1980.

Lazar, Seth. "Associative Duties and the Ethics of Killing in War." *Journal of Practical Ethics*. Accessed May 31, 2019. http://www.jpe.ox.ac.uk/papers/associative-duties-and-the-ethics-of-killing-in-war/.

Lebakeng, J. Teboho et al. "Epistemicide, Institutional Cultures and the Imperative for the Africanisation of Universities in South Africa." *Alternation* 13, no. 1 (2006): 70–87.

Luban, David. "Just War and Human Rights." *Philosophy and Public Affairs* 9, no. 2 (1980): 160–81.

Lutz, David, et al., eds. *War and Peace in Africa: Philosophy, Theology and the Politics of Confrontation*. Palo Alto, CA: Academica Press, 2014.

MacIntyre, Alasdair. "Is Patriotism a Virtue?" Lindley Lecture, University of Kansas, March 24, 1984. Accessed May 31, 2019. https://kuscholarworks.ku.edu/bitstream/handle/1808/12398/Is%20Patriotism%20a%20Virtue-1984.pdf.

Mandela, Nelson. *Conversations with Myself*. London: Pan Macmillan, 2010.

———. *Long Walk to Freedom*. London: Abacus, 1994.

———. *Nelson Mandela by Himself*. Johannesburg: Pan Macmillan, 2013.

———. *Notes to the Future*. New York: Atria, 2012.

———. "Statement by Nelson Mandela from the Dock at the Opening of the Defence Case in the Rivonia Trial." April 20, 1964. Accessed May 31, 2019. http://www.mandela.gov.za/mandela_speeches/before/640420_trial.htm.

———. "Statement by Nelson Mandela Read on His Behalf by His Daughter Zinzi at a UDF Rally to Celebrate Archbishop Tutu Receiving the Nobel Peace Prize." February 10, 1985. Accessed May 31, 2019. http://www.mandela.gov.za/mandela_speeches/before/850210_udf.htm.

———. *Ubuntu Told by Nelson Mandela*. Video, 1:37. Posted by Marc, March 6, 2012. http://www.youtube.com/watch?v=HED4h00xPPA.

Martin, Guy. *African Political Thought*. New York: Palgrave Macmillan, 2012.

Masolo, Dismas. *Self and Community in a Changing World*. Bloomington: Indiana University Press, 2010.

May, Larry. "The Principle of Just Cause." In *War: Essays in Political Philosophy*, edited by Larry May, 49–66. New York: Cambridge University Press, 2008.

McMahan, Jeff. "Aggression and Punishment." In *War: Essays in Political Philosophy*, edited by Larry May, 67–84. New York: Cambridge University Press, 2008.

———. "The Ethics of Killing in War." *Ethics* 114, no. 4 (2004): 693–733.

———. "Just Cause for War." *Ethics and International Affairs* 19, no. 3 (2005): 1–21.

Metz, Thaddeus. "African Ethics and Journalism Ethics." *Journal of Media Ethics* 30, no. 2 (2015): 74–90.

———. "An African Theory of Social Justice." In *Distributive Justice Debates in Political and Social Thought*, edited by Camilla Boisen and Matt Murray, 171–90. Abingdon: Routledge, 2016.

———. "African Values, Human Rights and Group Rights." In *African Legal Theory and Contemporary Problems*, edited by Oche Onazi, 131–51. Dordrecht: Springer, 2014.

———. "Developing African Political Philosophy: Moral-Theoretic Strategies." *Philosophia Africana* 14, no. 1 (2012): 61–83.

———. "Human Dignity, Capital Punishment, and an African Moral Theory." *Journal of Human Rights* 9, no. 1 (2010): 81–99.
———. "A Life of Struggle as Ubuntu." In *Nelson Rolihlahla Mandela: Decolonial Ethics of Liberation and Servant Leadership*, edited by Sabelo Ndlovu-Gatsheni and Busani Ngcaweni, 95–109. Trenton, NJ: Africa World Press, 2018.
———. "Reconciliation as the Aim of a Criminal Trial." *Constitutional Court Review* 9 (2019): 1–22.
———. "A Theory of National Reconciliation: Some Insights from Africa." In *Theorizing Transitional Justice*, edited by Claudio Corradetti, Nir Eisikovits, and Jack Rotondi, 119–35. Surrey: Ashgate, 2015.
———. "Toward an African Moral Theory." *Journal of Political Philosophy* 15, no. 3 (2007): 321–41.
Mofuoa, Khali. "The Exemplary Ethical Leadership of King Moshoeshoe of Basotho of Lesotho in the Nineteenth Century Southern Africa." *Journal of Public Administration and Governance* 5, no. 3 (2015): 21–35.
Mokgoro, Yvonne. "Ubuntu and the Law in South Africa." *Potchefstroom Electronic Law Journal* 1, no. 1 (1998): 15–26.
Murove, Munyaradzi Felix. "The Shona Ethic of Ukama with Reference to the Immortality of Values." *Mankind Quarterly* 48, no. 2 (2007): 179–89.
Nkondo, Gessler Muxe. "Ubuntu as a Public Policy in South Africa." *International Journal of African Renaissance Studies* 2, no. 1 (2007): 88–100.
Odora Hoppers, Catherine. "African Voices in Education." In *African Voices in Education*, edited by Philip Higgs et al., 1–11. Lansdowne: Juta, 2000.
Okeja, Uchenna. "War by Agreement." *Journal of Military Ethics* (forthcoming).
Oruka, Henry Odera. *Punishment and Terrorism in Africa*. 2nd ed. Nairobi: Kenya Literature Bureau, 1985.
Ramose, Mogobe. *African Philosophy through Ubuntu*. Harare: Mond Publishers, 1999.
Reichberg, Gregory. "Jus ad Bellum." In *War: Essays in Political Philosophy*, edited by Larry May, 11–29. New York: Cambridge University Press, 2008.
Shiffrin, Seana. "Wrongful Life, Procreative Responsibility, and the Significance of Harm." *Legal Theory* 5, no. 2 (1999): 117–48.
Sogolo, Godwin. *Foundations of African Philosophy*. Ibadan: Ibadan University Press, 1993.
Tutu, Desmond. *No Future without Forgiveness*. New York: Random House, 1999.
Vilakazi, H. W. "Education Policy for a Democratic Society." In *Black Perspective(s) on Tertiary Institutional Transformation*, edited by Sipho Seepe, 69–90. Florida Hills: Vivlia Publishers and the University of Venda, 1998.
Waddington, Conway. "Reconciling Just War Theory and Water-Related Conflict." *International Journal of Applied Philosophy* 26, no. 2 (2013): 197–212.
———. "Water Scarcity and Warfare." PhD diss., University of Johannesburg, 2018.
Walzer, Michael. *Just and Unjust Wars*. New York: Basic Books, 1977.
Wiredu, Kwasi. *Cultural Universals and Particulars: An African Perspective*. Bloomington: Indiana University Press, 1996.

Chapter Nine

The Classical Confucian Ideas of *Jus ad Bellum*

Cao Qin

In this essay, I will focus on the ancient Confucian ideas about war as an example of the traditional Chinese theory of *jus ad bellum*. More specifically, I will concentrate on the arguments of Confucius and Mencius—the two most respected figures in the Confucian tradition. I will borrow criteria from mainstream Western just war theory and see which one of them can be applied to those ancient Chinese sages. By highlighting the contrast between Confucius and Mencius in this aspect, I will try to explain the reason of their difference and explore the possible inspiration Mencius may bring to us.

The reason for using Confucius and Mencius as exemplars is similar to some recent scholars who had written on the same or similar topics. Confucius and Mencius lived in the Spring and Autumn Era (the eighth century BC to the fifth century BC) and the Warring States Era (the fifth century BC to 221 BC). Those were periods in which "China went through dramatic changes . . . that set the basic political framework for the following 2,000 years of Chinese history," and "the debates among political philosophers" during this period "contributed to these changes."[1] Those eras—especially the Warring States Era—were known as a period in which various schools of thought thrived, and Confucianism was only one among the many schools appeared during these periods. However, like Daniel A. Bell, I will limit my discussion to Confucianism—the "most influential East Asian political philosophy"[2]—and especially "to the values espoused by Confucius and Mencius," because the former's *Analects* is "the central founding text in the Confucian tradition" and the latter, "who elaborated and systematized Confucius's ideas, became its most famous exponent." Besides, Mencius also "continues to be the most influential theorist of war and just war in the Confucian tradition."[3] Therefore, I will use the text of *Analects* and *Mencius* as the primary source of the discussion in this essay.

However, arguments about war did not occupy a prominent place in these two books, so some readers may wonder what we can learn from their teachings. This is the question that I am trying to answer in the rest of this essay. I will demonstrate that, if we examine the ideas of Confucius and Mencius from the perspective of the modern theory of just war, especially with the concept of *jus ad bellum*, we can see that there was a crucial difference between them. The idea of legitimate authority in wars, which was central to Confucius's theory of just war, was abandoned by Mencius, who otherwise very much admired Confucius. For Mencius, the important thing was not who waged the war but whether the cause of the war was justified. Such transformation brings the possibility for legitimate revolutions and humanitarian interventions, and learning from it, I believe, is useful in an age in which state sovereignty usually prevails in the international arena.

CONFUCIUS AND THE LEGITIMATE AUTHORITY OF WAR

Neither Confucius nor Mencius spoke much on what we call *jus in bello* today (i.e., rules that regulate the conduct during war), at least not in *Analects* and *Mencius*.[4] This does not mean that they would say there are no moral rules in a war. It would be odd if a highly moralized theory like Confucianism is indifferent to the appropriateness of soldiers' conduct during wartime. They just did not propose more concrete and systematized suggestions about that aspect of war. However, they did say important things on the issue of *jus ad bellum*.

The contemporary idea of *jus ad bellum* usually includes six principles: (1) just cause, (2) right intentions, (3) legitimate authority, (4) last resort, (5) likelihood of success, and (6) proportionality.[5] A war is supposed to be fully just only if it can satisfy all these criteria. Clear indications of the last three principles cannot be found in Confucius's and Mencius's own words.[6] However, they did say something that can be related to the first three. More specifically, Confucius had a clear standing on the question of legitimate authority, though he had to compromise with the reality he was facing, whereas Mencius was eager to argue that right causes and intentions were crucial for the justification of wars.

The contemporary Western theories of just war have various historical sources, including the theological ideas of St. Augustine and Thomas Aquinas,[7] the aristocratic conventions rooted in the feudal societies, and the philosophical reflections from all those who saw the activity of war from a moral perspective. This mixture of origins is determined by the specific historical experiences of the Western world, especially Europe.[8] Similarly, the Confucian ideas of just war also reflected the relevant historical circumstances.

The philosophy of Confucius[9] has two facets: the ideas about personal morality and the ideas about social relationship, including political institutions. These two aspects are closely connected, but different interpretations of his thought tend to emphasize one or the other. On the one hand, Confucius taught us that we should be good people (e.g., be benevolent and righteous). On the other hand, he had a specific vision of the political organization of the ideal society. This part of his thought has been largely neglected in Chinese history.[10]

Confucius was born in a society far from his ideal concept of one. The Zhou dynasty, the model regime that he admired most, was very similar to medieval feudal Europe.[11] Under the rule of the King of Zhou—the "Tian Zi" (Son of Heaven)—there were various nobles who, like their European counterparts, were also divided into five classes: duke, marquis, count, viscount, and baron. Each of those nobles was granted a particular territory from the king, and they could give part of such territory to their own subjects. Ideally speaking, in this political system, wars should be conducted only by the highest authority. This was the one principle of *jus ad bellum* that Confucius explicitly emphasized. As he famously said, "When good government prevails in the empire, ceremonies, music, and punitive military expeditions proceed from the Son of Heaven. When bad government prevails in the empire, ceremonies, music, and punitive military expeditions proceed from the princes" (*Analects*, Book 6, Chapter 2).[12]

However, since the eighth century BC, the political situation of China was exactly one in which the military actions proceeded from the princes. The king still existed, but he was more like a symbol of the political order in the past. The princes began to act like independent agents, and they started to attack each other for power, glory, and wealth, without the permission of the Son of Heaven. The interprincipality system of that time was a quasi-anarchical one, to say the least.[13]

Under such circumstances, even a principled man like Confucius (some may say a man pragmatic enough like Confucius) had to make choices that seemed contrary to his own stated principles. One example was that, when a minister of another country murdered his prince, Confucius urged his own prince to undertake the duty of punishing that minister (*Analects*, Book 14, Chapter 22).[14] With this, we can see that Confucius did not always oppose military actions that "proceed from the princes" because that was practically the only way to realize some of the other rules of justice.

Moreover, sometimes Confucius went even further. He was, in one case at least, willing to support military actions that proceeded from someone who was not even a prince. In the year 502 BC, when he resided in the country Lu, a man called Kung-shan Fu-zao attempted to rebel against his superiors, and invited Confucius to visit him. Apparently, having connection with a person who clearly intended to disobey the traditional aristocratic order was something a Confucian should despise. Surprisingly, Confucius was inclined to pay the visit. Tsze-lu, one of his most prominent students, was quite disappointed at the master's decision. Confucius's justification for himself was that "Can it be without some reason that he [Kung-shan] has invited ME? If anyone employ [sic] me, may I not make an eastern Zhou?" (*Analects*, Book 17, Chapter 5).

It was mentioned above that the Zhou dynasty was the model regime in Confucius's theoretical world. What he meant was that, if some enlightened enough power holders gave him a chance, he might be able to help them establish a well-governed regime whose capital was supposed to be on the east of the capital of the Zhou dynasty in his time. However, Kung-shan was not even a prince and certainly not the Son of Heaven. He was no more than a subject of a particular prince. If he started a war by his own discretion, then by Confucius's criteria, it would definitely be a sign that "bad government prevails in the empire."

Nevertheless, Confucius recognized that he was not in a position to refuse the offers available just because they were made by illegitimate political actors. If he wanted to achieve something, he had to cooperate with people like Kung-shan if necessary. From Confucius's reaction to the incident of Kung-shan, we can see that, although his general moral philosophy was often believed to be more akin to contemporary theories of deontological or virtue ethics,[15] at least his idea of just war was closer to a consequentialist approach: if a particular action (helping someone who is not traditionally recognized as a legitimate ruler) can bring good results, it is worthy of doing.

In summary, for Confucius, ideally speaking, a just war ought to be one started by the legitimate authority, namely the Son of Heaven. However, this principle was rarely recognized in the world he lived in, so he had to make compromises. In the end, he was quite willing to be involved in wars in which the Son of Heaven played no role at all. But, if the principle of legitimate authority had to be abandoned, what other criteria can we use to assess the moral status of a war? Confucius did not give us an explicit answer.[16] It was Mencius who provided innovative standards in this aspect. It seems that the formal requirement of legitimate authority was quite unnecessary for him. Rather, it was the right reasons and right intentions that mattered.

THE RIGHT TO REBEL: MENCIUS ON REVOLUTIONARY WARS

Although the traditional political order had been largely eroded, the Spring and Autumn Era in ancient China was still much more aristocratic than all the other dynasties that had succeeded it. However, the Warring States Era witnessed one of the greatest social and political transformations in all of Chinese history. The states became increasingly absolutist, rather than aristocratic, and the most absolutist one—Chin—finally conquered the rest. In this process, the old ethics of war withered away together with the old regimes. The conventions honored in the heyday of the aristocratic age, which had already been largely eroded in Confucius's time, were finally abandoned with the coming of the absolutist era. We must read Mencius's arguments about war in this context.

Because the political order had been changed fundamentally in the Warring States Era, the principle of legitimate authority was even more outdated than in Confucius's time.[17] The answer to the question who had the right to use military force was quite clear: whoever possessed such force. Therefore, Mencius said little about that principle. He did complain that "there are no righteous wars" in the Spring and Autumn Era (*Mencius*, Book VII, Part II, Chapter 2) and claimed that, although the hegemonic princes in that era were already inferior to ancient kings, the rulers in his own time were even worse (*Mencius*, Book VI, Part II, Chapter 7). However, he blamed them not because of the fact that "punitive military expeditions proceed from the princes" but because they did not show benevolence in their actions. In other words, Mencius blamed them for substantive reasons, not procedural reasons. If a war were considered unjust, it was not because the participants did not meet some formal requirements (e.g., having the title of the Son of Heaven) but because their reasons and intentions were unsatisfactory. The political status of those participants has no weight in the evaluation of the moral status of the war. We may say that Mencius, as someone who was "[p]lacing moral hierarchy over political hierarchy,"[18] abandoned the principle of legitimate authority altogether.

Abandoning the idea of legitimate authority produced a positive side effect. The principle of legitimate authority has in effect often been translated as the idea that only formal state sovereigns have the right to conduct wars. One big problem of this principle is that some parties in military conflicts may not be able to receive the fair treatment they deserve. In modern warfare, this problem is most obvious when the rights of guerrillas and terrorists are in question, but the principle of legitimate authority can also be used to put domestic revolutionaries and anticolonial fighters in disadvantageous positions because they are not, formally speaking, agents who possess state sovereignty.[19] In the context of ancient China, that principle would likewise dictate that rebellion against a prince would be considered unjustified simply because the rebels were not qualified to start a war; such rebellion was definitely not something that "proceed[ed] from the Son of Heaven." However, when the limitation posed by the principle of legitimate authority was eliminated, justifications of revolutionary actions became possible. The main concern of the legitimacy of a war changed from the identity of the participants to the reasons for war. This led to the most influential part of Mencius's theory of just war, which is probably also the most relevant part for us today.

One of Mencius's most famous statements was that the war against a despot was just. When he resided in the Kingdom of Chi,[20] he was asked by the king about the ancient histories of regime change. According to the historians, Chau, the last king of the Shang dynasty, was an extremely cruel ruler and was killed by the founder of the Zhou dynasty in a revolutionary war.[21] In the tradition of the Confucian school (which saw the ethical and political system of the Zhou dynasty as the best one), that war was one of the paradigms of just war. However, no matter how righteous the rebels were, they were not able to change the inconvenient fact that, before they rebelled against the king of the Shang dynasty, they were still the subjects of the latter. The Confucian school was well known for its emphasis on the importance of class system—those who belong to the lower class should defer to those who belong to the higher one. Among all the possible class relationships, the most important one was the one between the monarch and his subjects. Therefore, the founding war of the Zhou dynasty was always a source of embarrassment for its supporters. On the one hand, they insisted that resisting the superiors—especially the monarchs—ought not to be allowed. On the other hand, the war they admired most was exactly the one in which the subjects overthrew the king.

It is under this background that the King of Chi asked Mencius, "Is it right for a subject to kill his monarch?" It is not clear whether the king was trying to embarrass the idealist or if he was merely curious. However, one thing was certain: the response of Mencius would undoubtedly define his intellectual reputation—even the reputation of the whole Confucian school—to a large extent.

The entire dialogue recorded in *Mencius* reads:

> The King Hsuan of Chi asked, saying, "Was it so, that Tang banished Chieh, and that King Wu smote Chau?" Mencius replied, "It is so in the records." The king said, "May a minister then put his sovereign to death?" Mencius said, "He who outrages the benevolence proper to his nature is called a robber; he who outrages righteousness is called a ruffian. The robber and ruffian we call a lone man [Yi Fu]. I have heard of the cutting off of the lone man Chau, but I have not heard of the putting a sovereign to death, in his case." (*Mencius*, Book I, Part II, Chapter 8)

So, according to Mencius, although people usually believed that killing their monarch was a crime (indeed, one of the most serious crimes one can commit), that was only true if your ruler were a good one. If he were a "lone man," a despot who is despised by all—a "Yi Fu"—then killing him was not only permissible but actually praiseworthy. The distinction between "Yi Fu" and legitimate ruler was to some extent parallel to the Western distinction between tyrant and legitimate king; thus, we may see Mencius as a defender of tyrannicide.[22]

More cynical people may tend to argue that Mencius's response was no more than an ad hoc justification for the legitimacy of the Zhou dynasty. However, if we look at the larger picture, we will understand that this was not the only occasion on which Mencius talked about rightful resistance to the superior. When he was asked whether virtuous subjects could "banish their sovereigns," he replied that they could do so if they were doing it for the right purpose (*Mencius*, Book VII, Part I, Chapter 31). Considering the moralistic attitude throughout the book, we have good reason to believe that Mencius's appeal to moral standards in wars is sincere.

It seems that, if we interpret Mencius's idea in terms of modern theories of just war, we can say that, out of the six principles of *jus ad bellum*, he focused on only two of them: just cause and right intentions. This was in sharp contrast to the doctrine Confucius once defended, which saw legitimate authority as the only relevant standard. Understandably, Mencius's idea was quite radical for his contemporaries, but, in a certain aspect, it can also be radical for us today. It is this radical aspect that I shall turn to in the next section.

HUMANITARIAN INTERVENTION

In the section above, we saw how Mencius justified revolutionary causes. Nevertheless, in many (or maybe we should say most) cases, even if a ruler is so wicked that he deserves to be overthrown by the mistreated ruled, the latter lack the means or the courage to rise up against the former. In such cases, it would be unrealistic to expect the people to end the tyranny by themselves; thus, the possibility of humanitarian intervention emerges. It is on this topic, I think, that Mencius can give us the most valuable inspiration.

Mencius's argument was very influential in Chinese history, and it shaped probably the most distinctive characteristic of the traditional Chinese just war theory: the idea that the paradigmatic case of a just war was a war of righteous uprising or humanitarian intervention, rather than a war of self-defense. The primary function of a just war was to secure the secular and materialistic needs of ordinary people. This is not to say that the factor of self-defense was unimportant. If a ruler of a country is sufficiently just, self-defense is undoubtedly a good reason to engage in warfare. However, for Mencius, the status of the war of self-defense is far less important than its status today, and this difference implies that he is probably much more radical than most of us today on the issue of humanitarian intervention.

In contemporary philosophical and political discussions concerning the legitimacy of humanitarian intervention, it has been widely recognized that the central difficulty, or paradox, of such intervention is the conflict between the principle of sovereignty and the principle of humanity.[23] State sovereignty has a prominent place in international relations. However, the principle of humanity has also claimed (though apparently has not earned yet) the same status since at least the end of WWII. These two principles may become incompatible in the case of humanitarian intervention because such intervention, while aiming at satisfying the principle of humanity, inevitably violates the principle of sovereignty. Therefore, if we insist on the traditional idea that a war of self-defense is always just,[24] on the one hand, and commit to the new idea that using war to stop genocide can be a just act, on the other hand, we will face the dilemma that in a war of humanitarian intervention, it is possible that both parties are just and deserve our moral support. This is a dilemma that would not occur to Mencius because sovereignty is not supposed to be that important in his theory.

One feature of traditional Chinese political thought was that it rarely glorified military virtue. War was seen as something inherently—though not always absolutely—bad: sometimes, they had to engage in wars to avoid larger evils, but, other things being equal, peace was always preferred to war.[25] The case was rather different in Western and other traditions. From Homer's description of heroic Greek warriors to the fascist worship of war in the twentieth century, there has been a trend (though usually not the mainstream one) in Western tradition to see military activities as honorable and praiseworthy in themselves. However, after the two destructive world wars of the past century, it seemed that the tendency in the Western world has turned to the other extreme. Although absolute pacifism has always been dismissed by most people as utopian and even counterproductive, the conventional presumption in the international arena nowadays is that we can hardly be too cautious on the decisions to go to war. Wars are supposed to be waged only as the last resort. In most if not all cases, to avoid wars between sovereign states, we are expected to refrain from struggling to gain some other good things, including human rights.[26]

Such sovereign fetishism was not found in the philosophy of Mencius. The most fundamental political good is the welfare of the people, not that of the state itself. Just as Mencius said, "the people are the most important element in a nation"; the state (*sheji*) is the next, and the prince (*sovereign*) is the lightest (*Mencius*, Book VII, Part II, Chapter 14).[27] Of course, Mencius should not thus be seen as a proto-democrat, but he did point out something worth considering (also something widely admitted in the Western world today provided that only *domestic* policies are concerned): the state is not a living organism that has its own irreducible will and welfare; its importance can be derived only from the importance of the people it consists of. In Mencius's mind, while the state is important and the prince ought to be respected, they need to be compromised when the well-being of the people is at stake. The contemporary international order, in contrast, is practically one in which *sheji* (i.e., the sovereignty of the state) is regarded as "the most important element." Although most states are willing or even eager to pay lip service to the 1948 UN Universal Declaration of Human Rights, they are very reluctant to downplay the absoluteness of state sovereignty, even when doing so would not affect their own interests directly.

Therefore, many participants in the discussion about humanitarian intervention claim that, when we have to decide whether to intervene, the principle of sovereignty should take priority.[28] Although few if any governments dare to argue that state sovereignty should always prevail, many of them are eager to deny the legitimacy of all the cases of humanitarian intervention in the past and to show skepticism whenever a new potential instance of humanitarian intervention is being discussed. If we adhere to Mencius's idea of just war instead, we will probably tend to be more tolerant to humanitarian intervention. For Mencius, the fundamental moral criterion for judging the justness of a war was the consequences it would bring. In specific cases, we may have reasons to doubt whether a particular instance of violating state sovereignty is just or prudent, but our assessment must be based on the influence such intervention may bring to the well-being of the relevant people. From this perspective, the burden of proof for the proponents of humanitarian intervention is likely to be considerably lighter.

According to Mencius's standard, all states with a sufficiently bad government are legitimate targets of intervention. The content of "bad governance" was not listed, but we can safely assume that the bar would be lower than the triggering conditions (e.g., genocide) of humanitarian intervention widely agreed in the current international society. This can make some of our contemporaries feel uncomfortable and anxious so that they may want to interpret Mencius in a more moderate way. For example, when trying to apply the Confucian war ethics to some of the events in our own time, Bell suggests that overthrowing Saddam Hussein[29] by a foreign army would not have been approved by Mencius because, from the Confucian perspective, merely "systematic violation of civil and political rights" (e.g., "denials of the right to free speech or the heavy-handed treatment of political dissenters in the name of social order") is not enough to justify intervention. A legitimate intervention can be launched only when the rulers "deliberatively deprive the people of the means of subsistence (by killing them, not feeding them, not dealing with a plague, etc.)."[30]

However, as we have mentioned above, according to Mencius himself, the war that overthrew King Chau of the Shang dynasty was a justified war. Chau was accused of committing many hideous crimes, including killing innocent people and being extremely luxurious. Yet none of his crimes can be seen as crimes that deliberatively deprived the people of the means of subsistence. Nonetheless, Mencius did not hesitate to claim that rebelling against him was just. Chau did kill some of his subjects brutally, but so did Saddam. If the gas attack against the Kurds cannot justify overthrowing Saddam's regime, as Bell insists, then Chau's regime should also be defensible in this aspect because there was no evidence that he ever systematically performed large-scale murder of any kind. But because Mencius did approve the war against Chau, we have no reason to say that he would disapprove a war against Saddam in principle.

Nevertheless, the argument above should not lead us to the conclusion that, if Mencius were alive today, he would approve the Iraq War. This is because he also takes the elements of right reason and right intention very seriously. He condemned wars that aimed at conquering new lands, calling them "leading on the land to devour human flesh," and claimed that even death "is not enough for such a crime" (*Mencius*, Book IV, Part I, Chapter 14). Those who worked hard to enlarge the territories of their kings are regarded as "robbers of the people," rather than "good ministers" (*Mencius*, Book VI, Part II, Chapter 9). Mencius's relevant attitude can be best exemplified by his reaction to the war between the kingdoms Chi and Yen. In the year 315 BC, the King of Chi invaded Yen. Before the adventure began, a minister of the king consulted with Mencius about the righteousness of the war, and the latter affirmed that it was OK to smite Yen.[31] However, when someone else asked Mencius whether he had advised the king to smite Yan, he replied in a rather ambiguous way. His explanation was that he said only that Yen might be smitten but not that Yen might be smitten by Chi:

> If he had asked me—"Who may smite it?" I would have answered him, "He who is the minister of the Heaven may smite it." Suppose the case of a murderer, and that one asks me—"May this man be put to death?" I will answer him—"He may." If he ask me—"Who may put him to death?" I will answer him—"The chief criminal judge may put him to death." But now with one Yen to smite another Yen:—how should I have advised this? (*Mencius*, Book II, Part II, Chapter 8)

Because Yen was ruled by someone illegitimate, it could have been the case that invading it was indeed just. However, for the invasion to have been just, it must have been conducted by someone who was righteous—some "minister of the Heaven," someone who could execute the (presumably good and just) will of God. If the invasion had been proved to be harmful to the people of Yen, it should not have been allowed. It turned out that the actual invasion—the one by the army of Chi—was exactly an invasion that did not fulfill the requirement set up by Mencius.[32] The invading army killed innocent civilians and showed disrespect to the "ancestral temple" and "precious vessels" of Yen (*Mencius*, Book I, Part II, Chapter 11). In the end, the army was defeated. This incident can give us a hint about what Mencius might say on cases like the Iraq War.

Therefore, if Mencius had had a chance to express his opinion on the Iraq War, he would probably have argued that, although Saddam was indeed "smitable," the Bush administration was not the proper agent to smite him. There was little evidence that the US government's intention was publicly justifiable. Besides, Mencius may have added that, because the Bush administration had just initiated the PATRIOT Act about seventeen months prior,[33] we would had have further reason to suspect whether defending human rights was really an important part of the administration's intention to go to war. However, he would not say that the Iraq War was an unjust one simply because the sovereignty of Iraq should be kept intact. In fact, he probably would not have regarded its sovereignty as something very important.[34] The problem of the Iraq War, he would say now, is not that the United States violated some particular formal rules, such as the supremacy of state sovereignty, but that it did not wage the war with sufficient benevolence.

MENCIUS AND JUST WAR THEORY TODAY

The ideas of Confucius and Mencius had dominated China for about two thousand years. However, since the early twentieth century, after China had suffered again and again from other countries that had very different cultures, more and more Chinese began to wonder whether their traditional wisdom was still applicable in the new age. Various doctrines from the West—liberalism, nationalism, socialism, and communism—were seen as the pills for the fatal illness of the old empire. Although it is not unreasonable to argue that many elements of the traditional culture still exist in Chinese politics today, there are certain areas in which those elements have little influence now. One of those areas is foreign affairs, in which a particularly cynical version of realism[35] has a dominant place. In the minds of most people, the guiding principle of the contemporary international arena is no more than the rule of the jungle (in both a descriptive and normative sense) and that it would be a gross mistake to bring moral discourse into war like Mencius did.

The key thesis of this folk realism is that, when it comes to war, talking about morality is nothing but a disguise of power politics; in particular, the idea of humanitarian intervention, which has been by far mostly practiced by Western countries, is just an ad hoc excuse for the pursuit of imperialistic powers' national interests. Therefore, banishing morality from international relations and wars is seen as part of the effort to resist the hegemony of the Western world in both practice and theory. However, in my opinion, this is a narrow vision. The proponents of such realism forget (or never really knew) that the modern theory of realism in international relations is precisely a product of European history, whereas the appeal to humanitarian intervention, in contrast, has its own roots in the ancient Chinese political philosophy.

Living in a transitional period, Confucius began to change the focus of just war theory from the status of the agents of war to the causes and consequences of war. Such a tendency was then inherited by Mencius. It is in this aspect that they can expand our visions. Indeed, the trend since WWII is, in some way, similar to the transformation of Chinese politics from Confucius's time to Mencius's. The traditional order (in one case, the old feudal system; in the other, the Westphalian system) has collapsed. With the memory of the horror of destructive wars, some people (e.g., Mencius) tried to set some new guiding rules for the interactions between states (including the wars between them). These rules are based on substantial moral principles (e.g., those about "benevolence" or "human rights"), which, though they already existed, were not generally applied in international relations and wars. Mencius's theory provides a new perspective on the question about the relationship between human beings and state sovereignty, a perspective that differs from both the dominant one in contemporary international relations and the individualistic one of some Western cosmopolitans.[36] It shows that liberal cosmopolitanism is not the only alternative to realism and that we do not have to make an either/or choice between them. We can reject the conventional state-centered paradigm without committing to individualism in the methodological and ontological levels.

Of course, here, I am not proposing Mencius's approach as *the* "right" or "just" one, but I do hope that the possibility it presents can help enlarge our imagination. In a pluralistic world where various cultures have very different understandings about the nature of human affairs, rejection of the presumably "Western" cosmopolitanism (a rejection that is justified in some cases) can often lead to cynical realism. For those who believe that the latter is undesirable, it is important to develop a more inclusive moral theory that can gain consensus from various parties. Learning from alternative theories like Mencius's might be helpful to such an enterprise.

Nevertheless, despite the important contribution to the just war theory that Mencius made, I want to discuss a drawback of his doctrine at the end of this essay. From the perspective of those who live in the modern world, one question (though perhaps a somewhat anachronistic one) still remains unsettled. The distinction between *jus ad bellum* and *jus in bello* was not very clear in Mencius. When he blamed those who waged unjust wars, in some cases, it seemed that he was condemning the cause of the wars, whereas, in other cases, it seemed that he was condemning the conduct of the officials and soldiers during wartime. But how about the case in which the cause is just but the conduct is not, that is, just wars (in the sense that the end of the war is justified) proceeded with unjust means, such as the bombings of Hamburg and Dresden by the Allied Forces[37] and the terrorist attacks in the Algerian national liberation movement?

With the conceptual distinction of *jus ad bellum* and *jus in bello*, we moderns can say that, although the cause of the war is just, some specific actions during it were not. But it seemed that such a distinction was not available for Mencius. He did blame the conduct of the soldiers in the war between Chi and Yen. However, it was not clear whether he blamed them because those actions were wrong by themselves or because they are the inevitable results of the wrong cause and thus reflected the unjustified attitude of the invasion army. An idealist like Mencius[38] probably believed that benevolent persons would show benevolence in all aspects of their actions so that an army fighting for a just cause would not do anything unjust during the combat. However, the experience of the twentieth century told us otherwise. It is difficult to imagine what Mencius would say today about the strategic bombings in WWII or the terrorist attacks of the Algerian nationalists.

Perhaps such a moral dilemma in war never occurred to Mencius, which is understandable. Because virtually none of the wars that happened in his lifetime could have counted as just, he did not have the opportunity to observe and judge the unjust means of fighting in just wars. Nevertheless, it is still a regrettable thing that he did not deal with this problem directly. Suppose that the distinction between *jus ad bellum* and *jus in bello* was available to Mencius, what would he say about the prospect of fighting a just war with unjust means? Say, if a benevolent, sage king has finally arrived, would he be allowed to conquer other countries (and bring them into a more prosperous state afterward) by fraud, betrayal, or even mass murder? Because he argued that rules regulating interpersonal relationships could be lessened in particular circumstances,[39] it is reasonable to assume that he would approve of extraordinary means in the case of emergency.[40] But how about the cases that are less emergent and hence less justified? For the soldiers who are fighting for a just cause, if they violate the principles of *jus in bello*, should we withdraw our support immediately, or should we withdraw our support only when such violations have become very serious? And where is the boundary between "very serious" and "not so serious"? These are all questions that Mencius did not encounter. A complete account of just war theory must address them. It is at this point that we need to go beyond Mencius, but it is also beyond the task of this paper.

CONCLUSION

The world system we have been living in for the past three centuries in which state sovereignty is the central value is very different from Confucius's feudal, aristocratic dreamland. However, in both his theory of just war and the mainstream theory in our age, the idea of legitimate authority occupies an important place. This fact raises a problem because, from the very start, some participants in military conflicts are very likely to be excluded from the candidates of legitimate authority, even when their actions can be morally justified. If the states are supposed to be the only legitimate agents in wars, then rising up against a tyrant or engaging in guerrilla warfare after the government has surrendered cannot be anything but crime.

Today, we cannot condemn revolutionaries and guerrilla fighters *merely* because they lack the alleged "legitimate authority." This kind of attitude is not only conservative but also reactionary. However, it is impossible to acknowledge the legitimate status of the morally praiseworthy nonstate combatants, unless the traditional principle of legitimate authority is revised or abandoned. This was precisely the step Mencius took, a step I believe we should also take.

BIBLIOGRAPHY

Altman, Andrew, and Christopher Heath Wellman. *A Liberal Theory of International Justice*. Oxford: Oxford University Press, 2009.

Atkins, E. M., and R. J. Dodaro, eds. *Augustine: Political Writings*. Cambridge: Cambridge University Press, 2001.

Bai, Tongdong. "The Political Philosophy of China." In *The Routledge Companion to Social and Political Philosophy*, edited by Gerald Gaus and Fred D'Agostino, 181–91. London: Routledge, 2013.

———. "Ren Quan Gao Yu Zhu Quan." *She Hui Ke Xue* 35, no. 1 (2013): 131–39.

Beitz, Charles R. *Political Theory and International Relations*. Princeton, NJ: Princeton University Press, 1979.

Bell, Daniel A. *Beyond Liberal Democracy: Political Thinking for an East Asian Context*. Princeton, NJ: Princeton University Press, 2006.

———. "East Asia and the West: The Impact of Confucianism on Anglo-American Political Theory." In *The Oxford Handbook of Political Theory*, edited by John S. Dryzek, Bonnie Honig, and Anne Phillips, 262–80. Oxford: Oxford University Press, 2006.

Brock, Gillian. *Global Justice: A Cosmopolitan Account*. Oxford: Oxford University Press, 2009.

Carr, E. H. *The Twenty Years' Crisis*. New York: Perennial, 2001.

Chong, Kim-chong. "Classical Confucianism (II): Meng Zi and Xun Zi." In *Routledge History of World Philosophies*. Vol. 3: *History of Chinese Philosophy*, edited by Bo Mou, 189–208. London: Routledge, 2009.

Coates, Anthony. "Just War." In *Political Concepts*, edited by Richard Bellamy and Andrew Mason, 211–24. Manchester: Manchester University Press, 2003.

Coppieters, Bruno, and Nick Fotion, eds. *Moral Constraints on War: Principles and Cases*. 2nd ed. New York: Lexington Books, 2008.

Fung, Yu-Lan. *A Short History of Chinese Philosophy*. New York: The Free Press, 1948.

Ivanhoe, Philip J., and Bryan W. van Norden, eds. *Readings in Classical Chinese Philosophy*. New York and London: Seven Bridges Press, 2001.
Liu, JeeLoo. *An Introduction to Chinese Philosophy*. Oxford: Blackwell, 2006.
Mattox, John Mark. *Saint Augustine and the Theory of Just War*. London and New York: Continuum, 2006.
Morgenthau, Hans. *Politics among Nations*. New York: Alfred A. Knopf, 1948.
Mou, Bo, ed. *Routledge History of World Philosophies*. Vol. 3: *History of Chinese Philosophy*. New York: Routledge, 2009.
Murnion, William E. "A Postmodern View of Just War." In *AMINTAPHIL: The Philosophical Foundations of Law and Justice*. Vol. 1, *Intervention, Terrorism, and Torture: Contemporary Challenges to Just War Theory*, edited by Steven P. Lee, 23–40. Dordrecht: Springer, 2007.
Nansen, Huang. "Confucius and Confucianism." In *Companion Encyclopedia of Asian Philosophy*, edited by Brian Carr and Indira Mahalingam, 481–96. London: Routledge, 1997.
Orend, Brian. "War." Stanford Encyclopedia of Philosophy. Published May 3, 2016. Accessed December 5, 2018. http://plato.stanford.edu/archives/spr2016/entries/war/.
Pogge, Thomas W. *World Poverty and Human Rights: Cosmopolitan Responsibilities and Reforms*. Cambridge: Polity, 2002.
Rawls, John. *The Law of Peoples*. Cambridge, MA: Harvard University Press, 1999.
Riegel, Jeffrey. "Confucius." Stanford Encyclopedia of Philosophy. Published July 3, 2002. Modified March 23, 2013. Accessed December 3, 2018. https://plato.stanford.edu/entries/confucius/.
Roetz, Heiner. *Confucian Ethics of the Axial Age*. Albany: SUNY Press, 1993.
Stacy, Helen. "Humanitarian Intervention and Relational Sovereignty." In *AMINTAPHIL: The Philosophical Foundations of Law and Justice*. Vol. 1: *Intervention, Terrorism, and Torture: Contemporary Challenges to Just War Theory*, edited by Steven P. Lee, 89–104. Dordrecht: Springer, 2007.
van Norden, Bryan. "Mencius." Stanford Encyclopedia of Philosophy. Published October 16, 2004. Modified December 3, 2014. Accessed December 3, 2018. https://plato.stanford.edu/entries/mencius/.
Waltz, Kenneth N. *Theory of International Politics*. New York: McGraw-Hill, 1979.
Walzer, Michael. *Arguing about War*. New Haven, CT: Yale University Press, 2004.
———. *Just and Unjust Wars*. New York: Basic Books, 2000.
Wheeler, Nicholas J. *Saving Strangers: Humanitarian Intervention in International Society*. Oxford: Oxford University Press, 2002.
Yao, Xinzhong. *An Introduction to Confucianism*. Cambridge: Cambridge University Press, 2000.

Chapter Ten

Just War and the Indian Tradition

Arguments from the Battlefield

Shyam Ranganathan

INTRODUCTION

Jeff McMahan in his remarkable *Killing in War*[1] draws a distinction between two senses of "war." In the first sense, war stands for a conflict between opposing parties. In the second sense, war is party relative, and some side may have a right of war (*jus ad bellum*), whereas others lack justification for war. In this sense, some parties fight a just war, whereas others fight an unjust war. According to McMahan, there is no radical difference between the moral considerations that operate outside of war and in war; the same moral considerations apply in both cases. Those who violate moral considerations fight an unjust war, whereas those who do not violate moral considerations fight a just war. Whereas Michael Walzer defended the idea that there is a logical independence between the considerations that justify going to war and the considerations pertaining to just conduct in war[2]—and the related idea that there is a moral equality among combatants such that fighting for the wrong side does not entail wrongdoing in the conduct of war—he argues that one's conduct in war does not count as just (*jus in bello*) if one fights for the wrong side and that one has no right to fight those whose cause is just.

The premise that produces McMahan's powerful conclusions is that *war does not create a new set of moral standards*; they are the same standards in peace and war that allow us to distinguish those whose cause and conduct in war are just and those whose cause and conduct are not just. If this is true, then fighting a just war would entail no need to get one's hands dirty—a requirement that Michael Walzer claimed earlier arises from the expedience of war and, later, only in cases of extreme emergency.[3]

While there are many notable contributions to just war theory from the Indian tradition, in this chapter I will consider what may be the most famous argument for just war defended in the *Bhagavad Gītā* (where the philosopher–deity Krishna provides an extended pep talk on just war and moral theory to his cousin Arjuna on the battlefield before the commencement of war) and implicitly explored in the wider epic from which it is from, the *Mahābhārata*.[4] This epic about a fratricidal war provides grounds for rejecting the idea that the justice of a war is elucidated by the fidelity of combatants to conventional standards of morality. Rather, the need for war arises from a breakdown of conventional morality, which identifies ethical considerations with the good. Such conventional moral considerations break down when they provide shelter for parties who endorse conventional morality as a weapon to undermine the conventionally moral. The conventionally moral whose cause is *prima facie* just must hence depart from conventional morality to rid themselves of this hostility and reset the moral order. Yet, according to the alternative moral paradigm that resets the moral order, the *Gītā* entails that we can agree with McMahan: the side of those whose cause is just have a right to fight, and those whose cause is unjust have no such right and do wrong by engaging in conflict. Those who fight for a just cause do not get their hands dirty by way of *transcendent* conditions of justice, though they get their hands dirty by conventional moral expectations. The point of convergence between the argument from the *Gītā* and McMahan is noteworthy, as is their divergence.

For McMahan, the conditions in war make no difference to what morality permits and that the justifications for killing people are the same in war as they are in other contexts, such as individual self-defense. On the approach we find in the *Gītā*, the conditions of just war, namely, the breakdown of conventional morality to mediate competing interests fairly by its conversion into a tool of oppressing the good by the wicked, entails that certain activities may be unjustified in peacetime, though just in war, if undertaken by those whose cause is just. Such activities could include proactive killing, including the killing of noncombatants providing material or emotional support to the unjust (which would not be allowed by conventional standards of self-defense); deceit; and the breaking of promises. I would suggest that this divergence is instructive and that the scenarios that we find discussed in the *Mahābhārata* that led to Krishna's advocating the radical departure from conventional morality should be taken seriously. In the Western tradition, it is difficult to think of arguments that highlight how conventional morality could be a tool of oppression. Nietzsche's *Genealogy of Morals* is an exception, wherein he argues that conventional morals are the values of slaves, conditioned by a context of oppression, and that the alternative is an ethics of the aristocratic self. Nietzsche himself showed an interest in Indian philosophy, and many of his ideas, such as the notion of eternal return and the superman *Übermensch*, who transcends the ordinary, have obvious Indian roots.[5] Indeed, the argument from the *Genealogy* also seems like a caricature of the argument in the *Gītā*. The main difference is that Krishna's argument in contrast does not require that we throw the baby out with the bath water; conventional morality need not be a tool of oppression, but, when it is, the alternative is the project of reestablishing a moral order, rid of moral parasites. Conventional moralists will object to such tactics by those whose cause is just as debasing; it would seem as though the moral line between the just and the unjust disappears. I think that the analysis of the breakdown of conventional morality provided by the *Gītā* and modeled in the *Mahābhārata* shows that this is mistaken; when it comes to such a just war, the conventional standards are now corrupt and cannot be used to judge the just. It would hence be wrong to assume that, if the just adopt techniques of the unjust, they hence fail at *jus in bello*. For instance, if Nazis attempt to use rights of free expression afforded by conventional moralities to protect their own hate speech or displays of racial hatred, by the display of fascist symbols, for instance, to the effect of inciting fear in racial minorities or Jews, it would not, on this argument, be wrong for antifascists to intimidate Nazis or punch or silence Nazis at random, whereas it would be wrong for Nazis to engage in such threatening behavior to attempt to defend themselves or even to be Nazis. The tactics of antifascists find justification in the *Gītā*. Of course, on standard conventional morality, including those of liberal societies, such tactics would be ruled out of bounds.

The *Mahābhārata* and the *Gītā* as they relate to just war have been discussed in the literature,[6] as have wider approaches to the question of just war in Indian literature.[7] My approach is distinct from the standard approach to talking about Indian thought in general.[8] I recommend that reading philosophy is about isolating perspectives and that we treat each perspective *P* as entailing a theory *T* about its controversial *t* claims and understanding the concept *t* as what competing theories of *T* disagree about. For instance, to read philosophy is to identify distinct perspectives in a dialectic or tract; identify a perspective's theory that entails all its claims about a topic, such as ethics; and identify the common concept of *ethics* as what competing theories of ethics disagree about. This approach contrasts with *interpretation*, which is explanation by way of what one takes to be true. In my preferred approach, which I call *explication*, we can remain agnostic about all substantive matters as we pursue research in philosophy.

One of the outcomes of explication is that we acknowledge that the various uses of the term "dharma" in Indian thought serve to articulate theories of dharma; the common concept of dharma is *the Right or the Good*; and, moreover, if we apply this method to contemporary philosophy in the Western tradition, we find that "ethics" has the same conceptual content. The contrary unprincipled approach is to treat one's perspective (and beliefs) as a frame to study Indian thought, and uses of terms, such as "dharma," are correlated with distinctions that we subjectively draw; this results in the multiplication of meanings associated with "dharma" and the ubiquitous claim that it is difficult to translate this term into English or any other language.

In endorsing explication, we are in a position to understand the dialectic of the *Mahābhārata*'s and the *Gītā*'s account of just war. The governing moral theory is what we could call yoga (i.e., discipline) or bhakti (i.e., devotion). According to this theory, the right action is defined by a regulative or procedural ideal (the Lord, defined by the characteristics of unconservatism and self-governance, which in the story is the character Krishna), and the good is the perfection of the practice of devotion to the ideal. Yoga not only provides the moral standards and practice to reestablish a moral order when conventional morality breaks down; it also reestablishes the moral order by dissolving the distinction between *jus ad bellum* and *jus in bello*; what justifies action is this approximation to the regulative or procedural ideal, and what makes it right is the same approximation.

In the next section, "The Great War and Its Background," I provide details about the *Mahābhārata* that are relevant to our inquiry into just war theory. In the third section, "Krishna's Response," I explicate Krishna's argument, which outlines an approach to self-defense in troubled times. The arguments here are frequently misunderstood. Krishna presents himself as the procedural ideal of just action, and readers often are distracted by the similarities between this case and theistic models of God offering advice and commands. Yet Krishna in the *Mahābhārata* is not a disjointed voice from the heavens, nor is Krishna merely a source of pithy, inspirational teachings. Krishna, a character on the ground, provides strategic advice in light of context-relative challenges in the *Mahābhārata* and systematic arguments in the *Gītā* and plays the role as the protagonist's charioteer, guiding the moral heroes into battle. In the context of a work of literature, the *Mahābhārata*, Krishna functions as the procedural ideal that allows us to navigate personal interests in a world of hostility. The entire work is hence a literary exploration of just war theory and yoga's relevance in particular. One major distinction is that Krishna presents himself not as good (indeed, much of his argument is a criticism of goodness as morally explanatory, and Krishna explicitly does bad things on purpose) but as right. Hence, following Krishna's example is not necessarily about doing what is good but rather a concern for what is right. (Indeed, one of the outcomes of the just war under Krishna's guidance in the *Mahābhārata* is the open question of whether the outcome was good, though it was right.) Because theology concerns the discourse on theism and God, for the theist, is primarily good, Krishna's proposed moral significance cannot be reduced to theism or theology. Unlike dialogues of Plato, where participants talk only philosophy, in this extended dialogue, we find characters acting out various parts of the story of just war. It is hence relevant to a global study of just war theory. In this chapter, and the third section, I only attempt to distil the argument; for the drama, one must read the epic. In the fourth section, I consider and respond to objections, and, in the fifth, I conclude.

Can all of this help us elucidate Hindu conceptions on ethics when entering war (*jus ad bellum*) and the rules when engaged in warfare (*jus in bello*)? This question is loaded and wades into areas of scholarship that are slightly beyond the scope of this chapter. For instance, the term "Hindu" was a term coined by the British to label indigenous Indian religion, and it is coextensive with the disagreements of philosophy.[9] With due caution not to overgeneralize the importance of this one argument to Hinduism, as such, it would not be an understatement to note that the argument from the *Gītā* may be the most influential argument on just war theory in the Indian tradition because the *Gītā* (and the *Mahābhārata* of which it is part) itself is one of the more influential and popular books of the Indian tradition (of late) and one of the very few on just war within this set.

THE GREAT WAR AND ITS BACKGROUND

The *Mahābhārata* (the "Great" war of the "Bhāratas") focuses on the fratricidal tensions and all-out war of two groups of cousins with a common ancestor, Bhārata: the Pāndavas, numbering five, the most famous of these brothers being Arjuna, all sons of Pāṇḍu, and the Kauravas, numerous, led by the oldest brother, Duryodhana, all sons of Dhṛtarāṣṭra. Dhṛtarāṣṭra, though older than Pāṇḍu and hence first in line for the throne, was born blind and hence sidelined in royal succession because it was reasoned that blindness would prevent Dhṛtarāṣṭra from ruling. Pāṇḍu, it so happens, was the first to have a son, Yudhiṣṭhira, rendering the throne all but certain to be passed down via Pāṇḍu's descendants. Yet Pāṇḍu dies prematurely, and Dhṛtarāṣṭra becomes king as the only appropriate heir to the throne because the next generation are still children.

As the sons of Pāṇḍu and Dhṛtarāṣṭra grow up, Pāṇḍu's sons distinguish themselves as excellent warriors and virtuous individuals, who are not without their flaws. The Kauravas in contrast are less able in battle but mostly without moral virtues or graces. The rivalry between the two sets of cousins is ameliorated only by the Pāṇḍavas' inclination to compromise and be deferential to their cousins—this despite attempts on the Pāṇḍavas' lives by the Kauravas. Matters turn for the worse when the Pāṇḍavas accept a challenge to wager their freedom in a game of dice, rigged by the Kauravas. The Pāṇḍavas seem unable to restrain themselves from participating in this foolish exercise because it is consistent with conventional past times of the rich and famous. After losing everything and even wagering their common wife, Draupadī, who is thereby publicly sexually harassed, their freedom is granted back by the Dhṛtarāṣṭra (who caves into the lament of the Pāṇḍavas' one common wife, Draupadī). But, once the challenge of the wager—taking a chance—is brought up again, the Pāṇḍavas lose everything (again) and must subsequently spend fourteen years in exile and the final year incognito and, if exposed, must repeat the fourteen years of exile. They complete the exile successfully and return to reclaim their portion of the kingdom, at which point the Kauravas refuse to allow the Pāṇḍavas any home area so that they might eke out a livelihood as rulers. Despite repeated attempts by the Pāṇḍavas at conciliation, mediated by their mutual cousin, Krishna, the Kauravas adopt a position of hostility, forcing the Pāṇḍavas into a corner where they have no choice but to fight. Alliances, loyalties, and obligations are publicly reckoned and distinguished, and the two sides agree to fight it out on a battlefield with their armies.

What is noteworthy about the scenario described in the *Mahābhārata* is that the Pāṇḍavas, but for imprudent decisions, conform their actions to standards of conventional moral expectations for people in their station and caste—including rising to the occasion of risky public challenges, as is the lot of warriors. Ever attempting both compromise and conciliation, their imprudent decisions are not the reason for their predicament, but rather the hostility of the Kauravas is the explanation. But for this hostility, exemplified by the rigged game of dice and the high-stakes challenge the Kauravas set, the Pāṇḍavas would have lived a peaceful existence and would never have been the authors of their own misfortune.

With all attempts at conciliation dashed by the Kauravas' greed and hostility, war is a *fait accompli*. Krishna agrees to be Arjuna's charioteer in the fateful battle, which will not only pit the Pāṇḍavas against the Kauravas but also the Pāṇḍavas against kin who fight on the side of the Kauravas for reasons of professional loyalty and not because of any sympathy for the Kauravas' plight. Indeed, to all who have any sense, the calamity that is to occur is a result of the Kauravas, who managed to pursue their program of aggression in part because of the Pāṇḍavas' commitment to moral standards of conciliation and compromise.

Arjuna laments the conditions that have brought him to this point. The details of the oncoming war are especially tragic. Arjuna and his four brothers (all sons of Pāṇḍu and thereby called the "Pāṇḍavas") were unjustly cheated out of their kingdom by their sociopathic cousins (the Kauravas), and the Pāṇḍavas had sought every diplomatic means of resolving the tension that would allow them to live the remainder of their lives peacefully. They initially sought the restoration of their entire wealth but later were willing to settle for a modest five villages to eke out a living. War was made inevitable not by the Pāṇḍavas' refusal to compromise, lack of deference, and willingness to make peace but by the Kauravas' tyrannical unwillingness to make peace. What makes the impending war especially tragic is that the Pāṇḍavas are faced with the challenge of fighting not only tyrannical relatives that they could not care less for; they must also fight loved ones and well-wishers, who, through obligations that arise out of patronage and professional loyalty to the throne, must fight with the tyrants. Bhīṣma, the grand-uncle of the Pāṇḍavas and the Kauravas and an invincible warrior (gifted or cursed with the freedom to choose when he will die), is an example of one such well-wisher. He repudiated the motives of the Kauravas and sympathized with the Pāṇḍavas, but because of an oath that preceded the birth of his tyrannical grandnephews (the Kauravas), he remained loyal to the throne on which the Kauravas' father, Dhṛtarāshtra, presided. Arjuna, who looked upon Bhīṣma and others like him as loving elders, had to subsequently fight him. The conflict and tender feelings between these parties was on display when, before the war, Arjuna's eldest brother, Yudhiṣṭhira, wanted the blessings of Bhīṣma on the battlefield to commence the war and Bhīṣma, his enemy and leader of the opposing army, blessed him with victory.[10]

Before the commencement of the battle, on the very battlefield with armies lined up in opposition and with Krishna as his charioteer, Arjuna loses heart and entertains three arguments against fighting.

First, if he were to fight the war, it would result in death and destruction on both sides, including the death of loved ones. Even if he succeeds, there would be no joy in victory because his family would largely have been decimated as a function of the war.[11] This is a consequentialist and, more specifically, utilitarian argument. Consequentialism is the theory that the ends justify the means. Utilitarianism is the version of consequentialism that holds that agent-neutral ends, such as the maximization of happiness or the minimization of pain, justify our actions. In the Indian tradition, the source of such arguments could be Buddhists, who are known for a consequentialist ethics,[12] or perhaps proponents of the Nyāya tradition.[13] Regardless of the cultural origins, according to utilitarianism, the right thing to do is justified by some agent-neutral good (harm reduction or the maximization of happiness), and, here, Arjuna's reasoning is that he should skip fighting to ensure the good of avoiding harm. It is worth noting that this argument on the basis of utilitarianism pans out only if fighting ends up making things worse; if war were the means to maximize happiness or minimize suffering, utilitarianism would justify war. In the case of the *Mahābhārata*, luck has it that the Pāṇḍavas are fewer in number than the Kauravas, and so it would seem that giving into the Kauravas would make more people happy and simply avoid the bloodshed and pain of war.

Second, if the battle is between good and evil, Arjuna's character is not that of the evil ones (the Kauravas), yet fighting a war would make him no better than his adversaries.[14] This is a virtue ethical argument. According to such arguments, the right thing to do is the result of a good, the virtues, or strength of character. In the Western tradition, virtue ethics is associated with Plato and Aristotle, who did not reason that war was unnecessary, and Plato in the *Republic* reasoned that a class of people in an ideal community are needed to wage war, namely, the guardians. In the Indian tradition, the thinkers who were the likely source of this virtue theoretic argument were the Jains, who regarded all action, especially and including action in deference to one's own physical interests, as wrong because such action further buries one's own virtue in practical schemes that run counter to the innate benign character of persons.[15] The idea that fighting evil renders oneself debased and evil (and that passivism is the appropriate response to evil) has a firm basis in Jain moral theory. The argument also resonates with the Christian idea in the Gospel of Matthew that the proper alternative to a retaliatory approach to offense is to turn the other cheek.

Third, war results in lawlessness, which undermines the virtue and safety of women and children (*Gītā*, 1.41). This might be understood as an elaboration of the first consequentialist argument: not only does war end in suffering, which should be avoided, but it also leads to undermining the personal safety of women and children and, because their safety is good, we ought to avoid war to protect it. But the argument can also be understood as a version of Kantian-style deontology.

An essential feature of deontology is the identification of goods, whether they are actions (i.e., duties) or freedoms (i.e., rights), as being what require justification on procedural grounds. A duty is hence not only something that is good to do and a right is not only something good to have, but one we have reason to do or allow. Such goods, duties, and rights constitute the social fabric and are justified (as Kant reasoned) in so far as they help us relate to each other in a kingdom of ends. Deontology is hence the inverse of consequentialism; whereas consequentialism holds that the good outcome justifies the procedure, the deontologist holds that some good state of affairs (i.e., actions and freedoms) are justified by a procedural consideration. But what consequentialism, deontology, *and* virtue ethics have in common is the idea that the good (i.e., the valuable outcome) is an essential feature of making sense of the right (thing to do). Morality defined or explained by way of the good is something that can be established as an outcome of reality and hence conventionalized. Thinking about morality by way of the good helps us identify an area of moral reasoning we might call *conventional morality*: actions motivated by good character (virtue ethics), good actions that we have good reason to do (deontology), and actions that are justified in so far as they promise to maximize the good as such (consequentialism).

What is surprising hence is that all of Arjuna's arguments against war make use of the *good*, and the theories he relies on fill out the content of what we could call conventional morality. According to conventional morality, we should do what is inspired by the virtues, avoid causing harm, and affirm the importance of good rules of interaction, whether they be characterized as rights or duties. War disrupts conventional morality as Arjuna laments. And this is indeed tragic in so far as conventional morality is organized around the *good*.

But there is indeed another side to the story, which Arjuna does not see and the *Mahābhārata* renders clear. It was conventional morality that made it possible for the Kauravas to exercise their hostility against the Pāṇḍavas by restricting and constraining the Pāṇḍavas. The Pāṇḍavas could have rid themselves of the Kauravas by killing them at any number of earlier times when they had the chance in times of peace, and everyone who survived would have been better off for having been rid of moral parasites as rulers and having the benevolent Pāṇḍavas instead. They could have accomplished this most easily by assassinating the Kauravas in secret or perhaps openly in public when they were not expecting it because the Kauravas never worried about nor protected themselves from such a threat, owing to the virtue of the Pāṇḍavas, whom they counted on. And yet the Pāṇḍavas' fidelity to conventional morality created a context for the Kauravas to ply their trade of deceit and hostility. The game of dice that snared the Pāṇḍavas is a metaphor for conventional morality itself: a social practice justified by prospects of a good outcome (consequentialism), organized around good rules that make the participation of all possible (deontology), and actions that follow from the courage and strength of its participants (virtue ethics).

The lesson of the *Mahābhārata* generalizes; conventional morality places constraints on people who are conventionally moral, and this enables the maleficence of those who act to undermine conventional morality by undermining those who bind themselves with it. Call the latter, who use conventional morality as a weapon against the conventionally moral, *moral parasites* (Kauravas) and the former, who are happy to be bound by conventional morality, *moral conventionalists* (Pāṇḍavas). The moral parasite is someone who, for instance, wishes you to be honest and to abide by conventions of transparency so they can steal from you. The moral parasite is someone who, for instance, wishes for you to behave in a manner that is courteous, kind, and accommodating so they can assault you, without resistance. The only way to end this relationship of parasitism is for the conventionally moral to give up on conventional morality and engage moral parasites in war. This would be a just war—*dharmyaṃ yuddham*—and the essence of a just war because the cause would be to rid the world of moral parasites. Yet, from the perspective of conventional morality, which encourages mutually accommodating behavior, this departure is wrong and bad. Indeed, relying purely on conventional standards that encourage social interaction for the promise of a good, an argument for pacifism is more easily constructed than an argument for war.

McMahan, from the perspective of the authors of the *Gītā* and *Mahābhārata*, is correct for noting that there is an important moral distinction to be drawn between those who fight for a just cause and those who do not. We might even note that the thrust of the argument from the *Gītā* agrees that those who fight for a just cause do no wrong but those who fight for an unjust cause are not morally equal to those who fight for a just cause—it is in an important sense wrong for them to fight the war. The liability requirement of discrimination, which holds that combatants must intentionally attack only those who are legitimate targets, is often thought to mark out *jus in bello* for all parties, and legitimate targets are often thought to be restricted to enemy combatants, clearly marked out from third parties, such as civilians. As McMahan notes, it is not at all clear how this applies to those who fight for an unjust cause because the injustice of the cause should undermine the propriety of attacking enemy (just) combatants. From the perspective of the *Gītā*, we could also agree to his conclusion that "the traditional criterion of liability to attack in war [from the West]—posing a threat to others—is unacceptable."[16] Everyone poses a threat to others in so far as we all stand in each other's way. He further elaborates:

> As I have presented it, the alternative conception of innocence is that one is innocent if one is neither morally responsible for nor guilty of a wrong. While the classical just war theorists focused on guilt, I think we should focus instead on moral responsibility. It is, I think, a mistake to suppose that noninnocence in the sense of moral guilt or culpability is necessary for liability to attack in war. Something less is sufficient: namely, moral responsibility for a wrong, particularly an objectively unjustified threat of harm. . . . [P]osing an objectively unjustified threat is not sufficient for liability in the absence of moral responsibility for that threat. In short, the criterion of liability to attack in war is moral responsibility for an objectively unjustified threat of harm.[17]

What the *Gītā* and *Mahābhārata* show, however, is that this threshold is too high. Moral parasites do something objectively wrong by being moral parasites, but the wrong is much less than a threat of harm; it is merely the imposition of conventional moral standards on others as a means of hostility. It is difficult to characterize this as an objectively unjustified threat of harm if one endorses conventional morality because moral conventionalists are paradoxically committed to agreeing to this imposition because they have their own reasons for endorsing it. That a thief desires us to be honest, for instance, does not undermine our reasons for being honest, and, for us, honesty may continue to be the best policy, even though it is in the advantage of the parasite.

In the *Mahābhārata* itself, it is most important that Krishna, the adviser of the Pāṇḍavas, steps in as their representative when they return from their exile and pursues peace and compromise to its logical extent. Krishna attempts to broker that the Pāṇḍavas should be given five villages for them to live in so that they can each sustain themselves as professional rulers of these communities. The Kauravas refuse, though they only took hold of the land in trust while the Pāṇḍavas were in exile. But now a new set of conventions has been created, with the Kauravas in charge of everything, and it is the imposition of this convention that constitutes the Kauravas' final assault as moral parasites. In this case, it is difficult for the Pāṇḍavas to see the move as an imposition of conventional morality (because it excludes them), and perhaps for this reason the Pāṇḍavas are inclined to fight. But the real reason war is inevitable is not for lack of conciliation on the part of the Pāṇḍavas but by virtue of the parasitism of the Kauravas.

KRISHNA'S RESPONSE

To recap, the *Mahābhārata* depicts just war as arising at the breakdown of conventional morality, between those who would protect and abide by such constraints and against those who would not. Before this breakdown, there is indeed a clear line that separates the innocent from the evil; not only is one side justified in its cause, but its conduct is creditable too, whereas the other side is not justified in its cause, and its conduct is discreditable. But, after the breakdown of conventional morality, when the virtuous are no longer willing to be constrained by the virtues themselves and are willing to engage in conduct outside the bounds of conventional morality and are hence motivated to engage in war, it is paradoxical to draw lines in the sand between sides; the *Mahābhārata*'s stress on the familial drama, which pits well-wishers against well-wishers, illustrates this point.[18] War might be *right* and hence *just*, but it is difficult to argue that it is good. The evil of war is shown by the desire of combatants in a war not for endless war (something we wish to preserve or maximize) but for victory, which is a good and also the cessation of war. So those who are committed to engaging in battle are hence not committed to the goodness of war but to its end. This shows that to transition from conventional morality to war is to leave the good as an organizing principle and to engage in an activity that is bad but also conventionally bad—with the distant hope of a good. In facilitating an understanding of the etiology of a just war, the *Mahābhārata* at once allows us to understand the moral distinction between those who fight justly (i.e., moral conventionalists) and those who do not (i.e., moral parasites), and yet the war that ensues constitutes a departure from the standards that would allow us to draw sides. And, whereas McMahan[19] argued that the moral considerations that exist before war are exactly those that allow us to understand the justice of one side during war, the *Mahābhārata* appears to deny this because the conventional moral considerations are structured around the good and war is crucially a bad thing characterized by several evils. Indeed, Arjuna's three arguments against war reviewed above—his consequentialist argument,[20] virtue ethical argument,[21] and deontological argument[22]—show the evil of war. Krishna's argument in response does not refute that war is bad: it trades on deflating the relevance of the good to rational deliberation.

Krishna's argument in the *Gītā* that concludes that Arjuna should fight his war and that such a war would be just provides a purely procedural approach to moral theorizing that does not involve or rely upon the good in any deep way. This allows Krishna to mark out a different set of moral considerations that survive the breakdown of conventional morality, which does depend on the good. This approach allows us to distinguish whose conduct and cause is just in war from those whose conduct and causes are unjust.

The first procedural ethic he defends is a form of deontology he calls *karma yoga*, the discipline of action. Action is itself purposeful, and the discipline of action is a practice of perfecting purposeful action. The argument is delivered generally as an argument for correct action in the face of uncertainty: no matter who you are, something counts as your duty, and the perfection of this duty is itself a good that relieves one from trouble.[23] Moreover, all people who uphold a transcendental moral order (including Krishna, who is depicted here as the Lord—the procedural ideal of right action, which in its essence is both unconservatism and self-governance) participate in this moral order by doing their duty. Krishna too, the procedural ideal, must participate in dutiful behavior, and the Lord's duties include *lokasaṃgraha* (the maintenance of the welfare of the world)[24] and to reestablish the moral order when it declines.[25] Whereas deontology can be part of a conventionalized picture of morality, *karma yoga* abstracts from conventional morality. One's duty can continue even at the breakdown of conventional moral expectations structured around the good because it is justified not by the good but by procedural considerations. But, as the reward of such behavior is duty itself, moral parasitism is limited in its capacity to treat one's own conscientious behavior as a tool of its hostility.

The next step is *bhakti yoga*, the discipline of devotion. Here, right action is defined by its conformity to a regulative ideal—Krishna himself—and, in doing what is right, we sacrifice a concern for the outcome as a means of worshipping the procedural ideal. This same theory is found elsewhere, articulated more clearly in the *Yoga Sūtra*; it is the moral theory of yoga (discipline) or *bhakti*.[26] According to this account, right action is defined by a procedural ideal—unconservatism and self-governance—and perfecting our practice of the right is the good. This theory differs from deontology in an important respect. Whereas deontology treats our duty as itself a good, justified by procedural considerations only, in yoga/bhakti, the right is defined by a procedural ideal, and hence we do not need to understand our moral practice in terms of the good.[27] In contrast to virtue ethics, consequentialism, and deontology, it alone accounts for morality without recourse to the good. The good is not a primitive notion, here, but one definable by way of the perfection of the right. So, whereas conventional morality is structured around the good, bhakti dispenses with the good.

A third moral practice that Krishna recommends is *jñāna yoga*: the discipline of thoughtfulness or knowledge. *Jñāna* yoga is the critical appreciation of the framework of moral action, which complements karma yoga's disinterest in trying to understand action as justified by outcome. It is the meta-ethical component of the shift away from conventional morality to a fully procedural approach to ethics. The essential element in this recipe is a move to thinking about morality in purely procedural terms, which cuts out the good as a primitive concept. This allows those who engage in just war, against moral parasites, to have a moral compass that is not that of conventional morality, which they had to leave behind to fight. Moreover, the moral compass of yoga—discipline, or proceduralism—is timeless in so far as we can understand its importance, even within the context of the breakdown of conventional morality.

In the moral framework of yoga, there is a way to clearly identify the *jus ad bellum* of just war. Previously we identified the just cause as the cause of ridding the world of moral parasites. This is reworked into a positive doctrine with yoga: our cause is just when we are devoted to the regulative ideal of unconservatism and self-governance and our conduct is thereby just; it is thereby not possible to have just conduct without a just cause. But this is a winning strategy in war because it involves giving up on conventional morality and engaging in belligerent action outside of the scope of convention but is also contrary to those who would attempt to constrain our potential. Moral parasites are deprived of their favored weapon, but this is a side effect of our own devotion to the Lord: unconservatism and self-governance. This requires that we follow the dialectic of Krishna, which begins with deontology but ends with the recommendation that we do not worry about morality, merely devotion to the procedural ideal (*Gītā*, 18:66). This seems paradoxical, but the paradox disappears when we appreciate that the moral standards we give up are conventional, tied to the good, and the one we embrace is ideal, tied to the regulative ideal.

The argument we find in the *Gītā* provides us a way to understand the logic of self-defense. The idea that we have a right to defend ourselves against aggression is widely acknowledged. But for pacifists, who take the stand that we should turn the other cheek, most would regard it as within our rights and perhaps even a requirement of justice that we defend ourselves against aggression, especially if this aggression is itself a departure from conventional morality, unprovoked or unjustified. Yet it is difficult to square with conventional moral expectation. Harming others does not follow from the conventional moral virtues; it is not a good end that could justify morality (unless one's idea of morality is sadism), and harming others is not a conventional moral duty. Yet this is what self-defense entails. It would seem that one's aggressor's departure from conventional morality, by adopting an aggressive or threatening posture, is what apparently justifies one's own departure from conventional expectations. And yet, so described, the right that we have to meet such hostility in kind assumes that we have departed the moral parameters of conventional morality. But now it appears that we have left behind the tools we would need to justify our actions. This is the predicament of the Pāṇḍavas against the Kauravas. Krishna's arguments for devotion provide the matrix for making sense of self-defense: it is a mere function of our devotion to unconservatism and self-governance and requires no permission or blessing from conventional morality. To talk about it as a right—a good freedom that we should protect—is to use the language of convention to capture something whose justification transcends the good. However, this procedural ideal—the Lord—is not proprietary but something we share as a governing interest as people who have an interest in their own unconservatism and self-governance. The ideal is something that we can organize and rally around as common cause. Parasites concerned only with their own good do not aspire to this common just cause and are instead tied to their vision of the good.

OBJECTIONS

One objection to the argument for a procedural approach to just war theory is that it not only licenses self-defense but apparently also preemptive measures. If we were to appreciate the motive of a party as moral parasitism, it would apparently be proper for us to confront, intimidate, or do away with such parasites, even if they had yet to break a moral convention and especially to prevent them from violating moral expectations. This seems like a problem if we understand just war by way of conventional morality. But, as noted, war does away with that. Moreover, intimidating and marginalizing moral parasites is part of the very moral procedure of devotion to unconservatism and self-governance, and, in so far as this can allow us to identify the just side in a conflict and to distinguish it from the moral parasites, we have no reason to object. The moral parasites, unlike the moral conventionalists, are motivated by the subjective goods of their hostility: their advantage. The moral conventionalist who takes up a procedural ethic is instead devoted in general to procedural considerations in morality. This suggests hence that the best just war is one where there is virtually little or no fighting; as in matters of health, the best measures would be preventive. This too seems strange if we adopt the posture of conventional morality but proper if we are proceduralists.

Consider also the case of anticolonial freedom fighters, who in the case of India or perhaps the civil rights movement in the United States, adopted tactics of unconservatism and self-governance that crippled conventional moral expectations as a means of deflating the power of moral parasites, such as British imperialists and racist policymakers of the United States. Gandhi is famous for his reliance on the *Bhagavad Gītā* for inspiration for his struggle. What is often not noted is that he drew inspiration and theory from the *Yoga Sūtra*,[28] which not only articulates the radical procedural approach to morality (yoga and bhakti) but also prescribes civil disobedience as a means of dealing with moral parasites.[29] M. L. King for his part was deeply influenced by the political theorizing of Gandhi, and he applied the same strategy in the US context. In the literature, citizen protests against hate groups and progressive political movements of liberation against colonialist or racist oppression are not treated as cases of war. Consider for instance Virginia Held's list of differing kinds of war: "world wars, small wars, civil wars, revolutions, and wars of liberation." Her comment that "terrorism resembles a small war"[30] is a characterization that excludes bloodless, nonviolent social confrontation. For any of these to be just, according to the considerations of the *Gītā*, they must involve a devotion to the regulative ideal, but then the justice of war is not to be measured in terms of casualties but in terms of the cause.

A second objection might be that the yogic or procedural approach to just war theory cannot explain the continuity of conflict in many areas of the world because surely some sides in these conflicts are just, and they should be far more successful if they manage to uproot the target of just war—moral parasites—by leaving aside conventional morality. The obvious response is that in most cases of sustained and perpetual conflict it is not clear whether any side has an uncontroversially just cause because all sides are tied to conventional morality to some measure. Each wishes their vision of the goods of morality to be imposed on the other, and this desire to impose such standards is an act of aggression. Such a mutual imposition might characterize a cold war or an active war of violence. Such wars are difficult to terminate because no side is motivated to revise the moral order but merely to sustain their vision of it.

A third objection is that just war understood as a procedural affair, as the *Gītā* describes it, licenses preemptive strikes that are unjustified. We might consider George W. Bush's bombing and takeover of Iraq on the (fabricated) supposed threat of weapons of mass destruction. Saddam Hussein could be described as a moral parasite who wanted to inflict a certain conventionalized vision on others for personal gain, and so it would have seemed just for the United States to attack Iraq. Yet this is widely regarded as a failure and hardly the paradigm case of a just war. Such scenarios of unjust preemptive strikes fail an important procedural test: unconservatism and self-governance as a procedural ideal that defines the right prevents us from thinking about campaigns as motivated by some good (say getting rid of Saddam Hussain) but rather fidelity to the regulative ideal. Hence, unjust preemptive strikes will fail to be just because they are motivated by some perceived good, such as the imposition of democracy, riddance of a perceived threat, or the rooting out of a dictator. The just cause is one that we can make sense of independent of threats. The Allied campaign against the Axis powers in WWII stands in sharp contrast. Here, the war was a function of the Allies' practice of reestablishing their own unconservatism and self-governance and thereby was just. In this case, the Axis powers had assumed a hostile position not only with respect to their own citizens (as in the case of Germany's persecution of its own minorities) but also with respect to their neighbors. The Allied intervention to disarm this hostility and put an end to the persecution of minorities was hence required to reestablish unconservatism and self-governance in general and the unconservatism and self-governance of the Allies. In the case of the Triple Entente versus the Triple Alliance in WWI, the origins of the war and cause of justice is murkier. Had either side sought to inculcate unconservatism and self-governance among all combatants, their cause would be just. The harsh conditions of the Treaty of Versailles that the French and British (of the Triple Entente) imposed on Germany (of the Triple Alliance) were punitive; they demanded an admission of German guilt for the war, and reparations undermined the cause of the Triple Entente because it rendered punishing the Germans the goal of the war, not the reestablishment of unconservatism and self-governance. That German resentment could lead to another world war is unsurprising; it was a function of a failure to resolve the war justly. The earlier annexation of the Balkan states of Bosnia and Herzegovina by the Austro-Hungarian Empire, thought to have motivated the Serbian nationalists to assassinate the Austro-Hungarian Archduke Ferdinand and commonly thought to be the start of WWI, constituted the imposition of a moral convention on a population that did not ask for it. This was an unjust action that tainted the cause of the Triple Alliance.

India's forceful reclamation of Goa from Portuguese rule (1961) was just; the Portuguese as colonizers were participating in the breakdown of conventional morality by the imposition of their laws as a means of controlling the local population. Portuguese control of Goa was hence unjust, and the Portuguese were hence not justified in resisting Indian takeover, which had the effect of returning local South Asian control to Goa. India's military intercession in Bangladesh's liberation from Pakistan (1971) was similarly justified; West Pakistan's violent attempt to wrest control of East Bengal, after a history of marginalization and imperial rule from the west, not only justified Bangladesh's break but also India's intercession on behalf of the breakaway East Bengal to establish unconservatism and self-governance for all concerned.

CONCLUSION

A famous Indian argument for *jus ad bellum* and *jus in bello* is presented in literary form in the *Mahābhārata*; it involves events and dynamics between two groups, moral conventionalists and moral parasites, that come to a head in the fateful battle, which the *Bhagavad Gītā* precedes. Arjuna's own lament is an internalization of the logic of conventional moral expectations that allowed moral parasitism, and Krishna's push for a purely procedural approach to moral reasoning that, in its radical form, does away with the good as a primitive of explanation provides the moral considerations that allow us to see that the *jus ad bellum* and *jus in bello* coincide. The just cause is the approximation to the procedural ideal, which is also just conduct. Hence, McMahan[31] would be correct in claiming that it is wrong for the unjust to attack the just. But it is also not obviously correct that it is the same set of moral considerations in war and peace that mark out the sides because peace is largely characterizable by conventional morality, which all are forced to abandon in war. Walzer[32] is correct that there are different sets of standards at play at war and peace and that getting hands dirty in immorality is a price worth paying in war,[33] but Walzer is thereby incorrect for a subtle reason: conventional standards by way of which *jus ad bellum* and *jus in bello* appear corrupt are themselves actually corrupt when the need for a just war arises. It is because moral parasites use conventional morality as a means of hostility and not as a means of fair, inclusive social interaction that conventional morality is corrupted and turned into a tool of the unjust. It is hence unjust to employ these standards to judge those whose cause is just, though such a judgment is conventional. In no way does *jus in bello* that breaks conventional moral standards lessen *jus ad bellum*. And indeed, the departure from conventional morality by those whose cause is just is decisive in undermining the cause of the unjust. Certainly, those who fight for a just cause thereby justly get their hands dirty by departing from conventional moral standards. But this is to the disadvantage of parasites who can function only in a climate where the conventionally good are constrained by conventional morality. Just war so understood deprives parasites of their weapon of choice. Just war thereby succeeds by the just imposing on the unjust the cruelties, disadvantages, or inconveniences rendered impossible by conventional morality.

BIBLIOGRAPHY

Allen, Nick. "Just War in the Mahābhārata." In *The Ethics of War: Shared Problems in Different Traditions*, edited by Richard Sorabji and David Rodin, 138–49. Hants, England: Ashgate Publishing Limited, 2006.

Brobjer, Thomas H. "Nietzsche's Reading about Eastern Philosophy." *Journal of Nietzsche Studies* 28 (2004): 3–35. http://www.jstor.org.ezproxy.library.yorku.ca/stable/20717839.

Chakrabarti, Kisor K. "Nyāya Consequentialism." In *The Bloomsbury Research Handbook of Indian Ethics*, edited by Shyam Ranganathan, 203–24. Bloomsbury Research Handbooks in Asian Philosophy. London: Bloomsbury Academic, 2017.

Clooney, Francis X. "Pain But Not Harm: Some Classical Resources toward a Hindu Just War Theory." In *Just War in Comparative Perspective*, edited by Paul Robinson, 109–26. Hampshire, England: Ashgate Publishing Limited, 2003.

Coady, C. A. J. "The Problem of Dirty Hands." Stanford Encyclopedia of Philosophy. Published April 29, 2009. Modified January 24, 2014. https://plato.stanford.edu/archives/spr2014/entries/dirty-hands/.

Goodman, Charles. *Consequences of Compassion: An Interpretation and Defense of Buddhist Ethics*. Oxford: Oxford University Press, 2009.

Held, Virginia. "Terrorism and War." *Journal of Ethics* 8, no. 1 (2004): 59–75.

The Mahābhārata: Abridged and Translated. Translated by John D. Smith. London: Penguin, 2009.

Mahābhāratam: Shriman Mahābhāratam. Part I. With Bharata Bhawadeepa by Nīlakaṇṭha. Edited by Ramchandrashastri Kinjawadekar. Vulgate, Bombay/Poona ed. Poona City, 1931.

McMahan, Jeff. *Killing in War*. Oxford: Oxford University Press, 2009.

Puri, Bindu. *Sophia Studies in Cross-cultural Philosophy of Traditions and Cultures*. Vol. 9: *The Tagore–Gandhi Debate on Matters of Truth and Untruth*. New Delhi: Springer, 2015.

Rāmānuja. *Śrī Rāmānuja Gītā Bhāṣya* (Edition and Translation). Translated by Svami Adidevanada. Madras: Sri Ramakrishna Math, 1991.

Ranganathan, Shyam. *Hinduism: A Contemporary Philosophical Investigation*, edited by Chad Meister and Charles Taliaferro. Investigating Philosophy of Religion. New York: Routledge, 2018.

———. "Patañjali's Yoga: Universal Ethics as the Formal Cause of Autonomy." In *The Bloomsbury Research Handbook of Indian Ethics*, edited by Shyam Ranganathan, 177–202. Bloomsbury Research Handbooks in Asian Philosophy. London: Bloomsbury Academic, 2017.

———. "Western Imperialism, Indology and Ethics." In *The Bloomsbury Research Handbook of Indian Ethics*, edited by Shyam Ranganathan, 1–122. Bloomsbury Research Handbooks in Asian Philosophy. London: Bloomsbury Academic, 2017.

Roy, Kaushik. "Just and Unjust War in Hindu Philosophy." *Journal of Military Ethics* 6, no. 3 (2007): 232–45.

Smith, David. "Nietzsche's Hinduism, Nietzsche's India: Another Look." *Journal of Nietzsche Studies* 28 (2004): 37–56. http://www.jstor.org.ezproxy.library.yorku.ca/stable/20717840.

Soni, Jayandra. "Jaina Ethics: Action and Non-Action." In *The Bloomsbury Research Handbook of Indian Ethics*, edited by Shyam Ranganathan, 155–76. Bloomsbury Research Handbooks in Asian Philosophy. London: Bloomsbury Academic, 2017.

Walzer, Michael. *Just and Unjust Wars*. Harmondsworth: Penguin, 1977.

———. "Political Action: The Problem of Dirty Hands." In *War and Moral Responsibility*, edited by Marshall Cohen, Thomas Nagel, and Thomas Scanlon, 62–82. Princeton, NJ: Princeton University Press, 1974.

Chapter Eleven

The Islamic War Ethic in Theory and Practice

Davis Brown

INTRODUCTION

Among the great debates over and within Islam today are whether Islam and the Islamic world are militant and whether the Islamic world will embrace a militant agenda in the future. Lewis, for example, highlights the moderate–extremist divide within the Islamic world over whether its woes are self-inflicted or inflicted upon it by others[1]—the latter warranting violence in response but the former not. Ayoob argues that mainstream Islamist parties, forming the "overwhelming majority" of Islamic political organizations, "by and large abjure violence."[2] But far too much literature—both Western and Muslim—is devoted to this question to explain away Islamic militarism as a fringe ideology. Abou el Fadl laments the encroachment of Islamic extremism and its imposition on mainstream Islam.[3]

This chapter explores the war ethic in Islamic thought. This is a difficult topic in the current sociopolitical environment. On one hand, most full professors are old enough to remember the rise of political Islam and the wave of Islamic terrorism from the 1980s through 9/11 and beyond. On the other hand, the several iterations of the Trump administration's travel ban (2017–present) have stoked accusations, long in the making, of widespread, unjustified Islamophobia in popular culture. While I agree with Islam apologists that terms like "jihad" are not well understood in non-Arabic-speaking cultures, the evidence has forced me to argue that the militaristic war ethic *does* prevail in Islamic thought, in both this chapter and other works. Those who profess that the Islamic war ethic is a misunderstood ethic of restraint will find little comfort in this chapter. Although other religions also have had roles in fueling interstate armed conflict, Islam has fueled more than its fair share since 1945, including the conflicts between Greece and Turkey, Israel and the Arab nations, Pakistan and India, and Somalia and Ethiopia.[4] The same is true for intrastate armed conflict. Toft finds that of forty-two religious civil wars from 1940 to 2000, 80 percent of them involved parties identifying with Islam, as opposed to 50 percent for Christianity and 16 percent for Hinduism.[5]

So what is going on? Are the statistics just cited spurious empirical anomalies, skewed by other political sentiments against Israel? Or are they skewed by some factor external to Islam, such as Western aggression against the Islamic world? My own empirical evidence, based on the dependent variable of armed conflict initiation, rather than simply involvement and controlling for Israel as the target, suggests that the correlation of Islam to interstate armed conflict initiation is not spurious.[6] This chapter's focus, however, is on the qualitative analysis of the Islamic war ethic. For substance, this is done via scripture, classical literature, and historical narrative. For its application, this is done in a case study. As detailed in the pages that follow, I argue that the Islamic war ethic overall is permissive relative to that of other religions and that the root of that permissiveness is Islam itself.

This chapter proceeds as follows. First is an introduction to the Islamic differentiation of Self and Other through the *dar al-harb*, *dar al-islam*, and the lesser-known *dar al-suhl*. Space does not permit adequate introduction of the underlying Islamic political theory. Second is an introduction to the concepts of self-defense and jihad in the Islamic war ethic. This section treats that war ethic in Islam as a whole, not in specific denomination or school (e.g., Hanafi and Maliki). Source material is included from authors who are Sunni, Shi'ite, and non-Muslim.[7] Third is a detailed illustration of Islam's effects on decisions for war and peace at the level of head of state; the selected case study is the Yom Kippur War of 1973, followed by the Egyptian–Israeli Peace Treaty of 1979. I argue that both of Egypt's preferences for war and then peace were rooted in Islam.

THE *DAR AL-HARB, DAR AL-ISLAM,* AND *DAR AL-SUHL*

In Islamic thought, the world is divided between the *dar al-harb*, abode of war/conflict, characterized by everything impious and undesirable, and the *dar al-islam*, the abode of submission to Islam, in which all those faults are righted.[8] Not only is this a recipe for Islamic hostility toward non-Islam, but it also generates a moral dilemma: whether the *dar al-islam* should be expanded by force.[9]

This tension is evident in principles of the Islamic law of nations. In Islam, international law was intended as a temporary institution only because

Islam's goal was to unite the world under its banner and, in doing so, bring about a universal peace.[10] This outlook is reflected in Islam's antipathy for perpetual treaties with non-Islam.[11] Ayatollah Khomeini, the former supreme religious leader of Iran, declared his opposition to treaties that contradicted Islam, and Sheikh Shaltut, rector of al-Azhar, asserted the right to denounce treaties that did not serve Islam's interest.[12] Accepting the authority of modern international law—a Western construction with roots in Christianity—offends the supremacy of Islamic law. This sentiment is reflected in reservations of many Muslim states to core provisions of the Convention on the Elimination of All Forms of Discrimination against Women (CEDAW).[13] Many Muslim states ratified the Convention but made reservations that nothing in the Convention would override Islamic law; this practice prompted several Western states to lodge objections to those reservations, claiming them to be fundamentally incompatible with CEDAW's object and purpose and therefore making the reserving states not genuine parties.[14]

The early jurisconsults constructed a third, often neglected, abode: the *dar al-suhl* (i.e., abode of treaty or conciliation). Conflict with non-Islam may be temporarily suspended when in Islam's interest—usually as a realistic acknowledgment of its contemporaneous relative weakness.[15] The Ottoman sultan's willingness to end the Crimean War and enter the Westphalian system[16] is best interpreted in this light, as is the Moroccan sultan's willingness to normalize peaceful relations with Europe.[17] However, the *dar al-suhl* has its limits. It allows Islamdom to capitulate to geopolitical realities, but, once those realities no longer require accommodating the *dar al-harb*, Islamic thought prescribes that such accommodation and conciliation should cease. The struggle for dominance may be revived whenever necessary.[18]

PRINCIPLES AND SUBSTANCE OF THE ISLAMIC WAR ETHIC

Islamic Conception of Self-Defense

Contemporary international law and most ethics of war acknowledge a nation's right of self-defense. The UN Charter releases a state from Article 2(4)'s general prohibition of using force when an armed attack occurs against it.[19] In the Christian just war tradition, war against another state is permitted "on account of some fault" (i.e., the criterion of "just cause").[20] Secular variants of the just war tradition preserve this right, though often limiting just cause to being attacked. Like most other *ad bellum* ethics, Islam permits force in self-defense. However, as the following pages show, the range of acts constituting an "attack" that justified self-defense is wider, making Islamic *jus ad bellum* more permissive.

In Islam's earliest days, Muhammad and his followers were weak, and God's revelations compelled him to persuade unbelievers but not fight them.[21] When the movement strengthened and its adversaries stepped up their efforts to destroy it, later revelations reversed the pacifist stance and sanctioned fighting.[22] The primary scriptural basis for this is Quran 22:39–40, which not only permits fighting against oppression but even requires it.[23] Several gentler translations of the Sword Verses (Quran 2:190–93, 9:5, 9:29) may be interpreted in this light. In addition, there is a duty to defend and protect the weak (i.e., fight for those who cannot defend themselves).[24]

But as Donner points out, whether the Quran limits violence to self-defense "is really left to the judgment of the exegete."[25] In fairness, the most militant Sword Verses cited by al-Qaeda and the likes (e.g., 9:5, kill the unbelievers wherever you find them) were specifically directed against the Quraysh tribe and its partisans. But translations and therefore interpretations vary widely. Pickthall, Dawood, and Muhammad Ali translate Quran 2:190 as a prohibition of *agg*ression, but newer translations of Haleem, Hilali and Khan, and Yusuf Ali interpret the same verse as prohibiting *trans*gression (of limits). The former prescribes force for defense only, but the latter constrains violence within the confines of *jus ad bellum* (i.e., the moral decision to engage in war) and *jus in bello* (i.e., conduct during warfare), which Islam itself prescribes. If, as other Quranic passages suggest, Muslims have broad discretion—or are required—to attack non-Muslims because of their unbelief, then Islamic *jus ad bellum* is rendered considerably more permissive. In addition, the verse might speak only to *jus in bello* and therefore not constrain the decision to attack (*jus ad bellum*).

The translations of Quran 2:191 vary widely in defining enemy wrongdoing that justifies the lesser wrongdoing of killing them. A plurality of translations known to this author employ the term "persecution," but others use "tumult and oppression," idolatry, or polytheism and apostasy. "Persecution" and "oppression" limit war to remediate *material* injuries, but idolatry, polytheism, and apostasy broaden the *casus belli* significantly.

The translations of Quran 2:193, articulating the objective of war, also vary widely. In the Haleem, Pickthall, and Muhammad Ali translations, the goal is to stop "persecution." These translations suggest that the purpose of fighting is defensive (i.e., relieve Muslims from material oppression by non-Muslims). In contrast, objectives of war in the other translations are more transcendental: in Dawood, the objectives are to eradicate "idolatry"; in Hilali and Khan, to eradicate "disbelief and worshipping of others along with Allâh"; and, in Yusuf Ali, to eradicate "tumult or oppression"—potentially very broad depending on the nature of "tumult."

The other objective in Quran 2:193, in Haleem's words, is to fight until "worship is devoted to God" (as opposed to entities other than God). Haleem's translation suggests that the goal of fighting is to propagate monotheism, or, put another way, eradicate polytheism; he claims that the verse speaks specifically to worship at the "sacred mosque" (apparently meaning the Kaaba).[26] Muhammad Ali's translation is softer: "until . . . religion is only for Allāh," which he interprets as "When persecution ceases, and men are not forced to accept or renounce a religion, being at liberty to profess any religion of the truth of which they are convinced."[27] Muhammad Ali asserts, incorrectly in my view, that this interpretation must be correct in light of other verses, such as 22:40 (fight to resist injustice),[28] which would be rendered meaningless under any other interpretation of 2:193. However, the context of both verses is resistance *by Muslims* against oppression, religious, or otherwise by *non-Muslims*. What Muhammad Ali really means is that *Muslims* be at liberty to choose their religions. An argument that Muslims should protect freedom of religion for non-Muslims, especially polytheists, is not persuasive in light of the Quran's overall hostility toward non-Muslims (especially polytheists). Other translations are more overtly militant. Yusuf Ali's translation is that "there *prevail* justice and faith in Allah" (emphasis added),[29] again suggesting promotion of monotheism and eradication of polytheism. Hilali and Khan go further, asserting that the goal is "(all and every kind of) worship is for Allâh (alone)"—Muslims must fight until all polytheism is eradicated, everywhere. Dawood's translation, "until . . . Allah's religion reigns supreme," suggests the goal of making Islam specifically the only religion, or at least the predominant one.

These variations generate ambiguities as to what acts are to be "defended" against. Sachedina suggests two: aggression and "moral wrong."[30] If "moral wrong" includes the failure to worship and obey the one true God, as is the position of many scriptural verses and Islamic priestly writings, then the concept of self-defense is broadened beyond what would be considered self-defense today. Islam then would permit offensive force to (1) eradicate polytheism, despite a lack of material injury toward Muslims, and (2) eliminate obstacles to the propagation of Islam.[31] As Sachedina puts it, the Quran "also requires Muslims to work toward establishing a just public order. At this point the jihad becomes an offensive endeavor in connection with efforts to bring about the kind of world order the Qur'an envisions."[32] Such objectives stray beyond the conventional definition of self-defense against an attack.

What Is Jihad, Exactly?

It is often asserted that the duty of *jihad* has a dual meaning. In its primary religious connotation, it means "the struggle of the soul to overcome the sinful obstacles that keep a person from God."[33] This is the inward-looking, passive "greater jihad." The use of force is the "lesser jihad"—"a form of punishment to be inflicted upon Islam's enemies and the renegades from the faith."[34]

I submit that the *lesser* jihad is the more accurate interpretation of the Islamic war ethic. The greater jihad is not a Quranic mandate but a juridical construction, emerging in the thirteenth century CE under formidable opposition.[35] Until then, war had been far more central in Islamic statecraft, and, as Cook notes, Islamic education heavily emphasizes *early* Muslim history, not later.[36] There is no basis for distinguishing the greater and lesser jihad in early Muslim history.

Many scholars argue that, even if the lesser jihad is its more valid interpretation, holy war was nevertheless *not* part of it. For example, Muslim expansion was motivated by "beneficent paternalism."[37] Or the Sword Verses legitimized force against only the Muslims' original persecutor[38] or against only *actively hostile* unbelievers.[39] However, Islamic practice was and is to *impose Islam's authority*, not merely inviting conversion.[40] The procedure, informed by the Quran and *hadith*, required that the Muslims first invite their opponents to convert to Islam or, for Scripturaries (i.e., Jews, Christians, and Sabeans), allow them to peacefully accept Muslim dominion and pay the *jizya* (poll tax). If the opponent accepts, the cause for jihad is negated. If not, the jihad may commence.[41] The adversaries then have *no* rights; Muslims may treat them as they wish (e.g., killing and enslaving). Satisfying the conditions necessary to negate the jihad means surrendering autonomy and self-determination—itself a cause for war.

Under the Prophet's leadership, the original jihad was undertaken to unify the Arabs. The Prophet participated personally in twenty-seven Muslim campaigns and directed another fifty-nine, all during the last nine years of his life (a total of about nine military engagements per year). The early Muslims were empowered to attribute their improbable military successes to divine ordination, and this belief emboldened them further.[42] Defeats and partial victories were viewed as divine tests of the Muslims' faith and resolve. This belief in their divinely ordained superiority induced the Muslims to enforce the unity of the ummah (community) when several tribes attempted to withdraw from it after Muhammad's passing (the Riddah Wars, 632–633 CE, which the Muslims viewed as a war to punish apostasy).

Islam's real expansion began under Caliph Umar in 634 CE. The notion that Islam should be the only religion was tolerated in Arabia. This served as Umar's "starting point," under his reign. As a result, the Muslims overran previously Christian domains of Syria, Egypt, and Armenia (of which only Armenia was able to retain its Christian identity) and conquered Persia (634–644 CE). Within a century, the Muslim caliphate completed its conquest of the Maghreb (710 CE) and Spain (718 AD).

Greater *in bello* Permissiveness

The basic *in bello* principle of distinction in traditional Islamic law is not significantly different from that of Christian-rooted secular international law—the most radical professions of al-Qaeda and its ilk notwithstanding. However, because it is expected that the Islamic world—now in a state of declined power relative to the West—would resort to the weapons of the weak as any similarly situated political entity would, it is apropos to highlight two concepts in Islamic warcraft that are not shared in secular war ethics.

One concept is the doctrine of *taqiyya*, in which Muslims are permitted to conceal their identities when they are at significant risk of persecution.[43] *Taqiyya* is a Shi'ite construction, formulated during a period of oppression by the Sunni majority so that the minority could preserve itself from extermination by avoiding direct confrontation with the majority. But, in addition to the "precautionary" category of *taqiyya* just described, the "arcane" category is employed "to carry out clandestine activity for furthering the religious goals, in times of weakness."[44] This form of *taqiyya* enables combatants to render themselves indistinguishable from noncombatants. For evidence of widespread use of *taqiyya* as a tactic of warfare by states, we need look no further than the long-standing practice of postrevolutionary Iran. Iran funds and supports terrorist organizations in Lebanon, such as Hezbollah. More recently, Iran supports Shi'ite paramilitary organizations in Iraq, such as the Kata'ib Hezbollah and Asa'ib Ahl al-Haq (i.e., League of the Righteous), both of which are designated terrorist organizations.

The other concept, which is also strong in Shi'ite tradition, is extolment of the martyr (*shahid*). Death in battle in the service of Islam is considered the surest path to the cleansing of sin and admission into heaven; all others must first face trial before being admitted.[45] The heavenly rewards are quite lavish, especially compared to those for Muslims dying of other causes.[46] They include extremely bountiful sexual pleasures for men, as described graphically in some *hadith* literature, such as the seventy beautiful virgins.[47]

The 1983 attack on the US Marine barracks in Beirut is an archetypical illustration of the combination of *taqiyya* and *shahid* into suicide attacks. Two Iranian-funded suicide truck bombers attacked US and French forces seconded to the Multinational Force (MNF) that was carrying out a peacekeeping mission in Lebanon. Only four months later, US forces withdrew from Lebanon entirely.[48] Because the tactic was demonstrated poignantly to be successful, non-Shi'ite entities have borrowed the Shi'ite theological basis for these tactics and adopted them as their own.[49]

SUMMARY

I have presented elsewhere a sliding scale of war ethics ranging from highly permissive to highly restrictive.[50] The substance of the war ethic of Islam outlined above yields the conclusion that it is permissive overall—certainly not militant on the scale of fascist war ethics but more permissive compared to the just war tradition and pacifist ethics.

As an increasingly militant form of Islam enters the Islamic mainstream,[51] we are seeing an empirically greater propensity not only of Islamic nonstate actors to resort to political violence[52] but also states in which Islam is dominant to be the first users of force in interstate disputes, thus initiating interstate armed conflicts.[53] This is so even after controlling for other political characteristics that are also affected by religion, such as regime type, economic prosperity, and proximity.[54]

If greater Islamic propensity to attack is attributable ultimately to antipathy toward non-Islam in Islamic thought, then what explains Muslim states' greater proneness to attack other Muslim states (beyond control factors, such as proximity)? Toft's argument centering on the practice of "outbidding"[55] seems persuasive. Because the Islamic *ummah* (i.e., community of believers) is no longer united, modern states vie for dominance within the Islamic world.

ANWAR SADAT AND WAR AND PEACE WITH ISRAEL

The case of Egyptian President Anwar Sadat is a useful illustration of religion's effect on a secular state's decision to make war and then peace. In 1973, Sadat launched the Yom Kippur War against Israel (styled the "War of Ramadan" in the Arab world) to recover the occupied Sinai peninsula. The assault was mostly successful; Egypt recaptured and held the east bank of the Suez Canal and inflicted heavy losses, but it was unable to push Israeli forces completely out of the territory. It is not surprising that Egypt had chosen to wage war with Israel, the Arab world's sworn enemy, especially for the purpose that it did. However, in 1979, Sadat signed the first full-fledged peace treaty between Israel and any Arab state.[56] This was out of character given the widespread internal *and external* opposition to peace with Israel. Why did Egypt do this? In addition to materialist reasons for both actions, the preferences of Egypt—and especially President Sadat—also were rooted in Islam.

Islamic Incentives for War with Israel

The ignominy of Egypt's 1967 defeat and occupation was a powerful psychological force on the country. Furthermore, Arab nationalism is a strong motivator in the Arab countries' hostility toward Israel. But I suggest that motivators to make war with Israel were not only Arab nationalism but also *Islamic* nationalism.

As discussed above, Islamic theories of statecraft are premised on Islamic superiority, which in turn necessitates Islamic strength relative to its neighbors. The Islamic world enjoyed such relative strength in its first thousand years, but in 1973 it was still quite weak. In addition, the Arab world took great offense at the introduction (imposition, in its view) of Israel into its midst in 1948. As (mostly Muslim) Arabs, the Egyptians were aggrieved, along with much of the rest of the Arab world, at the plight of the Palestinians. The Palestinians, who were Arabic-speaking and also mostly Muslim, were part of the *ummah*, and Islamic political theory stresses the importance of unity and brotherhood among all Muslims.[57] Not only this but also the existence of a non-Muslim nation in the heart of the Arab world fundamentally challenged the Islamic paradigm that Islam should enjoy hegemony, at least in its own region.[58] Anti-Semitism was likely also a factor in Arab antipathy toward Israel given the amount of emphasis on the duplicity and betrayal of the Jewish tribes during the early period of Islam that is placed in the Islamic historical narrative.[59] These factors created an incentive for the Arab world to reassert Islamic hegemony, at least regionally, by defeating Israel at a minimum (and preferably by eradicating it). This does not necessarily make Nasser, Sadat, and other Arab statesmen of that time "Islamist" in the sense that the word is used today; it means only that the Arab pride, wounded by the presence of Israel, was also Islamic pride.

Egypt's crushing defeat in 1967 was extremely humiliating. Public discourse was self-condemnatory and scathing, with demonstrations and public trials seeking to blame defeat on someone or something. "Everyone wallowed in a masochistic orgy of self-deprecation."[60] Egyptians were actually embarrassed of their nationality. A professional colleague of mine has recounted that, as a teenager in Great Britain (her father was with the Egyptian embassy there), her parents told her to claim that she was Spanish instead of Egyptian. Heikal, a one-time Egyptian official and associate of Sadat, writes:

> By 1973 Egypt had almost become the laughing stock of the Arab world. We claimed to be the leader and protector of the Arabs, but gave no lead to our own people and showed ourselves unable to protect our own country. . . . Each day that passed was a day of humiliation for Egypt.[61]

The result was a "remarkable revival" of Islam and Islamic values in Egypt and the rest of the Arab world. At an international conference hosted by al-Azhar University in 1968, scholars argued that "if only Muslims returned to the path of Islam, the 'glorious defeat' of 1967, as one of them bitterly termed it, could be turned into a long-overdue national catharsis."[62] And indeed, the Arab secularist movement began its wane after 1967.

Sadat's Faith and His Decision to Wage War

As with most modern states, Egypt's decision whether to go to war ultimately rested with its chief executive. In Egypt's case, that individual was Anwar Sadat. This section illustrates Islam's direct influence on the worldview and decision-making of President Sadat, through Sadat's own words and accounts of his own associates and external observers.

Sadat presented himself as secular, even Western oriented, but actually is documented as having been a pious, devout Muslim from his youth.[63] This important fact casts doubt on—and, in my opinion, refutes—the counterargument that the evidence recounted below is little more than insincere political propaganda. Sadat was hardly an Islamist and does not appear to have been overtly religious in his political activity before 1967. But, when Islam began to be reasserted after 1967, Sadat needed very little convincing, and he began displaying his own piety more openly.[64] He also personally felt the ignominy of Egypt's defeat.[65]

Egypt's 1967 defeat instilled in Sadat a new purpose. "That Egypt should survive became my dominant passion."[66] "Better to die honourably," he said, "than to live in humiliation."[67] He even characterized the liberation of the Sinai as a *holy* duty, saying, "we are required to sacrifice life in order to deserve life."[68] And further, "This is a war for our honour and self-respect."[69] To undo the shame, Sadat said, "the whole world, West and East, [had to] see whether or not we're able to liberate our land, whether or not we're able to fight."[70]

Sadat's public statements revealed his significant religious fervor for reversing Israel's victory over Egypt, and that fervor was infectious. In early 1971, Sadat invoked the idea of *jihad* against Israel in addressing the International Conference of Islamic Studies:

> This country has always resolutely stood in defense of Islam and of the Islamic Holy Places. This country will remain a solid stronghold in defense of the sanctity of Islam, however cruel the sacrifices prove to be. . . . Today, we ought to wage war against backwardness the way we are waging war against Zionism and Imperialism. . . . The war we are waging these days is the war we have learnt about in the Qur'an.[71]

And further, in the first Birthday of the Prophet address of his presidency, in 1971:

> In this battle that we are waging, we are required to provide ourselves with every weapon possible. . . . As I had told you before, Muhammad and his

Mission had supplied us with the most potent weapon—Faith.... Our people has [sic] always ultimately had the upper hand, even though it possessed no weapon other than faith.... We have learnt a lesson from Muhammad. In the course of history, whenever Arabs unified, they created their culture and occupied their place among nations; but, when they disunited, they were humiliated and they opened an inviting breach to foreigners and Imperialists.[72]

Finally, on the Birthday of the Prophet the following year, 1972:

This is a period of mighty trial, first and foremost for our Faith, the Faith of the Mission of the Prophet. We find ourselves in the most difficult ordeal that we could face in our lives. They want to shatter our faith.... We believe that Allah is on our side.... We believe, as commanded by Allah, that we are a nation elected above all nations.... We are preparing at present with all we have and with all our might to enter upon the glorious campaign.... I promise you that at the next Birthday we shall celebrate in this place not only the liberation of our country but also the defeat of Israeli arrogance and rampaging.[73]

In May 1973, when the mobilization of forces began, Sadat ordered the Egyptian media to quote "profusely" from the Quran[74] and enthusiastically backed the new war cry of the Egyptian army—"*Allah akbar*" ("God is great").[75] At the central command post on the eve of the war, Sadat participated in taking an oath on the Quran.[76] After the war, the Egyptian media were filled with stories of soldiers claiming to have seen Muhammad himself leading the troops across the canal on a white horse,[77] and Sadat himself spoke several times of the "miracles" of the war, which in his view could have materialized only with faith.[78]

The prospect of many casualties—win or lose—does not appear to have been a concern to Sadat. There are several possible reasons for this. One is that the major cities along the Suez Canal had already been evacuated and the fighting itself was expected to take place in a sparsely populated area (the Sinai desert); therefore, civilian casualties were likely to be light at the beginning of the war. On the other hand, however, had it become necessary to liberate by force the towns of El-Arish, Sharm el-Sheikh, and others, which were closer to the Israeli border, civilian casualties likely would have been heavier. There is no evidence that that prospect was a concern for Sadat, who, in the run-up to the war, often spoke of sacrifice.[79]

Sadat seemed concerned least of all about the prospect of Israeli casualties. As an Egyptian whose country was partially occupied by Israel, it is expected that he would find it necessary to inflict large-scale casualties on Israeli forces to regain territory that, under international law, rightfully belonged to Egypt. But Sadat's hostility to Israel appears to have run deeper than that which their identity as occupiers would have generated. His hostility cannot reasonably have been induced by Israeli atrocities in the Sinai (as

Bush's hostility to the Iraqi army was by their atrocities in Kuwait). There is no evidence of reports of atrocities during the occupation; indeed, the Israelis left the Sinai in a better condition than when they arrived.[80] It seems more likely that Sadat's deeper hostility toward the Israelis was induced by anti-Semitism, which appeared to be pervasive among Arab and Muslim states. In addition to Sadat's anti-Semitic statements cataloged above, Egyptian soldiers were also given personal booklets containing quotations from the Quran and other Islamic literature urging them to "pursue the Jews and not pity them."[81]

Finally, while Sadat's immediate aim was to regain Egyptian sovereignty over the Sinai, he continued to assume the role of advocate for the Arab cause in general and for the Palestinians in particular. Because Sadat regarded himself as the father figure for all of Egypt, he also believed that Egypt was "ordained" (in Israeli's words) to be the leader of the Arab world[82] and, therefore, it was his calling to assert the combined Arab states as the Sixth Power of the world.[83] Now, despite his incendiary speeches before the war,[84] the evidence is unclear as to whether Sadat fervently desired the destruction of Israel itself and/or the Jews, as opposed to merely driving Israeli forces out of Egyptian territory. However, it is clear that Sadat's grievances against Israel were not confined to the defeat and partial occupation of Egypt. In 1971, Sadat rejected entering into a separate peace with Israel, arguing that a necessary aspect of any comprehensive peace with Israel was the settling of grievances of all Arab states in addition to the Palestinian problem.[85] On October 16, 1973, with the war still in progress, Sadat told his parliament that the purpose of the war was not only to recover lands lost in 1967 (he did not specify which lands—Egyptian only or Jordanian and Syrian as well) but also to restore Palestinian rights.[86] These goals are also evident in Sadat's address to the Israeli Knesset in 1977: there would be no *separate* peace but rather a *comprehensive* peace based on the restoration of Arab lands and Palestinian rights.[87] Although such sentiments could have been driven partly by a personal craving for the power of hegemony, as classical realists would predict, this seems unlikely to have been the case for Sadat—biographical portraits of him do not depict a man with ambitions for personal political power. His interest in asserting Egyptian (and, by extension, Arab and Muslim) power appears to have been genuinely driven by his dedication to the well-being of the Arab world and, by extension, the Islamic *ummah*.

Thus, while nonreligious factors do generate the expectation that Egypt would eventually resort to war to recover its territory, such an expectation is also influenced by religious factors: the ignominy of defeat and domination by non-Muslims, especially Jews; the need to reassert Muslim hegemony; and the need to relieve the suffering (in Islam's eyes) of other Muslims within the *ummah*. Although Egypt's initiation of the Yom Kippur War was already predictable and the Arab nationalism that prompted it was difficult to disentangle from Islamic nationalism, I suggest that Islam made the outbreak of the war even *more* likely than it would otherwise have been.

Islamic Incentives for Peace with Israel

The war's outcome was positive yet mixed because Egypt was unable to recover its territory fully. It took a peace initiative for Egypt to complete its recovery. A series of cease-fire agreements culminated in the Egyptian–Israeli Peace Treaty of 1979, in which Egypt established relations with Israel that were at the time unprecedented in the Arab world. At first glance, it may be difficult to understand this move given the fervor (including religious fervor) with which Sadat blasted Israel and the United States before the war. Yet, as much as Egypt's initiation of the war was rooted in the influence of Islam, so was Sadat's initiative to forge a lasting peace with Israel.

Peace with Israel is made possible in Islamic statecraft under the doctrine of the *dar al-suhl* (i.e., the abode of conciliation), which was discussed earlier and is often overlooked. When Islamdom is too weak relative to the *dar al-harb* to dominate it, then the conflict may be temporarily suspended when in Islam's interest. In the case of Israel, entering into a peace treaty with Israel gained more for Egypt—and for Islamdom—than continuing to fight. Sadat acknowledged that the Arab world could not destroy Israel, treating Israel as a *fait accompli*:

> I said and I repeat again that Israel is a fact. An Arab President said that he had a plan to wipe Israel out within three hours, but three years or more have elapsed and he has failed to eliminate it. Moreover, twenty years have elapsed and Israel, far from being exterminated, remains a reality and stands firm.[88]

Having acknowledged that Egypt could not recover all of its lost territory by force, Sadat conveyed his willingness to accept peace with the Jewish state in exchange for border security.[89] Unable to defeat the Israeli *dar al-harb*, he was willing to settle for coexistence with an Israeli *dar al-suhl*.

However, entering into such a settlement first required demonstrating Egyptian strength or, at least, shattering Israel's sense of its own invincibility. This is what Sadat believed was the greatest achievement of the war.[90] The doctrine of *dar al-suhl* presupposes Islamic weakness relative to non-Islamdom but not Islamic impotence. Any Islamic conciliation with non-Islamdom would have to be reciprocated; otherwise, the relationship would become oppressive, which Islamic political theory cannot permit. Having forced Israel to respect Egypt, Sadat could now do likewise, and, henceforth, his bellicose condemnations of Israel in public speeches ended.[91]

In spite of the peace treaty, however, Israel still could not be brought within the *dar al-islam*. While no longer immediately hostile to Egypt, Israel still lay outside the abode of peace (or of Islam). And Sadat did not abandon his antipathy toward Jews, nor did he counsel other Arab states to do so.[92] It took several years for Sadat to be convinced of the need for any more permanent arrangement than a cease-fire, let alone for negotiating with Israel directly.[93] It took even longer—until 1978—for him to come around to the prospect of recognizing the *legitimacy* of Israel, as opposed to merely its existence.[94] Furthermore, as Israeli points out, Egyptian recognition of Israel and normalization of relations with it was not irrevocable.[95] Sadat said in 1975, in the same speech in which he acknowledged Egypt's inability to overcome Israel's strength, "Israel is a fact, and anyone who wishes to wipe her out—please go ahead and do it! I assure you that you will have my acclaim."[96] If Sadat had believed that Egypt and the rest of the Arab world could defeat and dominate Israel in the future without further compromise, he would have advocated precisely that. This position is well rooted in Islamic principles of statecraft; the *dar al-suhl* is not a perpetual accommodation of non-Islamdom, only a temporary one while Islamdom is unable to dominate the enemy on its own terms.

In sum, Egypt's peace with Israel was made possible by the ethic of war and peace in Islam—but only within its own parameters. Islam made that peace less likely than if Egypt had been a non-Muslim country. The first reason for this is the innate antipathy toward Jews in Islamic tradition, which significantly impeded negotiation with the Jewish state at all, let alone a settlement. The second reason is that the peace with Israel has the potential to unravel if the relative power of the two states is reversed. Israel understood this and needed security from further Egyptian attack in order to withdraw voluntarily; it therefore took a wholesale Egyptian demilitarization of the Sinai (i.e., its own territory) and the promise of a peacekeeping force to provide early warning and confidence-building measures (the Multinational Force and Observers) for Israel to agree to negotiate a peace treaty.[97]

CONCLUSION

This chapter has explored the Islamic war ethic and found it overall permissive. The strong distinction between Self and Other in Islamic thought, through the *dar al-harb* and *dar al-islam*, is a key building block in Islamic conceptions of both self-defense and just cause for offensive war. Islamic *jus ad bellum* permits the use of force to defend self and others against attack, as do most other *ad bellum* norms. However, the scriptural basis of self-defense can be—and often is—interpreted to include not only physical attacks or suppression of Muslims but also offenses against God—especially worshipping other gods—that do not constitute physical attack or suppression of Muslims. In addition, the scripture does not appear to admit the possibility of just defense of non-Muslims, and the timbre of much of the literature casts doubt on whether Islamic thought admits such a right for non-Muslims.

The just causes for offensive war in Islamic thought are similarly broad. In fairness, other nonpacifist religious war ethics admit to the possibility of just cause for attacking other nations (beyond self-defense), which literal interpretations of *jus ad bellum* in international law do not do. Even the just war tradition is more permissive than the UN Charter. But, in defining just causes for offensive war, Islamic thought privileges Islamic dominance and evangelization. Jihad to propagate Islam and exert dominion over non-Muslims is permissible. These traits render the Islamic war ethic, both defensive and offensive, relatively permissive. Space does not permit presentation of empirical evidence, but I have presented some such evidence elsewhere.

This chapter also has highlighted some *in bello* doctrines that render the range of acceptable methods and means of warfare more permissive in Islamic thought than is the norm in today's *in bello* legal and ethical regimes.

An extended case study on the Yom Kippur War and Egyptian–Israeli Peace Treaty illustrates Islam's causal effect. Religions wield strong causal influences on *ad bellum* outcomes on religionist state leaders and such as the case with Islam too. Islam's influence on the theocratic leadership of Iran is obvious—too obvious to generalize. But its influence on mainstream Muslim state leaders, such as Anwar Sadat, is more appropriate as a generalizable illustration, albeit requiring deeper probing to see.

One final note: I am sensitive to the fact that this chapter does not portray Islam in a positive light. There is ample literature arguing that the Islamic war ethic is misunderstood and actually is innocuous or, at least, no less aggressive than war ethics of other religions. Sizgorich, for example, argues that the Islamic Arabs' early jihadic expansion was constructed socially by the practice of nations around it.[98] Abu Zahra claims that Islamic thought permits fighting only in self-defense and never to propagate the faith.[99] Ayoob seeks to dispel the "myth," in his words, that political Islam is inherently violent.[100] Space does not permit a specific refutation of these claims, beyond this chapter's existing contents. But, against the argument that this chapter's depiction of Islam mischaracterizes Islamic fundamentalism as mainstream, I submit evidence that more fundamentalist war ethic is becoming, or even *is*, the mainstream. Haddad and Khashan, cited above, surveyed Muslims in Lebanon—hardly a fundamentalist country—and found that half of the respondents supported the 9/11 attacks and more than one-third supported a follow-up attack with weapons of mass destruction.[101] Tibi—a Muslim originally from Syria—has expressed concerns similar to mine.[102] Perhaps we are seeing an internal contestation for the soul of Islam. In any case, these findings certainly should not become the basis for a pattern of bigotry against individual Muslims or Muslim-dominated states. However, to bury this inconvenient truth is to embrace the political at the expense of science.

These findings must be presented as they are, not as we would wish them to be.

BIBLIOGRAPHY

Abou el Fadl, Khaled. *The Great Theft*. New York: HarperOne, 2007.
Aboul-Enein, Youssef, and Sherifa Zuhur. *Islamic Rulings on Warfare*. Strategic Studies Institute Monograph. Carlisle, PA: US Army War College, 2004.
Abu Zahra, Muhammad. *Concept of War in Islam*. Translated by Muhammad al-Hady and Taha Omar. Cairo: Société Orientale de Publicité-Press, 1961.
Acosta, Benjamin. "The Suicide Bomber as Sunni-Shi'i Hybrid." *Middle East Quarterly* 17, no. 3 (2010): 13–20.
Aquinas, Thomas. *Summa Theologica*. Chicago: Encyclopedia Britannica, 1952.
Aslan, Reza. *No God But God: The Origins, Evolutions, and Future of Islam*. New York: Random House, 2005.
Ayoob, Mohammed. *The Many Faces of Political Islam*. Ann Arbor, MI: University of Michigan Press, 2011.
Ball, Terence, Richard Dagger, and Daniel O'Neil. *Political Ideologies and the Democratic Ideal*. Boston: Pearson, 2014.
Brown, Davis. "The Influence of Religion on Interstate Armed Conflict: Government Religious Preference and First Use of Force, 1946–2002." *Journal for the Scientific Study of Religion* 55, no. 4 (2017): 800–20.
———. "A Typology of War Ethics." *Journal of Military Ethics* 16, no. 3–4 (2017): 145–56.
Brown, Davis, and Patrick James. "The Religious Characteristics of States Dataset: Classic Themes and New Evidence." *Journal of Conflict Resolution* 62, no. 6 (2018): 1340–76.
Bukay, David. "The Religious Foundations of Suicide Bombings." *Middle East Quarterly* 13, no. 4 (2006): 27–36.
CNN. "Beirut Marine Barracks Bombing Fast Facts." Modified March 21, 2019. https://www.cnn.com/2013/06/13/world/meast/beirut-marine-barracks-bombing-fast-facts/index.html?no-st=9999999999.
Cook, David. "Islamism and Jihadism." *Totalitarian Movements and Political Religions* 10, no. 2 (2009): 177–87.
———. *Understanding Jihad*. Berkeley: University of California Press, 2005.
Donner, Fred. "The Sources of Islamic Conceptions of War." In *Just War and Jihad: Historical and Theoretical Perspectives on War and Peace in Western and Islamic Traditions*, edited by John Kelsay and James Turner Johnson, 31–69. Westport, CT: Greenwood Press, 1991.
Enayat, Hamid. *Modern Islamic Political Thought*. Austin, TX: University of Texas Press, 1982.
Firestone, Reuven. "Conceptions of Holy War in Biblical and Qur'ānic Tradition." *Journal of Religious Ethics* 24, no. 1 (1996): 99–123.
al-Ghunaimi, Mohammed Talaat. *The Muslim Conception of International Law and the Western Approach*. The Hague: Martinus Nijhoff, 1968.
Haddad, Simon, and Hilal Khashan. "Islam and Terrorism: Lebanese Muslim Views on September 11." *Journal of Conflict Resolution* 46, no. 6 (2002): 812–28.
Heikal, Mohammed. *The Road to Ramadan*. New York: Quadrangle/New York Times, 1975.
Horowitz, Michael. "Nonstate Actors and the Diffusion of Innovations." *International Organization* 64, no. 1 (2010): 33–64.
Israeli, Raphael. *Man of Defiance: A Political Biography of Anwar Sadat*. Totowa, NJ: Barnes & Noble Books, 1985.
———. "The Role of Islam in President Sadat's Thought." *Jerusalem Journal of International Relations* 4, no. 4 (1980): 1–12.
Kelsay, John. *Arguing the Just War in Islam*. Cambridge, MA: Harvard University Press, 2007.
Khadduri, Majid. *War and Peace in the Law of Islam*. Baltimore: Johns Hopkins University Press, 1955.

Kushner, H. W. "Suicide Bombers: Business as Usual." *Studies in Conflict and Terrorism* 19, no. 4 (1996): 329–37.
Lewis, Bernard. *What Went Wrong?* New York: Perennial, 2002.
Martin, Richard. "The Religious Foundations of War, Peace, and Statecraft in Islam." In *Just War and Jihad: Historical and Theoretical Perspectives on War and Peace in Western and Islamic Traditions*, edited by John Kelsay and James Turner Johnson, 91–117. Westport, CT: Greenwood Press, 1991.
Mayer, Ann Elizabeth. "War and Peace in the Islamic Tradition and International Law." In *Just War and Jihad: Historical and Theoretical Perspectives on War and Peace in Western and Islamic Traditions*, edited by John Kelsay and James Turner Johnson, 195–226. Westport, CT: Greenwood Press, 1991.
Pipes, Daniel. *In the Path of God: Islam and Political Power*. New York: Basic Books, 1983.
Quandt, William. *Camp David: Peacemaking and Politics*. Washington, DC: Brookings Institution, 1986.
The Quran. Ahmed Ali. *Al-Qur'ān: A Contemporary Translation*. Translated by Ahmed Ali. Princeton: Princeton University Press, 2001.
———. Dawood. *The Koran*. 4th rev. ed. Translated by N. J. Dawood. New York: Penguin Books, 1974.
———. Haleem. *The Qur'an: English Translation and Parallel Arabic Text*. Rev. ed. Translated by M. A. S. Abdel Haleem. New York: Oxford University Press, 2010.
———. Hilali and Khan. *Translation of the Meanings of the Noble Qur'an in the English Language*. Translated by Muhammad Taqî-ud-Dîn Al-Hilâlî and Muhmmad Muhsin Khân. Medina, Saudi Arabia: King Fahd Complex for the Printing of the Holy Qur'an, 1998/9.
———. Muhammad Ali. *The Holy Qur'ān: Arabic Text with English Translation and Commentary*. Translated by Maulana Muhammad Ali. Dublin, OH: Ahmadiyya Anjuman Isha'at Islam, 2002.
———. Pickthall. *The Meaning of the Glorious Koran*. Translated by Mohammad Marmaduke Pickthall. New York: Mentor, n.d.
———. Yusuf 'Ali. *The Meaning of the Holy Qur'ān*. 11th ed. Translated by 'Abdullah Yūsuf 'Alī. Beltsville, MD: Amana Publications, 2009.
Rapoport, David. "Messianic Sanctions for Terror." *Comparative Politics* 20, no. 2 (1988): 195–213.
Sachedina, Abdulaziz. "From Defensive to Offensive Warfare: The Use and Abuse of Jihad in the Muslim World." In *Religion, Law and the Role of Force: A Study of Their Influence on Conflict and on Conflict Resolution*, edited by J. I. Coffey and Charles Mathewes, 23–37 (Ardsley, NY: Transnational Publishers, 2002).
Sadat, Anwar. *In Search of Identity: An Autobiography*. New York: Harper & Row, 1977.
Sizgorich, Thomas. "Sanctified Violence: Monotheist Militancy as the Tie That Bound Christian Rome and Islam." *Journal of the American Academy of Religion* 77, no. 4 (2009): 895–921.
Sonbol, Amira. "Norms of War in Sunni Islam." In *World Religions and Norms of War*, edited by Vesselin Popovski, Gregory Reichberg, and Nicholas Turner, 282–302. Tokyo: United Nations University Press, 2009.
Thayer, Bradley, and Valerie Hudson. "Sex and the Shaheed." *International Security* 34, no. 4 (2010): 37–62.
Tibi, Bassam. *Islamism and Islam*. New Haven, CT: Yale University Press, 2012.
———. "War and Peace in Islam." In *The Ethics of War and Peace: Religious and Secular Perspectives*, edited by Terry Nardin, 128–145. Princeton, NJ: Princeton University Press, 1996.
Toft, Monica Duffy. "Getting Religion? The Puzzling Case of Islam and Civil War." *International Security* 31, no. 4 (2007): 97–131.
Walker, Paul. "Taqiyah." In *Oxford Encyclopedia of the Modern Islamic World*. Vol. 4: *Sata-Zurk*, edited by John Esposito, 186–87. New York: Oxford University Press, 1995.
Weeramantry, C. G. *Islamic Jurisprudence: An International Perspective*. New York: St. Martin's Press, 1988.

Chapter Twelve

Just War Thinking in Chinese Buddhism

Tong Sau Lin and King-Fai Tam

INTRODUCTION

Buddhism has always been thought of as a religion that promotes compassion and peace. In the history of Buddhism, rarely is any large-scale war waged in the name of defending itself from attack. However, this should not be taken to mean that Buddhism is blind to the ubiquitous reality of war. In fact, the Buddha spoke of his views on war many times. He is not completely opposed to war, but is more concerned with why and how one should enter war.[1] In other words, he is much more interested in promoting an appropriate and reasonable view of war.

Generally speaking, Buddhist teachings strongly oppose the use of violence. From a Buddhist perspective, any course of action that initiates a war or leads to the involvement in it would be considered immoral. On the other hand, whenever violence appears to be the only resolution of conflicts and therefore unavoidable, Buddhism will conditionally recognize the justifications of the use of force, including military campaigns, as long as they do not spring out from personal hatred or animosity.

Among the many sects of Buddhism, this chapter will focus on Chinese Buddhism in exploring the Buddhist view of war and the relationship between Chinese monks and the history of war. Specifically, it will look at the role Buddhist monks played in the War of Resistance against Japanese Aggression in the 1930s and 1940s as a way to understand whether the fundamental Buddhist stance toward warfare constitutes something that corresponds to the just war thinking in the West.

THE BUDDHIST STANCE TOWARD WAR

This section will begin by delineating an underlying contradiction in the Buddhist view of war. It looks at the first of the five precepts in Buddhism, which spell out categorically "the abstinence from killing" and that the Buddha practices in the many instances where he intervenes to avert war. Yet, when violence becomes unavoidable and war becomes the only way to resolve conflicts, Buddhism justifies the use of military force, giving rise to the idea of righteous war and killing with compassion. These precepts will be covered in their respective parts.

NONVIOLENCE AND NEGATION OF WAR

From the earliest days of the establishment of Buddhism, it has always been one of its core tenets to propagate compassion and oppose killing and violence. Because war represents an extreme form of killing and violence, in essence, then, there exist irresolvable contradictions between Buddhist thoughts and the violent behavior in war.

"Abstain from killing"—such is the moral principle that has been held in high regard since the beginning of primitive Buddhism. It comes from the concept of *ahiṃsā*, which was promoted by various religions in Indian society of the sixth century BCE. The first of the fundamental five precepts for Buddhist cultivation is precisely the abstinence from killing:

> I undertake to observe the rule
> to abstain from taking life;
> to abstain from taking what is not given;
> to abstain from sensuous misconduct;
> to abstain from false speech;
> to abstain from intoxicants as tending to cloud the mind.[2]

The first precept is explained by Buddhaghoṣa, a fifth-century Indian Theravāda Buddhist commentator, in this way: "Taking life" means to murder "anything that lives." It refers to the termination of life. "Anything that lives" refers to "anything that has the life-force." "Taking life" is then the conscious act of terminating the life of anything that one perceives as having life, or to bring to end the life force that resides in it.[3]

It can be seen, therefore, that the precept of abstinence from killing includes not only the killing of human lives but also all other forms of lives, including one's own. Moreover, not only should one not kill, but one should not abet others in killing or derive any form of satisfaction from the killing.[4] This applies to monks and lay believers alike, a precept that one should adhere to throughout one's life. Violation of the precept disqualifies one as a Buddhist.

Dhammapada, an early Buddhist text of 423 poems with brief summaries of the Buddha's teachings, encapsulates the fundamental virtues of Buddhism of compassion, equanimity, and benevolence toward all beings, which lie at the heart of the basic rules of social behavior:

> One should conquer anger by non-anger;
> One should conquer evil by good;
> One should conquer miserliness by giving;
> One should conquer a liar by truth.[5]

These rules make it only too clear that "an eye for an eye and a tooth for a tooth" is not the way to combat evil according to Buddhist beliefs. War, in this sense, is not recommended as a way to do away with conflicts and hatred.

A similar injunction against killing accompanied by a recommendation to forgo violence is found in *Suttanipāta*:

> Kill not any beings nor cause them to be killed,
> and do not approve of them having been killed,
> put by the rod for all that lives—
> whether they are weak, or strong in the world.[6]

What is the psychological reason behind the abstinence from killing? As is clearly stated in *Dhammapada*:

> All tremble at punishment; all fear death. Having made the comparison with oneself, one should not kill or cause to kill.[7]

All sentient beings are in fear of death and suffering, and those with compassion would even feel the suffering that they witness in other people. For this very reason, they would certainly not inflict it onto others but would in fact seek to relieve others of their suffering.

Contrary to the feelings of compassion and empathy, according to Buddhism, the root causes of conflict, violence, and the attendant suffering are greed (*rāga*), hatred (*dveṣa*), and delusion or ignorance (*moha*) of the dynamics of human behavior.

According to the law of karma, the consequence of taking a life is an inferior, gloomy, sorrowful reincarnation.[8] People who involve themselves in killing and die as a result of violence in the battlefield will be reincarnated into a specific hell because they harbor feelings of anger and evil thoughts at their dying moments.[9]

Buddhism does not recommend combatting violence with violence but rather dissolving evil and anger with compassion and patience (*khanti*). In his various reincarnations, the Buddha is a model of compassion and patience in his conduct. According to *Khantivādi-Jātaka*, in one of his former lives, he was a Bodhisattva dedicated to the cultivation of *khanti*. He was dismembered by the angry King Kalābu, but he bore no grudge against the king.

Instead, he pitied him.[10] Earlier in his current reincarnation, even though his disciple and cousin, Devadatta, repeatedly plotted against him, he held no anger against him but instead tried different ways to change Devadatta's ways.

It is, therefore, seen that the Buddhist attitude to war and violence derives primarily from the first of the five precepts, incumbent on monks and laity alike, not to take life nor to be party to the taking of lives.

THE HISTORICAL BUDDHA'S INTERVENTIONS IN WAR

When confronted directly by violence and war, however, the Buddha does not wait passively for the violent party to change his ways. E. B. Cowell notes the three occasions when the Buddha actively intervened to forestall war. The first was when King Ajātasattu was planning to invade the Vajjian Kingdom. Before he sent his troops to battle, King Ajātasattu sent his prime minister, Vassakāra, to ask for the Buddha's advice. Vassakāra was asked to remember everything the Buddha said in order to relate it to the throne. In his report, Vassakāra said that the Buddha discouraged the king from waging war, pointing out that the Vajjians could not be defeated as long as they abided by the seven welfare conditions that the Buddha had taught them. Accordingly, the king abandoned his plan to invade the Vajjian Kingdom.[11]

On another occasion, the Buddha mediated a dispute between his relatives before it broke out into a full-scale war. The story is told in *Kuṇāla-Jātaka*, where a conflict arose between the Sākyas on the paternal side of the Buddha's family and the Koliyas on the maternal side over the distribution of water of the Rohiṇī River. After the two families failed to come to a reconciliation, their armies gathered along the river to get ready for a showdown. The Buddha intervened at this point, asking why they should want to destroy their best warriors over something as worthless as water. In the end, he succeeded in persuading both sides of the pointlessness of the war, and a conflict was thus averted.[12]

On the third occasion, when the Buddha learned that King Virūḍhaka of Kosala was getting ready to attack the land of the Sākyas, he sat down under a withered tree by the road where the army had to pass. King Virūḍhaka saw the Buddha, and he stopped to ask, "Buddha, why are you sitting here under the withered tree? Not far down the road, there is a luxuriant tree with branches and leaves that will shade you from the sun." The Buddha replied, "The shade from the tree is nothing like the shade from the kings." King Virūḍhaka understood the implication of Buddha's words. He turned around and led his troops home.

In this way, the Buddha stopped the troops three times. On the fourth time, knowing that there was no way that the Sākyas could avoid their karma, he decided not to intervene any more.[13]

The above three wars are prompted by the expansion of the military to settle arguments over self-interests and resources that originate from selfish desires and result in the harm and suffering of innocent bystanders. This is the kind of war that Buddhism is vehemently against.

THE WHEEL TURNER KING AND THE CONCEPT OF RIGHTEOUS WAR

Buddhism is opposed to offensive military buildup and condemns militarism in strong terms.[14] However, as *Madhyamāgama* puts it, "For their own desires, people are in conflicts with each other as nations are in conflicts with each other. And because of their conflicts and their hatred for each other, various means of warfare came to be used and cause further harm."[15] In recognition of war as an unavoidable phenomenon in the human world, the Buddha chooses to take it seriously rather than deny its existence and to approach it with a reasonable state of mind.

The Buddha's first attempt at stopping war by means of practicing compassion and patience might not be effective, however. For example, in the third battle described above, the Buddha in the end could not stop the invading force of King Virūḍhaka, and the Sākyas were wiped out as a result. Moreover, not all wars are aggressive in nature; some are raised in defense against invasions. Can one expect those who are invaded to practice compassion and patience when their lives are being threatened? Do they not have the right to fight force with force? In the early Buddhist scriptures, Buddhism does not require indiscriminately its believers to forswear violence completely.[16] Under certain circumstances, violence is necessary. In *Aggañña Sutta*, it is said that rulers are chosen by the people to use proper force to punish the evil and to protect the order of society and the lives and property of the people. This is the origin of the kṣatriya class.[17] Moreover, the Buddha does not disallow soldiers from becoming his followers. People such as King Bimbisāra are all military leaders, for example. Once, the four ministers of King Prasenajit came to bid the Buddha farewell before a military expedition. The Buddha said to them, "You receive an official's salary from the King to do what is proper. This is an auspicious endeavor."[18] In this way, Buddhism affirms the functions of the military and the duties of the soldiers.

While it is not recommended that a country expand its military to invade others, one has to resort to the Buddhist expedient wisdom to neutralize the threat and the destruction of war to protect the lives and welfare of the people. Such skillful measures to nip a war in the bud before it becomes a large-scale conflict reduces destruction to a minimum. The *Ummagga Jātaka* refers to wars to forestall further wars as *dharmayuddha* (righteous war). The Buddhist use of the term *dharmayuddha* may be somewhat different from what is given in the Hindu epic *Bhagavad-Gita*, but one can get a glimpse from it of the Buddhist ethics of warfare, which is otherwise rarely seen in the Buddhist text.[19]

Buddhism believes that a benevolent leader needs a well-prepared army to protect the lives and wealth of the people so they can live in harmony and peace. In the ideal country of the Buddhist legend, there is the figure *Cakravartin* (the Wheel Turner King). He is a sacred king who rules the human world in accordance with the Buddhist dharma but, at the same time, possesses an "unsullied army" (i.e., an army that is motivated by the highest ideal). Only then can *Cakravartin* crush all the unjust violence in the world, ensuring peaceful existence for all.[20] *Cakravartin* also has the important charge of defending the Buddhist dharma. For this, he also needs a strong army to guard his territory and overcome threats from outside. Although Buddhism upholds the importance of peace and opposes violence, it does not forbid rulers from possessing an army or recommend the disbandment of the armed force. Even King Aśoka, regarded as the avatar of *Cakravartin*, showed no sign of cutting down military preparation after the destructive war at Kalinga.[21]

Cakravartin went to war not to expand his military might or to satisfy his selfish desires but rather to protect the dharma and disseminate its teachings. *Cakkavatti-Sīhanāda Sutta* relates how, after *Cakravartin* conquered the east with his four wheels and fourfold army, he taught the local people to abstain from killing, stealing, false speech, and licentiousness. He also told them to stay away from alcohol and be moderate in their diet, thereby spreading the word of love to all people and creatures on earth.[22] It would seem war can bring out good effects from the perspective of Buddhism.

In the Chinese *Tripiṭaka* is included the Jain text *Dasazhe niqianzi suoshuo jing* (*the Mahāsatya-nirgrantha-sūtra*). Nirgrantha, the leader of Jainism, believes that a good king has to love his people. Even when it becomes necessary for him to punish them, he "should not terminate their lives and cut off all roots." When a country is invaded and experiences internal turmoil, the king should try to deal with the invaders in nonviolent ways. When all fails, then he should raise an army with prudence:

> At this moment, go to the battle with three thoughts in mind. Which three? One: this is a recalcitrant king [that we are fighting against]. He personally commits murder with no compassion. Besides, he does not take any measures to prevent others from committing murder. I should try to stop such kind of killing among people. This is the first thought to protect the sentient beings. Two: I should take expedient measures to vanquish the recalcitrant king with-

out using troops and horses to fight him. Three: I should use expedient measures to capture the king without really taking his life.

If the king has gone through such deliberations and planning and still cannot avoid conflicts, then the only thing left to him is to go to battle.[23]

Is a king who goes into battle after giving it due prudent considerations guilty of killing and hence should initiate a course of retribution? Nirgrantha argues that, because the king has contemplated the three compassionate thoughts and enters into war as a last resort, war is committed only as a skillful action. In this way, even if he ends up killing in the war, the crime is minimal, and the king can be absolved of the crime with repentance. This Jain view of war is affirmed by Buddhism, which can be seen as the Buddhist version of the discourse on *jus ad bellum* (i.e., the right to go to war). The focus is on whether people involve themselves in war with the right intention. King Dutugemunu of Sri Lanka, for example, was upheld as the model of entering a war with the right intention.

According to the *Mahāvaṃsa*, a fifth- to sixth-century CE mytho-historical narrative, King Dutugemunu of the second century BCE engages in a war with the invading Damila (Tamil) not out of resentment or hatred but rather out of a wish to protect the relics of the Buddha and dharma. King Dutugemunu knows too well that war is an unavoidable measure. He often expresses contrition over the killing that he commits during the war. After he kills King Elara of Damila, he cremates his body, arranges an extravagant funeral for him, and erects a monument in his honor. During the funeral, music is banned throughout the country. King Dutugemunu demonstrates respect and compassion for the defeated party in a war and does not turn arrogant or lose sight of the right mindfulness because he wins the war.[24]

KILLING WITH COMPASSION, KILLING ONE TO SAVE MANY

Under normal circumstances, Buddhism is opposed to violence, but, when *Cakravartin* killed in a battle, he did so with the proper goal in mind and, for that reason, was not condemned but won the approval of Buddhism. It is clear, therefore, that the Buddhist moral codes reflect the teleological and relativistic nature of the Buddhist ethics. An action can be wrong in nature but be undertaken out of good intentions. In evaluating and appraising its moral consequences and its rightness or wrongness, one has to keep in mind its long-term benefit and its immediate results and focus on the motive and intention (*cetana*) behind it.

In this way, a gap is cracked open in the first precept of Buddhism of "abstaining from killing." As long as the goal is legitimate and the thought correct, killing is but a skillful action that leads to no evil karma. For example, to kill one to save many or to kill with compassion to prevent others from committing evil is permitted by Buddhism. For example, *Dafangguang shanqiao fangbianjing* has a story: When the Buddha was a merchant in his previous life, he killed an evil person who had a plan to kill five hundred merchants. Thus, the Buddha's action saved the lives of those who would have been murdered.[25] Whether killing would constitute a crime depends on the initial thought. It is the condition of the common people to regard evil with indignation, but a buddha has to show compassion even for those who are bad and vicious. He would rather have them killed and fall into hell himself so that they would not commit a serious crime and get entrapped in the better results of their bad deeds. A compassionate act like this does not represent a breach of the precept but produces an immense merit.[26]

As shown above, early Buddhism—Theravāda Buddhism and Mahāyāna Buddhism—are alike in emphasizing the importance of nonviolence. They require people to abstain from any form of killing. However, under certain circumstances, Buddhism allows killing and provides a legal basis for violence and the taking of lives. Conceptually, then, Buddhism and violence do not lie in complete opposition; in reality, one often finds links between Buddhism and violence. While Buddhism promotes harmony and peace, it is by no means unconditionally pacifist.

CHINESE BUDDHISM AND WARFARE IN HISTORY

Since the early days of primitive Buddhism, the monks have always been instructed to stay away from war. The Buddha forbids people who join the order to enter army camps. According to the *Sūtra of Brahma's Net* (*Brahmajāla Sutta*), monks who watch military training or participate in military parades, maneuvers, and reviews are considered to have broken the precepts.[27] Furthermore, monks are not supposed to take part in the discussion of topics related to military affairs.[28] Monks and the laity should not trade in arms.[29] Even more stringent is the early prohibition that disallows soldiers to join the Buddhist order perhaps to prevent them from bringing their former disagreements and feuds into their religion.[30]

The strict precept, however, did not cut off the contact between monks and war. Monks were involved in politics during the Sri Lankan civil war of 1983–2009 and were opposed to negotiations and cease-fires. Instead, they opted for military solutions to the conflict.[31]

Similarly, in Chinese history, there are incidents where monks rose in arms. In 515 AD, Fa Qing, a Buddhist monk, gathered 50,000 people in Jizhou (in today's Hebei) during the Northern Wei period and rose in the name of Buddhism against the rule of the authorities.[32] In 618, the end of the Sui dynasty, another monk Gao Tansheng revolted, formed his own state, and declared himself the Mahāyāna Emperor. A few months later, he was murdered in turn.[33]

However, in Chinese history, the incidents were rare where monks came to revolt against the central authority. Rather, in cases where monks were involved in military actions in China, one is more likely to find acts of bravery and loyalty in defense of their country or religion. For example, Zhen Bao, the monk of Mount Wutai in the Northern Song, organized a group of followers into a defensive force. They trained themselves in martial arts and assisted the official army to resist the aggression of the Jurchens. In 1126, the Jurchens took Mount Wutai, "razing the temples and hostels." Zhen Bao led his fellow monks in a bloody combat with the Jurchens until he was captured. Refusing to yield, in the end he "serenely gave himself up for execution."[34] During the reign of Jiajing of the Ming dynasty, the Japanese pirates came to attack Hangzhou. Tianzhen and Tianchi of Shaolin Temple led a group of forty monk–soldiers against the pirates and defeated them.[35] The tradition of Buddhist monks coming to the defense of the country against foreign aggression went throughout Chinese history. Even in the twentieth century, examples are not lacking, as in an incident in 1933.[36]

There is scriptural basis for such acts of bravery against foreign aggression. *Dasheng bensheng xindi guanjing* speaks of four favors that a Buddhist must return: the favors from the parents, the favors from all sentient beings, the favors from the kings, and the favors from the Three Treasures.[37] The favors from the kings refer to those one receives from the rulers. In the Chinese cultural setting, where Confucianism with its emphasis on the patriarchal tradition and the interest of the country occupies a core position, Chinese Buddhism has never become a religion with an elevated status above political authority. On the contrary, Buddhism has to be beholden to the court before it can continue to exist and develop. In the words of Dao An of the Eastern Jin period, "It is difficult for religions to exist independently of the master of the country."[38] It is not easy for Buddhism, an imported religion, to get accepted by the public in China with its strong cultural roots, which is why Dao An believed that the support from those in power would be a big help to the spread of Buddhism. But, once the fate of the country is in question or when the court withdraws its support, Buddhism also suffers. This is a concept commonly accepted by Chinese Buddhists, hence, the widespread currency of the idea of "Protecting the country" (*huguo*) among the Buddhists. This may of course be simply based on the idea of repaying the king for his patronage, but, more importantly, it reflects the recognition, culturally and historically determined, that, without the king, the religion itself would be in danger.

Buddhists have never stopped rendering service to the state and society in Chinese history. In their morning and evening recitations, Buddhists have always kept "the prosperity of the country and the contentment of the people" in their prayers. And, when the country was under threat or natural disasters occurred, Buddhist groups would organize service to chant *Renwang boruo boluomi huguo jing*, a book of scripture that people turn to in requesting blessings for the peace of the country. In many places in China, temples are named "Temple in Protection of the Country" (*Huguosi*) as a sign of the monks' support of the state. In the grand hall of these temples, placards are placed with the words "May the ruling king live for thousands and thousands of years" inscribed on them. In the Republican era, the words "Ruling emperor" were changed to "The Republic of China."[39]

CHINESE BUDDHIST MONKS AND THE WAR OF RESISTANCE AGAINST JAPANESE AGGRESSION IN THE 1930S AND 1940S

The September 18 Incident of 1931 marked the beginning of the Second Sino-Japanese War. Full-scale conflicts broke out between the two countries in 1937, which lasted eight years, until Japan surrendered in 1945. In this national struggle for survival, Buddhist monks, together with the rest of the nation, were involved either voluntarily or involuntary in the effort in resisting Japanese aggression.

What role should monks play in the War of Resistance is a question that occupied the mind of the people at the time. The tradition of "Protecting the Country" mentioned above provides the religious basis for the monks' involvement in the war. But the purview of "Protecting the Country" is broad, covering anything that can benefit the state and the people, such as providing disaster relief, taking care of the sick and injured, or applying with renewed vigor to one's spiritual cultivation. Whether there is a need to risk violating the important precept of "abstaining from killing" became a debated issue, especially when the central government stipulated in 1936 that all monks had to join the army and ordered in 1939 that monks and nuns who joined the army had to go to combat on the front line.[40] The conflict between defending the country and violating the precept became all the more stark.

In an article, Fa Fang, probably a monk, succinctly lays out the issues that monks joining the army have to contend with: If a monk is drafted into the army, he is in danger of violating the precepts, but if he dodges the draft, he will not be able to fulfill his duty of defending the country. If he renounces his precepts before joining the army, it is unlikely that he would come to accept the precepts again. If one engages only in the work of caring for the injured but stands aside to allow the battle to go on, one might be guilty of abetting killing, which amounts to violating the precepts, just the same. There is of course the option of killing with compassion or with an indeterminate mind (*avyākṛta-citta*), but it is one thing to understand it conceptually and quite another to put it into practice. Fa Fang, in the end, does not provide answers to these questions.[41]

Faced with the dilemma, there were monks who preferred giving up their lives, rather than breaking the precepts. When they found out that they were about to be recruited for military training, some hanged themselves and others deserted.[42] In the meantime, Buddhist publications at the time were imbued with the spirit of defending the country, and Buddhist leaders called upon monks and nuns to immerse themselves in the resistance forces. Yi Tuo wrote in an article, "The country is now under threat. When we find ourselves in this dual circumstances (二重環境), [we have to declare] we love our country, but we have to love Buddhism more; we love Buddhism, but we need to love our country more!"[43] Similarly, Yue Yao stated in the foreword of the special issue "Protecting the Country by the Sangha" in *Fohaideng*, "Monks like ourselves are members of the Republic of China. All our daily needs, clothing, food, shelter and means of transportation, are all dependent on the country. Now that we are facing a national disaster, can we afford to stand aside and watch?"[44] With the intensification of the Japanese aggression, more and more voices joined in to echo the call for Buddhists to participate in the war efforts.

Was there a consensus, then, on how monks should resist the aggression of the Japanese at that time? A wide range of opinions existed. Jing Guang insisted that monks should not involve themselves personally in military actions because they should not go against the precept of not killing; they should instead turn to the tasks of medical aid.[45] Ren Xing asserted that all monks are citizens of the highest caliber of the country and their patriotism should not fall behind that of other people. At the same time, if one is to prioritize the many duties of defending one's country, care of the injured should come first and then the practice of the rituals of protecting the country and the chanting of the *Prajñāpāramitā-sūtra*. The most active role would of course be to fight on the front line, but, without the proper training or organization, the monks would only get in the way of serious combat.[46] The views above represent the monks who were opposed to involvement in combat and other direct military actions. On the other hand, other monks attempted to negotiate for a practicable compromise between joining the army and adhering to the precepts. Yi Sheng, for example, indicated two proper ways for the monks to join the defense efforts, what he called the mundane, or this-worldly way (*lokiya*) and the other-worldly way (*lokuttara*). If one opts for the former, then the proper thing to do is to withdraw from the Buddhist order before joining the army. In this way, one can avoid violating the precept of killing. If one opts for the latter, one should do one's best to realize the holy fruit, that is, ultimate enlightenment, at which time, one can exercise the supernatural power (*abhijñā*) in defending the country and squashing the enemies.[47]

On the other hand, Tai Xu, China's Buddhist leader at the time, unequivocally called upon monks to join the rank of the resisting forces. In sharp contrast to the more conservative views summarized above, he pointed out in an article that "[i]f the country cannot protect itself from invasion, if there is no safeguard for its people, if there is no peace in our lives, there is no way we can speak of repaying the favors we receive from our parents and society. That is why we need to love and protect our country. Defending the country should be our first task." And of the many kinds of work of defending the country, joining the army is the most important:

> There are now hundreds of thousands of monks in China. Except for those who clearly have the ability to be scholar monks, ministry monks [monks in charge of the administration of the temples] and senior and virtuous monks [venerable retired monks] and others who are too old, too young, too sick or too infirmed, all others healthy able-bodied monks should go and sacrifice for the country instead of remaining in the temple and defiling the name of Buddhism as they cannot in other ways take up the role of the "treasure of sangha" to preserve the purity of Buddhism. To join the army to fight the violent enemy is in fact beneficial both to Buddhism and the country.

Those who could not join the army were then expected to devote themselves to the originally given religious task of spreading the word of Buddhism and serving people as well as attending to the injured.[48]

How would one then resolve the dilemma of killing in the battlefield and the Buddhist injunction against killing? Jue Xian, who shared Tai Xu's position of calling for the enlistment of the 730,000 monks and nuns in China, argued that, if one kills with the mindset of the Bodhisattva, who killed a bandit to save five hundred merchants, one is stopping a violent act in the defense of the country and the welfare of the people and is therefore not in violation of the Buddhist injunction. On the contrary, if one refrains from doing anything in the face of evil, it is tantamount to the negation of the Buddhist dharma. Quoting Jiun Onko, a Japanese monk, "It is not a crime to kill what harms the country; not only is it not a crime; it is a meritorious act." Jue Xian then argued, "The righteous army is inspired by kindliness and justice. That is why, even when it kills hundreds and thousands of enemies, its merits increase more than tenfold." What deserves special note here is that he makes a point of reminding the "armed comrades" to be careful not to be misled by the "bandits." They should follow the right leaders, that is, Commissioner Chiang Kai-shek, the highest military commander of the nation, and Master Tai Xu, the commander-in-chief of the Buddhist volunteer troops. Only by taking orders from them can the monks and nuns be unified and direct their invincible force against the enemies.[49]

In this public exchange of ideas, those arguing for direct involvement in the war had the upper hand. As Buddhist monks and nuns participated in the war efforts, what were their specific tasks?

- Medical work, for example, the Rescue Crew of the Monks in the Provisional Capital (陪都僧侶救護隊), established in March 1940.[50]
- Propaganda work, for example, the International Propaganda Team of Chinese Buddhism (中國佛教國際宣傳隊) made up of young monks.[51]
- Donation of money and material resources, for example, the Buddhist Association of Quanzhou in Fujian (福建省泉州佛教會) requested that monks fast for three days. The money thus saved was donated in the form of an airplane named "Buddhism" (佛教號).[52]
- Repentance Ceremony, for example, during the war, Shanghai Buddhists established an organization for praying for the protection of the country and the cessation of calamities.[53]
- Joining the army or the guerrillas, for example, Master Zhen Wei of Tongshan Temple joined the guerrillas, capturing four Japanese soldiers in the grand hall of the temple in 1942.[54] Monks of Mt. Wutai also joined the guerrillas, making Mt. Wutai the first guerrilla headquarters in China.[55]

From the currently available sources, it is impossible to estimate the actual number of monks who actively involved themselves in the War of Resistance. However, we can see that, among those who did, their activities were quite extensive, ranging from medical aid to propaganda, monetary and material donations, and combat as well as religious ceremonies. We will not know how many of them succeeded in putting aside the feeling of uncertainty and anxiety of violating the precept of not taking life and threw themselves wholeheartedly into the resistance. Similarly, we are not in a position to judge whether they were motivated by the Mahāyāna Bodhisattva spirit or by nationalist feelings. More certain is the fact that they were willing to see themselves as members of the citizenry when the state came under military invasion. In their mind, their religious and secular identities must have intertwined, which made it possible for them to accept that monks can take part in warfare and still adhere to the Buddhist instructions. That, however, does not mean that their resistance actions necessarily were governed by these considerations.

SUMMARY: JUST WAR THINKING IN CHINESE BUDDHISM

Buddhism advocates love toward all sentient beings. Violence will only beget suffering and bad karma for the self and others. Therefore, even when violence is unavoidable, it should take a second place to nonviolence. For someone to move from a nonviolent to a violent position, as monks did in their involvement in war, there has to be a justification as well as remorse.[56] The Buddhist opposition to violence runs through its view of war. Simply put, it stands in opposition to wars that are fought out of selfish reasons and a desire to pillage, but Buddhism also provides justifications for the proper use of force, for example, defending oneself when attacked, upholding the dharma, and stopping acts of evil and saving lives. Buddhism therefore is not intransigent in its stance against killing but in fact allows that, under certain circumstances (for example, out of compassion, where the killing of one evil life might save myriad other lives), it is legitimate to go against the precept. In the absence of other better options, war can be entertained as a protective, or defensive, measure. This is, of course, different from encouraging the use of warfare. Perhaps it is more correct to say that, while accepting that violence is bad, when it cannot be avoided, "defensive violence is less bad than aggressive violence."[57]

Buddhist precepts (*śīla*) have often been thought to be externally imposed restrictions and injunctions. In fact, the main purpose of precepts is to remind believers that, to reap good results, one has to put in place good causes.

In volume 13 of Nāgārjuna's *Mahāprajñāpāramita—śastra*, *śīla* is defined as "vigilance in doing good deeds."[58] The four conditions of *śīla* are chastity, calmness, quietness, and a state of extinguishment (i.e., where one is no longer perturbed by the passions).[59]

Thus, the point is not to emphasize the penalty that results from the violation of the precepts but rather to point out what type of actions will result in bad karma and lead to the suffering of the sentient beings. Buddhism therefore emphasizes moral autonomy rather than a set of heteronomous commandments. The focus of the precepts is not only on the overt behavior but also includes the motive and intention behind it. For example, whether the taking of life constitutes a serious crime depends not only on the act of killing but also on the motivation of the killer. If the killing is done without intention, by mistake, or in a state of mental confusion, then the crime associated with it might not be regarded as so serious; it might not even be thought of as a crime at all.[60]

Because of the fact that the Buddhist ethic stresses the moral autonomy of the individual, it permits people to interpret the spirit, not only the letter of the precepts, and act in response to it on the basis of their experience and standpoint. In this way, war, which is not allowed by the precepts, can be rationalized under "reasonable" circumstances. Is such a position equivalent to just war theory (*jus bellum justum*)?

Just war theory deals with the justification of why and how wars are fought, that is, the just reasons to go to war (*jus ad bellum*) and the just conduct in war (*jus in bello*). The former refers to a set of moral constraints on the justifiability of resorting to military actions, and the latter refers to a set of moral constraints on the justifiability of the conduct in war.[61] Therefore, a just war refers to a war thought to be motivated by just causes and conducted in a humane way.[62]

Both *Cakkavatti-Sīhanāda Sutta* and the *Mahāsatya-nirgrantha-sūtra*, mentioned above, have pointed out that a ruler should not enter war in a cavalier way. Rather, he has to be motivated by a legitimate reason, such as compassion, and give due deliberation to the action of war beforehand. Similar discussions to those on justice of war (*jus ad bellum*) are therefore evident in the Buddhist scriptures, but little mention is made of the proper conduct of the military action (*jus in bello*) in the course of war. As far as that is concerned, the discussion of war in Buddhism is at best only one sided. In contrast with *dharmayuddha* (righteousness of warfare) of Hinduism, Buddhism has yet to develop a well-defined theory on just war.[63] Some scholars would even argue that, unlike the Christian tradition, there is no place in Buddhism for a holy, or a just, war.[64]

Even though Buddhism initially does not show much interest in just war theory, the lack of a central doctrinal authority, on the one hand, and the emphasis on autonomy rather than heteronomy, on the other, in Buddhism means that it is open to the contemplation of the question of the justice of war. Moreover, attempts can be found in the early Buddhist scriptures to define what is appropriate and legal in a war. These attempts are sporadic but are enough to pave the way for believers toward the development of a set of just war thinking in their social involvement in subsequent periods. The Buddhists in Sri Lanka, for example, constructed a rich war ideology based on Theravāda canonical literature and postcanonical works, primarily the *Mahāvaṃsa*. Putting aside the question as to whether the Sri Lankan war ideology as such constitutes a complete just war theory, in so far that it stipulates that Buddhists must not deviate from the dharma, even in war, it is not too different from just war theory in its goals.[65]

Chinese Buddhism has incorporated both Mahāyāna and Theravāda teachings and precepts from Indian Buddhism, and its view on warfare is not much different from Hinduism in that neither develops a systematic just war theory. In the case of Chinese Buddhism, the discourse of "protecting the country" puts the question in a different light. If the country were destroyed, Buddhism would be eliminated as well—such is the consensus among the Chinese monks since antiquity. In times of peace, they seek to repay the ruler's favor; in times of war, they come out to defend the country, which is equivalent to defending Buddhism. That is to say that defending the legitimate political authority and the people to save the country from disasters becomes the legal reason for monks to participate in war, a concept that takes precedence over religious teachings and precepts. The fervor to love and protect their country pervaded in Buddhist circles during the War of Resistance against Japanese Aggression and became the major motivation for them to fight and kill the enemy, making them turn a blind eye to the precepts that should have taken them away from war. Nevertheless, compared to the Japanese Buddhist monks, who rarely considered the contradictions between war and the precept of no killing and instead actively supported the invasive war that Japan was waging against other countries, Chinese monks, with their respect for the precepts, had difficulty in accepting unconditionally the idea of "killing with compassion."[66]

There is no uniform just war thinking in Chinese Buddhism. Often, under the influence of the political situation of the time, different parties express what they consider to be conditions under which Buddhists can participate in war. Most based their opinions on the fundamental positions of Buddhism, such as altruism, and, for that reason, they do not consider the ethics of the conduct of war from the point of view of *jus in bello*. This perhaps is the shortcoming of just war thinking in Chinese Buddhism. On the other hand, the core values in Buddhist ethics are kindness (*maitrī*) and pity (*karuṇā*). The former aims to make others happy, and the latter sets out to eliminate the suffering of others. To reduce suffering to its minimum is to magnify joy to its maximum. As long as it conforms to this motivation and helps the realization of this goal, any human behavior, violence and war included, will not be condemned and will be allowed when it is put to good use. Buddhist just war thinking is hence not complete in and of itself, but that fact should not prevent it from incorporating the latest just war theory, thereby becoming an engaging discourse on the discussion of war.

BIBLIOGRAPHY

CBETA *Taisho*, Vol. 1, No. 11.
CBETA *Taisho*, Vol. 1, No. 26.
CBETA *Taisho*, Vol. 2, No. 99.
CBETA *Taisho*, Vol. 2, No. 125.
CBETA Taisho, Vol. 3, No. 154.
CBETA *Taisho*, Vol. 3, No. 159.
CBETA *Taisho*, Vol. 9, No. 272.
CBETA *Taisho*, Vol. 12, No. 346.
CBETA *Taisho*, Vol. 17, No. 721.
CBETA *Taisho*, Vol. 25, No. 1509.
CBETA *Taisho*, Vol. 30, No. 1579.
CBETA *Taisho*, Vol. 50, No. 2059.
CBETA X77, No. 1524.
Bartholomeusz, Tessa J. *In Defense of Dharma: Just-War Ideology in Buddhist Sri Lanka*. London and New York: Routledge Curzon, 2002.
Brown, Garrett, Iain McLean, and Alistair McMillan, eds. *The Concise Oxford Dictionary of Politics and International Relations*. 4th ed. Oxford: Oxford University Press, 2018.
Chatterjee, D. K., ed. *Encyclopedia of Global Justice*. Dordrecht: Springer, 2011.
Conze, Edward, trans. *Buddhist Scriptures*. Baltimore: Penguin Books, 1959.
Cowell, E. B., ed., H. T. Francis and R. A. Neil, trans. *The Jātaka or Stories of the Buddha's Former Births*, Book IV. Oxford: Pali Text Society, 1995.

Deegalle, Mahinda. "The Buddhist Traditions of South and Southeast Asia." In *Religion, War, and Ethics: A Sourcebook of Textual Traditions*, ed. Gregory M. Reichberg and Henrik Syse, 544–96. New York: Cambridge University Press, 2004.
Dhammika Sutta, Suttanipāta 2:14, *Khuddaka Nikāya*. Sutta Central. Accessed December 22, 2018. https://suttacentral.net/snp2.14/en/mills.
Du Doucheng (杜斗城), ed. 正史佛教資料類編 (*Collected Materials on Buddhism in Orthodox History*). CBETA H01, 2, no. 1.
E Kou (惡口). "寫在護國息災法會之後" ("Writing after the Ritual of Defending the Nation"). 佛海燈 (*Lamp of the Buddhist Sea*) 2, no. 2: 1.
Fa Fang (法舫). "僧尼應否服國民兵役?" ("Should Monks and Nuns Serve the Draft?"). 海潮音 (*The Sound of Waves*) 17, no. 8: 1–2.
Fumihiko, Sueki. "Chinese Buddhism and the Anti-Japan War." *Japanese Journal of Religious Studies* 37, no. 1 (2010): 9–20.
Hare, E. M., trans. *The Book of the Gradual Sayings* (*Aṅguttara-Nīkāya*). London: Pali Text Society, 1934.
Jackson, D. M. "Jus ad Bellum" and "Jus in Bello." In *Encyclopedia of Global Justice*, ed. D. K. Chatterjee. Dordrecht: Springer, 2011.
Jayasuriya, Laksiri. "Just War Tradition and Buddhism." *International Studies* 46, no. 4 (2009): 423–38.
Jing Guang (淨光). "現代中國佛教青年應具之幾種觀點" ("A Few Viewpoints Buddhist Youth in Modern Times Should Adopt"). 海潮音 (*The Sound of Waves*) 18, no. 1 (1937): 33–36.
Jue Xian (覺先). "僧訓武裝護國論" ("On Arming the Monks in Defense of the Nation"). 佛海燈 (*Lamp of the Buddhist Sea*) 2, no. 4: 3–6.
Le Guan (樂觀). "一個無名英雄和尚" ("An Anonymous Young Monk Hero"). 海潮音 (*The Sound of Waves*) 28, no. 8: 20–21.
———. 僧侶抗戰工作史 (*History of the Work of Monks in the War of Resistance*). Taipei, 1980.
Master Sheng-yen (聖嚴法師). 戒律學綱要 (*The Essentials of the Study of Precepts*). Taipei: Dharma Drum Publishing Corp., 1999.
Nanamoli, Bhikku, and Bhikku Bodhi, trans. *The Middle Length Discourses of the Buddha: A New Translation of the Majjhima Nikaya*. Boston: Wisdom Publications, 1995.
Ramaiah, G. Sundara, et al., eds. *Buddhism and Peace: An Interdisciplinary Study*. Visakhapatnam: Andhra University Press, 1991.
Ravi, Komarraju. "Buddhism and Just War." In *Buddhism and Peace: An Interdisciplinary Study*, ed. G. Sundara Ramaiah et al., 77–83. Visakhapatnam: Andhra University Press, 1991.
Reichberg, Gregory, and M. Henrik Syse, eds. *Religion, War, and Ethics: A Sourcebook of Textual Traditions*. New York: Cambridge University Press, 2004.
Ren Xin (仁心). "抗戰聲中的佛教徒" ("The Buddhists in the Cries of Defending the Nation"). 海潮音 (*The Sound of Waves*) 18, no. 9 (1937): 1–2.
Rhys Davids, T. W., and C. A. F. Rhys Davids, trans. *Dialogues of the Buddha*. London: Pali Text Society, 1977.
Sarao, K. T. S. *The Dhammapada: A Translator's Guide*. New Delhi: Munshiram Manoharlal Publishers, 2009.
Sheng Sheng (生生). "走出經堂與惡魔搏鬥—抗戰熱潮泛濫五台" ("Stepping Out of the Buddhist Hall to Combat the Demon—The Heated Waves of War of Resistance Sweeping over Wutai"). 獅子吼 (*The Lion's Roar*) 1, no. 2: 28–29.
Soothill, William Edward, and Lewis Hodous, eds. *A Dictionary of Chinese Buddhist Terms*. Accessed December 22, 2018. https://www.buddhistdoor.org/tc/dictionary/details/sila-sila-morality-precept-virtue.
Tai Xu (太虛). "勸全國佛教青年組護國團" ("On Advising Young Buddhists of the Country to Form Organizations in Defending the Nation"). 海潮音 (*The Sound of Waves*) 14, no. 5: 7–13.
Tan Yun (曇雲). "僧伽護國雜談" ("Random Words of Saṅgha Defending the Nation"). 佛海燈 (*Lamp of the Buddhist Sea*) 2, no. 5–6: 25–26.

Venerable Zhenhua (震華法師). 僧伽護國史 (*History of Saṅgha Defending the Nation*). Shanghai: Foxue shuju, 1934.

Walshe, Maurice, trans. *The Connected Discourses of the Buddha: A Translation of the Dīgha-Nīkāya*. Boston: Wisdom Publications, 1995.

———. *The Long Discourses of the Buddha: A Translation of the Dīgha-Nikāya*. Boston: Wisdom Publications, 1995.

Xue Yu (學愚). *Buddhism, War, and Nationalism: Chinese Monks in the Struggle against Japanese Aggressions, 1931–1945* (in Chinese). Hong Kong: The Chinese University Press, 2011.

Yi Sheng (一乘). "僧伽護國的正途" ("The Correct Path of Saṅgha in Defending the Nation"). 佛海燈 (*Lamp of the Buddhist Sea*) 2, no. 4: 11–15.

Yi Tuo (伊陀). "從一個民族英雄的青年和尚說起" ("Beginning with the Story of a Young Monk—A Hero of the People"). 海潮音 (*The Sound of Waves*) 18, no. 5 (1937): 98–99.

Yin Shun (印順). 佛在人間 (*The Buddha in the Human World*). Taipei: Zhengwen chubanshe, 1984.

Yue Yao (月耀). "僧伽護國專號卷首語" ("Foreword to the Special Issue of Saṅgha Defending the Nation"). 佛海燈 (*Lamp of the Buddhist Sea*) 2, no. 4: 1.

Notes

FOREWORD

1. This is the central argument of Alex J. Bellamy, *World Peace (And How We Can Achieve It)* (Oxford: Oxford University Press, 2019), 1.
2. Christopher Coker, *Barbarous Philosophers: Reflections on the Nature of War from Heraclitus to Heisenberg* (London: Hurst and Co., 2010), 12–13; and Azar Gat, *Military Thought in the Nineteenth Century* (Oxford: Oxford University Press, 1992), 67.
3. Matt Ridley, *The Origins of Virtue* (London: Viking, 1996), 6.
4. John Maynard Smith, *The Theory of Evolution*, 3rd ed. (London: Penguin, 1975), 312.
5. Ridley, *Origins of Virtue*, 181.
6. Claude Levi-Strauss, *Structural Anthropology* (New York: Doubleday, 1963), 21–37.
7. David Sloan-Wilson, *Darwin's Cathedral: Evolution, Religion and the Nature of Society* (Chicago: University of Chicago Press, 2007), 179–80.
8. Peter Kropotkin, *Mutual Aid: A Factor of Evolution* (New York: Dover, 2009 [1902]), 8–12.
9. Siep Stuurman, *The Invention of Humanity: Equality and Cultural Difference in World History* (Cambridge, MA: Harvard University Press, 2017), 1–2.
10. Frans De Waal, *Primates and Philosophers: How Morality Evolved* (Princeton, NJ: Princeton University Press, 2016), 54; and Ridley, *Origins of Virtue*, 174.
11. Michael Walzer, *Just and Unjust Wars: A Moral Argument with Historical Illustrations* (New York: Basic Books, 1977), 44.
12. William Graham Sumner, "War" [1903], in *War and Other Essays* (New Haven, CT: Yale University Press, 1919), 3–20.
13. Hannah Arendt, *On Violence* (London: Harcourt, 1970), 5.
14. George Orwell, *The Lion and the Unicorn: Socialism and the English Genius* (London: Penguin, 1970 [first published 1941]), 37.

INTRODUCTION

1. To provide one example, chapter 11 on non-Western Islamic perspectives of just war theory will avoid traditional political critiques.

2. John Langan, "The Elements of St. Augustine's Just War Theory," *The Journal of Religious Ethics* 12, no. 1 (1984): 19.

3. Robert L. Holmes, "A Time for War? Augustine's Just War Theory Continues to Guide the West," *Christianity Today* (September 1, 2001).

4. Langan, "Elements," 36.

5. Michael Walzer, *Just and Unjust Wars: A Moral Argument with Historical Illustrations*, 3rd ed. (New York: Basic Books, 2000).

6. Jeff McMahan, "Innocence, Self-Defense and Killing in War," *Journal of Political Philosophy* 2/3 (1994).

7. *Stanford Encyclopedia of Philosophy*, "War," May 3, 2016; *Internet Encyclopedia of Philosophy* "Just War Theory."

8. Chenyang Li, "Confucian Harmony in Dialogue with African Harmony: A Response," *African and Asian Studies* 15, no. 1 (2016); Daniel A. Bell and Thaddeus Metz, "Confucianism and Ubuntu: Reflections on a Dialogue between Chinese and African Traditions," *Journal of Chinese Philosophy* 38 (2011).

9. Tongdong Bai, "What to Do in an Unjust State? On Confucius's and Socrates's Views on Political Duty," *Dao* 9, no. 4 (2010); Joseph Chan, *Confucian Perfectionism: A Political Philosophy for Modern Times*, reprint ed. (Princeton, NJ, and Oxford: Princeton University Press, 2015); Mario Wenning, "Kant and Daoism on Nothingness," *Journal of Chinese Philosophy* 38, no. 4 (2011).

10. United Nations Summit Outcome Document, "2005 World Summit Outcome," *UN General Assembly Doc.* A/RES/60/1, 60th session, October 24, 2005, paras. 138–139.

11. See chapter 5 for the examination of just war theory, with the support of LOAC, in the contexts of these three non-Western settings.

1. ANARCHISM AND JUST WAR THEORY

1. For a particularly in-depth analysis of anti-authoritarianism in anarchist thought, see Paul McLaughlin, *Anarchism and Authority: A Philosophical Introduction to Classical Anarchism* (London: Routledge, 2016).

2. See Andrew Fiala, "Anarchism and Pacifism," in *Brill's Companion to Anarchism and Philosophy*, ed. Nathan Jun (Leiden: Brill, 2017), 152–70.

3. Anne Schwenkenbecher, "Rethinking Legitimate Authority," in *The Routledge Handbook of Ethics and War: Just War Theory in the Twenty-First Century*, ed. Fritz Allhoff, Nicholas G. Evans, and Adam Henschke (London: Routledge 2013), 161; Andrew Fiala, *Against Religion, Wars, and States: The Case for Enlightenment Atheism, Just War Pacifism, and Liberal-Democratic Anarchism* (Lanham, MD: Rowman & Littlefield, 2013), 117–18.

4. Mikhail Bakunin, *The Political Philosophy of Bakunin*, ed. G. P. Maximoff (New York: Free Press, 1953), 224.

5. Ibid.

6. Andrew Robinson, "The State as a Cause of War: Anarchist and Autonomist Critiques of War," in *The Ashgate Research Companion to War: Origins and Prevention*, ed. Oleg Kobtzeff and Hall Gardner (Aldershot, UK: Ashgate, 2013), 131.

7. Ibid.

8. Ibid., 132.

9. Ibid., 131. See also Fiala, "Anarchism and Pacifism," 161–62.

10. Yoram Dinstein, *War, Aggression and Self-Defence*, 4th ed. (Cambridge: Cambridge University Press, 2005), 3.

11. Lassa Oppenheim, *International Law*, vol. 2: *International Law, A Treatise*, ed. Hersh Lauterpacht (London: Longmans, Green & Co., 1952), 202. Cf. Robert Bledsoe and Bolesław Boczek, eds., *The International Law Dictionary* (Oxford: ABC-CLIO, 1987), 343; James Fox, ed., *Dictionary of International and Comparative Law*, 3rd ed. (New York: Oceana Publications Inc., 2003), 356.

12. Fritz Allhoff, Nicholas G. Evans, and Adam Henschke, eds., "Introduction: Not Just Wars: Expansions and Alternatives to the Just War Tradition," in *The Routledge Companion of Ethics and War* (New York: Routledge, 2013), 1.

13. McLaughlin, *Anarchism and Authority*, 56.

14. Ibid.

15. A. J. Simmons, *Boundaries of Authority* (Oxford: Oxford University Press, 2016), 16.

16. Martin van Crevald, *The Rise and Decline of the State* (Cambridge: Cambridge University Press, 1999), 1.

17. Ibid., 17.

18. Schwenkenbecher, "Rethinking Legitimate Authority," 161–62.

19. St. Thomas Aquinas, *Summa Theologica*, ed. and trans. Fathers of the English Dominican Province (New York: Benziger Brothers, 1946), II–II, Q. 40, A.1.

20. Simmons, *Boundaries of Authority*, 21–22.

21. Eric Heinze and Brent Steele, eds., *Ethics, Authority and War: Non-State Actors in the Just War Tradition* (New York: Palgrave Macmillan, 2009), 1.

22. Ibid.

23. Ibid. For example, although Article 4 of the Third Geneva Convention (1949) explicitly mentions nonstate actors, such as "[m]embers of . . . militias and members of other volunteer corps, including those of organized resistance movements," it does not consider such actors to be lawful combatants unless they "fulfill the following conditions: (a) that of being commanded by a person responsible for his subordinates; (b) that of having a fixed distinctive sign recognizable at a distance; (c) that of carrying arms openly; and (d) that of conducting their operations in accordance with the laws and customs of war" (Third Geneva Convention Relative to the Treatment of Prisoners of War of 12 August 1949, Part 1, Article 4, 92–93). In other words, parties to armed conflicts must be sufficiently akin to state actors in their overall demeanor and conduct to qualify as "lawful" combatants.

24. Anarchists, of course, were among the first political actors to be labeled "terrorists" beginning in the 1890s. For additional historical context, see Richard Bach Jensen, *The Battle against Anarchist Terrorism: An International History, 1878–1934* (Cambridge: Cambridge University Press, 2014); Constance Bantman, "The Era of Propaganda by the Deed," in *The Palgrave Handbook of Anarchism*, ed. Carl Levy and Matthew S. Adams (Basingstoke, UK: Palgrave Macmillan, 2018), 371–87; and Michael Loadenthal, *The Politics of Attack: Communiqués and Insurrectionary Violence* (Manchester, UK: Manchester University Press, 2018), chapter 2.

25. Bruce Hoffman, *Inside Terrorism* (New York: Columbia University Press, 2006), 1.

26. Ibid., 41.

27. This problem is vividly illustrated, for example, in the ongoing failure of the UN General Assembly to adopt a uniform definition of terrorism.

28. Heinze and Steele, *Ethics, Authority and War*, 2.

29. Third Geneva Convention Relative to the Treatment of Prisoners of War of 12 August 1949, Part 1, Article 4, 92–93.

30. This presumption is evident, for example, in Chapter VII, Article 51 of the Charter of the UN, according to which "Nothing in the present Charter shall impair the inherent right of individual or collective self-defence if an armed attack occurs against a Member of the United Nations, until the Security Council has taken measures necessary to maintain international peace and security. Measures taken by Members in the exercise of this right of self-defence shall be immediately reported to the Security Council and shall not in any way affect the authority and responsibility of the Security Council under the present Charter to take at any time such action as it deems necessary in order to maintain or restore international peace and security."

31. Bakunin, *The Political Philosophy of Bakunin*, 365; cf. ibid., 249; Rudolf Rocker, *Nationalism and Culture* (Montreal: Black Rose Books, 1998), 63.

32. Ibid., 139.

33. Ibid., 365.

34. Errico Malatesta, *Anarchy*, ed. Vernon Richards (London: Freedom Press, 1974), 12; Bakunin, *The Political Philosophy of Bakunin*, 159; Peter Kropotkin, *Anarchism: A Collection of Revolutionary Writings*, ed. Roger Baldwin (Mineola, NY: Dover, 1970), 51.

35. Nathan Jun, "Freedom," in *Anarchism: A Conceptual Approach*, ed. Benjamin Franks, Nathan Jun, and Leonard Williams (London: Routledge, 2018), 44–59.

36. Ibid., 53–54.

37. Ibid., 54–55.

38. Ibid., 52–53.

39. Ibid., 53.

40. Emma Goldman, *Red Emma Speaks*, ed. Alix Kates Shulman (Amherst, NY: Humanity Books, 1998), 121.

41. Ibid.

42. Emma Goldman, *Anarchism and Other Essays* (New York: Mother Earth Publishing Company, 1910), 67.

43. Ibid.

44. Mikhail Bakunin, *The Basic Bakunin*, ed. Robert Cutler (Buffalo: Prometheus Books, 1992), 236.

45. Iris Marion Young, *Justice and the Politics of Difference* (Princeton, NJ: Princeton University Press, 1990), 38.

46. Ibid.; cf. Ann Cudd, *Analyzing Oppression* (Oxford: Oxford University Press, 2006), 52.

47. Nathan Jun, "The State," in *The Palgrave Handbook of Anarchism*, ed. Carl Levy and Matthew S. Adams (Basingstoke, UK: Palgrave Macmillan, 2018), 38.

48. Nathan Jun, "On Philosophical Anarchism," *Radical Philosophy Review* 19, no. 3 (2016): 559.

49. Daniel Guérin, *No Gods, No Masters*, trans. Paul Sharkey (Oakland, CA: AK Press, 1998), 57.

50. Pierre-Joseph Proudhon, *The General Idea of the Revolution in the Nineteenth Century* [1851], trans. John Beverly Robinson (London: Freedom Press, 1923), 294; cf. Bakunin, *God and the State* (Mineola, NY: Dover, 1970), 10; Malatesta, *Anarchy*, 12.

51. Jun, "The State," 39; cf. Kropotkin, *Anarchism: A Collection of Revolutionary Writings*, 181; Pierre-Joseph Proudhon, *What Is Property?* (London: William Reeves, 1969), 43.

52. McLaughlin, *Anarchism and Authority*, 28.

53. Bakunin, *The Political Philosophy of Bakunin*, 358; Proudhon, *What Is Property?*, 43.

54. Jun, "The State," 39. For a more detailed comparison of anarchism and Marxism on this issue, see Lucien van der Walt, "Anarchism and Marxism," in *Brill's Companion to Anarchism and Philosophy*, ed. Nathan Jun (Leiden: Brill, 2017), 505–58.

55. Karl Marx and Friedrich Engels, *The Marx-Engels Reader*, ed. Robert Tucker (New York: Norton, 1978), 475.

56. Vladimir Lenin, *The Essential Works of Lenin*, ed. Henry Christman (New York: Dover, 1987), 274.

57. Bakunin, *The Political Philosophy of Bakunin*, 365.

58. Jun, "The State," 31; cf. Bakunin, *The Political Philosophy of Bakunin*, 165.

59. Mikhail Bakunin, *Bakunin on Anarchy*, ed. Sam Dolgoff (New York: Alfred A. Knopf, 1972), 76, 229–30; Alexander Berkman, *What Is Anarchism?* (Oakland, CA: AK Press, 2003), 65; Goldman, *Red Emma Speaks*, 98; Uri Gordon, "Power and Anarchy," in *New Perspectives on Anarchism*, ed. Nathan Jun and Shane Wahl (Lanham, MD: Lexington Books, 2009), 45; Peter Kropotkin, "Words of a Rebel," in *No Gods, No Masters*, ed. Daniel Guérin, trans. Paul Sharkey (Oakland, CA: AK Press), 301; Malatesta, *Anarchy*, 37; Errico Malatesta, *Fra Contadini: A Dialogue on Anarchy*, trans. Jean Weir (London: Bratach Dubh Editions, 1981), 26; Rudolf Rocker, *Anarcho-Syndicalism: Theory and Practice* (Oakland, CA: AK Press, 2004), 33; Rocker, *Nationalism and Culture*, 35.

60. Robinson, "The State as Cause of War," 132.

61. Goldman, *Red Emma Speaks*, 115.

62. Bakunin, *The Political Philosophy of Bakunin*, 211.

63. Malatesta, *Anarchy*, 14.

64. Kropotkin, *Anarchism: A Collection of Revolutionary Writings*, 98; cf. Goldman, *Anarchism and Other Essays*, 113.
65. Bakunin, *Bakunin on Anarchy*, 328.
66. Robinson, "The State as a Cause of War," 132.
67. Ibid.
68. Ibid.
69. Bakunin, *Bakunin on Anarchy*, 337.
70. Ibid, 133.
71. Ibid., 337.
72. Errico Malatesta, *Life and Ideas*, ed. Vernon Richards (Oakland, CA: PM Press, 2015), 228. Countless examples attest to the truth of this claim, ranging from the Russian tsars' deliberate fomenting of pogroms in the Pale of Settlement to Slobodan Milosevic's instigation of ethnic cleansing in the former Yugoslavia.
73. Bakunin, *The Political Philosophy of Bakunin*, 365.
74. Malatesta, *Life and Ideas*, 228.
75. Uri Gordon, *Anarchy Alive! Anti-Authoritarian Politics from Practice to Theory* (London: Pluto Books, 2008), 79.
76. Alexander Berkman, *The Bolshevik Myth* (London: Pluto Press, 1989), 3.
77. Gordon, *Anarchy Alive!*, 49.
78. Benjamin Franks, "Prefiguration," in *Anarchism: A Conceptual Approach*, ed. Benjamin Franks, Nathan Jun, and Leonard Williams (London: Routledge, 2018), 29.
79. Vicente Ordóñez, "Direct Action," in *Anarchism: A Conceptual Approach*, ed. Benjamin Franks, Nathan Jun, and Leonard Williams (London: Routledge, 2018), 75–76.
80. Benjamin Franks, "Vanguards and Paternalism," in *New Perspectives on Anarchism*, ed. Nathan Jun and Shane Wahl (Lanham, MD: Lexington Books, 2009), 99.
81. Peter Kropotkin, *Fugitive Writings*, ed. George Woodcock (Montreal: Black Rose Books, 1993), 41.
82. Malatesta, *Life and Ideas*, 83.
83. Ibid., 170.
84. Ibid.
85. Peter Kropotkin, *Direct Struggle against Capital: A Peter Kropotkin Anthology*, ed. Iain McKay (Oakland, CA: AK Press, 2014), 533.
86. Uri Gordon, "Revolution," in *Anarchism: A Conceptual Approach*, ed. Benjamin Franks, Nathan Jun, and Leonard Williams (London: Routledge, 2018), 88.
87. Ibid.
88. Ibid.
89. Gordon, *Anarchy Alive!*, 90, 93.
90. For an overview of the anarcho-pacifist tradition, see Fiala, "Anarchism and Pacifism."
91. Gordon, *Anarchy Alive!*, 98.
92. Malatesta, *Life and Ideas*, 45.
93. Ibid., 50.
94. Ibid., 226.
95. Ibid., 50.
96. Ibid., 49.
97. Johann Most, *The Social Monster* (New York: Bernhard and Schenck, 1890), 10.
98. Alexander Berkman, *Now and After: The ABC of Anarchist Communism* (New York: Vanguard Press, 1929), 222.
99. Bakunin, *The Political Philosophy of Bakunin*, 374.
100. Mikhail Bakunin, *Michael Bakunin: Selected Writings*, ed. Arthur Lehning (London: Cape, 1973), 204.
101. Gordon, "Revolution," 91.
102. Bakunin, *Michael Bakunin: Selected Writings*, 198.
103. Ibid., 178.
104. See Bakunin, *Bakunin on Anarchy*, 259–73.
105. Ibid., 264.
106. Ibid., 264–65.

107. George Woodcock, *Anarchism: A History of Libertarian Ideas and Movements* (Toronto: University of Toronto Press, 2009), 242.
108. Bakunin, *Bakunin on Anarchy*, 266.
109. Gordon, "Revolution," 92.
110. Errico Malatesta, *The Method of Freedom: An Errico Malatesta Reader*, ed. Davide Turcato (Oakland, CA: AK Press, 2014), 65.
111. Ibid., 66.
112. For a representative account of this development in the context of France, see Woodcock, *Anarchism*, 247–69.
113. Rocker, *Anarcho-Syndicalism*, 78.
114. Woodcock, *Anarchism*, 268.
115. In the United States alone, more than 20,000 strikes took place during this period. See Florence Peterson, Strikes in the United States, 1880–1936: Bulletin of the United States Bureau of Labor Statistics, No. 651 (Washington, DC: United States Government Publishing Office, 1937), 21.
116. Alfredo Bonnano, quoted in Gordon, "Revolution," 93.
117. Loadenthal, *The Politics of Attack*, 40.
118. Ibid.
119. Ibid., 47–49.
120. Ibid., 43–44.
121. Nathan Jun, *Anarchism and Political Modernity* (London: Bloomsbury, 2012), 110.
122. Gordon, "Revolution," 93.
123. Ibid., 93–94.

2. "THE ONLY JUSTIFIABLE WAR"

1. Michael Walzer, *Just and Unjust Wars: A Moral Argument with Historical Illustrations*, 5th ed. (New York: Basic, 2015), 97–100, 81–85.
2. Ibid., 203–4, 262–67.
3. Karl Marx, *The Portable Karl Marx*, ed. Eugene Kamenka (New York: Penguin, 1983), 224.
4. Walzer, *Just and Unjust Wars*, 121.
5. Ibid., 64.
6. Ibid., 66.
7. Michael Hardt and Antonio Negri, *Empire* (Cambridge, MA: Harvard University Press, 2000), 12–13.
8. Richard Seymour, *The Liberal Defence of Murder* (London: Verso, 2012), 36–49.
9. Ibid., 13, 213–14.
10. Ibid., 157–58, 205–11, 225–29, 285–90.
11. While China continues to designate itself as following a variety of Marxism, I do not view its leadership as following Marxist principles in any meaningful respect. See Ahmed Shawki, "China: Deng's Legacy," *International Socialist Review* 2, Fall 1997, accessed June 2, 2019, http://www.isreview.org/issues/02/China_Part2.shtml.
12. Karl Marx and Friedrich Engels, *The Marx-Engels Reader*, 2nd ed., ed. Robert C. Tucker (New York: W. W. Norton, 1978), 60.
13. Ibid., 228.
14. Ibid., 203.
15. Ibid., 220.
16. Ibid., 492.
17. Marx, *The Portable Karl Marx*, 648.
18. Karl Marx, "Address of the International Working Men's Association to Abraham Lincoln, President of the United States of America," *The Bee-Hive Newspaper* 169, 1865, accessed June 2, 2019, https://www.marxists.org/archive/marx/iwma/documents/1864/lincoln-letter.htm.

19. Rosa Luxemburg, *The Accumulation of Capital* (London: Routledge, 1951), accessed June 2, 2019, https://www.marxists.org/archive/luxemburg/1913/accumulation-capital/; Nicolai Bukharin, *Imperialism and World Economy* (New York: International Publishers, 1929).

20. Vladimir Lenin, *Imperialism, The Highest Stage of Capitalism* (Moscow: Progress Publishers, 1963), accessed June 2, 2019, https://www.marxists.org/archive/lenin/works/1916/imp-hsc/; Anthony Brewer, *Marxist Theories of Imperialism: A Critical Survey* (New York: Routledge, 1990); Andrew Ryder, "Multiculturalism and Oppression: The Marxist Perspectives of Fraser, Lenin, and Fanon," in *Philosophies of Multiculturalism: Beyond Liberalism*, ed. Luis Cordeiro-Rodrigues and Marko Simendic (New York: Routledge, 2017).

21. Vladimir Lenin, *Collected Works*, vol. 21: *Socialism and War: The Attitude of the Russian Social Democratic Labour Party Towards the War* (Peking: Foreign Languages Press, 1970), 295–338, accessed June 2, 2019, https://www.marxists.org/archive/lenin/works/1915/s+w/index.htm.

22. Vladimir Lenin, *Collected Works*, vol. 28: *The Proletarian Revolution and the Renegade Kautsky* (Moscow: Progress Publishers, 1977), 227–325.

23. Vladimir Lenin, *Collected Works*, vol. 26: *On the Slogan to Transform the Imperialist War into a Civil War* (Moscow: Progress Publishers, 1977), 337, accessed June 2, 2019, https://www.marxists.org/archive/lenin/works/1914/sep/00.htm.

24. Walzer, *Just and Unjust Wars*, 87–91.

25. Giorgi Dimitrov, "Unity of the Working Class against Fascism," accessed June 2, 2019, https://www.marxists.org/reference/archive/dimitrov/works/1935/unity.htm.

26. Erich Wollenberg, "Just Wars in the Light of Marxism," *New International* 3, no. 1 (1936): 2–5, accessed June 2, 2019, https://www.marxists.org/history/etol/newspape/ni/vol03/no01/wollenberg.htm.

27. Isaac Deutscher, *The Prophet Armed: Trotsky 1879–1921* (London: Verso, 2003), 337–70.

28. Doug Enaa Greene, "The Communist Order of Samurai: Leon Trotsky and the Red Army," *Links: International Journal of Socialist Renewal*, published May 17, 2016, http://links.org.au/node/4691.

29. Tony Cliff, "Trotsky on Substitutionism," accessed June 2, 2019, https://www.marxists.org/archive/cliff/works/1960/xx/trotsub.htm.

30. Deutscher, *The Prophet Armed*, 389.

31. Leon Trotsky, *Terrorism and Communism* (London: Verso, 2007), 121–64.

32. Leon Trotsky, *Problems of Everyday Life* (New York: Pathfinder, 1973), 205.

33. UN Documents, Geneva Conventions of 12 August 1949 and Protocols Additional to the Conventions, accessed June 2, 2019, http://www.un-documents.net/gc.htm; United Nations Office for Disarmament Affairs, Protocol for the Prohibition of the Use in War of Asphyxiating, Poisonous or Other Gases, and of Bacteriological Methods of Warfare, accessed June 2, 2019, https://www.un.org/disarmament/wmd/bio/1925-geneva-protocol/.

34. Deutscher, *The Prophet Armed*, 400.

35. Ibid., 396.

36. Ibid., 397.

37. Ibid., 399.

38. Leon Trotsky, *Fascism: What It Is and How to Fight It* (New York: Pioneer Publishers, 1964), accessed June 2, 2019, https://www.marxists.org/archive/trotsky/works/1944/1944-fas.htm.

39. Dan La Botz, *What Went Wrong? The Nicaraguan Revolution: A Marxist Analysis* (Boston: Brill, 2016), 52.

40. Che Guevara, *Che Guevara Reader: Writings on Guerrilla Strategy, Politics and Revolution*, ed. David Deutschmann (Melbourne: Ocean Press, 1997), 19–72.

41. Régis Debray, *Revolution in the Revolution? Armed Struggle and Political Struggle in Latin America* (New York: Grove Press, 1967).

42. Debray, *Revolution in the Revolution?*, 32.

43. La Botz, *What Went Wrong?*, 130.

44. Ibid., 140–70.

45. Walzer, *Just and Unjust Wars*, 176–96.

46. Ibid., 87–90.
47. Ibid., 181.
48. Joseph Hansen, "In Defense of the Leninist Strategy of Party Building," *International Information Bulletin* 3, published April 1971, accessed June 2, 2019, https://www.marxists.org/archive/hansen/1971/indef.htm.
49. Quoted in ibid.
50. Livio Maitan, "Major Problems of the Latin American Revolution: A Reply to Régis Debray," *International Socialist Review* 28, no. 5 (1967): 1–22, accessed June 2, 2019, https://www.marxists.org/history/etol/writers/maitan/1967/05/debray.htm.
51. Hugo Blanco, *Land or Death: The Peasant Struggle in Peru* (New York: Pathfinder, 1972), 20.
52. Ibid., 27.
53. Ibid., 28.
54. Ibid., 30.
55. Ibid., 56.
56. Ibid., 58–59.
57. Ibid., 63.
58. Ibid., 64.
59. Hugo Blanco, "Militia or Guerrilla Movement?," in *Marxism in Latin America from 1909 to the Present*, ed. Michael Löwy (New York: Prometheus, 1992), 258.
60. Blanco, *Land or Death*, 145.
61. Ibid., 39.
62. Hugo Blanco, *We the Indians: The Indigenous People of Peru and the Struggle for Land* (London: Merlin Press, 2018), 16–17.
63. Hugo Blanco, "Indigenous People Are the Vanguard of the Fight to Save the Earth," *Links: International Journal of Socialist Renewal*, published October 13, 2009, http://links.org.au/node/1304.
64. While Blanco remains a somewhat obscure figure outside Peru, his work has recently achieved a reappraisal, including brief appreciative essays in 2010 by Eduardo Galeano and Raúl Zibechi. See Blanco, *We the Indians*, 7, 180.

3. A PACIFIST CRITIQUE OF JUST WAR THEORY

1. See Robert L. Holmes, "The Metaethics of Pacifism and Just War Theory," *The Philosophical Forum* 46, no. 1 (2015): 14.
2. Michael Neu, *Just Liberal Violence: Sweatshops, Torture, War* (London: Rowman & Littlefield, 2018).
3. See Robert L. Holmes, *Pacifism: A Philosophy of Nonviolence* (London: Bloomsbury, 2017).
4. Richard Jackson, "Pacifism: The Anatomy of a Subjugated Knowledge," *Critical Studies on Security* 6, no. 2 (2018): 160–75; Richard Jackson, "Pacifism and the Ethical Imagination," *International Politics* 56, no. 2 (2019): 212–27.
5. Robert Phillips and Duane Cady, *Humanitarian Intervention: Just War vs. Pacifism* (Lanham, MD: Rowman & Littlefield, 1996), 34.
6. Neu, *Just Liberal Violence*; Holmes, *Pacifism*; Cheyney Ryan, "Pacifism, Just War, and Self-Defense," *Philosophia* 41 (2013): 977–1005; Dustin Howes, "The Failure of Pacifism and the Success of Nonviolence," *Perspectives on Politics* 11, no. 2 (2013): 427–66; Duane Cady, *From Warism to Pacifism: A Moral Continuum*, 2nd ed. (Philadelphia, PA: Temple University Press, 2010); Dustin Howes, *Toward a Credible Pacifism: Violence and the Possibilities of Politics* (Albany, NY: SUNY Press, 2009).
7. See Todd May, *Nonviolent Resistance: A Philosophical Introduction* (Cambridge, UK: Polity, 2015).
8. Robert L. Holmes, *The Ethics of Nonviolence: Essays by Robert L. Holmes*, ed. P. Cicovacki (New York: Bloomsbury, 2013), 159.

9. Cheyney Ryan, "Pacifism(s)," *Philosophical Forum* 46, no. 1 (2015): 33; Neu, *Just Liberal Violence*.

10. Colin Bird, *An Introduction to Political Philosophy* (Cambridge, UK: Cambridge University Press, 2007), 239.

11. See Dustin Howes, "The Just War Masquerade," *Peace Review: A Journal of Social Science* 27, no. 3 (2015): 379–87.

12. Holmes, *The Ethics of Nonviolence*, 160.

13. See Kimberly Hutchings, "Pacifism Is Dirty: Towards an Ethico-Political Defence," *Critical Studies on Security* 6, no. 2 (2018): 176–92.

14. Neu, *Just Liberal Violence*, 10–13.

15. Laurie Calhoun, "How Violence Breeds Violence: Some Utilitarian Considerations," *Politics* 22, no. 2 (2002): 98.

16. I discuss some of the limitations of the individual attacker analogy in Jackson, "Pacifism and the Ethical Imagination," 216.

17. Ryan, "Pacifism(s)," 33.

18. For a useful discussion of the long-term consequences of war and its preparation, see Calhoun, "How Violence Breeds Violence"; and Phillips and Cady, *Humanitarian Intervention*.

19. Andrew Alexandra, "Political Pacifism," *Social Theory and Practice* 29, no. 4 (October 2003): 604.

20. Calhoun, "How Violence Breeds Violence."

21. Michael Neu, "Why There Is No Such Thing as Just War Pacifism and Why Just War Theorists and Pacifists Can Talk Nonetheless," *Social Theory and Practice* 37, no. 3 (July 2011): 429. See also, Hutchings, "Pacifism Is Dirty."

22. Neu, *Just Liberal Violence*.

23. Ibid.

24. Neu, *Just Liberal Violence*; Calhoun, "How Violence Breeds Violence."

25. Holmes, "The Metaethics of Pacifism and Just War Theory," 5.

26. Eduardo Aboultaif, "Just War and the Lebanese Resistance to Israel," *Critical Studies on Terrorism* 9, no. 2 (2016): 334–55.

27. For discussions on this point, see Holmes, *The Ethics of Nonviolence*, 185; and May, *Nonviolent Resistance*, 49–52.

28. See Molly Wallace, *Security without Weapons: Rethinking Violence, Violent Action, and Civilian Protection* (Abingdon, UK: Routledge, 2016), 33–40.

29. Hannah Arendt argued that "power and violence are opposites; where the one rules absolutely, the other is absent. . . . Violence can destroy power; it is utterly incapable of creating it." Hannah Arendt, *On Violence* (New York: Harcourt, Brace and World, 1970), 56.

30. Stellan Vinthagen, *A Theory of Nonviolent Action: How Civil Resistance Works* (London: Zed Books, 2015), 193–94.

31. See Stephen Biddle, *Military Power: Explaining Victory and Defeat in Modern Battle* (Princeton, NJ: Princeton University Press, 2004).

32. See Ivan Arreguin-Toft, *How the Weak Win Wars: A Theory of Asymmetric Conflict* (New York: Cambridge University Press, 2005).

33. Richard Jackson and Helen Dexter, "The Social Construction of Organised Political Violence: An Analytical Framework," *Civil Wars* 16, no. 1 (2014): 1–23.

34. See Wallace, *Security without Weapons*, 61–62; and Elaine Scarry, "Injury and the Structure of War," *Representations* 10 (Spring 1985): 1–51.

35. Elizabeth Frazer and Kimberley Hutchings, "On Politics and Violence: Arendt Contra Fanon," *Contemporary Political Theory* 7 (2008): 104.

36. Craig Ihara, "Pacifism as a Moral Idea," *The Journal of Value Inquiry* 22 (1988): 275.

37. Calhoun, "How Violence Breeds Violence," 103.

38. Arendt, *On Violence*, 80.

39. Neu, *Just Liberal Violence*.

40. Cady, *From Warism to Pacifism*, 56.

41. Graham Parsons, "The Incoherence of Walzer's Just War Theory," *Social Theory and Practice* 38, no. 4 (October 2012): 663.

42. See, among others, Neu, *Just Liberal Violence*; Neu, "Why There Is No Such Thing as Just War Pacifism"; Howes, "The Just War Masquerade"; Ryan, "Pacifism, Just War, and Self-Defense"; Holmes, "The Metaethics of Pacifism and Just War Theory"; Jeff McMahan, "Rethinking the 'Just War,' Part 1," *New York Times Opinionator*, November 11, 2012, https://opinionator.blogs.nytimes.com/2012/11/11/rethinking-the-just-war-part-1/; Parsons, "The Incoherence of Walzer's Just War Theory"; and Phillips and Cady, *Humanitarian Intervention*.

43. Jeff McMahan, "Rethinking the 'Just War,' Part 2," *New York Times Opinionator*, November 12, 2012, https://opinionator.blogs.nytimes.com/2012/11/12/rethinking-the-just-war-part-2/.

44. Parsons, "The Incoherence of Walzer's Just War Theory," 666.

45. Ibid., 681.

46. McMahan, "Rethinking the 'Just War,' Part 2."

47. Parsons, "The Incoherence of Walzer's Just War Theory," 682.

48. Neu, *Just Liberal Violence*, 5; original emphasis.

49. Ibid.

50. Judith Butler, *Precarious Life: The Powers of Mourning and Violence* (London: Verso, 2006).

51. I discuss and dismiss many of the most common arguments raised against pacifism in Jackson, "Pacifism and the Ethical Imagination." See also Jackson, "Pacifism: The Anatomy of a Subjugated Knowledge."

52. Cady, *From Warism to Pacifism*, 103; emphasis added.

53. Holmes, *The Ethics of Nonviolence*, 196.

54. See, among many others, Maciej J. Bartkowski, ed., *Recovering Nonviolent History: Civil Resistance in Liberation Struggles* (Boulder, CO: Lynne Rienner Publishers, 2013); Sharon Nepstad, *Nonviolent Revolutions: Civil Resistance in the Late 20th Century* (New York: Oxford University Press, 2011); Adam Roberts and Timothy Garton Ash, eds., *Civil Resistance and Power Politics: The Experience of Non-Violent Action from Gandhi to the Present* (Oxford: Oxford University Press, 2009); Kurt Schock, *Unarmed Insurrections: People Power Movements in Nondemocracies* (Minneapolis: University of Minnesota Press, 2005).

55. The data set on which a great deal of current research on successful nonviolent movements is based is described in Erica Chenoweth and Maria Stephan, *Why Civil Resistance Works: The Strategic Logic of Nonviolent Conflict* (New York: Columbia University Press, 2011). It can be viewed directly at Nonviolent and Violent Campaigns and Outcomes (NAVCO) Data Project based at Denver University, http://www.du.edu/korbel/sie/research/chenow_navco_data.html.

56. Cady, *From Warism to Pacifism*, 95.

57. Holmes, *The Ethics of Nonviolence*, 167.

58. See Cady, *From Warism to Pacifism*, 96–99.

59. See Schock, *Unarmed Insurrections*; and Chenoweth and Stephan, *Why Civil Resistance Works*.

60. Holmes, *The Ethics of Nonviolence*, 164.

61. Ibid., 165.

62. Ibid., 162.

63. Chenoweth and Stephan, *Why Civil Resistance Works*.

64. Oliver Kaplan, *Resisting War: How Communities Protect Themselves* (Cambridge, UK: Cambridge University Press, 2017); Graham Kemp and Douglas Fry, *Keeping the Peace: Conflict Resolution and Peaceful Societies around the World* (London: Routledge, 2003).

65. Wallace, *Security without Weapons*; Rachel Julian and Christine Schweitzer, "The Origins and Development of Unarmed Civilian Peacekeeping," *Peace Review: A Journal of Social Justice* 27, no. 1 (2015): 1–8.

66. Robert Burrowes, *The Strategy of Nonviolent Defense: A Gandhian Approach* (New York: State University of New York Press, 1996); Grazina Miniotaite, "Lithuania: From Non-Violent Liberation towards Non-Violent Defence?" *Peace Research: The Canadian Journal of Peace Studies* 48, no. 4 (1996): 19–36.

67. Karuna Mantena, "Another Realism: The Politics of Gandhian Nonviolence," *American Political Science Review* 106, no. 2 (2012): 455–70.

68. See Richard Jackson, "Commentary & Debate: CTS, Counterterrorism and Nonviolence," *Critical Studies on Terrorism* 10, no. 2 (2017): 357–69; Carol Goerzig, *Talking to Terrorists: Concessions and the Renunciation of Violence* (Abingdon: Routledge, 2010).
69. Jackson, "Pacifism and the Ethical Imagination."

4. UNDERTAKING CRITICAL LEGAL THEORY TO EXAMINE JUST WAR INTERVENTION

1. Shadia B. Drury, *Aquinas and Modernity: The Lost Promise of Natural Law* (Lanham, MD: Rowman & Littlefield, 2008), 67.
2. John Mark Mattox, "The Just War Tradition in Late Antiquity and the Middle Ages," in *The Cambridge Handbook of the Just War*, ed. Larry May (Cambridge: Cambridge University Press, 2018), 31.
3. Richard J. Regan, *Just War: Principles and Cases* (Washington, DC: The Catholic University of America Press, 1996), 17–18.
4. Natalino Ronzitti, "Reparation and Compensation," in *Research Handbook on International Conflict and Security Law*, ed. Nigel D. White and Christian Henderson (Cheltenham, Glos: Edward Elgar, 2013), 638.
5. Brian Orend, *The Morality of War* (Peterborough, ON: Broadview Press, 2006), 105.
6. Heather Widdows, *Global Ethics: An Introduction* (London: Routledge, 2014), 182–83.
7. N. Fotion, *Military Ethics* (Stanford, CA: Hoover Institution Press, 1990), 34; Richard D. White Jr., "Military Ethics," in *Handbook of Administrative Ethics*, 2nd ed., ed. Terry L. Cooper (New York, Marcel Dekker, Inc., 2001), 634.
8. Colleen Murphy and Linda Radzik, "*Jus Post Bellum* and Political Reconciliation," in *Jus Post Bellum and Transitional Justice*, ed. Larry May and Elizabeth Edenberg (Cambridge: Cambridge University Press, 2013), 306.
9. Erika De Wet, *The Chapter VII Power of the United Nations Security Council* (Portland, OR: Hart Publishing, 2004), 99.
10. These norms, which include piracy, slavery, crimes against humanity, and genocide, are held in customary international law as peremptory norms (*jus cogens*), which are deemed heinous if breached.
11. Critical legal theory initially emerged during the 1970s in the United States. Matthew H. Kramer, *Critical Legal Theory and the Challenge of Feminism: A Philosophical Reconception* (Lanham, MD: Rowman & Littlefield, 1995), 39.
12. William Paul Simmons, *Human Rights Law and the Marginalized Other* (Cambridge: Cambridge University Press, 2011), xv.
13. However, under this article, the UN can intervene within the national jurisdiction of states if enforcement measures due to a threat to peace and security are exercised under Chapter VII of the UN Charter.
14. United States Commission on International Religious Freedom, *Annual Report of the United States Commission on International Religious Freedom* (Washington, DC: Diane Publishing Co., 2010), 34.
15. In contrast, pacifists argue that war cannot be morally justified.
16. Hans Joachim Morgenthau, *Politics among Nations* (New York: Alfred A. Knopf, 1956), 4; Kenneth N. Waltz, *Theory of International Politics* (New York: McGraw-Hill, 1979), 91.
17. Morgenthau, *Politics*, 4; Waltz, *Theory*, 126.
18. Morgenthau, *Politics*, 186.
19. Morgenthau, *Politics*, 14–16.
20. Waltz, *Theory*, 131.
21. Michael Mastanduno, "Do Relative Gains Matter? America's Response to Japanese Industrial Policy," *International Security* 16, no. 1 (1991): 78.

22. Jack Donnelly, *Realism and International Relations* (Cambridge: Cambridge University Press, 2000), 58.
23. Waltz, *Theory*, 105.
24. Mustafa Aydin and Kostas Ifantis, "Introduction," in *Turkish-Greek Relations: The Security Dilemma in the Aegean*, ed. Mustafa Aydin and Kostas Ifantis (London: Routledge, 2004), 2; Glenn Diesen, *EU and NATO Relations with Russia: After the Collapse of the Soviet Union* (London: Routledge, 2015), 3.
25. Nukhet A. Sandal and Jonathan Fox, *Religion in International Relations Theory: Interactions and Possibilities* (Oxon: Routledge, 2013), 89.
26. Denise Garcia, *Disarmament Diplomacy and Human Security: Regimes, Norms and Moral Progress in International Relations* (New York: Routledge, 2011), 21.
27. Alexandros Petersen, *Integration in Energy and Transport: Azerbaijan, Georgia, and Turkey* (Lanham, MD: Lexington Books, 2016), 66.
28. Robert Jackson and Georg Sørensen, *Introduction to International Relations: Theories and Approaches*, 6th ed. (Oxford: Oxford University Press, 2016), 107.
29. James L. Richardson, *Contending Liberalisms in World Politics: Ideology and Power* (Boulder, CO: Lynne Rienner Publishers, 2001), 75.
30. Annie Herro, *UN Emergency Peace Service and the Responsibility to Protect* (London: Routledge, 2015), 20.
31. This later led to Boutros-Ghali's emphasizing that powerful states needed to do more to protect vulnerable persons to prevent another genocide (Boutros Boutros-Ghali, "Supplement to an Agenda for Peace: Position Paper of the Secretary-General on the Occasion of the Fiftieth Anniversary of the United Nations," UN Doc. A/50/60-S/1995/1, January 3, 1995). To specify, Boutros-Ghali argued that, when the UNSC decided to expand UNAMIR in May 1994, none of the nineteen governments deployed standby troops as agreed (Boutros-Ghali, "Supplement," para. 43). The nonarrival of forthcoming troops hindered the credibility of the UNSC (Boutros-Ghali, "Supplement," para. 99).
32. Kofi Nsia-Pepra, *UN Robust Peacekeeping: Civilian Protection in Violent Civil Wars* (New York: Palgrave Macmillan, 2014), 52.
33. Touko Piiparinen, *The Transformation of UN Conflict Management: Producing Images of Genocide from Rwanda to Darfur and Beyond* (Oxon: Routledge, 2010), 23–25.
34. Alain Destexhe, *Rwanda and Genocide in the Twentieth Century* (East Haven, CT: Pluto Press, 1995), ix.
35. Jared A. Cohen, *One Hundred Days of Silence: America and the Rwanda Genocide* (Lanham, MD: Rowman & Littlefield, 2007), 14.
36. Paul Robert Bartrop, *A Bibliographical Encyclopedia of Contemporary Genocide: Portraits of Evil and Good* (Santa Barbara, CA: ABC-CLIO, 2012), 180.
37. Ewen MacAskill, "Sudan's Darfur Crimes Not Genocide, Says UN Report," *The Guardian*, February 1, 2005, accessed February 7, 2019, https://www.theguardian.com/world/2005/feb/01/sudan.unitednations.
38. Hilary Andersson, "China 'Is Fuelling War in Darfur,'" *BBC News*, July 13, 2008.
39. Christina Gabriela Badescu, *Humanitarian Intervention and the Responsibility to Protect: Security and Human Rights* (London: Routledge, 2011), 46–47.
40. The 1977 Additional Protocol II to the Geneva Conventions expands the rules of law in war to apply in noninternational armed conflict situations.
41. UN Summit Outcome Document, "2005 World Summit Outcome," UN General Assembly Doc. A/RES/60/1, 60th session, October 24, 2005, paras. 138–39.
42. Ibid.
43. Report of the Secretary-General, "Implementing the Responsibility to Protect," UN General Assembly Doc. A/63/677, 63rd session, January 12, 2009.
44. Reg G. Grant, *1001 Battles That Changed the Course of History* (New York: Chartwell Books, 2017), 942.
45. Michael Waltzer, *Arguing about War* (New Haven, CT: Yale Nota Bene, 2005), 99.
46. Jeff L. Holzgrefe, "The Humanitarian Intervention Debate," in *Humanitarian Intervention: Ethical, Legal and Political Dilemma*, ed. Jeff L. Holzgrefe and Robert O. Keohane (Cambridge: Cambridge University Press, 2003), 18.

47. Simon Chesterman, *Just War or Just Peace? Humanitarian Intervention and International Law* (Oxford: Oxford University Press, 2001), 228.
48. Badescu, *Humanitarian Intervention*, 1.
49. Marc W. Herold, "Urban Dimensions of the Punishment of Afghanistan by US Bombs," in *Cities, War, and Terrorism: Towards an Urban Geopolitics*, ed. Stephen Graham (Malden, MA: Blackwell Publishing, 2004), 326–27.
50. Lyombe S. Eko, *New Media, Old Regimes: Case Studies in Comparative Communication Law and Policy* (Lanham, MD: Rowman & Littlefield, 2012), 393–94.
51. Nina Burri, *Bravery or Bravado? The Protection of News Providers in Armed Conflict* (Leiden: Brill Nijhoff, 2015), 151.
52. International Criminal Tribunal for the Former Yugoslavia, "Final Report to the Prosecutor by the Committee Established to Review the NATO Bombing Campaign against the Federal Republic of Yugoslavia," ICTY, 2000, para. 50, 90–91, accessed May 21, 2019, http://www.icty.org/en/press/final-report-prosecutor-committee-established-review-nato-bombing-campaign-against-federal.
53. Independent International Commission on Kosovo, *The Kosovo Report* (Oxford: Oxford University Press, 2008), 4.
54. David M. Malone and Karin Wermester, "Boom and Bust? The Changing Nature of UN Peacekeeping," *International Peacekeeping* 7, no. 4 (2000): 49.
55. Nicholas J. Wheeler, *Saving Strangers* (Oxford: Oxford University Press, 2000), 41.
56. Judith Gardam, *Necessity, Proportionality and the Use of Force by States* (Cambridge: Cambridge University Press, 2004), 86.
57. Will Worley, "9/11 Anniversary: Rare Images Show the Aftermath of World Trade Centre Attack That Killed 2,997," *The Independent*, September 11, 2018, accessed February 5, 2019, https://www.independent.co.uk/news/world/americas/9-11-anniversary-images-aftermath-world-trade-center-terror-attack-responders-emergency-al-qaeda-a8530611.html.
58. William M. Spellman, *A Concise History of the World since 1945: States and Peoples* (New York: Palgrave Macmillan, 2006), 140. The killing of Bin Laden provides the debate around *military necessity*, *distinction*, and *proportionality*.
59. Ali Wardak and John Braithwaite, "Crime and War in Afghanistan. Part II: Jeffersonian Alternative?" *British Journal of Criminology* 53 (2013): 203.
60. Frederick H. Gareau, *State Terrorism and the United States: From Counterinsurgency to the War on Terror* (London: Zed Books, 2004), 191.
61. Jennifer Leaning, "Was the Afghan Conflict a Just War?" *British Medical Journal* 324, no. 7333 (2002): 353–55.
62. Nake M. Kamrany and Jessica Greenhalgh, "Afghanistan War Is Not a Just War?" *Huffington Post*, July 6, 2013, accessed February 7, 2019, https://www.huffingtonpost.com/nake-m-kamrany/afghanistan-war-just-war_b_3220799.html.
63. Michael Scheuer, *Osama Bin Laden* (Oxford: Oxford University Press, 2011), 131.
64. Timor Sharan, "The Dynamics of Elite Networks and Patron-Client Relations in Afghanistan," in *Elites and Identities in Post-Soviet Space*, ed. David Lane (Oxon: Routledge, 2012), 193.
65. Kamrany and Greenhalgh, "Afghanistan."
66. Spellman, *A Concise History*, 140; Thomas G. Paterson et al., *American Foreign Relations*, vol. 2: *A History since 1895*, 7th ed. (Boston: Wadsworth Cengage Learning, 2010), 487.
67. Kamrany and Greenhalgh, "Afghanistan."
68. Noam Chomsky, *9/11* (New York: Pluto Press, 2001), 34, 103–104.
69. Human Rights Watch, *Human Rights Watch World Report 2000: Events of 1999 (November 1998–October 1999)* (New York: Human Rights Watch, 2000), 167; Rosemarie Skaine, *The Women of Afghanistan under the Taliban* (Jefferson, NC: McFarland and Company, Inc., 2002), 65.
70. David Cutler, "Timeline: Invasion, Surge, Withdraw; U.S. Forces in Iraq," *Reuters*, December 18, 2011, accessed January 29, 2019, https://www.reuters.com/article/us-iraq-usa-pullout/timeline-invasion-surge-withdrawal-u-s-forces-in-iraq-idUSTRE7BH08E20111218.

71. Ipek Danju, Yasar Maasoglu, and Nahide Maasoglu, "The Reasons behind U.S. Invasion of Iraq," *Procedia—Social and Behavioral Sciences* 81 (2013): 683.

72. Eric Victor Larson and Bogdan Savych, *Misfortunes of War: Press and Public Reactions to Civilian Deaths in Wartime* (Santa Monica, CA: RAND Corporation, 2007), 175.

73. Simon Cottle, *Global Crisis Reporting: Journalism in the Global Age* (Maidenhead, Berkshire: Open University Press, 2009), 5.

74. John Chilcot et al., *The Report of the Iraq Inquiry: Executive Summary*, Report of a Committee of Privy Counsellors, HC 264, July 6 (London: House of Commons, 2016), https://assets.publishing.service.gov.uk/government/uploads/system/uploads/attachment_data/file/535407/The_Report_of_the_Iraq_Inquiry_-_Executive_Summary.pdf.

75. Eric Stover, Victor Peskin, and Alexa Koenig, *Hiding in Plain Sight: The Pursuit of War Criminals from Nuremberg to the War on Terror* (Oakland, CA: University of California Press, 2016), 200, 204–205.

76. Military necessity to use prohibited weapons and illicit modes of warfare to override the rules of *jus in bello* is a contentious area when analyzing the interventions in Kosovo and Afghanistan. Under critical legal theory, it can be argued that the international relations of NATO and the United States in both interventions had driven the use of force and concept of military necessity to override *jus in bello*, particularly in relation to proportionality.

5. AN EXAMINATION OF NIGERIAN, SRI LANKAN, AND GUATEMALAN CIVIL WARS IN LIGHT OF THE LAW OF ARMED CONFLICT

1. The just war theory now has a third component, *jus post bellum* (postwar justice), which deals with just reconciliation and reconstruction in the aftermath of conflict. This third component is not the primary focus of this chapter.

2. Cf. Peter P. Ekeh, "Colonialism and the Two Publics in Africa: A Theoretical Statement," *Comparative Studies in Society and History* 17, no. 1 (1975): 91–112.

3. Adewale Ademoyega, *Why We Struck: The Story of the First Nigerian Coup* (Ibadan: Evans Brothers, 1981), 1–10.

4. Frederick Forsyth, *The Making of an African Legend: The Biafran Story* (New York: Penguin Books, 1969), 257.

5. Ibid.

6. Alexander Madiebo, *The Nigerian Revolution and the Biafran War* (Enugu: Fourth Dimension Publishers, 1980).

7. H. B. Momoh, ed., *The Nigerian Civil War: 1967–1970: History and Reminiscences* (Ibadan: Sam Bookman Publishers, 2000).

8. Rajan Hoole et al., *The Broken Palmyra—The Tamil Crisis in Sri Lanka: An Inside Account* (Claremont: The Sri Lanka Studies Institute, 1990).

9. Adele Balasingham, *The Will to Freedom—An Inside View of Tamil Resistance*, 2nd ed. (Mitcham, UK: Fairmax Publishing, 2003).

10. Gordon Weiss, *The Cage: The Fight for Sri Lanka and the Last Days of the Tamil Tigers* (New York: Random House, 2011).

11. Stephen M. Streeter, *Managing the Counterrevolution: The United States and Guatemala, 1954–1961* (Athens, OH: Ohio University Press, 2000), 5–12.

12. Michael McClintock, *The American Connection: State Terror and Popular Resistance in Guatemala* (London: Zed Books, 1985), 20–35.

13. Victor Perera, *Unfinished Conquest: The Guatemalan Tragedy* (California: University of California Press, 1993).

14. Beatriz Manz, *Paradise in Ashes: A Guatemalan Journey of Courage, Terror, and Hope* (Oakland: University of California Press, 2004).

15. Greg Grandin, *The Last Colonial Massacre: Latin America in the Cold War* (Chicago: University of Chicago Press, 2011).

16. Peter P. Ekeh, *Colonialism and Social Structure: An Inaugural Lecture* (Ibadan: Ibadan University Press, 1983), 2–3.
17. Chinua Achebe, *There Was a Country: A Personal History of Biafra* (New York: Penguin Group, 2012), 2.
18. Luís Cordeiro-Rodrigues, "Towards a Tutuist Ethics of War: Ubuntu, Forgiveness and Reconciliation," *Politikon* 45, no. 3 (2018): 426.
19. Robert Kolb and Richard Hyde, *An Introduction to the International Law of Armed Conflicts* (Oxford: Hart Publishing, 2008), 47.
20. Ibid.
21. Ibid., 49.
22. S. Elizabeth Bird and Fraser M. Ottanelli, *The Asaba Massacre: Trauma, Memory, and the Nigerian Civil War* (Cambridge: Cambridge University Press, 2017), 21–61.
23. Emma Okocha, *Blood on the Niger: The First Black on Black Genocide* (New York: Gomslam Books, 2012).
24. Forsyth, *The Making of an African Legend*, 256–69.
25. Achebe, *There Was a Country*, 228–35.
26. Forsyth, *The Making of an African Legend*, 257.
27. For details, see Francis Boyle, *The Tamil Genocide by Sri Lanka: The Global Failure to Protect Tamil Rights* (Atlanta: Clarity Press, 2010); and Permanent Peoples' Tribunal, *Peoples' Tribunal on Sri Lanka: 07–10 December 2013* (Bremen: Permanent Peoples' Tribunal and the International Human Rights Association, 2014), 15–38.
28. For details, see Amnesty International, *Guatemala: All the Truth, Justice for All*, published May 13, 1998, accessed December 22, 2018, https://www.refworld.org/docid/3ae6a9ba4.html; and Victoria Sanford, *Buried Secrets: Truth and Human Rights in Guatemala* (New York: Palgrave Macmillan, 2003), 147–79.
29. International Crisis Group, "War Crimes in Sri Lanka," *Asia Report*, No. 191, May 17 (Brussels: ICG, 2010), 10–32.
30. Shlomi Yass, "Sri Lanka and the Tamil Tigers: Conflict and Legitimacy," *Military and Strategic Affairs* 6, no. 2 (2014): 73.
31. American University, Washington College of Law, *Justice for Genocide: Sri Lanka's Genocide against Tamils* (Washington, DC: UNROW Human Rights Impact Litigation Clinic, 2014), 14–19.
32. International Crisis Group, "War Crimes," 20.
33. Ibid., 25.
34. See Patrick Ball, Herbert F. Spirer, and Louise Spirer, *Making the Case: Investigating Large Scale Human Rights Violations Using Information Systems and Data Analysis* (Washington, DC: American Association for the Advancement of Science, 2000); Charles D. Brockett, *Political Movements and Violence in Central America* (Cambridge: Cambridge University Press, 2005), 194–229, 265–91; Todd Landman, *Studying Human Rights* (London: Routledge, 2006); Peter Winn, *Americas: The Changing Face of Latin America and the Caribbean* (Berkeley: University of California Press, 2006); Kirsten Weld, *Paper Cadavers: The Archives of Dictatorship in Guatemala* (Durham, NC: Duke University Press, 2014).
35. For detailed discussions on these ideas, see Douglas Anthony, "Ours Is a War of Survival: Biafra, Nigeria and Arguments about Genocide, 1966–70," *Journal of Genocide Research* 16, no. 2–3 (2014): 205–25; Marie-Luce Desgrandchamps, "Dealing with 'Genocide': The ICRC and the UN during the Nigeria–Biafra War, 1967–70," *Journal of Genocide Research* 16, no. 2–3 (2014): 281–97; Roy Doron, "Marketing Genocide: Biafran Propaganda Strategies during the Nigerian Civil War, 1967–70," *Journal of Genocide Research* 16, no. 2–3 (2014): 227–46; Brian McNeil, "And Starvation Is the Grim Reaper: The American Committee to Keep Biafra Alive and the Genocide Question during the Nigerian Civil War, 1968–70," *Journal of Genocide Research* 16, no. 2–3 (2014): 317–36; Kevin O'Sullivan, "Humanitarian Encounters: Biafra, NGOs and Imaginings of the Third World in Britain and Ireland, 1967–70, *Journal of Genocide Research* 16, no. 2–3 (2014): 299–315; and Brad Simpson, "The Biafran Secession and the Limits of Self-Determination," *Journal of Genocide Research* 16, no. 2–3 (2014): 337–54.

36. Thaddeus Metz, "Toward an African Moral Theory," *Journal of Political Philosophy* 15, no. 3 (2007): 321–41.

6. AFRICAN FEMINISTS' CRITIQUE OF JUST WARS AND THE REALITY OF AFRICAN WOMEN IN WARS

1. Naomi Malone, "From Just War to Just Peace: Re-Visioning Just War Theory from a Feminist Perspective," master's thesis, University of South Florida, 2004, 2, https://scholarcommons.usf.edu/cgi/viewcontent.cgi?article=2145&context=etd.
2. Lucinda Peach, "An Alternative to Pacifism? Feminism and Just-War Theory," *Hypatia* 9, no. 2 (1994): 155–56.
3. Malone, "From Just War," 49.
4. Ibid., 19.
5. Laura Sjoberg, "Gendered Realities of the Immunity Principle: Why Gender Analysis Needs Feminism," *International Studies Quarterly* 50, no. 4 (2006): 908.
6. Jiri Krcek, "What's Wrong with Just War Theory? Examining the Gendered Bias of a Longstanding Tradition," *Inquiries Journal* 4, no. 5 (2012): 2.
7. Robin Schott, "Gender and 'Postmodern War,'" *Hypatia* 11, no. 4 (2009): 22.
8. UN Outreach Programme on the Rwanda Genocide and United Nations, Department of Public Information, accessed June 7, 2019, https://www.un.org/en/preventgenocide/rwanda/preventing-genocide.shtml.
9. International Criminal Tribunal for the Former Yugoslavia, UN Security Council Resolution 827, May 25, 1993, accessed May 19, 2019, http://www.icty.org/en/documents/statute-tribunal.
10. UN Outreach Programme.
11. Marie Pauline Eboh, "From Fowl to Feminism: Snippets of Gynist Issues in Non-Gendered Narrative," in *Discourses in African Philosophy*, ed. Ike Odimegwu, Martin Asiegbu, and Maurice Izunwa (Akwa: Fab Anieh Nigeria Ltd., 2015), 13.
12. Carol Gilligan, *In a Different Voice* (Cambridge, MA: Harvard University Press, 1982), 174.
13. Nawal El Saadawi, "War against Women and Women against War: Waging War on the Mind," *The Black Scholar: Journal of Black Studies and Research* 38, no. 2–3 (2008): 27–32; Asma Abdel Halim, "Attack with a Friendly Weapon," in *What Women Do in Wartime: Gender and Conflict in Africa*, ed. Meredeth Turshen and Clotilde Twagiramariya (New York: Zed, 1998), 87–88.
14. Malone, "From Just War," 23; Sharon A. Omotosho, "African Womanist View of Just War Theory in Tunde Kelani's Narrow Path," *African Notes: Bulletin of the Institute of African Studies* 42, no. 1–2 (2018): 69.
15. Michael Walzer, *Just and Unjust Wars: A Moral Argument with Historical Illustrations*, 2nd ed. (New York: Basic Books, 1992), 61–62.
16. Omotosho, "African Womanist View of Just War Theory," 57.
17. J. O. Akin Sofoluwe, "Heroes and Heroines in African Classical Thought," in *African Myths and Legends of Gender*, ed. S. B. Oluwole and J. O. Akin Sofoluwe (Lagos: Ark Publishers, 2014), 22–36.
18. Sophie Bosede Oluwole, "Short Notes on the Characters," in *African Myths and Legends of Gender*, ed. Sophie Bosede Oluwole and J. O. Akin Sofoluwe (Lagos: Ark Publishers, 2014), 17.
19. Annette Madden, *In Her Footsteps* (New York: Gramercy Books, 2001).
20. Wole Soyinka, *The Seven Signposts of Existence: Knowledge, Honour, Justice and Other Virtues* (Ibadan: Bookcraft, 1999).
21. Ibid., 13.

22. Aljazeera News, "France Admits Torture during Algeria Independence War," published September 13, 2018, accessed December 18, 2018, https://www.aljazeera.com/news/2018/09/france-admits-torture-algeria-war-independence-180913140641963.html.

23. Cynthia Cockburn, "The Gendered Dynamics of Armed Conflict and Political Violence," in *Victims, Perpetrators or Actors? Gender, Armed Conflict and Political Violence*, ed. Caroline Moser and Fiona C. Clark (London: Zed Books, 2001); Amina Mama and Margo Okazawa-Rey, "Editorial: Militarism, Conflict and Women's Activism," *Feminist Africa* 10 (2008): 1–8, http://www.agi.ac.za/sites/default/files/image_tool/images/429/feminist_africa_journals/archive/10/feminist_africa_10.pdf.

24. UN Outreach Programme.

25. African Sun News, "About Wars and Post-War Conflicts," accessed May 19, 2019, http://africasunnews.com/wars.html.

26. Malone, "From Just War," 19.

27. Legit, "10 Things You Should Know about Biafra and the Biafran War," accessed February 14, 2019, https://www.legit.ng/629644-10-things-need-know-biafra-biafran-war.html.

28. VOA News, "UN Says, Women, Children Are Biggest Victims of War," November 2, 2009, accessed January 30, 2019, https://www.voanews.com/a/a-13-2009-03-08-voa9-68678402/408727.html.

29. Sofoluwe, "Heroes and Heroines," 27–35.

30. VOA News, "UN Says."

31. Aurora Brossault, "South Sudan: Working with Communities to Help Victims of Sexual Violence," published April 8, 2016, accessed June 7, 2019, https://www.icrc.org/en/document/south-sudan-communities-help-victims-sexual-violence.

32. UN Women, "The Contribution of UN Women to Increasing Women's Leadership and Participation in Peace and Security and in Humanitarian Response," published September 2013, http://www.unwomen.org/en/about-us/evaluation/~/media/3A55D8A0FCB64F98997D99A95A616F6A.ashx.

33. Brossault, "South Sudan."

34. VOA News, "UN Says."

35. Jo Adetunji, "The Democratic Republic of Congo: Forty-Eight Women Raped Every Hour in Congo, Study Finds," *The Guardian*, May 12, 2011, accessed June 7, 2019, https://www.theguardian.com/world/2011/may/12/48-women-raped-hour-congo.

36. UN Outreach Programme.

37. Global Nonviolent Action Database, "Liberian Women Act to End Civil War," published October 22, 2010, accessed May 19, 2019, https://nvdatabase.swarthmore.edu/content/liberian-women-act-end-civil-war-2003.

38. Frantz Fanon, *A Dying Colonialism*, trans. Haakon Chevalier (New York: Grove, 1967), 66.

39. Aaronete M. White, "All the Men Are Fighting for Freedom, All the Women are Mourning Their Men, But Some of Us Carried Guns: Fanon's Psychological Perspectives on War and African Women Combatants," *Journal of Women in Culture and Society* 32, no. 4 (2007): 877–78, accessed January 19, 2019, https://genderandsecurity.org/sites/default/files/aaronette_white_working_paper_302.pdf.

40. White, "All the Men Are Fighting for Freedom," 877–78.

41. Hun Sinem, "An Evaluation of Feminist Critiques of Just War Theory," *DEP* 24 (2014): 76–86, accessed January 19, 2019, https://www.unive.it/media/allegato/dep/n24-2014/Ricerche/05_Hun.pdf.

42. Peach, "An Alternative to Pacifism?," 35.

43. Carol Cohn, "Emasculating America's Linguistic Deterrent," in *Rocking the Ship of State: Toward a Feminist Peace Politics*, ed. Adrienne Harris and Ynestra King (Boulder, CO: Westview Press, 1989), 160.

44. Virginia Held, *The Ethics of Care: Personal, Political, and Global* (Oxford: Oxford University Press, 2005), 31; Sjoberg, "Gendered Realities," 905.

7. FEMINIST CARE POLITICAL THEORY AND CONTEMPORARY JUST WAR THEORY

1. Augustine, Ambrose, and Aquinas are the founding fathers of historic JWT. "Their prescription for Just War was a formula for enablement, not deterrence." Robert Emmet Meagher, *Killing from the Inside Out* (Eugene, OR: Cascade Books, 2014), 9.

2. Traditional JWT has a foundational premise that morality applies in war but that, within the scope of war, morality is separate, unique, and *different* in smaller or greater degrees from the morality of self-defense or the morality of defending others. One of the principal contemporary texts on JWT is Michael Walzer's *Just and Unjust Wars* (New York: Basic Books, 1977). Walzer's *statist* approach views war through the lens of a separate set of moral codes and thus a separate morality such that wars are governed by distinct moral codes from what governs ordinary life. Jeff McMahan, in *Killing in War* (Oxford: Oxford University Press, 2009), revises Walzer's lens and proposes that there is not a separate moral code for war and for ordinary life but rather one continuous moral code, although the moral situations that occur in war are rare in ordinary life. Jeff McMahan revises traditional JWT and argues that the moral codes that apply in war are the *same* moral codes that apply outside it, although perhaps, outside war, these moral codes are rarely applied.

3. Walzer, *Just and Unjust Wars*.

4. McMahan, *Killing in War*.

5. Gertrud Nunner-Winkler, "Two Moralities? A Critical Discussion of an Ethic of Care and Responsibility versus an Ethic of Rights and Justice," in *An Ethic of Care*, ed. Mary Jeanne Larrabee (New York: Routledge, 1993), 143–56.

6. Richard N. Haas, *War of Necessity, War of Choice: A Memoir of Two Iraq Wars* (New York: Simon and Schuster, 2009), 268–70.

7. November 29, 1990, the United Nations Security Council Resolution 678 authorized UN member states to "Restore international peace and security in the area." Resolution 660, adopted the day after Iraq invaded Kuwait, imposed a full import and export embargo on all the territories controlled by Iraq and demanded that Iraq withdraw unconditionally from Kuwait. In January 1991, a UN-authorized military coalition led by the United States, called Operation Desert Storm, was launched to force Iraq out of Kuwait. In this chapter, the UN embargo will be referred to as *multilateral sanctions*.

8. David Cortright and George A. Lopez, *Sanctions and the Search for Security: Challenges to UN Action* (Boulder, CO: Lynne Rienner Publishers, 2002), 65.

9. Laura Sjoberg, *Gender, Justice, and the Wars in Iraq* (Oxford: Lexington Books, 2006), 189.

10. The Ba'ath policy, as communicated to the Iraqi people, had multiple components, including an idea of Arabism writ large, the imagination of what Arabism could and should mean to the Iraqi people, a wider political discourse of cultural practices, and the economic stresses being resolved by Iraq's (rightful, according to the propaganda) access of Kuwaiti oil. See Hamdi A. Hassan, *The Iraqi Invasion of Kuwait: Religion, Identity and Otherness in the Analysis of War and Conflict* (London: Pluto Press, 1999), especially 181–90.

11. The Ba'ath party had a variety of slogans blaming Kuwait, referring to Kuwait as waging an "economic war" against Iraq, and Saddam Hussein's quote that Kuwait was responsible for stealing the milk out of Iraqi children's mouths. Ibid.

12. Zachary A. Selden, *Economic Sanctions as Instruments of American Foreign Policy* (Westport, CT: Praeger Publishers, 1999).

13. The Weinberger doctrine conceives of the necessity of public support for American foreign military interventions, especially in reaction to American disapproval of Vietnam. Citizen support for a military action overseas is different from civilian involvement and dialogue about eminent military threats to their own lives. An impartial dialogue coalition comprising stakeholder states is discussed on military legal analysis of reasons to go to war in Allen Buchanan and Robert Keohane, "Pre-Commitment Regimes for Intervention: Supplementing the Security Council," *Ethics & International Affairs* 25, no. 1 (Spring 2011): 41–63.

14. Walzer recognizes the problematic and perhaps unsympathetic and, ultimately, irresponsible ways JWT can offer moral characterizations of *jus post bellum* but says that JWT does not sustain its critique of itself. Michael Walzer, "The Triumph of Just War Theory (and the Dangers of Success)," *Social Research* 69, no. 4 (2002): 940.

15. McMahan says that the case helps most of us see that a morally absolute position against interrogation torture is untenable. Jeff McMahan, "Torture in Principle and in Practice," *Public Affairs Quarterly* 22, no. 2 (2008): 94.

16. From the UN Convention against Torture, Article 1.1: "Any act by which severe pain or suffering, whether physical or mental, is intentionally inflicted on a person for such purposes as obtaining from him or a third person, information or a confession, punishing him for an act he or a third person has committed or is suspected of having committed, or intimidating or coercing him or a third person, or for any reason based on discrimination of any kind, when such pain or suffering is inflicted by or at the instigation of or with the consent or acquiescence of a public official or other person acting in an official capacity. It does not include pain or suffering arising only from, inherent in or incidental to lawful sanctions." United Nations Human Rights, "Convention against Torture and Other Cruel, Inhuman or Degrading Treatment or Punishment," United Nations Treaty Series, 1465 (December 10, 1984): 85, accessed March 12, 2019, https://www.ohchr.org/EN/ProfessionalInterest/Pages/CAT.aspx.

17. David Luban, "Liberalism and the Unpleasant Question of Torture," *Virginia Law Review* 91, no. 6 (2005): 1425–61. Dissenting voices against the moral permissibility of torture tend to locate their arguments in rights-based claims about the moral agency of the torture victim.

18. Darius Rejali, *Torture and Democracy* (Princeton, NJ: Princeton University Press, 2009).

19. In "Torture in Theory and in Practice," McMahan refers to the detainee as a *terrorist*, indicating that the detainee is not just an actor acting for a just cause.

20. Jeremy Waldron's meta-analysis on contemporary moral debate about torture, which shows that moral theorists begin from the supposition that interrogation torture is, in certain cases, morally permissible, morally justified, immoral yet justified, or morally excusable. Many have challenged the TTB's moral and practical legitimacy as wildly unrealistic—that it fails to provide the mechanisms from which we would form an absolute moral prohibition against torture or that it gives us (the wrong reasons) for bending the torture victim's will against itself, a Kantian criticism. These criticisms largely conclude that, in both practical reality and sincere philosophical analysis, the case cannot do any good moral work because it is such an unrealistic case posing as a legitimate probability and it elicits moral intuitions that appear scalable but are in reality not scalable nor transferrable. Jeremy Waldron, *Torture, Terror, and Trade-Offs: Philosophy for the White House* (Oxford: Oxford University Press, 2012).

21. The prevailing characterization by moral philosophers finds that psychological interrogation torture is considered "morally justified," "immoral yet justified," or "morally excusable." Waldron, *Torture, Terror, and Trade-Offs*, introduction.

22. Alejandro Gándara, "Memorias de los Monstruos," *El Mundo*, published November 11, 2011, accessed May 19, 2019, https://www.elmundo.es/blogs/elmundo/escorpion/2011/11/17/memorias-de-los-monstruos.html.

23. Joshua A. S. Phillips, *None of Us Were Like This Before: American Soldiers and Torture* (New York: Verso Books, 2010).

24. Ibid., 188.

25. Ibid., 188–95.

26. Recognizing that many feminist philosophers have argued for an intractable conceptual dichotomy between moral theories of care and moral theories of justice. This dichotomy can be broken down as JWT evolves. See Nunner-Winkler, "Two Moralities?"

8. AN AFRICAN THEORY OF JUST CAUSES FOR WAR

1. See the papers in David Lutz et al., eds., *War and Peace in Africa: Philosophy, Theology and the Politics of Confrontation* (Palo Alto, CA: Academica Press, 2014); Colin Chasi, "Ubuntu and Freedom of Expression: Considering Children and Broadcast News Violence in a Violent Society," *Journal of Media Ethics* 30, no. 2 (2015): 91–108; Colin Chasi, "Provisional Notes on Ubuntu for Journalists Covering War," *International Communication Gazette* 78, no. 8 (2016): 802–17; Colin Chasi, "Tutuist Ubuntu and Just War," *Politikon* 45, no. 2 (2017): 232–44; Deane-Peter Baker, "Rebellion and African Ethics," *Journal of Military Ethics* 15, no. 4 (2016): 288–98; Luís Cordeiro-Rodrigues, "African Views of Just War in Mandela and Cabral," *Journal of Speculative Philosophy* 32, no. 4 (2018): 657–73; Luís Cordeiro-Rodrigues, "Towards a Tutuist Ethics of War: Ubuntu, Forgiveness and Reconciliation," *Politikon* 45, no. 3 (2018): 426–35; Uchenna Okeja, "War by Agreement," *Journal of Military Ethics* (forthcoming).

2. The closest that much of the African moral–philosophical literature had come was to include discussions of capital punishment and some appeals to defensive force. See, e.g., Henry Odera Oruka, *Punishment and Terrorism in Africa*, 2nd ed. (Nairobi: Kenya Literature Bureau, 1985); Egbeke Aja, "Crime and Punishment: An Indigenous African Experience," *Journal of Value Inquiry* 31, no. 3 (1997): 353–68; Peter Kasenene, *Religious Ethics in Africa* (Kampala: Fountain Publishers, 1998), 41; Mogobe Ramose, *African Philosophy through Ubuntu* (Harare: Mond Publishers, 1999), 120; Oladele Abiodun Balogun, "A Philosophical Defence of Punishment in Traditional African Legal Culture," *Journal of Pan African Studies* 3, no. 3 (2009): 43–54; and Thaddeus Metz, "Human Dignity, Capital Punishment, and an African Moral Theory," *Journal of Human Rights* 9, no. 1 (2010): 81–99.

3. Okeja, "War by Agreement."

4. For Afro-centric discussion of the conditions of legitimate authority to initiate a war, see Okeja, "War by Agreement," who argues that there must be consensual agreement among at least those who would fight, and Cordeiro-Rodrigues, "African Views of Just War," who argues that this authority need not be a state. And for African theoretical discussion of *jus post bellum*, see essays in Lutz, *War and Peace in Africa*, as well as Cordeiro-Rodrigues, "Towards a Tutuist Ethics of War," 432–33, which I mention in the conclusion of this chapter along with *jus in bello*, on which there is still almost nothing at all.

5. Except, most clearly, for certain cases of punishment of the guilty and redirection of impersonal threats.

6. Ideas from this section have been cribbed from various previous publications, especially Thaddeus Metz, "African Ethics and Journalism Ethics," *Journal of Media Ethics* 30, no. 2 (2015): 74–90; and Thaddeus Metz, "An African Theory of Social Justice," in *Distributive Justice Debates in Political and Social Thought*, ed. Camilla Boisen and Matt Murray (Abingdon: Routledge, 2016), 171–90. What is new about this chapter is not the African moral theory but rather its application to the conditions of just war.

7. For different approaches to sub-Saharan morality, see Bujo, who takes vital force to be a basic value to be promoted, and Gyekye, who treats the common good as foundational. Bénézet Bujo, "Differentiations in African Ethics," in *The Blackwell Companion to Religious Ethics*, ed. William Schweiker (Malden, MA: Blackwell, 2005), 423–37; Kwame Gyekye, "African Ethics," Stanford Encyclopedia of Philosophy, published September 9, 2010, accessed May 31, 2019, http://plato.stanford.edu/entries/african-ethics/.

8. Kasenene, *Religious Ethics in Africa*, 21.

9. Desmond Tutu, *No Future without Forgiveness* (New York: Random House, 1999), 35.

10. Munyaradzi Felix Murove, "The Shona Ethic of Ukama with Reference to the Immortality of Values," *Mankind Quarterly* 48, no. 2 (2007): 181.

11. Dismas Masolo, *Self and Community in a Changing World* (Bloomington: Indiana University Press, 2010), 240.

12. Initially distinguished and reconstructed in Thaddeus Metz, "Toward an African Moral Theory," *Journal of Political Philosophy* 15, no. 3 (2007): 321–41.

13. Segun Gbadegesin, *African Philosophy* (New York: Peter Lang, 1991), 65.
14. Yvonne Mokgoro, "Ubuntu and the Law in South Africa," *Potchefstroom Electronic Law Journal* 1, no. 1 (1998): 17.
15. Kwame Gyekye, *Beyond Cultures* (Washington, DC: The Council for Research in Values and Philosophy, 2004), 16.
16. Pantaleon Iroegbu, "Beginning, Purpose and End of Life," in *Kpim of Morality Ethics*, ed. Pantaleon Iroegbu and Anthony Echekwube (Ibadan: Heinemann Educational Books, 2005), 442.
17. Gessler Muxe Nkondo, "Ubuntu as a Public Policy in South Africa," *International Journal of African Renaissance Studies* 2, no. 1 (2007): 91.
18. Thaddeus Metz, "A Theory of National Reconciliation: Some Insights from Africa," in *Theorizing Transitional Justice*, ed. Claudio Corradetti, Nir Eisikovits, and Jack Rotondi (Surrey: Ashgate, 2015), 119–35.
19. Thaddeus Metz, "Developing African Political Philosophy: Moral-Theoretic Strategies," *Philosophia Africana* 14, no. 1 (2012): 61–83.
20. Anthony Appiah, "Ethical Systems, African," *Routledge Encyclopedia of Philosophy*, accessed May 31, 2019, https://www.rep.routledge.com/articles/thematic/ethical-systems-african/v-1.
21. The reasoning here parallels a familiar Kantian justification for coercion in, for example, Thomas Hill, Jr., *Virtue, Rules, and Justice* (Oxford: Oxford University Press, 2012), 310–12.
22. Or, in a case that McMahan has mentioned, it can be permissible for someone who unjustly initiated an attack to use force to fend off a response to his initial attack that is also unjust, for example, disproportionate. Jeff McMahan, "The Ethics of Killing in War," *Ethics* 114, no. 4 (2004): 712–13.
23. As per ibid.
24. Notice that this principle does not say that it is categorically wrong to be severely discordant in respect of innocents because I acknowledge exceptions, such as redirections of impersonal threats from runaway trolleys and incoming asteroids. The case of innocent threats is harder and briefly discussed in the conclusion.
25. Thaddeus Metz, "Reconciliation as the Aim of a Criminal Trial," *Constitutional Court Review* 9 (2019): 1–22.
26. The next few paragraphs borrow from Thaddeus Metz, "A Life of Struggle as Ubuntu," in *Nelson Rolihlahla Mandela: Decolonial Ethics of Liberation and Servant Leadership*, ed. Sabelo Ndlovu-Gatsheni and Busani Ngcaweni (Trenton, NJ: Africa World Press, 2018), 104–5.
27. Nelson Mandela, *Nelson Mandela by Himself* (Johannesburg: Pan Macmillan, 2013), 233.
28. Nelson Mandela, *Conversations with Myself* (London: Pan Macmillan, 2010), 79.
29. Nelson Mandela, *Long Walk to Freedom* (London: Abacus, 1994), 336.
30. Mandela, *Long Walk to Freedom*, 325.
31. Ibid., 338.
32. Ibid., 322.
33. Nelson Mandela, "Statement by Nelson Mandela from the Dock at the Opening of the Defence Case in the Rivonia Trial," April 20, 1964, accessed May 31, 2019, http://www.mandela.gov.za/mandela_speeches/before/640420_trial.htm.
34. Nelson Mandela, "Statement by Nelson Mandela Read on His Behalf by His Daughter Zinzi at a UDF Rally to Celebrate Archbishop Tutu Receiving the Nobel Peace Prize," February 10, 1985, accessed May 31, 2019, http://www.mandela.gov.za/mandela_speeches/before/850210_udf.htm.
35. Mandela, *Long Walk to Freedom*, 320–22, 618; Mandela, *Conversations with Myself*, 249; Nelson Mandela, *Notes to the Future* (New York: Atria, 2012), 22–23.
36. Mandela, *Long Walk to Freedom*, 325, 336; see also 441.
37. Michael Hobbes, "How Did Zimbabwe Become So Poor—and Yet So Expensive?," *The New Republic*, published January 5, 2014, accessed May 31, 2019, https://newrepublic.com/article/115925/zimbabwe-prices-why-are-they-high-new-york-citys.
38. Ibid.

39. Another reason for doubting that violence, intimidation, and forcible ejection were justified is that it is not clear that they were necessary to effect land reform. The historical details are contested, but, *if* it is true that the British government had still been willing in 1998 to fund a peaceful and pro-poor approach to it adequately (as per Holland), then the invasions perhaps were not essential to effect land reform. Heidi Holland, *Dinner with Mugabe: The Untold Story of a Freedom Fighter Who Became a Tyrant* (Johannesburg: Penguin Books, 2008), 94–98, 101, 228.

40. Chasi, "Ubuntu and Freedom of Expression," 101.

41. Chasi, "Provisional Notes on Ubuntu," 810.

42. Cordeiro-Rodrigues, "Towards a Tutuist Ethics of War," 431.

43. See Seana Shiffrin, "Wrongful Life, Procreative Responsibility, and the Significance of Harm," *Legal Theory* 5, no. 2 (1999): 117–48.

44. Cf. Conway Waddington, "Reconciling Just War Theory and Water-Related Conflict," *International Journal of Applied Philosophy* 26, no. 2 (2013): 197–212; and Conway Waddington, "Water Scarcity and Warfare," PhD diss., University of Johannesburg, 2018.

45. Godwin Sogolo, *Foundations of African Philosophy* (Ibadan: Ibadan University Press, 1993), 124.

46. Ibid., 121–29.

47. Francis Kasoma, "The Foundations of African Ethics (Afriethics) and the Professional Practice of Journalism," *Africa Media Review* 10, no. 3 (1996): 107–8.

48. Nelson Mandela, *Ubuntu Told by Nelson Mandela*, video, 1:37, posted by Marc, March 6, 2012, accessed May 31, 2019, http://www.youtube.com/watch?v=HED4h00xPPA; Julius Gathogo, "African Philosophy as Expressed in the Concepts of Hospitality and Ubuntu," *Journal of Theology for Southern Africa* 130, no. 1 (2008): 39–53.

49. Kwasi Wiredu, *Cultural Universals and Particulars: An African Perspective* (Bloomington: Indiana University Press, 1996), 157–71; Gyekye, "African Ethics."

50. Redirecting impersonal threats might be another matter; however, on which see Seth Lazar, "Associative Duties and the Ethics of Killing in War," *Journal of Practical Ethics*, accessed May 31, 2019, http://www.jpe.ox.ac.uk/papers/associative-duties-and-the-ethics-of-killing-in-war/. The bulk of his analysis suggests that it is often permissible to redirect impersonal lethal threats, such as incoming meteors, toward innocent strangers to protect loved ones. However, warfare instead normally involves a person himself employing deadly force, and so extension of the analogies to warfare is limited.

51. As well as some of the work of Seth Lazar, "Associative Duties and the Ethics of Killing in War."

52. Recall the basics of the Responsibility to Protect doctrine accepted at the 2005 World Summit, that each state must protect its people from genocide, war crimes, crimes against humanity, and ethnic cleansing; other states must help a given state to do so; and, if a given state is manifestly failing to protect its people in these ways, other states may intervene.

53. For a medieval expression of the point at the interpersonal level, consider the remark ascribed to Ambrose that "he who fails to ward off injury from an associate if he can do so, is quite as blamable as he who inflicts it." Quoted in Gregory Reichberg, "*Jus ad Bellum*," in *War: Essays in Political Philosophy*, ed. Larry May (New York: Cambridge University Press, 2008), 23.

54. Michael Walzer, *Just and Unjust Wars* (New York: Basic Books, 1977), 61–62.

55. Thomas Hurka, "Proportionality and Necessity," in *War: Essays in Political Philosophy*, ed. Larry May (New York: Cambridge University Press, 2008), 132.

56. However, incursion into a state's territory would justify war if it were an indication of more incursions to come and hence real subordination and harm to people.

57. As Waddington has pointed out in "Reconciling Just War Theory" and "Water Scarcity and Warfare."

58. See, e.g., Kenneth Kaunda, *Kaunda on Violence* (London: Collins, 1980), 157, 179–83; and Cordeiro-Rodrigues, "African Views of Just War in Mandela and Cabral," 669.

59. Khali Mofuoa, "The Exemplary Ethical Leadership of King Moshoeshoe of Basotho of Lesotho in the Nineteenth Century Southern Africa," *Journal of Public Administration and Governance* 5, no. 3 (2015): 28, 32.

60. Jeff McMahan, "Just Cause for War," *Ethics and International Affairs* 19, no. 3 (2005): 1–21; Jeff McMahan, "Aggression and Punishment," in *War: Essays in Political Philosophy*, ed. Larry May (New York: Cambridge University Press, 2008), 78–79.

61. Thomas Hurka, "Liability and Just Cause," *Ethics and International Affairs* 21, no. 2 (2007): 201–202; Hurka, "Proportionality and Necessity," 131–32.

62. And the admitted fact that some African theorists have appealed to general deterrence as a legitimate way to protect communal relationships (e.g., Aja, "Crime and Punishment," 360; Balogun, "A Philosophical Defence of Punishment," 52).

63. See, e.g., Daniel Farrell, "Capital Punishment and Societal Self-Defense," in *Philosophy and Its Public Role*, ed. William Aiken and John Haldane (Charlottesville, VA: Imprint Academic, 2004), 241–56.

64. Being discordant toward another as necessary to rebut his initial discordance can, in rare circumstances, mean doing so to deter others when they are acting together as part of an unjust plan (see Metz, "Human Dignity," 90).

65. David Luban, "Just War and Human Rights," *Philosophy and Public Affairs* 9, no. 2 (1980): 160–81.

66. Larry May, "The Principle of Just Cause," in *War: Essays in Political Philosophy*, ed. Larry May (New York: Cambridge University Press, 2008), 49–66.

67. A third difference worth considering is the salience of group rights in the African philosophical and legal tradition. The bearers of human rights are normally understood to be individuals, but if groups, as distinct from their members, also have rights, that would likely influence thought about just causes for war. I do not pursue this line because I suspect that what appear to be group rights are ultimately individual rights. See Thaddeus Metz, "African Values, Human Rights and Group Rights," in *African Legal Theory and Contemporary Problems*, ed. Oche Onazi (Dordrecht: Springer, 2014), 142–44. However, I believe the issue merits more reflection, particularly because it seems possible for groups *qua* groups to exhibit identity and solidarity.

68. Compare this view with appeals to the moral significance of a common life in Walzer, *Just and Unjust Wars*, 54, and of community in Alasdair MacIntyre, "Is Patriotism a Virtue?," Lindley Lecture, University of Kansas, March 24, 1984, accessed May 31, 2019, https://kuscholarworks.ku.edu/bitstream/handle/1808/12398/Is%20Patriotism%20a%20Virtue-1984.pdf.

69. Basil Davidson as quoted in Guy Martin, *African Political Thought* (New York: Palgrave Macmillan, 2012), 78.

70. Amilcar Cabral, "National Liberation and Culture," in *Unity and Struggle: Speeches and Writings*, ed. PAIGC, trans. Michael Wolfers (New York: Monthly Review Press, 1979), esp. 143, 148, 151, 153.

71. Ibid., 141.

72. Ibid., 151.

73. H. W. Vilakazi, "Education Policy for a Democratic Society," in *Black Perspective(s) on Tertiary Institutional Transformation*, ed. Sipho Seepe (Florida Hills: Vivlia Publishers and the University of Venda, 1998), 76.

74. Catherine Odora Hoppers, "African Voices in Education," in *African Voices in Education*, ed. Philip Higgs et al. (Lansdowne: Juta, 2000), 5.

75. J. Teboho Lebakeng et al., "Epistemicide, Institutional Cultures and the Imperative for the Africanisation of Universities in South Africa," *Alternation* 13, no. 1 (2006): 70.

76. Tutu, *No Future without Forgiveness*, 35.

77. Kaunda, *Kaunda on Violence*, 89.

78. Ibid., 117; see also 88, 131.

79. See also note 4 above for mention of *jus ad bellum* topics beyond just cause.

80. See, e.g., Cordeiro-Rodrigues, "Towards a Tutuist Ethics of War," 432–33.

81. Ibid., 433.

82. Tutu, *No Future without Forgiveness*, 33–60.

83. Government of the Republic of Colombia and the Revolutionary Armed Forces of Colombia—People's Army, "Final Agreement to End the Armed Conflict and Build a Stable

and Lasting Peace," published November 24, 2016, accessed May 31, 2019, http://especiales.presidencia.gov.co/Documents/20170620-dejacion-armas/acuerdos/acuerdo-final-ingles.pdf.

84. Metz, "Reconciliation as the Aim of a Criminal Trial."

85. For comments on a prior draft of this chapter, I thank an anonymous referee for Rowman & Littlefield, Luís Cordeiro-Rodrigues, Danny Singh, and participants in a workshop on Just War Theory in an African Context held at the University of Johannesburg in 2016.

9. THE CLASSICAL CONFUCIAN IDEAS OF *JUS AD BELLUM*

1. Tongdong Bai, "The Political Philosophy of China," in *The Routledge Companion to Social and Political Philosophy*, ed. Gerald Gaus and Fred D'Agostino (London: Routledge, 2013), 182.

2. Daniel A. Bell, "East Asia and the West: The Impact of Confucianism on Anglo-American Political Theory," in *The Oxford Handbook of Political Theory*, ed. John S. Dryzek, Bonnie Honig, and Anne Phillips (Oxford: Oxford University Press, 2006), 264.

3. Daniel A. Bell, *Beyond Liberal Democracy: Political Thinking for an East Asian Context* (Princeton, NJ: Princeton University Press, 2006), 31. For more on the historical status of Mencius, see Kim-chong Chong, "Classical Confucianism (II): Meng Zi and Xun Zi," in *Routledge History of World Philosophies*, vol. 3: *History of Chinese Philosophy*, ed. Bo Mou (London: Routledge, 2009), 189–90.

4. In *Li Chi* (*Book of Rites*), it was recorded that Confucius once praised someone who restrained himself from killing too many people in a battle. We may compare this with the modern *jus in bello* principle of proportionality.

5. See, for example, Bruno Coppieters and Nick Fotion, eds., *Moral Constraints on War: Principles and Cases*, 2nd ed. (New York: Lexington Books, 2008), part 1; Anthony Coates, "Just War," in *Political Concepts*, ed. Richard Bellamy and Andrew Mason (Manchester: Manchester University Press, 2003), 215; Brian Orend, "War," Stanford Encyclopedia of Philosophy, published May 3, 2016, accessed December 5, 2018, http://plato.stanford.edu/archives/spr2016/entries/war/. Personally, I believe that only the principles of just cause and proportionality are proper criteria for judging the moral status of wars. However, due to space limitations, I have to refrain from explaining the problems of the other principles here (except the principle of legitimacy, which will be discussed later).

6. Mencius did once suggest that, if a small country were facing the threat of a larger one and had virtually no chance to successfully defend itself, then the prince of this small country could resign from his position (*Mencius*, Book I, Part II, Chapter 15). This may sound like the principles of last resort or the likelihood of success. However, that was supposed to be only a noble thing to do, not a moral obligation.

7. See E. M. Atkins and R. J. Dodaro, eds., *Augustine: Political Writings* (Cambridge: Cambridge University Press, 2001), 205–26; John Mark Mattox, *Saint Augustine and the Theory of Just War* (London and New York: Continuum, 2006), especially 44–91; William E. Murnion, "A Postmodern View of Just War," in *AMINTAPHIL: The Philosophical Foundations of Law and Justice*, vol. 1: *Intervention, Terrorism, and Torture: Contemporary Challenges to Just War Theory*, ed. Steven P. Lee (Dordrecht: Springer, 2007), 25–27; and the literature cited in Michael Walzer, *Arguing about War* (New Haven, CT: Yale University Press, 2004), 197, n. 1.

8. Walzer, *Arguing about War*, 3–5; Murnion, "A Postmodern View of Just War," 25–27.

9. See Yu-Lan Fung, *A Short History of Chinese Philosophy* (New York: The Free Press, 1948), chapter 4. This chapter is still a reliable and accessible brief introduction to the thought of Confucius. For a general review of Confucianism, see Xinzhong Yao, *An Introduction to Confucianism* (Cambridge: Cambridge University Press, 2000).

10. Huang Nansen, "Confucius and Confucianism," in *Companion Encyclopedia of Asian Philosophy*, ed. Brian Carr and Indira Mahalingam (London and New York: Routledge, 1997),

483–84; Philip J. Ivanhoe and Bryan W. van Norden, eds., *Readings in Classical Chinese Philosophy* (New York and London: Seven Bridges Press, 2001), 22.

11. For a brief introduction of the historical background of Confucius's philosophy, see Bo Mou, ed., *Routledge History of World Philosophies*, vol. 3: *History of Chinese Philosophy* (London and New York: Routledge, 2009), 113–14.

12. Throughout the essay, I will use the translation by the British missionary James Legge. Although it may seem too old today, and certainly contains some mistakes or misinterpretations, I believe that, for all the quotes of Confucius and Mencius mentioned here, Legge's translation is still good enough for the discussion we are engaging in now.

13. Yao, *An Introduction to Confucianism*, 21; Nansen, "Confucius and Confucianism," 483; Ivanhoe and Norden, *Readings in Classical Chinese Philosophy*, 23; Jeffrey Riegel, "Confucius," Stanford Encyclopedia of Philosophy, published July 3, 2002, modified March 23, 2013, accessed December 3, 2018, https://plato.stanford.edu/entries/confucius/.

14. "Chan Chang murdered the Duke Chien of Chi. Confucius bathed, went to court, and informed the Duke Ai, saying, 'Chan Chang has slain his sovereign. I beg that you will undertake to punish him.'"

15. For Confucius as a deontologist, see Heiner Roetz, *Confucian Ethics of the Axial Age* (Albany: SUNY Press, 1993). For Confucius as a theorist of virtue ethics, see JeeLoo Liu, *An Introduction to Chinese Philosophy* (Oxford: Blackwell, 2006), 72, and the literatures mentioned in Mou, *History of Chinese Philosophy*, 130, n. 10.

16. Perhaps, for Confucius, wars that help restore the traditional aristocratic social order can count as just ones. That is why, as we have seen above, he supported a war that punished someone who killed a prince and was willing participate in a potential war that might help rebuild an ideal country.

17. Bryan van Norden, "Mencius," Stanford Encyclopedia of Philosophy, published October 16, 2004, modified December 3, 2014, accessed December 3, 2018, https://plato.stanford.edu/entries/mencius/.

18. Liu, *An Introduction to Chinese Philosophy*, 86.

19. This problem had not been formally and fully addressed until the Common Article 3 to the Geneva Convention in 1949, which includes rules of noninternational armed conflicts.

20. During Confucius's lifetime, most of the princes in the various countries were still satisfied with the titles given by the King of the Zhou dynasty, such as duke or count. However, in Mencius's time, the rulers of the few remaining large states got rid of that outdated hierarchical institution and enthroned themselves as kings. Therefore, although the principalities were referred to as countries in the section above, it is appropriate to call them kingdoms in the context of the Warring States Era.

21. Calling that war a "revolutionary" one is not as anachronistic as it may seem because the very words "Ge Ming" ("revolution" in Chinese) were used to describe the rebellion against the Shang dynasty by members of the Confucian school and that rebellion had been an inspiration for many instances of political resistance in later Chinese history, including the one that ended the institution of monarchy in 1911.

22. However, more accurately speaking, the despot Mencius had in mind was not exactly like the tyrant in the classical Western tradition. In the ancient Greek and Roman context, the term "tyrant" was used to refer to someone who gained political power in unlawful or unjust ways. There was no inevitable conceptual linkage between tyrant and bad governance. But a despot, in both the traditional Western sense and Mencius's sense, referred to the way of governing, rather than the source of power. Tyrannicide and many other concepts used in this article are originated from the Western tradition and do not have precise counterparts in ancient Chinese political thought. When I use words such as "justice," "sovereignty," and "absolutism," I do so more for the convenience of the readers than for implying that the ideas of Confucius and Mencius should be understood in terms of the meaning of those Western and modern concepts.

23. Gillian Brock, *Global Justice: A Cosmopolitan Account* (Oxford: Oxford University Press, 2009), 173.

24. At least, when such a war can satisfy the other criteria of *jus ad bellum*, for example, the principle of the likelihood of success.

25. Confucius displayed such an attitude in various places in the *Analects*, for example, Book VII, Chapter 12, and Book XIV, Chapter 17.

26. This can be seen from the three cases of what we may call quasi-humanitarian intervention in the 1970s. During India's invasion of Pakistan (1971), Tanzania's invasion of Uganda (1979), and Vietnam's invasion of Cambodia (1979), it is fair to say that, generally speaking, following the defeat of the despotic regimes, the citizens of the invaded countries were actually better off (though this was not the main intention of the invaders). Nevertheless, the three wars were condemned by international society and the UN because they were violations of the principle of the priority of state sovereignty. For accounts of those wars from a moral perspective, see Nicholas J. Wheeler, *Saving Strangers: Humanitarian Intervention in International Society* (Oxford: Oxford University Press, 2002), chapters 2–4.

27. I have modified Legge's translation here because he took the meaning of *sheji* too literally.

28. For example, *The Responsibility to Protect*, an influential report produced by the International Commission on Intervention and State Sovereignty, argued that "[t]he starting point . . . should be the principle of non-intervention. This is the norm any departure from which has to be justified," . . . "[t]ough threshold conditions should be satisfied before military intervention is contemplated." Andrew Altman and Christopher Heath Wellman, *A Liberal Theory of International Justice* (Oxford: Oxford University Press, 2009), 97. This is consistent with the spirit of the UN Charter; see Helen Stacy, "Humanitarian Intervention and Relational Sovereignty," in *AMINTAPHIL: The Philosophical Foundations of Law and Justice*, vol. 1: *Intervention, Terrorism, and Torture*, ed. Steven P. Lee (Dordrecht: Springer, 2007), 89, 91. In fact, some believe that the "weight of opinion among international lawyers" is that humanitarian intervention "is not part of international law"; Altman and Wellman, *A Liberal Theory of International Justice*, 210.

29. Of course, the initial reason for the Iraq War in 2003 given by the US government was that Saddam possessed weapons of mass destruction, but because that reason had been discredited, defending human rights became the only possible justification for the war. So, for the sake of argument, we will concentrate on this reason, which is more relevant to the discussion here anyway.

30. Bell, *Beyond Liberal Democracy*, 46–47.

31. The King of Yen gave his throne to one of his ministers. This was widely seen as an inappropriate act by the rulers of other kingdoms and Mencius. This again shows that Mencius did approve of intervening in countries whose rulers did not "deliberatively deprive the people of the means of subsistence."

32. However, according to Sima Qian's *Shih Chi* (*Historical Records*), Mencius did, in the beginning, recommend that the King of Chi launch the invasion (Book 34). If that were true, perhaps he once held the hope that the king could indeed be the "minister of the Heaven."

33. The PATRIOT Act was passed soon after the terrorist attacks on September 11, 2001. The Act expanded, among other things, the power of governmental agencies to access the information of private citizens; it has been criticized for the negative effects on civil rights it has brought.

34. Mencius frequently talked about the prospect (or the historical experience) of the world—the world that ancient Chinese people knew—being conquered and unified by a virtuous and benevolent ruler. Apparently, the sovereignty of the conquered countries was not a concern.

35. The idea of realism in international theory can be traced back to the famous "Melian Dialogue" in Thucydides's *History of the Peloponnesian War*. Two early modern texts of political philosophy that influenced the development of realism are Machiavelli's *Prince* and Chapter 13 of Hobbes's *Leviathan*. The most representative works of realism in the twentieth century include E. H. Carr, *The Twenty Years' Crisis* (New York: Perennial, 2001); Hans Morgenthau, *Politics among Nations* (New York: Alfred A. Knopf, 1948); and Kenneth N. Waltz, *Theory of International Politics* (New York: McGraw-Hill, 1979).

36. Say, the theories of Charles R. Beitz, *Political Theory and International Relations* (Princeton, NJ: Princeton University Press, 1979) and Thomas Pogge, *World Poverty and Human Rights: Cosmopolitan Responsibilities and Reforms* (Cambridge: Polity, 2002).

37. For discussions about the moral aspects of strategic bombings in WWII (and the decision to drop an atomic bomb on Hiroshima), see Michael Walzer, *Just and Unjust Wars* (New York: Basic Books, 2000), chapter 16; and John Rawls, *The Law of Peoples* (Cambridge, MA: Harvard University Press, 1999), 98–103.

38. It can be argued that he was not always hopelessly idealistic; see the analysis of his conversation with various princes in Tongdong Bai, "Ren Quan Gao Yu Zhu Quan," *She Hui Ke Xue* 35, no. 1 (2013): 132–34. Nevertheless, it is hard to deny that Mencius was often too unrealistic on many moral and political issues.

39. For example, although (according to the morality back then) you are not allowed to touch the body of your sister-in-law in normal circumstances, when she is about to drown, to save her life, you can leave the rules aside and grab her hand and drag her out (*Mencius*, Book IV, Part I, Chapter 17).

40. The British RAF's bombing of German cities in 1940 and 1941 has been widely regarded as a typical example of such an emergency because, in the words of Rawls, "Germany could not be allowed to win the war" (Rawls, *The Law of Peoples*, 99).

10. JUST WAR AND THE INDIAN TRADITION

1. Jeff McMahan, *Killing in War* (Oxford: Oxford University Press, 2009).
2. Michael Walzer, *Just and Unjust Wars* (Harmondsworth: Penguin, 1977), 21.
3. Cf. C. A. J. Coady, "The Problem of Dirty Hands," *Stanford Encyclopedia of Philosophy*, published April 29, 2009, modified January 24, 2014, accessed November 21, 2018, https://plato.stanford.edu/archives/spr2014/entries/dirty-hands/.
4. The *Mahābhārata*, or Great Bhārata (a traditional term for India but, in this case, the ancestor of two opposing sets of cousins), is one of India's two Sanskrit epics, the other being the *Rāmāyaṇa*; both took final form by the start of the Common Era. Both feature incarnations of the god Vishnu. In the *Rāmāyaṇa*, Vishnu's incarnation, the protagonist Rāma, lacks self-awareness of his divine status and attempts to navigate moral dilemmas and challenges in an exemplary manner while adhering to prevailing rules of ethical behavior. In the *Mahābhārata*, Vishnu's incarnation possesses self-awareness, is a relatively minor character in the story, and recommends breaking some rules of ethical behavior for reasons we shall track.
5. Thomas H. Brobjer, "Nietzsche's Reading about Eastern Philosophy," *Journal of Nietzsche Studies* 28 (2004), 3–35; cf., for a slightly different account, David Smith, "Nietzsche's Hinduism, Nietzsche's India: Another Look," *Journal of Nietzsche Studies* 28 (2004).
6. Nick Allen, "Just War in the Mahābhārata," in *The Ethics of War: Shared Problems in Different Traditions*, ed. Richard Sorabji and David Rodin (Hants, England: Ashgate Publishing Limited, 2006), 138–49.
7. Francis X. Clooney, "Pain But Not Harm: Some Classical Resources toward a Hindu Just War Theory," in *Just War in Comparative Perspective*, ed. Paul Robinson (Hampshire, England: Ashgate Publishing Limited, 2003), 109–26; Kaushik Roy, "Just and Unjust War in Hindu Philosophy," *Journal of Military Ethics* 6, no. 3 (2007).
8. Shyam Ranganathan, "Western Imperialism, Indology and Ethics," in *The Bloomsbury Research Handbook of Indian Ethics*, ed. Shyam Ranganathan, Bloomsbury Research Handbooks in Asian Philosophy (London: Bloomsbury Academic, 2017).
9. Shyam Ranganathan, *Hinduism: A Contemporary Philosophical Investigation*, ed. Chad Meister and Charles Taliaferro, Investigating Philosophy of Religion (New York: Routledge, 2018).
10. *Mahābhārata*, 6.43.
11. *Gītā*, 1.34–36.
12. Charles Goodman, *Consequences of Compassion: An Interpretation and Defense of Buddhist Ethics* (Oxford: Oxford University Press, 2009).
13. Kisor K. Chakrabarti, "Nyāya Consequentialism," in *The Bloomsbury Research Handbook of Indian Ethics*, ed. Shyam Ranganathan, Bloomsbury Research Handbooks in Asian Philosophy (London: Bloomsbury Academic, 2017).

14. *Gītā*, 1.38–39.
15. Jayandra Soni, "Jaina Ethics: Action and Non-Action," in *The Bloomsbury Research Handbook of Indian Ethics*, ed. Shyam Ranganathan, Bloomsbury Research Handbooks in Asian Philosophy (London: Bloomsbury Academic, 2017).
16. McMahan, *Killing in War*, 16.
17. Ibid., 34–35.
18. Cf. *Mahābhārata*, 6.43.
19. McMahan, *Killing in War*.
20. *Gītā*, 1.34–36.
21. Ibid., 1.38–39.
22. Ibid., 1.41.
23. Ibid., 2.38, 47, 18.47.
24. Ibid., 3.24.
25. *Gītā*, IV.7–8.
26. Shyam Ranganathan, "Patañjali's Yoga: Universal Ethics as the Formal Cause of Autonomy," in *The Bloomsbury Research Handbook of Indian Ethics*, ed. Shyam Ranganathan, Bloomsbury Research Handbooks in Asian Philosophy (London: Bloomsbury Academic, 2017).
27. *Gītā*, 9.27–33.
28. Bindu Puri, *Sophia Studies in Cross-cultural Philosophy of Traditions and Cultures*, vol. 9: *The Tagore–Gandhi Debate on Matters of Truth and Untruth* (New Delhi: Springer, 2015).
29. *Yoga Sūtra*, II.33–35.
30. Virginia Held, "Terrorism and War," *Journal of Ethics* 8, no. 1 (2004).
31. McMahan, *Killing in War*, chapter 1.
32. Walzer, *Just and Unjust Wars*, 21.
33. Ibid., 267–68; Michael Walzer, "Political Action: The Problem of Dirty Hands," in *War and Moral Responsibility*, ed. Marshall Cohen, Thomas Nagel, and Thomas Scanlon (Princeton, NJ: Princeton University Press, 1974).

11. THE ISLAMIC WAR ETHIC IN THEORY AND PRACTICE

1. Bernard Lewis, *What Went Wrong?* (New York: Perennial, 2002).
2. Mohammed Ayoob, *The Many Faces of Political Islam* (Ann Arbor, MI: University of Michigan Press, 2011), 1.
3. Khaled Abou el Fadl, *The Great Theft* (New York: HarperOne, 2007).
4. Daniel Pipes, *In the Path of God: Islam and Political Power* (New York: Basic Books, 1983), 3.
5. Monica Duffy Toft, "Getting Religion? The Puzzling Case of Islam and Civil War," *International Security* 31, no. 4 (2007): 97.
6. See, e.g., Davis Brown, "The Influence of Religion on Interstate Armed Conflict: Government Religious Preference and First Use of Force, 1946–2002," *Journal for the Scientific Study of Religion* 55, no. 4 (2017): 800–20. Not all of my empirical results have been published yet.
7. The Ibadi branch, along with the Ahmadiyya Muslim Community, are not known to be represented among the sources and authors.
8. Quran 10:25; see also Bassam Tibi, "War and Peace in Islam," in *The Ethics of War and Peace: Religious and Secular Perspectives*, ed. Terry Nardin (Princeton, NJ: Princeton University Press, 1996), 129–30.
9. Richard Martin, "The Religious Foundations of War, Peace, and Statecraft in Islam," in *Just War and Jihad: Historical and Theoretical Perspectives on War and Peace in Western and Islamic Traditions*, ed. John Kelsay and James Turner Johnson (Westport, CT: Greenwood Press, 1991), 108.

10. Majid Khadduri, *War and Peace in the Law of Islam* (Baltimore: Johns Hopkins University Press, 1955), 44–45.

11. Quran 5:51, 9:1–4; Mohammed Talaat al-Ghunaimi, *The Muslim Conception of International Law and the Western Approach* (The Hague: Martinus Nijhoff, 1968), 160–61.

12. Ann Elizabeth Mayer, "War and Peace in the Islamic Tradition and International Law," in *Just War and Jihad: Historical and Theoretical Perspectives on War and Peace in Western and Islamic Traditions*, ed. John Kelsay and James Turner Johnson (Westport, CT: Greenwood Press, 1991), 201. The sources do not name any specific treaty, suggesting that Khomeini and Shaltut were speaking in general terms.

13. Convention on the Elimination of All Forms of Discrimination against Women (CEDAW), December 18, 1979, 1249 UNTS 13, accessed May 30, 2019, https://www.un.org/womenwatch/daw/cedaw/cedaw.htm.

14. States Parties to CEDAW, 14th meeting, 23 June 2006, Item 6 of Provisional Agenda, UN Doc. CEDAW/SP/2006/2, accessed May 30, 2019, https://undocs.org/en/CEDAW/SP/2006/2.

15. See Tibi, "War and Peace in Islam," 130.

16. General Treaty for the Re-Establishment of Peace (Austria, France, Great Britain, Prussia, Russia, Sardinia, and Turkey), March 30, 1856 [Treaty of Paris], 46 BFSP 8, 114 CTS 409, 410. The Westphalian state system, dating from 1648, is the modern community of states today but was a prima facie Christian cultural construct; therefore, non-Christian states originally lay outside it. The Ottoman Empire's entry into the Westphalian system represented a capitulation to the West—an acknowledgment of the reality of its relative material weakness.

17. See Tibi, "War and Peace in Islam," 134–35.

18. Khadduri, *War and Peace*, 65.

19. UN Charter, art. 51.

20. Thomas Aquinas, *Summa Theologica*, pt. ii–ii, q. 40, art. 1 (Chicago: Encyclopedia Britannica, 1952).

21. Quran 15:94–95, 16:125.

22. Reuven Firestone, "Conceptions of Holy War in Biblical and Qur'ānic Tradition," *Journal of Religious Ethics* 24, no. 1 (1996): 112.

23. Reza Aslan, *No God But God: The Origins, Evolutions, and Future of Islam* (New York: Random House, 2005), 84; Amira Sonbol, "Norms of War in Sunni Islam," in *World Religions and Norms of War*, ed. Vesselin Popovski, Gregory Reichberg, and Nicholas Turner (Tokyo: United Nations University Press, 2009), 289.

24. Sonbol, "Norms," 289. Weeramantry asserts that Muslims have a duty to defend non-Muslims as well. C. G. Weeramantry, *Islamic Jurisprudence: An International Perspective* (New York: St. Martin's Press, 1988), 115. However, Sonbol would limit that duty to defending Jews and Christians only.

25. Fred Donner, "The Sources of Islamic Conceptions of War," in *Just War and Jihad: Historical and Theoretical Perspectives on War and Peace in Western and Islamic Traditions*, ed. John Kelsay and James Turner Johnson (Westport, CT: Greenwood Press, 1991), 47.

26. Quran, Haleem trans., 2:193 note c.

27. Quran, Muhammad Ali trans., 2:193 note 193a.

28. Kelsay and Sonbol arrive at the same interpretation of Quran 22:40, as do I, that fighting is justified to resist injustice. John Kelsay, *Arguing the Just War in Islam* (Cambridge, MA: Harvard University Press, 2007), 24; Sonbol, "Norms," 288.

29. "Justice and faith" is Yusuf Ali's translation of the Arabic word *dīn*, which implies many meanings. The syntax of the original Arabic version of 2:193 is "until there is *dīn* for Allah."

30. Abdulaziz Sachedina, "From Defensive to Offensive Warfare: The Use and Abuse of Jihad in the Muslim World," in *Religion, Law and the Role of Force: A Study of Their Influence on Conflict and on Conflict Resolution*, ed. J. I. Coffey and Charles Mathewes (Ardsley, NY: Transnational Publishers, 2002), 39–42, citing Quran 8:39, 2:193.

31. Mayer, "War and Peace," 204–205; see also Youssef Aboul-Enein and Sherifa Zuhur, *Islamic Rulings on Warfare* (Carlisle, PA: US Army War College, 2004), 11.

32. Sachedina, "From Defensive," 39.

33. Aslan, *No God But God*, 81.
34. Khadduri, *War and Peace*, 59.
35. Among its most vehement critics was the scholar Taqi ad-Din Ahmed Ibn Taymiyya, whose extreme conservatism inspired the Wahhabi movement, now official in Saudi Arabia and also influential in radical Islam. Sonbol, "Norms," 297.
36. David Cook, *Understanding Jihad* (Berkeley: University of California Press, 2005), 42–43.
37. Reported in Kelsay, *Arguing the Just War*, 38.
38. Aslan, *No God But God*, 84; Sachedina, "From Defensive," 42–43; al-Ghunaimi, *Muslim Conception*, 166–67.
39. Sonbol, "Norms," 296.
40. Kelsay, *Arguing the Just War*, 45–46.
41. Khadduri, *War and Peace*, 96, citing Quran 17:18 and *hadith*.
42. Especially the Battle of Badr (624 CE), in which only two years after the Hejira (i.e., Muhammad's flight from Mecca to Medina), Muhammad's outnumbered forces were able to defeat and slay prominent members of the Quraysh tribe, which had persecuted the Muslims in Mecca. Cook, *Understanding Jihad*, 7.
43. Paul Walker, "Taqiyah," in *Oxford Encyclopedia of the Modern Islamic World*, vol. 4: *Sata-Zurk*, ed. John Esposito (New York: Oxford University Press, 1995), 186–87.
44. Hamid Enayat, *Modern Islamic Political Thought* (Austin, TX: University of Texas Press, 1982), 177.
45. Khadduri, *War and Peace*, 61–62; Cook, *Understanding Jihad*, 15.
46. Quran 3:14–15; 158, 169–71; see also David Rapoport, "Messianic Sanctions for Terror," *Comparative Politics* 20, no. 2 (1988): 195–213; H. W. Kushner, "Suicide Bombers: Business as Usual," *Studies in Conflict and Terrorism* 19, no. 4 (1996): 329–37; Tibi, "War and Peace," 138; Kelsay, *Arguing the Just War*, 26. Enayat curiously glosses over this dimension of martyrdom, instead, for reasons unknown, confining his exposition to martyrdom as vicarious atonement. Enayat, *Modern Islamic*, 181–90.
47. Cook, *Understanding Jihad*, 26–28; David Bukay, "The Religious Foundations of Suicide Bombings," *Middle East Quarterly* 13, no. 4 (2006): 27–36, citing Quran 44:514; 52:17–20; 55:47–72 *passim*; 56:224. See also Bradley Thayer and Valerie Hudson, "Sex and the Shaheed," *International Security* 34, no. 4 (2010): 37–62, attributing the appeal of suicide tactics to young Muslim men who, for whatever reason, believe themselves unlikely to find mates and procreate in this life.
48. CNN, "Beirut Marine Barracks Bombing Fast Facts," modified March 21, 2019, accessed May 1, 2019, https://www.cnn.com/2013/06/13/world/meast/beirut-marine-barracks-bombing-fast-facts/index.html?no-st=9999999999.
49. David Cook, "Islamism and Jihadism," *Totalitarian Movements and Political Religions* 10, no. 2 (2009): 184–86; Benjamin Acosta, "The Suicide Bomber as Sunni-Shi'i Hybrid," *Middle East Quarterly* 17, no. 3 (2010): 13–20; Michael Horowitz, "Nonstate Actors and the Diffusion of Innovations," *International Organization* 64, no. 1 (2010): 33–64.
50. Davis Brown, "A Typology of War Ethics," *Journal of Military Ethics* 16, no. 3–4 (2017): 145–56.
51. See, e.g., Simon Haddad and Hilal Khashan, "Islam and Terrorism: Lebanese Muslim Views on September 11," *Journal of Conflict Resolution* 46, no. 6 (2002): 820.
52. Toft, "Getting Religion?"
53. Brown, "The Influence of Religion on Interstate Armed Conflict."
54. See Davis Brown and Patrick James, "The Religious Characteristics of States Dataset: Classic Themes and New Evidence," *Journal of Conflict Resolution* 62, no. 6 (2018): 1340–76.
55. See Toft, "Getting Religion?"
56. Treaty of Peace between the State of Israel and the Arab Republic of Egypt (Egypt–Israel), March 26, 1979, 1138 UNTS 59, 72.
57. See Donner, "The Sources of Islamic Conceptions of War," 51.
58. See Terence Ball, Richard Dagger, and Daniel O'Neil, *Political Ideologies and the Democratic Ideal* (Boston: Pearson, 2014), 298–314.
59. See Kelsay, *Arguing the Just War in Islam*, 25; Aslan, *No God But God*, 89–94.

60. Raphael Israeli, *Man of Defiance: A Political Biography of Anwar Sadat* (Totowa, NJ: Barnes & Noble Books, 1985), 46.
61. Mohammed Heikal, *The Road to Ramadan* (New York: Quadrangle/New York Times, 1975), 205.
62. Israeli, *Man of Defiance*, 46.
63. Ibid., *passim*.
64. Ibid., 47.
65. Anwar el-Sadat, *In Search of Identity: An Autobiography* (New York: Harper & Row, 1977), 176–84. Sadat's sense of shame, along with that of his nation, may also have been exacerbated by his own anti-Semitic tendencies. Sadat, like many others, often spoke derogatorily of Israel, Jews, and Zionists as if they were all the same. Raphael Israeli, "The Role of Islam in President Sadat's Thought," *Jerusalem Journal of International Relations* 4, no. 4 (1980): 8; Israeli, *Man of Defiance, passim*.
66. Sadat, *In Search of Identity*, 184.
67. Quoted in Israeli, *Man of Defiance*, 9.
68. Ibid., 49.
69. Ibid., 72.
70. Ibid., 75.
71. Quoted in Israeli, "The Role of Islam," 6. This is Israeli's interpretation of the speech.
72. Israeli, "The Role of Islam," 6.
73. Ibid., 7.
74. Ibid., 197. This was the first of three mobilizations on the Suez Canal that were designed to lull Israel into the false belief that Egypt was merely saber-rattling and not genuinely committed to war. To Israel's surprise, Egypt actually attacked on the third mobilization.
75. Israeli, *Man of Defiance*, 11, 48.
76. Heikal, *The Road to Ramadan*, 37. The idea appears to have been initiated by one of Sadat's generals; the oath was for everyone to make his utmost effort.
77. Israeli, *Man of Defiance*, 48.
78. Ibid., 11.
79. For example, in an October 1, 1973, directive to the commander-in-chief of the Egyptian armed forces: "[O]nly a people armed with faith in freedom and the willingness to make the necessary sacrifices could have shouldered [the burdens of defeat and occupation by Israel]." Sadat, *In Search of Identity*, 326.
80. While living in the Sinai from June 1992 to June 1993, I heard many locals actually praise the Israelis, who started industries there. For example, a major boost to the local economy consisted of peach orchards grafted on almond trees so they could grow in the desert—an innovation brought to the region by the Israelis.
81. Israeli, *Man of Defiance*, 112.
82. Ibid., 168.
83. Ibid., 86, 127.
84. See, e.g., on the Birthday of the Prophet in 1972; Israeli, "The Role of Islam," 7–8.
85. Israeli, *Man of Defiance*, 66; see also, 89.
86. Ibid., 116.
87. Sadat, *In Search of Identity*, 334–35.
88. Quoted in Israeli, *Man of Defiance*, 141.
89. Heikal, *The Road to Ramadan*, 224; Israeli, *Man of Defiance*, 116. Sadat also sought the recovery of other Arab lands and Palestinian self-determination. It was not until the 1978 Camp David negotiations that Sadat realized that, to secure the Sinai, he had to drop the other matters. William Quandt, *Camp David: Peacemaking and Politics* (Washington, DC: Brookings Institution, 1986), 236.
90. Israeli, *Man of Defiance*, 75.
91. Ibid., 133.
92. Ibid., 11.
93. Ibid., 62.
94. Quandt, *Camp David*, 227.
95. Israeli, "The Role of Islam," 11.

96. Quoted in Israeli, *Man of Defiance*, 141.
97. Framework for the Conclusion of a Peace Treaty between Egypt and Israel (Egypt–Israel–United States), n.d., reprinted in Quandt, *Camp David*, 381–83.
98. Thomas Sizgorich, "Sanctified Violence: Monotheist Militancy as the Tie That Bound Christian Rome and Islam," *Journal of the American Academy of Religion* 77, no. 4 (2009): 895–921.
99. Muhammad Abu Zahra, *Concept of War in Islam*, trans. Muhammad al-Hady and Taha Omar (Cairo: Société Orientale de Publicité-Press, 1961).
100. Ayoob, *The Many Faces of Political Islam*.
101. Haddad and Khashan, "Islam and Terrorism," 821.
102. Bassam Tibi, *Islamism and Islam* (New Haven, CT: Yale University Press, 2012).

12. JUST WAR THINKING IN CHINESE BUDDHISM

1. Yin Shun, *Fo zai renjian (The Buddha in the Human World)* (Taipei: Zhengwen chubanshe, 1984), 301.
2. Edward Conze, trans., *Buddhist Scriptures* (Baltimore: Penguin Books, 1959), 70.
3. Mahinda Deegalle, "The Buddhist Traditions of South and Southeast Asia," in *Religion, War, and Ethics: A Sourcebook of Textual Traditions*, ed. Gregory M. Reichberg and Henrik Syse (New York: Cambridge University Press, 2004), 547.
4. CBETA *Taisho*, Vol. 1, No. 11, 223a.
5. K. T. S. Sarao, *The Dhammapada: A Translator's Guide* (New Delhi: Munshiram Manoharlal Publishers, 2009), Chapter 17, Kodhavaggo, 274–75.
6. *Dhammika Sutta, Suttanipāta* 2:14, *Khuddaka Nikāya*. Sutta Central, accessed December 22, 2018, https://suttacentral.net/snp2.14/en/mills.
7. Sarao, *The Dhammapada*, Chapter 10, Daṇḍavaggo, 161.
8. Bhikku Nanamoli and Bhikku Bodhi, trans., *The Middle Length Discourses of the Buddha: A New Translation of the Majjhima Nikaya* (Boston: Wisdom Publications, 1995), 1053–54.
9. CBETA *Taisho*, Vol. 2, No. 99, 227–28a.
10. No. 313, "Khantivādi-Jātaka," in *The Jātaka or Stories of the Buddha's Former Births*, book IV, vol. III, ed. E. B. Cowell, trans. H. T. Francis and R. A. Neil (Oxford: Pali Text Society, 1995), 26–28.
11. T. W. Rhys Davids and C. A. F. Rhys Davids, trans., *Dialogues of the Buddha* (London: Pali Text Society, 1977), "*Mahā Parinibbāna Suttanta*," Chapter 1, 78–81.
12. "Kuṇāla-Jātaka," in *The Jātaka or Stories of the Buddha's Former Births*, vol. V, ed. E. B. Cowell, trans. H. T. Francis and R. A. Neil (Oxford: Pali Text Society, 1995), 219–20.
13. CBETA *Taisho*, Vol. 2, No. 125, 690b–91c.
14. Komarraju Ravi, "Buddhism and Just War," in *Buddhism and Peace: An Interdisciplinary Study*, ed. G. Sundara Ramaiah et al. (Visakhapatnam: Andhra University Press, 1991), 78.
15. CBETA *Taisho*, Vol. 1, No. 26, 585a.
16. Xue Yu, *Buddhism, War, and Nationalism: Chinese Monks in the Struggle against Japanese Aggressions, 1931–1945* (in Chinese) (Hong Kong: The Chinese University Press, 2011), 25.
17. Maurice Walshe, trans., *Aggañña Sutta: Sutta 27, The Long Discourses of the Buddha: A Translation of the Dīgha-Nikāya* (Boston: Wisdom Publications, 1995), 412–13.
18. CBETA *Taisho*, Vol. 3, No. 154, 102a.
19. Degalle, "The Buddhist Traditions of South and Southeast Asia," 575–79.
20. CBETA *Taisho*, Vol. 17, No. 721, 317a.
21. Komarraju Ravi, "Buddhism and Just War," 80–81.
22. Walshe, *Cakkavatti-Sīhanāda Sutta, The Long Discourses of the Buddha*, 395–403.

23. CBETA *Taisho*, Vol. 9, No. 272, 338a.
24. Tessa J. Bartholomeusz, *In Defense of Dharma: Just-War Ideology in Buddhist Sri Lanka* (London and New York: Routledge Curzon, 2002), 58–59.
25. CBETA *Taisho*, Vol. 12, No. 346, 175c.
26. *Yogācārya-bhūmi-śāstra*, chapter 41, CBETA *Taisho*, Vol. 30, No. 1579, 517b.
27. Walshe, *Brahmajāla Sutta*, Sutta 1, *The Long Discourses of the Buddha*, 68–72.
28. Maurice Walshe, trans., *The Connected Discourses of the Buddha: A Translation of the Dīgha-Nīkāya* (Boston: Wisdom Publications, 1995), 1843.
29. E. M. Hare, trans., *The Book of the Fives*, Chapter XVIII, §VII (177), *The Book of the Gradual Sayings (Aṅguttara-Nīkāya)* (London: Pali Text Society, 1934), 153; Walshe, *Brahmajāla Sutta*, Sutta 1, *The Long Discourses of the Buddha*, 68–72.
30. Degalle, "The Buddhist Traditions of South and Southeast Asia," 546.
31. Bartholomeusz, *In Defense of Dharma*, 32.
32. Du Doucheng, ed., *Zhengshi fojiao ziliao leibian* (*Collected Materials on Buddhism in Orthodox History*), CBETA H01, Vol. 2, No. 1, 69a–70a.
33. Ibid., 105a.
34. CBETA X77, No. 1524, 522b.
35. Venerable Zhenhua, *Sengqie huguoshi* (*History of Saṅgha Defending the Nation*) (Shanghai: Foxue shuju, 1934), 89.
36. Ibid., 117.
37. CBETA *Taisho*, Vol. 3, No. 159, 297a.
38. CBETA *Taisho*, Vol. 50, No. 2059, 351c.
39. Xue Yu, *Buddhism, War, and Nationalism*, 103.
40. Ibid., 261.
41. Fa Fang, "Sengni yingfou fu guomin bingyi?" ("Should Monks and Nuns Serve the Draft?"), *Haichaoyin* (*The Sound of Waves*) 17, no. 8: 1–2.
42. Tan Yun, "Sengqie huoguo zaitan" ("Random Words of Saṅgha Defending the Nation"), *Fohaideng* (*Lamp of the Buddhist Sea*) 2, no. 5–6: 25–26.
43. Yi Tuo, "Cong yige minzu yingxiong de qingnian heshang shuoqi" ("Beginning with the Story of a Young Monk—A Hero of the People"), *Haichaoyin* 18, no. 5 (1937): 98–99. The term "dual circumstances" probably refers to the different pulls that Buddhist believers must feel between their love for the country and their love for the religion.
44. Yue Yao, "Sengqie huguo zhuanji jueshouyu" ("Foreword to the Special Issue of Saṅgha Defending the Nation"), *Fohaideng* 2, no. 4: 1.
45. Jing Guang, "Xiandai zhongguo qingnian yingju zhi jizhong guandian" ("A Few Viewpoints Buddhist Youth in Modern Times Should Adopt"), *Haichaoyin* 18, no. 1 (1937): 33–36.
46. Ren Xin, "Kangdi sheng zhong de fojiaotu" ("The Buddhists in the Cries of Defending the Nation"), *Haichaoyin* 18, no. 9 (1937): 1–2.
47. Yi Sheng, "Sengqie huguo de zhengtu" ("The Correct Path of Saṅgha in Defending the Nation"), *Fohaideng* 2, no. 4: 11–15.
48. Tai Xu, "Quan quanguo fojiao qingnian zu huguotuan" ("On Advising Young Buddhists of the Country to Form Organizations in Defending the Nation"), *Haichaoyin* 14, no. 5: 7–13.
49. Jue Xian, "Sengxun wuzhuang huguo lun" (On Arming the Monks in Defense of the Nation"), *Fohaideng* 2, no. 4: 3–6.
50. Le Guan, "Peidu senglü jiuhudui chengli wuzhounian jinian ganyan" ("Remarks on the Fifth Anniversary of the Establishment of the Rescue Crew of the Monks in the Provisional Capital"), *Senglü kangzhan gongzuoshi* (*History of the Work of Monks in the War of Resistance*) (Taipei, 1980), 106–9.
51. Le Guan, "Zhongguo fojiao guoji xuanchuandui xuanyan" ("The Manifesto of the International Propaganda Team of Chinese Buddhism"), *Senglü kangzhan gongzuoshi* (Taipei, 1980), 44–45.
52. Xue Yu, *Buddhism, War, and Nationalism*, 224.
53. E Kou, "Xiezai huguo fahui zhihou" ("Writing after the Ritual of Defending the Nation"), *Fohaideng* 2, no. 2: 1.

54. Le Guan, "Yige wumingde yingxiong heshang" ("An Anonymous Young Monk Hero"), *Haichaoyin* 28, no. 8: 20–21.

55. Xue Yu, *Buddhism, War, and Nationalism*, 266–68; Sheng Sheng, "Zouchu jingtang yu emo bodou: kangzhan rechao fanlan wutai" ("Stepping Out of the Buddhist Hall to Combat the Demon—The Heated Waves of War of Resistance Sweeping over Wutai"), *Shizihou* (*The Lion's Roar*) 1, no. 2: 28–29.

56. Bartholomeusz, *In Defense of Dharma*, 46.

57. Peter Harvey, as cited in Laksiri Jayasuriya, "Just War Tradition and Buddhism," *International Studies* 46, no. 4 (2009): 432.

58. CBETA *Taisho*, Vol. 25, No. 1509, 153b.

59. William Edward Soothill and Lewis Hodous, eds., *A Dictionary of Chinese Buddhist Terms*, accessed December 22, 2018, https://www.buddhistdoor.org/tc/dictionary/details/sila-sila-morality-precept-virtue.

60. Master Sheng-yen, *Jiel ü xue gangyao* (*The Essentials of the Study of Precepts*) (Taipei: Dharma Drum Publishing Corp., 1999), 101–2.

61. D. M. Jackson, "Jus ad Bellum" and "Jus in Bello," in *Encyclopedia of Global Justice*, ed. D. K. Chatterjee (Dordrecht: Springer, 2011).

62. Garrett Brown, Iain McLean, and Alistair McMillan, eds., "Just War," in *The Concise Oxford Dictionary of Politics and International Relations*, 4th ed. (Oxford: Oxford University Press, 2018).

63. Komarraju Ravi, "Buddhism and Just War," 82.

64. Laksiri Jayasuriya, "Just War Tradition and Buddhism," 430.

65. Bartholomeusz, *In Defense of Dharma*, 14–21.

66. Sueki Fumihiko, "Chinese Buddhism and the Anti-Japan War," *Japanese Journal of Religious Studies* 37, no. 1 (2010): 17.

Index

Afghanistan, 71–73, 75, 76
African ethic/moral thought, 133–137
Afro-communal (approach), 132, 141, 142, 144, 146, 148, 149–150, 152
anarchism, 11, 16, 16–18; conventional warfare, 19–20; violence, 20–26
Aquinas, Thomas, 62, 76, 158
Augustine, Saint, 2, 158

Bakunin, Mikhail, 16, 19, 23–24
Blanco, Hugo, 39–41
Buddha, Siddhartha Gautama, 209, 210, 211, 212–213, 213, 215, 216

Charter of the United Nations, 1945, 63–64, 70, 71–72, 73–74, 193, 205
civil war, definition, 82
Clausewitz, Carl von, xv
colonialism, African, 102, 141, 149; Kaunda, Kenneth, 150–151
Confucius, 2, 3, 157–158, 159, 159–160, 165, 167, 168, 170, 217
critical legal theory, 64–65, 70

Darfur, 68

feminism, 96–97; African, 98–99, 109; care political theory, 116–119, 120, 121, 124, 126, 127, 127–128

Gītā, Bhagavad, 174–175, 176–177, 180, 182, 184, 185, 187, 189
Guatemalan civil war, 1960–1996, 85–86
Guevara, Che, 39

Hoffman, Bruce, 14

Iraqi invasion, 2003, 53, 73–74, 166, 166–167; Gulf War, 1990–1991, 120–121

Jihad, 195–196, 205; Sadat, Anwar, 198, 199, 200–202, 203, 205

Kant, Immanuel, xv
karma, 211, 213, 215, 221, 222; *karma yoga*, 184, 185
Kosovo, NATO intervention, 69–70

Law of Armed Conflict, 87–92
Lenin, Vladimir Illich, 34–35
liberalism, 32, 66; institutional, 67, 75
LOAC. *See* Law of Armed Conflict

Mahābhārata, 2, 174–175, 176–177, 177, 178, 179, 181–182, 182, 183, 189
Mandela, Nelson, and the African National Congress, 140–141
Marx, Karl, 33–34
Marxist revolutionary war, 33, 34, 42

McMahan, Jeff, 3, 132, 146, 173–174, 174, 182, 183, 187, 189
Mencius, xii, 2, 7, 157–158, 158, 160–163, 163–164, 164–167, 168–169, 170
morality, xiv, 1, 3
Morgenthau, Hans, 65–66
Muhammad, Prophet, 193, 196, 200, 201
Myanmar, 5, 65

Nazism, 55–56
Neu, Michael, 48, 53
Nietzsche, Friedrich Wilhelm, 174
Nigerian civil war, 1967–1970, 83–84, 103–104, 108
nonstate actors: violence, 14; protection, 15; al-Qaeda, 13, 71, 72, 73, 194, 197
nonviolence, 210–212
normative theory/legitimacy, 13, 126, 132, 135–136, 137, 144, 151, 167

Oppenheim, Lassa, 12
Ositadimma principle, 92

pacifism, xi, 54–56, 57
Paris Commune, 1871, 24, 25, 34
political/legitimate authority, 12, 13, 52, 160, 161–162, 170

Quran, 193–195, 196, 201

rape, war crime, 97, 99, 105, 107–108, 108, 109, 110, 116, 137
realism, xi, 65–66, 73, 76, 167

responsibility to protect, 67–69, 68–69, 73, 76
Robinson, Andrew, 11, 12
Rwanda, genocide, 5–6, 61, 67–68, 68, 75, 103, 108

Second Sino-Japanese War, 1937–1945, 218–221
self-defense, 32, 36, 38, 39–41, 42, 49, 52, 53, 56, 63, 64, 71, 116, 152, 163, 164, 174, 176, 185, 186, 192, 193, 195, 204, 205; Islamic, 193–195
Seymour, Richard, 32
Srebrenica, massacre, 68
Sri Lankan civil war, 1983–2009, 85
Stalin, Joseph, 35
Syria, 48, 49

Taliban, 71, 72–73
terrorism, definition, 14–15
ticking time bomb scenario, 123–127, 127
Trotsky, Leon, 35–39
TTB. *See* ticking time bomb scenario

violence, 49–51, 143, 191, 194

Walzer, Michael, xiv, 31–32, 35, 39, 55, 99, 122, 132, 173, 189

Yom Kippur War, 1973, 192, 198, 202, 205

Zimbabwe, 141–142; Mugabe, Robert, 141

About the Editors and Contributors

Danny Singh (co-editor for this volume) is senior lecturer in Criminology & Sociology at Teesside University. He has previously taught at the University of York's Department of Politics and at Leeds Beckett University. He has published on interventions in war-torn states leading to police and judicial reform and anticorruption. These journals include *Conflict, Security & Development, Journal of Intervention and Statebuilding, Journal of Developing Societies, Crime, Law and Social Change, Policy Studies, The Journal of Legal Pluralism and Unofficial Law*, and *The Police Journal*. He is currently working on a monograph, titled *Investigating Corruption in the Afghan Police Force: Instability and Insecurity in Post-Conflict Societies*.

Luís Cordeiro-Rodrigues (co-editor for this volume) holds a PhD from the University of York and is currently associate professor at the Department of Philosophy, Yuelu Academy, Hunan University, China. He has published widely on multiculturalism, just war theory, and animals. His main publications are two edited books, *Philosophies of Multiculturalism: Beyond Liberalism* (2017) and *Animals, Race and Multiculturalism*, and articles on *Critical Studies on Terrorism, Journal of Speculative Philosophy, Theoria*, and *Journal of Agricultural and Environmental Ethics*.

Alex J. Bellamy is currently director of the Asia Pacific Centre for the Responsibility to Protect (R2P), which is part of the University of Queensland's School of Political Science and International Studies. He is also senior adviser at the International Peace Institute and Fellow of the Academy of Social Sciences. He has published books, chapters, and journal articles within the field of R2P, peacekeeping, international security, terrorism, conflict studies, and just war theory.

Nathan Jun is associate professor and coordinator of the philosophy program at Midwestern State University in Wichita Falls, Texas. Dr. Jun specializes in political theory and the history of political thought with a particular emphasis on the anarchist and revolutionary socialist traditions. He has published more than three dozen articles, book chapters, and reviews as well as ten books, most recently, *Proletarian Days: A Hippolyte Havel Reader* (2018), *Anarchism: A Conceptual Approach* (2018), and *A Companion to Anarchism and Philosophy* (2017).

Andrew Ryder is adjunct faculty at the John V. Roach Honors College of Texas Christian University. He has written several articles on decolonization and multiculturalism. He is currently co-authoring a manuscript, titled *Consciousness beyond the Human: Mesoamerican Dialogues in Race, Gender and Ecology*.

Richard Jackson is director of the National Centre for Peace and Conflict Studies (NCPACS) and professor of peace studies at the University of Otago, New Zealand. He is the founding editor and current editor-in-chief of the journal *Critical Studies on Terrorism* and the author and editor of eleven books and more than sixty journal articles and book chapters on terrorism, war, political violence, pacifism, and conflict resolution. His current research focuses on pacifism and nonviolence in international relations.

Jonathan O. Chimakonam, PhD, teaches at the University of Pretoria, South Africa. His research interests cover the areas of African philosophy, logic, philosophy of mind, environmental ethics, and postmodern/postcolonial thought. He aims to break new grounds in African philosophy by formulating a system that unveils new concepts and opens new vistas for thought (conversational philosophy); a method that represents a new approach to philosophizing in African and intercultural philosophies (conversational thinking); and a system of logic that grounds both (Ezumezu). His articles have appeared in refereed and accredited international journals. He is an author, co-author, editor, and co-editor of several books, including *Ezumezu: A System of Logic for African Philosophy and Studies* (2019); *New Conversations on the Problems of Identity, Consciousness and Mind* (with U. Egbai, S. Segun, and A. Attoe, 2019); *Atuolu Omalu: Some Unanswered Questions in Contemporary African Philosophy* (2015); *African Philosophy and Environmental Conservation* (2017); *African Philosophy and the Epistemic Marginalisation of Women* (with Louise du Toit, 2018); *Ka Osi So Onye: African Philosophy in the Post Modern Era* (with Edwin Etieyibo, 2018); and *The Death Penalty from an African Perspective: Views from Zimbabwean and Nigerian Philosophers* (with Fainos Mangena, 2017). He is the convener of the professional African philosophy society, The Conversational School of Philosophy (CSP) and the founding editor of *Filosofia Theoretica: Journal of African Philosophy, Culture and Religions*. He is winner of Jens Jacobsen Research Award for Outstanding Research in Philosophy by the International Society for Universal Dialogue. He is African philosophy area editor in the *Internet Encyclopedia of Philosophy*. Jonathan is working on a new manuscript in African philosophy.

Victor C. A. Nweke is currently a researcher/PhD candidate at the Institute of Cultural Studies, University of Koblenz-Landau, Germany. His major research interest includes African philosophy, global normative theory, intercultural philosophy, and philosophy of logic. He is working on his PhD as a member of a multidisciplinary normative project, "Diversity, Power and Justice: Transcultural Perspectives," funded by the DFG (Deutsche Forschungsgemeinschaft, the German Research Foundation). His peer-reviewed publications (articles and chapters in academic journals and edited books) attempt to interrogate and (re)conceptualize articulate perspectives on right conduct and optimal human flourishing using salient ideas in African philosophy as a crucial point of departure. Victor is also an affiliate researcher with the Conversational School of Philosophy (CSP), University of Calabar, Nigeria.

Olajumoke M. Akiode holds a PhD degree in applied ethics and sociopolitical philosophy from the University of Lagos, where she left to accept the appointment to the research director cum executive director position of the Center for Ethics and Sustainable Development (CESD), an independent research organization based in Lagos. Her research interests include applied ethics, sociopolitical philosophy, feminism, African philosophy, gender equality and social inclusion (GESI), postmodernism, and sustainability.

Heleana Theixos, PhD, University of Miami, is assistant professor of philosophy at Heidelberg University and a professional ethicist specializing in moral injury on and off the battlefield. Theixos studied with Alasdair MacIntyre on virtue ethics, Nel Noddings on care ethics, and Jeff McMahan on just war theory. While much feminist philosophy and care ethics is interested in victims of harm, Theixos primarily applies theoretical resources to perpetrators of harm. Academic and professional publications include moral injury and bullies in primary school, military interrogators, slaughterhouse workers, and US Border Patrol agents. Theixos collaborates actively outside academia, acting as a consultant on moral injury for trial attorneys, medical professionals, and government and nongovernmental think tanks.

Thaddeus Metz hails from the United States, where he received his PhD from Cornell University in 1997. He began living in South Africa in 1999, and in 2004 joined the Philosophy Department at the University of the Witwatersrand, Johannesburg. In 2009, he became professor (research focus) at the University of Johannesburg, where he is currently distinguished professor (2015–2019, 2020–2024). Professor Metz has published about two hundred and fifty scholarly works in value theory, comparative philosophy, and moral, political, and legal philosophy. Recent books include *Jurisprudence in an African Context* (with David Bilchitz and Oritsegbubemi Oyowe, 2017) and *Agwa Oma N'Echiche Ndi Afrikana Nkowa Nke* (*An Account of African Moral Thought*, a collection of essays translated into Igbo and edited by Lawrence Ogbo Ugwuanyi, 2018).

Cao Qin received a PhD in politics at the University of Manchester and is currently an associate professor in the School of Philosophy of Nankai University. His major research fields include contemporary political philosophy and the history of political thought.

Shyam Ranganathan is faculty at the Department of Philosophy and at the York Center for Asian Research, York University, Toronto. His research and writing span areas relevant to the study of non-Western and, especially, Indian moral philosophy, including the philosophy of language (translation theory), theoretical ethics (normative and metaethics), and Asian philosophy (especially South Asian philosophy). He is the author of numerous peer-reviewed papers, monographs, and edited volumes, and is the translator of *Patañjali's Yoga Sūtra* (2008).

Davis Brown (PhD, University of Virginia, 2012) is senior research associate with the Association of Religion Data Archives and nonresident fellow of the Baylor University Institute for Studies of Religion. His research focuses on ethics of war, *jus ad bellum*, and religion and state. He is the author of *The Sword, the Cross, and the Eagle* (Rowman & Littlefield, 2008) and has a new book on religion and armed conflict under contract.

Tong Sau Lin is a visiting lecturer of the Department of Cultural and Religious Studies at the Chinese University of Hong Kong. She received her doctorate in Buddhism from Sun Yat-Sen University. She was a research fellow of the faculty of Buddhism at Komazawa University in Tokyo. Her publications include *Xin de Zhihui: Boye Boluomiduo Xinjing Xiyi* (*Wisdom of the Heart: A Reinterpretation of the Heart Sutra*), *Fanwen Fodian Duban* (*Sanskrit Buddhist Sutras: A Reader's Guide*), and *Sengzhao de Foxue Lijie yu Geyi Fojiao* (*Sengzhao's Understanding of Buddhist Doctrine and Geyi Buddhism*). Her research interests include Sanskrit Buddhist texts, Chinese Buddhist philosophy, and Buddhism and contemporary society, and she is currently studying the Buddhist views on suicide.

King-Fai Tam is retired from the Hong Kong Polytechnic University, having taught previously in various universities in the United States and Hong Kong. He received his training in English and comparative literature from the Chinese University of Hong Kong and East Asian studies from Princeton University. He has a broad research interest in Chinese literature, film, popular culture, and translation, including the depiction of war; the modern Chinese essay; political humor; and popular literary genres, such as detective fiction and spy fiction. Among his publications is an edited volume of articles, *Chinese and Japanese Films on the Second World War*. In 2018, he received a fellowship from the Netherlands Institute for Advanced Study in the Humanities and Social Sciences in Amsterdam, where he researched daily life in Hong Kong under the Japanese occupation in World War II.

www.ingramcontent.com/pod-product-compliance
Lightning Source LLC
Chambersburg PA
CBHW031547300426
44111CB00006BA/204